INTRODUCTION TO TRAGEDY

EDWARD J. GORDON

Yale University

HAYDEN BOOK COMPANY, INC.
Rochelle Park, New Jersey

The author would like to thank the proprietors for permission to quote from copyrighted works, as follows:

Antigone, Jean Anouilh. Adapted and translated by Lewis Galantière. Copyright 1946 by Random House, Inc. Reprinted from *Four Contemporary French Plays*, by permission of the publisher.

Beyond the Horizon, Eugene O'Neill. Copyright 1920 and renewed 1948 by Eugene O'Neill. Reprinted from *Ah, Wilderness! and Two Other Plays*, by Eugene O'Neill, by permission of Random House, Inc.

Oedipus, the King, Sophocles. Translated by Bernard M. W. Knox. Copyright © 1959 by Bernard W. Knox. Reprinted by permission of Washington Square Press, division of Simon & Schuster, Inc.

ISBN 0-8104-5786-5 (soft-bound edition)
        0-8104-5787-3 (hard-bound edition)
Library of Congress Catalog Card Number 73-7001
Copyright © 1973

Printed in the United States of America

1 2 3 4 5 6 7 8 9   PRINTING

73 74 75 76 77 78   YEAR

Contents

INTRODUCTION
TO
TRAGEDY

Introduction

This book is about tragedy, a literary form that probes the nature of man or, more particularly, the reasons why man suffers. Since tragedy also deals with how man faces his misfortunes, it helps us to define what man is and what he can be. In much of your education to this point and in most of your life hereafter, you have been and will be asking questions about the meaning of life. The questions usually come up when things are not going well. The measure of a man is how he faces the moments when life gets rough.

In moments of difficulty where do we put the blame, on ourselves or on some outside force? The distinction can be seen in some frivolous examples, even though they are not subjects for tragedy. The student who turns up with a D on a report card will invariably say of his teacher, *"He* gave me a D." But if the situation is better, the student will say, *"I* got a B." The man who backs his car into a tree will often blame the car or the tree. Many people obviously think that difficulty comes from outside the individual and that success comes from inside. Writers of tragedy make no such simple-minded distinctions.

Tragedy deals with the great questions: Why does man suffer? What part of that suffering is caused by fate? What is fate? Does the meaning of the term "fate" change at different moments in history? What portion of the suffering is brought on by a man's own character? What is man's reaction to his plight? Does he stand and fight back or does he go down whimpering, full of pity for himself? Does the suffering of the tragic character affect the society in which he lives? What difference does it make? What are the great tragic moments of life? How should an audience react to tragedy?

We raise such questions in schools largely through the books that we read. But anyone who teaches English faces the inevitable question that comes from the back of the room, "Why do we have to read this stuff?" And "stuff" in this context often means some of the great tragedies of the Western World: sections of the *Bible;* plays by Sophocles, Shakespeare, Ib-

1

sen, O'Neill, Anouilh, or Miller; novels by Melville, Hawthorne, Dostoevsky, Hardy, Conrad, Hemingway, or Faulkner.

In answer, one can only echo those who have said that the purpose of a liberal education is that we may know ourselves, that we may know *why* we do what we do, why we *are* what we are. Only then can we be free.

And there is a further consideration in the reading of great books. A book will continue to be read only if people see in it reflections of their own situations or of those whom they know. Few of us will be like Socrates or Antigone; our thoughts may never disturb a state to the point where we will be killed for those beliefs. But most of us will, at one time or another, be up against an authority that we may consider unjust. When we see how a situation in a book is similar to a situation that we know, we can see the book as a metaphor, as a comparison in some way with our own lives.

And if we see a book as metaphor, we may see that it makes comments on our own lives. If, for example, a young man refuses to be drafted into the army because he does not believe in killing others for any reason, he is caught between the authority of the state and his own conscience. Any struggle between authority and conscience can make a situation ripe for tragedy. We see a similar situation acted out in "The Trial of Socrates" and in *Antigone*. When a young man reads these moments of lonely debate, he may see them as metaphors of his own predicament. They are lonely moments because when one arrives at the point of tragedy, the moment when one is trapped by circumstances, one is alone. With no one else to depend on, a man must be himself. What that *self* is we may partially find out through the literature of tragedy. Whitehead, a philosopher, has said that man goes on acting the same way because no other way of acting has ever occurred to him. When one finishes reading some tragedies, he may see the difference between acting heroically and acting basely—and that should be a good enough reason for reading on.

We have purposely shunned "defining" tragedy in any detailed way. The defining will come through your own experiencing of the variety of ways in which the tragic mode presents itself. What follows are introductions to, and questions on, ten tragedies written from about 2,500 years ago to twenty-five years ago. For six of the selections we include the texts; for the other four, easily available in inexpensive paperback editions, we include only introductions and questions. (If we included all of the texts, this book would be too bulky to handle.)

The following editions are recommended for the four texts not included here, although any complete edition will serve:

> *Hamlet,* William Shakespeare: in Hayden Shakespeare Series, edited
> by Maynard Mack and Robert W. Boynton, Hayden Book Co.,
> 50 Essex St., Rochelle Park, N. J. 07662

An Enemy of the People, Henrik Ibsen: in *Four Great Plays,* Bantam
Books, 666 Fifth Ave., New York, N. Y. 10019.

Heart of Darkness, Joseph Conrad: New American Library, 1301
Avenue of the Americas, New York, N. Y. 10019.

Death of a Salesman, Arthur Miller: Viking Press, 625 Madison
Ave., New York, N. Y. 10022.

The Book of Job

(5th Century B.C.)

THE *Book of Job* is usually considered the greatest piece of Hebrew literature that has come down to us. As a poem it is one of the classics of world literature and also a great moment in the history of tragedy. Written in either the fifth century B.C. or, more probably, in the fourth century, it is concerned, as is all tragedy, with asking how we reconcile the suffering of an innocent man with the idea of a just God.

Tragedy, as a type of literature, evolved from man's attempts to understand what was happening to him as he lived his life. Around him he saw evil and suffering, and in his attempt to understand the purpose of life and his place in the universe, he tried to work out answers to why people suffer. Does suffering have a purpose? Is there order in the universe, or does suffering strike haphazardly, affecting bad and good alike? Does man bring suffering on himself through his own character (the choices he can control) or is suffering caused by fate (the choices he cannot control)?

Western man's first attempts to understand the nature of evil are found in the Bible. At first there was the simple notion that suffering was a punishment from God for an evil act, that punishment was a form of divine retribution visited on an individual. If he suffered, he had obviously done something wrong. But as man thought more about this theory, he found that it did not fit the facts of life. Good men *did* suffer, and evil men *did* prosper. Of course the obvious answer to this latter observation was that the man who seemed to be good must have some secret sin—and who could prove that he did not? But many men, Job for one, could truthfully ask, "Why do I, a good man, suffer?"

A good man could be told that he was suffering for the sins of his father, for the sins of his tribe, and so on. However, in spite of such answers, man persisted in asking the simple question: What is the purpose of suffering? And each time he asked the question, the answer became more complex. Now it was easy to conclude that if a man suffered, he had committed a sin, even if that sin was unknown to his society. But what of the evil people who did not suffer? The answer: Reward and punishment will be meted out in an afterlife. However, such an answer could not satisfy all men, and the problem of evil remained a constant dilemma. Man continued to feel a power outside himself that to some extent controlled his actions. He saw that the simpler, earlier explanations were not enough to explain the cause of evil; and with the writer of *Ecclesiastes,* he could say:

> I returned, and saw under the sun, that the race is not to the swift, nor the battle to the strong, neither yet bread to the wise, nor yet riches to men of understanding, nor yet favor to men of skill; but time

and chance happeneth to them all. For man also knoweth not his time: as the fishes that are taken in an evil net, and as the birds that are caught in the snare; so are the sons of men snared in an evil time, when it falleth suddenly upon them.[1]

One can trace various attitudes toward suffering through the books of the Bible. The early Hebrews, who worshipped many gods, explained suffering or prosperity as the result of the gods' displeasure or pleasure. A sacrifice to a god might bring rain, a good crop, or victory in war. A man's moral actions did not seem to matter.

Later, with the acceptance of the idea of one God in Israel, came the Hebraic concept of morality: the way a man lived *did* matter. This idea also raised the problem of how a good man could suffer. The major explanation was that suffering was the consequence of past sin. But the Hebrews at this time were thinking not of individual men but rather of a whole tribe that could suffer for the sins of one of its members. Such thinking was hard to contradict, since every group had at least one member who had sinned. But in a later development of society, the individual became more important than the group. In *The Book of Jeremiah* (15:17-18) we read:

> I sat not in the assembly of the mockers, nor rejoiced;
>> I sat alone because of thy hand:
>> for thou hast filled me with indignation.
> Why is my pain perpetual,
>> and my wound incurable, which refuseth to be healed?
> Wilt thou be altogether unto me as a liar,
>> and as waters that fail?

In other words, why me? The assumption behind such thinking is that there is a just God who deals with individual lives. His fairness became a matter for man to consider and evolved into one of the main concerns of the Old Testament. So now we have arrived at a point where individual sin, and not the sins of the tribe, can be considered as the cause of man's suffering.

Another aspect of the suffering theme that can be found in the Bible is that one cannot judge a man's life at a given moment. You must wait and see before judging whether a man is truly prospering. (You will find this idea also in the closing lines of *Oedipus the King.*) Consider, for example, these few excerpts from the 37th Psalm (1-2, 7, 10-11):

---

[1] *Ecclesiastes* 9: 11-12. (The quotations here, and the text which follows this introduction, are from the King James Version of the Bible [1611]. The first number in a Biblical reference indicates the chapter, whereas the numbers following the colon indicate the verses within the chapter. Thus, to refer to Chap. 9, verses 11 through 12, we write "9: 11-12.")

> Fret not thyself because of evildoers,
>> neither be thou envious against the workers of iniquity.
> For they shall soon be cut down like the grass,
>> and wither as the green herb.
>
> Rest in the Lord, and wait patiently for him:
>> fret not thyself because of him who prospereth in his way, because of the man who bringeth wicked devices to pass.
>
> For yet a little while, and the wicked shall not be:
>> Yea, thou shalt diligently consider his place, and it shall not be.
> But the meek shall inherit the earth;
>> and shall delight themselves in the abundance of peace.

This idea led logically to its extension, that man will be rewarded or punished in an afterlife.

Finally came the idea that suffering can be a form of discipline, that it can educate a man and redeem him or his society. The theme of many books, even those written today, is that suffering will make a man better. The idea is expressed in *The Second Book of Isaiah,* in a section on the suffering servant, especially in Chap. 53: 3-5:

> He is despised and rejected of men;
>> a man of sorrows, and acquainted with grief:
> and we hid as it were our faces from him;
>> he was despised, and we esteemed him not.
> Surely he hath borne our griefs,
>> and carried our sorrows:
> yet we did esteem him stricken,
>> smitten of God, and afflicted.
> But he was wounded for our transgressions,
>> he was bruised for our iniquities:
> the chastisement of our peace was upon him;
>> and with his stripes we are healed.

Against this background, then, we can turn to *The Book of Job,* a book that expresses doubt about the traditional ways of explaining human suffering. Job's friends are arguing some of the orthodox beliefs that we have just traced through the Bible, mainly that man suffers for his own sins. However, they are arguing backwards. They assume that since Job is suffering, he must have sinned. Job argues that he has not. Sin may lead to suffering, but one cannot assume that all who suffer have sinned.

Resemblances between *The Book of Job* and Greek tragedy have led some to believe that it may have been written by one who had seen a Greek tragedy. *Job* begins with a prose prologue, often called the "Prologue in Heaven," between God and Satan; and it ends with a prose epilogue. In between (Chaps. 3 through 42: 6) is the "Poem of Job." We can also think of it as drama in that the ideas are expressed in dialogue form, between God and Satan, between Job and God, and between Job and his three friends, Eliphaz, Bildad, and Zophar. (Elihu's speeches, which we have omitted, were probably not written by the original author of the book.) The speeches by Job and his friends make up what in a play might be called acts, and they express the kinds of confrontations that make up the essence of drama. There is also the suggestion of a setting, for after the prologue the action (2: 8) takes place on an ash heap: ". . . he took him a potsherd to scrape himself withal; and he sat down among the ashes."

Once Job's suffering begins, we do not find the close cause-and-effect relation that we find in Greek drama; one scene does not happen *because* of the previous scene. We do, however, find a story that progresses by action and reaction. As each of the friends acts by trying to persuade Job to a particular belief, he reacts by arguing against that belief. The total effect of the book is an argument against the idea that suffering is the result of a person's having done evil or that a good man prospers and an evil man suffers.

The book can be considered tragedy because it has much of the structure of what has since come to be called tragic drama. We see a man of high estate, a leading member of his community, brought from prosperity to ruin. The argument is whether he fell through his own character (the elements of his life that he could control) or through fate (the supernatural elements of his life that he could not control). Job, who has lost family, home, property, and health, has his back to the wall. He needs some explanation for the catastrophes. However, he does not accept the traditional Hebraic beliefs that his friends present. Standing on the edge of chaos, Job wants to know why he suffers.

Like all great characters in tragedies, Job fights back against his fate. If he had merely accepted his destiny, he would excite only our pity, not our admiration. In his challenge to God (13: 15), Job knows the great risk that he takes:

> Though he slay me, yet will I trust him:
> but I will maintain my own ways before him.

Another element of tragedy that is present in *Job* is that the question being debated concerns us all: why do good people suffer? Great tragedies ask questions; they do not answer them. They become lessons in the art of living. There is a mystery about life. A great book does not solve that mystery; it presents it. The awesome thing about Job himself is not that he has such a capacity for suffering, but rather that in the face of such suffering he can stand on his own two feet and speak his mind. He helps us to define what it is to be a man.

The Book of Job

There was a man in the land of Uz, whose name was Job; and
that man was perfect and upright, and one that feared God, and es-
chewed evil. And there were born unto him seven sons and three
daughters. His substance also was seven thousand sheep, and three
thousand camels, and five hundred yoke of oxen, and five hundred she
asses, and a very great household; so that this man was the greatest of
all the men of the east. And his sons went and feasted in their houses,
every one his day; and sent and called for their three sisters to eat and
to drink with them. And it was so, when the days of their feasting 5
were gone about, that Job sent and sanctified them, and rose up early
in the morning, and offered burnt offerings according to the number
of them all: for Job said, It may be that my sons have sinned, and
cursed God in their hearts. Thus did Job continually.

Job's Character

Now there was a day when the sons of God came to present
themselves before the LORD, and Satan came also among them. And
the LORD said unto Satan, Whence comest thou? Then Satan answered
the LORD, and said, From going to and fro in the earth, and from
walking up and down in it. And the LORD said unto Satan, Hast thou
considered my servant Job, that there is none like him in the earth, a
perfect and an upright man, one that feareth God, and escheweth evil?
Then Satan answered the LORD, and said, Doth Job fear God for
nought? Hast not thou made an hedge about him, and about his house, 10
and about all that he hath on every side? thou hast blessed the work of
his hands, and his substance is increased in the land. But put forth
thine hand now, and touch all that he hath, and he will curse thee to
thy face. And the LORD said unto Satan, Behold, all that he hath is in
thy power; only upon himself put not forth thine hand. So Satan went
forth from the presence of the LORD.

His Afflictions

And there was a day when his sons and his daughters were eating and drinking wine in their eldest brother's house: and there came
a messenger unto Job, and said, The oxen were plowing, and the asses

feeding beside them: and the Sabeans fell upon them, and took them ₁₅
away; yea, they have slain the servants with the edge of the sword; and
I only am escaped alone to tell thee. While he was yet speaking, there
came also another, and said, The fire of God is fallen from heaven,
and hath burned up the sheep, and the servants, and consumed them;
and I only am escaped alone to tell thee. While he was yet speaking,
there came also another, and said, The Chaldeans made out three
bands, and fell upon the camels, and have carried them away, yea,
and slain the servants with the edge of the sword; and I only am escaped alone to tell thee. While he was yet speaking, there came also
another, and said, Thy sons and thy daughters were eating and drinking wine in their eldest brother's house: and, behold, there came a
great wind from the wilderness, and smote the four corners of the
house, and it fell upon the young men, and they are dead; and I only
am escaped alone to tell thee.

Then Job arose, and rent his mantle, and shaved his head, and ₂₀
fell down upon the ground, and worshipped, and said, Naked came I
out of my mother's womb, and naked shall I return thither: the LORD
gave, and the LORD hath taken away; blessed be the name of the
LORD. In all this Job sinned not, nor charged God foolishly.

2 Again there was a day when the sons of God came to present ₁
themselves before the LORD, and Satan came also among them to present himself before the LORD. And the LORD said unto Satan, From
whence comest thou? And Satan answered the LORD, and said, From
going to and fro in the earth, and from walking up and down in it.
And the LORD said unto Satan, Hast thou considered my servant Job,
that there is none like him in the earth, a perfect and an upright man,
one that feareth God, and escheweth evil? and still he holdeth fast his
integrity, although thou movedst me against him, to destroy him without cause. And Satan answered the LORD, and said, Skin for skin, yea,
all that a man hath will he give for his life. But put forth thine hand ₅
now, and touch his bone and his flesh, and he will curse thee to thy
face. And the LORD said unto Satan, Behold, he is in thine hand; but
save his life.

So went Satan forth from the presence of the LORD, and smote
Job with sore boils from the sole of his foot unto his crown. And he
took him a potsherd to scrape himself withal; and he sat down among
the ashes. Then said his wife unto him, Dost thou still retain thine integrity? curse God, and die. But he said unto her, Thou speakest as ₁₀
one of the foolish women speaketh. What? shall we receive good at the
hand of God, and shall we not receive evil? In all this did not Job sin
with his lips.

His Friends

> Now when Job's three friends heard of all this evil that was come upon him, they came every one from his own place; Eliphaz the Temanite, and Bildad the Shuhite, and Zophar the Naamathite: for they had made an appointment together to come to mourn with him and to comfort him. And when they lifted up their eyes afar off, and knew him not, they lifted up their voice, and wept; and they rent every one his mantle, and sprinkled dust upon their heads toward heaven. So they sat down with him upon the ground seven days and seven nights, and none spake a word unto him: for they saw that his grief was very great.

THE DEBATE

3   *Job's Outburst*

> After this opened Job his mouth, and cursed   1
> his day. And Job spake, and said,

> Let the day perish wherein I was born,
> And the night in which it was said,
> There is a man child conceived.
> Let that day be darkness;
> Let not God regard it from above,
> Neither let the light shine upon it.
> Let darkness and the shadow of death stain it;   5
> Let a cloud dwell upon it;
> Let the blackness of the day terrify it.
> As for that night, let darkness seize upon it;
> Let it not be joined unto the days of the year,
> Let it not come into the number of the months.
> Lo, let that night be solitary,
> Let no joyful voice come therein.
> Let them curse it that curse the day,
> Who are ready to raise up their mourning.
> Let the stars of the twilight thereof be dark;
> Let it look for light, but have none;
> Neither let it see the dawning of the day:
> Because it shut not up the doors of my mother's   10
>   womb,
> Nor hid sorrow from mine eyes.

Why died I not from the womb?
Why did I not give up the ghost when I came out
    of the belly?
Why did the knees prevent me?
Or why the breasts that I should suck?
For now should I have lain still and been quiet,
I should have slept: then had I been at rest,
With kings and counsellors of the earth,
Which built desolate places for themselves;
Or with princes that had gold,   15
Who filled their houses with silver:
Or as an hidden untimely birth I had not been;
As infants which never saw light.
There the wicked cease from troubling;
And there the weary be at rest.
There the prisoners rest together;
They hear not the voice of the oppressor.
The small and great are there;
And the servant is free from his master.

Wherefore is light given to him that is in   20
    misery,
And life unto the bitter in soul;
Which long for death, but it cometh not;
And dig for it more than for hid treasures;
Which rejoice exceedingly,
And are glad, when they can find the grave?
Why is light given to a man whose way is hid,
And whom God hath hedged in?
For my sighing cometh before I eat,
And my roarings are poured out like the waters.
For the thing which I greatly feared is come upon   25
    me,
And that which I was afraid of is come unto me.
I was not in safety, neither had I rest, neither was
    I quiet;
Yet trouble came.

4   *Eliphaz Speaks*

Then Eliphaz the Temanite answered and   1
said,

If we assay to commune with thee, wilt thou
be grieved?
But who can withhold himself from speaking?
Behold, thou hast instructed many,
And thou hast strengthened the weak hands.
Thy words have upholden him that was falling,
And thou hast strengthened the feeble knees.
But now it is come upon thee, and thou faintest;   5
It toucheth thee, and thou art troubled.
Is not this thy fear, thy confidence,
Thy hope, and the uprightness of thy ways?
Remember, I pray thee, who ever perished, being
innocent?
Or where were the righteous cut off?
Even as I have seen, they that plow iniquity,
And sow wickedness, reap the same.
By the blast of God they perish,
And by the breath of his nostrils are they con-
sumed.
The roaring of the lion, and the voice of the fierce   10
lion,
And the teeth of the young lions, are broken.
The old lion perisheth for lack of prey,
And the stout lion's whelps are scattered abroad.

Now a thing was secretly brought to me,
And mine ear received a little thereof.
In thoughts from visions of the night,
When deep sleep falleth on men,
Fear came upon me, and trembling,
Which made all my bones to shake.
Then a spirit passed before my face;   15
The hair of my flesh stood up:
It stood still, but I could not discern the form
thereof:
An image was before mine eyes,
There was silence, and I heard a voice, saying,
Shall mortal man be more just than God?
Shall a man be more pure than his maker?
Behold, he put no trust in his servants;
And his angels he charged with folly:
How much less in them that dwell in houses of
clay,
Whose foundation is in the dust,

Which are crushed before the moth?
They are destroyed from morning to evening: 20
They perish for ever without any regarding it.
Doth not their excellency which is in them go
    away?
They die, even without wisdom.

5   Call now, if there be any that will answer   1
    thee;
And to which of the saints wilt thou turn?
For wrath killeth the foolish man,
And envy slayeth the silly one.
I have seen the foolish taking root:
But suddenly I cursed his habitation.
His children are far from safety,
And they are crushed in the gate,
Neither is there any to deliver them.
Whose harvest the hungry eateth up,   5
And taketh it even out of the thorns,
And the robber swalloweth up their substance.
Although affliction cometh not forth of the dust,
Neither doth trouble spring out of the ground;
Yet man is born unto trouble,
As the sparks fly upward.

    I would seek unto God,
And unto God would I commit my cause:
Which doeth great things and unsearchable;
Marvellous things without number:
Who giveth rain upon the earth,   10
And sendeth waters upon the fields:
To set up on high those that be low;
That those which mourn may be exalted to safety.
He disappointeth the devices of the crafty,
So that their hands cannot perform their enter-
    prise.
He taketh the wise in their own craftiness:
And the counsel of the froward is carried head-
    long.
They meet with darkness in the daytime,
And grope in the noonday as in the night.
But he saveth the poor from the sword, from their
    mouth,   15

And from the hand of the mighty.
So the poor hath hope,
And iniquity stoppeth her mouth.

Behold, happy is the man whom God correct-
   eth:
Therefore despise not thou the chastening of the
   Almighty:
For he maketh sore, and bindeth up:
He woundeth, and his hands make whole.
He shall deliver thee in six troubles:
Yea, in seven there shall no evil touch thee.
In famine he shall redeem thee from death: 20
And in war from the power of the sword.
Thou shalt be hid from the scourge of the tongue:
Neither shalt thou be afraid of destruction when it
   cometh.
At destruction and famine thou shalt laugh:
Neither shalt thou be afraid of the beasts of the
   earth.
For thou shalt be in league with the stones of the
   field:
And the beasts of the field shall be at peace with
   thee.
And thou shalt know that thy tabernacle shall be
   in peace;
And thou shalt visit thy habitation, and shalt not
   sin.
Thou shalt know also that thy seed shall be great,   25
And thine offspring as the grass of the earth.
Thou shalt come to thy grave in a full age,
Like as a shock of corn cometh in in his season.
Lo this, we have searched it, so it is;
Hear it, and know thou it for thy good.

6   *Job's Answer*

But Job answered and said,   1

Oh that my grief were thoroughly weighed,
And my calamity laid in the balances together!
For now it would be heavier than the sand of the
   sea:

Therefore my words are swallowed up.
For the arrows of the Almighty are within me,
The poison whereof drinketh up my spirit;
The terrors of God do set themselves in array
    against me.
Doth the wild ass bray when he hath grass?   5
Or loweth the ox over his fodder?
Can that which is unsavoury be eaten without salt?
Or is there any taste in the white of an egg?
The things that my soul refused to touch
Are as my sorrowful meat.

    Oh that I might have my request;
And that God would grant me the thing that I long
    for!
Even that it would please God to destroy me;
That he would let loose his hand, and cut me off!
Then should I yet have comfort;   10
Yea, I would harden myself in sorrow: let him not
    spare;
For I have not concealed the words of the Holy
    One.
What is my strength, that I should hope?
And what is mine end, that I should prolong my
    life?
Is my strength the strength of stones?
Or is my flesh of brass?
Is not my help in me?
And is wisdom driven quite from me?

    To him that is afflicted pity should be
    shewed from his friend;
But he forsaketh the fear of the Almighty.
My brethren have dealt deceitfully as a brook,   15
And as the stream of brooks they pass away;
Which are blackish by reason of the ice,
And wherein the snow is hid:
What time they wax warm, they vanish:
When it is hot, they are consumed out of their
    place.
The paths of their way are turned aside;
They go to nothing, and perish.
The troops of Tema looked,

The companies of Sheba waited for them.
They were confounded because they had hoped;   20
They came thither, and were ashamed.
For now ye are nothing;
Ye see my casting down, and are afraid.
Did I say, Bring unto me?
Or, Give a reward for me of your substance?
Or, Deliver me from the enemy's hand?
Or, Redeem me from the hand of the mighty?

Teach me, and I will hold my tongue:
And cause me to understand wherein I have erred.
How forcible are right words!   25
But what doth your arguing reprove?
Do ye imagine to reprove words,
And the speeches of one that is desperate, which
      are as wind?
Yea, ye overwhelm the fatherless,
And ye dig a pit for your friend.
Now therefore be content, look upon me;
For it is evident unto you if I lie.
Return, I pray you, let it not be iniquity;
Yea, return again, my righteousness is in it.
Is there iniquity in my tongue?   30
Cannot my taste discern perverse things?

7   Is there not an appointed time to man upon earth?   1
Are not his days also like the days of an hireling?
As a servant earnestly desireth the shadow,
And as an hireling looketh for the reward of his
      work:
So am I made to possess months of vanity,
And wearisome nights are appointed to me.
When I lie down, I say,
When shall I arise, and the night be gone?
And I am full of tossings to and fro unto the
      dawning of the day.
My flesh is clothed with worms and clods of dust;   5
My skin is broken, and become loathsome.
My days are swifter than a weaver's shuttle,
And are spent without hope.
O remember that my life is wind:
Mine eye shall no more see good.

The eye of him that hath seen me shall see me no
    more:
Thine eyes are upon me, and I am not.
As the cloud is consumed and vanisheth away:
So he that goeth down to the grave shall come up
    no more.
He shall return no more to his house,   10
Neither shall his place know him any more.

        Therefore I will not refrain my mouth;
I will speak in the anguish of my spirit;
I will complain in the bitterness of my soul.
Am I a sea, or a whale,
That thou settest a watch over me?
When I say, My bed shall comfort me,
My couch shall ease my complaint;
Then thou scarest me with dreams,
And terrifiest me through visions:
So that my soul chooseth strangling,   15
And death rather than my life.
I loathe it; I would not live alway:
Let me alone; for my days are vanity.
What is man, that thou shouldest magnify him?
And that thou shouldest set thine heart upon him?
And that thou shouldest visit him every morning,
And try him every moment?
How long wilt thou not depart from me,
Nor let me alone till I swallow down my spittle?
I have sinned; what shall I do unto thee, O thou   20
    preserver of men?
Why hast thou set me as a mark against thee,
So that I am a burden to myself?
And why dost thou not pardon my transgression,
    and take away mine iniquity?
For now shall I sleep in the dust;
And thou shalt seek me in the morning, but I shall
    not be.

8   *Bildad's Speech*

        Then answered Bildad the Shuhite, and said,   1

        How long wilt thou speak these things?

And how long shall the words of thy mouth be like
    a strong wind?
Doth God pervert judgment?
Or doth the Almighty pervert justice?
If thy children have sinned against him,
And he have cast them away for their transgres-
    sion;
If thou wouldest seek unto God betimes,   5
And make thy supplication to the Almighty;
If thou wert pure and upright;
Surely now he would awake for thee,
And make the habitation of thy righteousness
    prosperous.
Though thy beginning was small,
Yet thy latter end should greatly increase.

    For enquire, I pray thee, of the former age,
And prepare thyself to the search of their fathers:
(For we are but of yesterday, and know nothing,
Because our days upon earth are a shadow:)
Shall not they teach thee, and tell thee,   10
And utter words out of their heart?

    Can the rush grow up without mire?
Can the flag grow without water?
Whilst it is yet in his greenness, and not cut down,
It withereth before any other herb.
So are the paths of all that forget God;
And the hypocrite's hope shall perish:
Whose hope shall be cut off,
And whose trust shall be a spider's web.
He shall lean upon his house, but it shall not   15
    stand:
He shall hold it fast, but it shall not endure.
He is green before the sun,
And his branch shooteth forth in his garden.
His roots are wrapped about the heap,
And seeth the place of stones.
If he destroy him from his place,
Then it shall deny him, saying, I have not seen
    thee.
Behold, this is the joy of his way,
And out of the earth shall others grow.

Behold, God will not cast away a perfect   20
man,
Neither will he help the evil doers:
Till he fill thy mouth with laughing,
And thy lips with rejoicing.
They that hate thee shall be clothed with shame;
And the dwelling place of the wicked shall come
to nought.

9   *Job's Reply*

Then Job answered and said,   1

I know it is so of a truth:
But how should man be just with God?
If he will contend with him,
He cannot answer him one of a thousand.
He is wise in heart, and mighty in strength:
Who hath hardened himself against him, and hath
prospered?
Which removeth the mountains, and they know   5
not:
Which overturneth them in his anger.
Which shaketh the earth out of her place,
And the pillars thereof tremble.
Which commandeth the sun, and it riseth not;
And sealeth up the stars.
Which alone spreadeth out the heavens,
And treadeth upon the waves of the sea.
Which maketh Arcturus, Orion, and Pleiades,
And the chambers of the south.
Which doeth great things past finding out;   10
Yea, and wonders without number.
Lo, he goeth by me, and I see him not:
He passeth on also, but I perceive him not.
Behold, he taketh away, who can hinder him?
Who will say unto him, What doest thou?

If God will not withdraw his anger,
The proud helpers do stoop under him.
How much less shall I answer him,
And choose out my words to reason with him?
Whom, though I were righteous, yet would I not   15
answer,

But I would make supplication to my judge.
If I had called, and he had answered me;
Yet would I not believe that he had hearkened
      unto my voice.
For he breaketh me with a tempest,
And multiplieth my wounds without cause.
He will not suffer me to take my breath,
But filleth me with bitterness.
If I speak of strength, lo, he is strong:
And if of judgment, who shall set me a time to
      plead?
If I justify myself, mine own mouth shall condemn   20
      me:
If I say, I am perfect, it shall also prove me per-
      verse.
Though I were perfect, yet would I not know my
      soul:
I would despise my life.
This is one thing, therefore I said it,
He destroyeth the perfect and the wicked.
If the scourge slay suddenly,
He will laugh at the trial of the innocent.
The earth is given into the hand of the wicked:
He covereth the faces of the judges thereof;
If not, where, and who is he?

      Now my days are swifter than a post: 25
They flee away, they see no good.
They are passed away as the swift ships:
As the eagle that hasteth to the prey.
If I say, I will forget my complaint,
I will leave off my heaviness, and comfort myself:
I am afraid of all my sorrows,
I know that thou wilt not hold me innocent.
If I be wicked,
Why then labour I in vain?
If I wash myself with snow water,   30
And make my hands never so clean;
Yet shalt thou plunge me in the ditch,
And mine own clothes shall abhor me.
For he is not a man, as I am, that I should answer
      him,
And we should come together in judgment.

Neither is there any daysman betwixt us,
That might lay his hand upon us both.
Let him take his rod away from me,
And let not his fear terrify me:
Then would I speak, and not fear him;   35
But it is not so with me.

10   My soul is weary of my life;   1
I will leave my complaint upon myself;
I will speak in the bitterness of my soul.
I will say unto God, Do not condemn me;
Shew me wherefore thou contendest with me.
Is it good unto thee that thou shouldest oppress,
That thou shouldest despise the work of thine
        hands,
And shine upon the counsel of the wicked?
Hast thou eyes of flesh?
Or seest thou as man seeth?
Are thy days as the days of man?   5
Are thy years as man's days,
That thou enquirest after mine iniquity,
And searchest after my sin?
Thou knowest that I am not wicked;
And there is none that can deliver out of thine
        hand.
Thine hands have made me and fashioned me
Together round about; yet thou dost destroy me.
Remember, I beseech thee, that thou hast made
        me as the clay;
And wilt thou bring me into dust again?
Hast thou not poured me out as milk,   10
And curdled me like cheese?
Thou hast clothed me with skin and flesh,
And hast fenced me with bones and sinews.
Thou hast granted me life and favour,
And thy visitation hath preserved my spirit.
And these things hast thou hid in thine heart:
I know that this is with thee.
If I sin, then thou markest me,
And thou wilt not acquit me from mine iniquity.
If I be wicked, woe unto me;   15
And if I be righteous, yet will I not lift up my
        head.

I am full of confusion;
Therefore see thou mine affliction;
For it increaseth. Thou huntest me as a fierce lion:
And again thou shewest thyself marvellous upon
    me.
Thou renewest thy witnesses against me,
And increasest thine indignation upon me;
Changes and war are against me.

  Wherefore then hast thou brought me forth
    out of the womb?
Oh that I had given up the ghost, and no eye had
    seen me!
I should have been as though I had not been;
I should have been carried from the womb to the
    grave.
Are not my days few? cease then,   20
And let me alone, that I may take comfort a little,
Before I go whence I shall not return,
Even to the land of darkness and the shadow of
    death;
A land of darkness, as darkness itself;
And of the shadow of death, without any order,
And where the light is as darkness.

11   *Zophar's Speech*

  Then answered Zophar the Naamathite, and   1
said,

  Should not the multitude of words be an-
    swered?
And should a man full of talk be justified?
Should thy lies make men hold their peace?
And when thou mockest, shall no man make thee
    ashamed?
For thou hast said, My doctrine is pure,
And I am clean in thine eyes.
But oh that God would speak,   5
And open his lips against thee;
And that he would shew thee the secrets of wis-
    dom,
That they are double to that which is!
Know therefore that God exacteth of thee less than
    thine iniquity deserveth.

Canst thou by searching find out God?
Canst thou find out the Almighty unto perfection?
It is as high as heaven; what canst thou do?
Deeper than hell; what canst thou know?
The measure thereof is longer than the earth,
And broader than the sea.
If he cut off, and shut up,   10
Or gather together, then who can hinder him?
For he knoweth vain men:
He seeth wickedness also; will he not then con-
    sider it?
For vain man would be wise,
Though man be born like a wild ass's colt.

If thou prepare thine heart,
And stretch out thine hands toward him;
If iniquity be in thine hand, put it far away,
And let not wickedness dwell in thy tabernacles.
For then shalt thou lift up thy face without spot;   15
Yea, thou shalt be steadfast, and shalt not fear:
Because thou shalt forget thy misery,
And remember it as waters that pass away:
And thine age shall be clearer than the noonday;
Thou shalt shine forth, thou shalt be as the morn-
    ing.
And thou shalt be secure, because there is hope;
Yea, thou shalt dig about thee, and thou shalt take
    thy rest in safety.
Also thou shalt lie down, and none shall make
    thee afraid;
Yea, many shall make suit unto thee.
But the eyes of the wicked shall fail.   20
And they shall not escape,
And their hope shall be as the giving up of the
    ghost.

Job's Reply

And Job answered and said,   1

No doubt but ye are the people,
And wisdom shall die with you.
But I have understanding as well as you;
I am not inferior to you:
Yea, who knoweth not such things as these?

I am as one mocked of his neighbour,
Who calleth upon God, and he answereth him:
The just upright man is laughed to scorn.
He that is ready to slip with his feet   5
Is as a lamp despised in the thought of him that is
    at ease.
The tabernacles of robbers prosper,
And they that provoke God are secure;
Into whose hand God bringeth abundantly.
But ask now the beasts, and they shall teach thee;
And the fowls of the air, and they shall tell thee:
Or speak to the earth, and it shall teach thee:
And the fishes of the sea shall declare unto thee.
Who knoweth not in all these
That the hand of the Lord hath wrought this?
In whose hand is the soul of every living thing,   10
And the breath of all mankind.

Doth not the ear try words?
And the mouth taste his meat?
With the ancient is wisdom;
And in length of days understanding.
With him is wisdom and strength,
He hath counsel and understanding.
Behold, he breaketh down, and it cannot be built
    again:
He shutteth up a man, and there can be no open-
    ing.
Behold, he withholdeth the waters, and they dry   15
    up:
Also he sendeth them out, and they overturn the
    earth.
With him is strength and wisdom:
The deceived and the deceiver are his.
He leadeth counsellors away spoiled,
And maketh the judges fools.
He looseth the bond of kings,
And girdeth their loins with a girdle.
He leadeth princes away spoiled,
And overthroweth the mighty.
He removeth away the speech of the trusty,   20
And taketh away the understanding of the aged.
He poureth contempt upon princes,

And weakeneth the strength of the mighty.
He discovereth deep things out of darkness,
And bringeth out to light the shadow of death.
He increaseth the nations, and destroyeth them:
He enlargeth the nations, and straiteneth them
    again.
He taketh away the heart of the chief of the people
    of the earth,
And causeth them to wander in a wilderness where
    there is no way.
They grope in the dark without light,   25
And he maketh them to stagger like a drunken
    man.

13   Lo, mine eye hath seen all this,   1
Mine ear hath heard and understood it.
What ye know, the same do I know also:
I am not inferior unto you.

        Surely I would speak to the Almighty,
And I desire to reason with God.
But ye are forgers of lies,
Ye are all physicians of no value.
O that ye would altogether hold your peace!   5
And it should be your wisdom.
Hear now my reasoning,
And hearken to the pleadings of my lips.
Will ye speak wickedly for God?
And talk deceitfully for him?
Will ye accept his person?
Will ye contend for God?
Is it good that he should search you out?
Or as one man mocketh another, do ye so mock
    him?
He will surely reprove you,   10
If ye do secretly accept persons.
Shall not his excellency make you afraid?
And his dread fall upon you?
Your remembrances are like unto ashes,
Your bodies to bodies of clay.

    Hold your peace, let me alone, that I may
    speak,

And let come on me what will.
Wherefore do I take my flesh in my teeth,
And put my life in mine hand?
Though he slay me, yet will I trust in him: 15
But I will maintain mine own ways before him.
He also shall be my salvation:
For an hypocrite shall not come before him.
Hear diligently my speech,
And my declaration with your ears.
Behold now, I have ordered my cause;
I know that I shall be justified.
Who is he that will plead with me?
For now, if I hold my tongue, I shall give up the
    ghost.

Only do not two things unto me: 20
Then will I not hide myself from thee.
Withdraw thine hand far from me:
And let not thy dread make me afraid.
Then call thou, and I will answer:
Or let me speak, and answer thou me.
How many are mine iniquities and sins?
Make me to know my transgression and my sin.
Wherefore hidest thou thy face,
And holdest me for thine enemy?
Wilt thou break a leaf driven to and fro?   25
And wilt thou pursue the dry stubble?
For thou writest bitter things against me,
And makest me to possess the iniquities of my
    youth.
Thou puttest my feet also in the stocks, and look-
    est narrowly unto all my paths;
Thou settest a print upon the heels of my feet.
And he, as a rotten thing, consumeth,
As a garment that is moth eaten.

14   Man that is born of a woman   1
Is of few days, and full of trouble.
He cometh forth like a flower, and is cut down:
He fleeth also as a shadow, and continueth not.
And dost thou open thine eyes upon such an one,
And bringest me into judgment with thee?
Who can bring a clean thing out of an unclean?
    Not one.

Seeing his days are determined, the number of his   5
    months are with thee,
Thou hast appointed his bounds that he cannot
    pass;
Turn from him, that he may rest,
Till he shall accomplish, as an hireling, his day.

    For there is hope of a tree, if it be cut down,
    that it will sprout again,
And that the tender branch thereof will not cease.
Though the root thereof wax old in the earth,
And the stock thereof die in the ground;
Yet through the scent of water it will bud,
And bring forth boughs like a plant.
But man dieth, and wasteth away: 10
Yea, man giveth up the ghost, and where is he?
As the waters fail from the sea,
And the flood decayeth and drieth up:
So man lieth down, and riseth not:
Till the heavens be no more, they shall not awake,
Nor be raised out of their sleep.

    O that thou wouldest hide me in the grave,
That thou wouldest keep me secret, until thy wrath
    be past,
That thou wouldest appoint me a set time, and re-
    member me!
If a man die, shall he live again?
All the days of my appointed time will I wait,
Till my change come.
Thou shalt call, and I will answer thee: 15
Thou wilt have a desire to the work of thine
    hands.
For now thou numberest my steps:
Dost thou not watch over my sin?
My transgression is sealed up in a bag,
And thou sewest up mine iniquity.

    And surely the mountain falling cometh to
    nought,
And the rock is removed out of his place.
The waters wear the stones:
Thou washest away the things which grow out of
    the dust of the earth;

And thou destroyest the hope of man.
Thou prevailest for ever against him, and he pass-   20
eth:
Thou changest his countenance, and sendest him
away.
His sons come to honour, and he knoweth it not;
And they are brought low, but he perceiveth it not
of them.
But his flesh upon him shall have pain,
And his soul within him shall mourn.

15   *Eliphaz Speaks*

Then answered Eliphaz the Temanite, and   1
said,

Should a wise man utter vain knowledge,
And fill his belly with the east wind?
Should he reason with unprofitable talk?
Or with speeches wherewith he can do no good?
Yea, thou castest off fear,
And restrainest prayer before God.
For thy mouth uttereth thine iniquity,   5
And thou choosest the tongue of the crafty.
Thine own mouth condemneth thee, and not I:
Yea, thine own lips testify against thee.

Art thou the first man that was born?
Or wast thou made before the hills?
Hast thou heard the secret of God?
And dost thou restrain wisdom to thyself?
What knowest thou, that we know not?
What understandest thou, which is not in us?
With us are both the grayheaded and very aged   10
men,
Much elder than thy father.
Are the consolations of God small with thee?
Is there any secret thing with thee?
Why doth thine heart carry thee away?
And what do thy eyes wink at,
That thou turnest thy spirit against God,
And lettest such words go out of thy mouth?
What is man, that he should be clean?

And he which is born of a woman, that he should
    be righteous?
Behold, he putteth no trust in his saints;   15
Yea, the heavens are not clean in his sight.
How much more abominable and filthy is man,
Which drinketh iniquity like water?

      I will shew thee, hear me;
And that which I have seen I will declare;
Which wise men have told
From their fathers, and have not hid it:
Unto whom alone the earth was given,
And no stranger passed among them.
The wicked man travaileth with pain all his days,   20
And the number of years is hidden to the oppres-
    sor.
A dreadful sound is in his ears:
In prosperity the destroyer shall come upon him.
He believeth not that he shall return out of dark-
    ness,
And he is waited for of the sword.
He wandereth abroad for bread, saying, Where is
    it?
He knoweth that the day of darkness is ready at
    his hand.
Trouble and anguish shall make him afraid;
They shall prevail against him, as a king ready to
    the battle.
For he stretcheth out his hand against God,   25
And strengtheneth himself against the Almighty.
He runneth upon him, even on his neck,
Upon the thick bosses of his bucklers:
Because he covereth his face with his fatness,
And maketh collops of fat on his flanks.
And he dwelleth in desolate cities,
And in houses which no man inhabiteth,
Which are ready to become heaps.
He shall not be rich, neither shall his substance
    continue,
Neither shall he prolong the perfection thereof
    upon the earth.
He shall not depart out of darkness;   30
The flame shall dry up his branches,

And by the breath of his mouth shall he go away.
Let not him that is deceived trust in vanity:
For vanity shall be his recompence.
It shall be accomplished before his time,
And his branch shall not be green.
He shall shake off his unripe grape as the vine,
And shall cast off his flower as the olive.
For the congregation of hypocrites shall be deso-
    late,
And fire shall consume the tabernacles of bribery.
They conceive mischief, and bring forth vanity,   35
And their belly prepareth deceit.

16   *Job's Reply*

          Then Job answered and said,   1

          I have heard many such things:
Miserable comforters are ye all.
Shall vain words have an end?
Or what emboldeneth thee that thou answerest?
I also could speak as ye do:
If your soul were in my soul's stead,
I could heap up words against you,
And shake mine head at you.
But I would strengthen you with my mouth,   5
And the moving of my lips should assuage your
    grief.

          Though I speak, my grief is not assuaged:
And though I forbear, what am I eased?
But now he hath made me weary:
Thou hast made desolate all my company.
And thou hast filled me with wrinkles, which is a
    witness against me:
And my leanness rising up in me beareth witness
    to my face.
He teareth me in his wrath, who hateth me:
He gnasheth upon me with his teeth;
Mine enemy sharpeneth his eyes upon me.
They have gaped upon me with their mouth;   10
They have smitten me upon the cheek reproachfully;

They have gathered themselves together against
  me.
God hath delivered me to the ungodly,
And turned me over into the hands of the wicked.
I was at ease, but he hath broken me asunder:
He hath also taken me by my neck, and shaken me
  to pieces,
And set me up for his mark.
His archers compass me round about,
He cleaveth my reins asunder, and doth not spare;
He poureth out my gall upon the ground.
He breaketh me with breach upon breach,
He runneth upon me like a giant.
I have sewed sackcloth upon my skin,   15
And defiled my horn in the dust.
My face is foul with weeping,
And on my eyelids is the shadow of death;
Not for any injustice in mine hands:
Also my prayer is pure.

    O earth, cover not thou my blood,
And let my cry have no place.
Also now, behold, my witness is in heaven,
And my record is on high.
My friends scorn me: 20
But mine eye poureth out tears unto God.
O that one might plead for a man with God,
As a man pleadeth for his neighbour!
When a few years are come,
Then I shall go the way whence I shall not return.

17   My breath is corrupt, my days are extinct,   1
The graves are ready for me.
Are there not mockers with me?
And doth not mine eye continue in their provoca-
  tion?

    Lay down now, put me in a surety with thee;
Who is he that will strike hands with me?
For thou hast hid their heart from understanding:
Therefore shalt thou not exalt them.
He that speaketh flattery to his friends,   5
Even the eyes of his children shall fail.

He hath made me also a byword of the peo-
ple;
And aforetime I was as a tabret.
Mine eye also is dim by reason of sorrow,
And all my members are as a shadow.
Upright men shall be astonied at this,
And the innocent shall stir up himself against the
hypocrite.
The righteous also shall hold on his way,
And he that hath clean hands shall be stronger and
stronger.
But as for you all, do ye return, and come now: 10
For I cannot find one wise man among you.
My days are past, my purposes are broken off,
Even the thoughts of my heart.
They change the night into day:
The light is short because of darkness.
If I wait, the grave is mine house:
I have made my bed in the darkness.
I have said to corruption, Thou art my father:
To the worm, Thou art my mother, and my sister.
And where is now my hope?   15
As for my hope, who shall see it?
They shall go down to the bars of the pit,
When our rest together is in the dust.

18   *Bildad's Speech*

Then answered Bildad the Shuhite, and said,   1

How long will it be ere ye make an end of
words?
Mark, and afterwards we will speak.
Wherefore are we counted as beasts,
And reputed vile in your sight?
He teareth himself in his anger:
Shall the earth be forsaken for thee?
And shall the rock be removed out of his place?

Yea, the light of the wicked shall be put out,   5
And the spark of his fire shall not shine.
The light shall be dark in his tabernacle,
And his candle shall be put out with him.

The steps of his strength shall be straightened,
And his own counsel shall cast him down.
For he is cast into a net by his own feet,
And he walketh upon a snare.

. . . .

His remembrance shall perish from the earth,
And he shall have no name in the street.
He shall be driven from light into darkness,
And chased out of the world.
He shall neither have son nor nephew among his
    people,
Nor any remaining in his dwellings.
They that come after him shall be astonied at his   20
    day,
As they that went before were affrighted.
Surely such are the dwellings of the wicked,
And this is the place of him that knoweth not God.

19   *Job's Reply*

     Then Job answered and said,   1

     How long will ye vex my soul,
And break me in pieces with words?
These ten times have ye reproached me;
Ye are not ashamed that ye make yourselves
    strange to me.
And be it indeed that I have erred,
Mine error remaineth with myself.
If indeed ye will magnify yourselves against me,   5
And plead against me my reproach:
Know now that God hath overthrown me,
And hath compassed me with his net.

     Behold, I cry out of wrong, but I am not
    heard:
I cry aloud, but there is no judgment.
He hath fenced up my way that I cannot pass,
And he hath set darkness in my paths.
He hath stripped me of my glory,
And taken the crown from my head.

He hath destroyed me on every side, and I am   10
    gone:
And mine hope hath he removed like a tree.
He hath also kindled his wrath against me,
And he counteth me unto him as one of his ene-
    mies.
His troops come together, and raise up their way
    against me,
And encamp round about my tabernacle.

He hath put my brethren far from me,
And mine acquaintance are verily estranged from
    me.
My kinsfolk have failed,
And my familiar friends have forgotten me.
They that dwell in mine house, and my maids,   15
    count me for a stranger:
I am an alien in their sight.
I called my servant, and he gave me no answer;
I intreated him with my mouth.
My breath is strange to my wife,
Though I intreated for the children's sake of mine
    own body.
Yea, young children despised me;
I arose, and they spake against me.
All my inward friends abhorred me:
And they whom I loved are turned against me.
My bone cleaveth to my skin and to my flesh,   20
And I am escaped with the skin of my teeth.
Have pity upon me, have pity upon me, O ye my
    friends;
For the hand of God hath touched me.
Why do ye persecute me as God,
And are not satisfied with my flesh?

Oh that my words were now written!
Oh that they were printed in a book!
That they were graven with an iron pen and lead
In the rock for ever!
For I know that my redeemer liveth,   25
And that he shall stand at the latter day upon the
    earth:
And though after my skin worms destroy this
    body,

Yet in my flesh shall I see God:
Whom I shall see for myself,
And mine eyes shall behold, and not another;
Though my reins be consumed within me.
But ye should say, Why persecute we him,
Seeing the root of the matter is found in me?
Be ye afraid of the sword:
For wrath bringeth the punishments of the sword,
That ye may know there is a judgment.

20 *Zophar's Speech*

Then answered Zophar the Naamathite, and 1
said,

Therefore do my thoughts cause me to an-
swer,
And for this I make haste.
I have heard the check of my reproach,
And the spirit of my understanding causeth me to
answer.
Knowest thou not this of old,
Since man was placed upon earth,
That the triumphing of the wicked is short, 5
And the joy of the hypocrite but for a moment?
Though his excellency mount up to the heavens,
And his head reach unto the clouds;
Yet he shall perish for ever like his own dung:
They which have seen him shall say, Where is he?
He shall fly away as a dream, and shall not be
found:
Yea, he shall be chased away as a vision of the
night.

. . . .

The heaven shall reveal his iniquity;
And the earth shall rise up against him.
The increase of his house shall depart,
And his goods shall flow away in the day of his
wrath.
This is the portion of a wicked man from God,
And the heritage appointed unto him by God.

21   *Job's Reply*

But Job answered and said,   1

Hear diligently my speech,
And let this be your consolations.
Suffer me that I may speak;
And after that I have spoken, mock on.
As for me, is my complaint to man?
And if it were so, why should not my spirit be
   troubled?
Mark me, and be astonished,   5
And lay your hand upon your mouth.
Even when I remember I am afraid,
And trembling taketh hold on my flesh.
Wherefore do the wicked live,
Become old, yea, are mighty in power?
Their seed is established in their sight with them,
And their offspring before their eyes.
Their houses are safe from fear,
Neither is the rod of God upon them.
Their bull gendereth, and faileth not;   10
Their cow calveth, and casteth not her calf.
They send forth their little ones like a flock,
And their children dance.
They take the timbrel and harp,
And rejoice at the sound of the organ.
They spend their days in wealth,
And in a moment go down to the grave.
Therefore they say unto God, Depart from us;
For we desire not the knowledge of thy ways.
What is the Almighty, that we should serve him?   15
And what profit should we have, if we pray unto
   him?
Lo, their good is not in their hand:
The counsel of the wicked is far from me.

How oft is the candle of the wicked put out!
And how oft cometh their destruction upon them!
God distributeth sorrows in his anger.
They are as stubble before the wind,
And as chaff that the storm carrieth away.
God layeth up his iniquity for his children:

He rewardeth him, and he shall know it.
His eyes shall see his destruction,   20
And he shall drink of the wrath of the Almighty.
For what pleasure hath he in his house after him,
When the number of his months is cut off in the
     midst?
Shall any teach God knowledge?
Seeing he judgeth those that are high.
One dieth in his full strength,
Being wholly at ease and quiet.
His breasts are full of milk,
And his bones are moistened with marrow.
And another dieth in the bitterness of his soul,   25
And never eateth with pleasure.
They shall lie down alike in the dust,
And the worms shall cover them.

     Behold, I know your thoughts,
And the devices which ye wrongfully imagine
     against me.
For ye say, Where is the house of the prince?
And where are the dwelling places of the wicked?
Have ye not asked them that go by the way?
And do ye not know their tokens,
That the wicked is reserved to the day of destruc-   30
     tion?
They shall be brought forth to the day of wrath.
Who shall declare his way to his face?
And who shall repay him what he hath done?
Yet shall he be brought to the grave,
And shall remain in the tomb.
The clods of the valley shall be sweet unto him,
And every man shall draw after him,
As there are innumerable before him.
How then comfort ye me in vain,
Seeing in your answers there remaineth falsehood?

22   *Eliphaz Speaks*

     Then Eliphaz the Temanite answered and   1
said,

     Can a man be profitable unto God,

As he that is wise may be profitable unto himself?
Is it any pleasure to the Almighty, that thou art
    righteous?
Or is it gain to him, that thou makest thy ways
    perfect?
Will he reprove thee for fear of thee?
Will he enter with thee into judgment?
Is not thy wickedness great?   5
And thine iniquities infinite?
For thou hast taken a pledge from thy brother for
    nought,
And stripped the naked of their clothing.
Thou hast not given water to the weary to drink,
And thou hast withholden bread from the hungry.
But as for the mighty man, he had the earth;
And the honourable man dwelt in it.
Thou hast sent widows away empty,
And the arms of the fatherless have been broken.
Therefore snares are round about thee,   10
And sudden fear troubleth thee;
Or darkness, that thou canst not see;
And abundance of waters cover thee.

. . . .

    Acquaint now thyself with him, and be at
    peace:
Thereby good shall come unto thee.
Receive, I pray thee, the law from his mouth,
And lay up his words in thine heart.
If thou return to the Almighty, thou shalt be built
    up,
Thou shalt put away iniquity far from thy taber-
    nacles.
Then shalt thou lay up gold as dust,
And the gold of Ophir as the stones of the brooks.
Yea, the Almighty shall be thy defence,   25
And thou shalt have plenty of silver.
For then shalt thou have thy delight in the Al-
    mighty,
And shalt lift up thy face unto God.
Thou shalt make thy prayer unto him, and he shall
    hear thee,

And thou shalt pay thy vows.
Thou shalt also decree a thing, and it shall be es-
tablished unto thee:
And the light shall shine upon thy ways.
When men are cast down, then thou shalt say,
There is lifting up;
And he shall save the humble person.
He shall deliver the island of the innocent: 30
And it is delivered by the pureness of thine hands.

23   *Job's Reply*

Then Job answered and said,   1

Even to day is my complaint bitter:
My stroke is heavier than my groaning.
Oh that I knew where I might find him!
That I might come even to his seat!
I would order my cause before him,
And fill my mouth with arguments.
I would know the words which he would answer   5
me,
And understand what he would say unto me.
Will he plead against me with his great power?
No; but he would put strength in me.
There the righteous might dispute with him;
So should I be delivered for ever from my judge.
Behold, I go forward, but he is not there;
And backward, but I cannot perceive him:
On the left hand, where he doth work, but I can-
not behold him:
He hideth himself on the right hand, that I cannot
see him:
But he knoweth the way that I take: 10
When he hath tried me, I shall come forth as gold.

My foot hath held his steps,
His way have I kept, and not declined.
Neither have I gone back from the commandment
of his lips;
I have esteemed the words of his mouth more than
my necessary food.
But he is in one mind, and who can turn him?

And what his soul desireth, even that he doeth.
For he performeth the thing that is appointed for
    me:
And many such things are with him.
Therefore am I troubled at his presence: 15
When I consider, I am afraid of him.
For God maketh my heart soft,
And the Almighty troubleth me:
Because I was not cut off before the darkness,
Neither hath he covered the darkness from my
    face.

24   Why, seeing times are not hidden from the   1
    Almighty,
Do they that know him not see his days?
Some remove the landmarks;
They violently take away flocks, and feed thereof.
They drive away the ass of the fatherless,
They take the widow's ox for a pledge.
They turn the needy out of the way:
The poor of the earth hide themselves together.
Behold, as wild asses in the desert,   5
Go they forth to their work; rising betimes for a
    prey:
The wilderness yieldeth food for them and for
    their children.
They reap every one his corn in the field:
And they gather the vintage of the wicked.
They cause the naked to lodge without clothing,   10
That they have no covering in the cold.
They are wet with the showers of the mountains,
And embrace the rock for want of a shelter.
They pluck the fatherless from the breast,
And take a pledge of the poor.
They cause him to go naked without clothing,
And they take away the sheaf from the hungry;
Which make oil within their walls,
And tread their winepresses, and suffer thirst.
Men groan from out of the city,
And the soul of the wounded crieth out:
Yet God layeth not folly to them.

They are of those that rebel against the light;
They know not the ways thereof,

Nor abide in the paths thereof.
The murderer rising with the light killeth the poor
     and needy,
And in the night is as a thief.
The eye also of the adulterer waiteth for the twi-   15
     light,
Saying, No eye shall see me:
And disguiseth his face.
In the dark they dig through houses,
Which they had marked for themselves in the day-
     time:
They know not the light.
For the morning is to them even as the shadow of
     death:
If one know them, they are in the terrors of the
     shadow of death.

     He is swift as the waters;
Their portion is cursed in the earth:
He beholdeth not the way of the vineyards.
Drought and heat consume the snow waters:
So doth the grave those which have sinned.
The womb shall forget him; the worm shall feed   20
     sweetly on him;
He shall be no more remembered;
And wickedness shall be broken as a tree.
He evil entreateth the barren that beareth not:
And doeth not good to the widow.
He draweth also the mighty with his power:
He riseth up, and no man is sure of life.
Though it be given him to be in safety, whereon he
     resteth;
Yet his eyes are upon their ways.
They are exalted for a little while, but are gone
And brought low; they are taken out of the way as
     all other,
And cut off as the tops of the ears of corn.
And if it be not so now, who will make me a liar,   25
And make my speech nothing worth?

25   *Bildad's Speech*

     Then answered Bildad the Shuhite, and said,   1

Dominion and fear are with him,
He maketh peace in his high places.
Is there any number of his armies?
And upon whom doth not his light arise?
How then can man be justified with God?
Or how can he be clean that is born of a woman?
Behold even to the moon, and it shineth not;   5
Yea, the stars are not pure in his sight.
How much less man, that is a worm?
And the son of man, which is a worm?

26   *Job's Reply*

But Job answered and said,   1

How hast thou helped him that is without
    power?
How savest thou the arm that hath no strength?
How hast thou counselled him that hath no wis-
    dom?
And how hast thou plentifully declared the thing
    as it is?
To whom hast thou uttered words?
And whose spirit came from thee?

Dead things are formed   5
From under the waters, and the inhabitants there-
    of.
Hell is naked before him,
And destruction hath no covering.
He stretcheth out the north over the empty place,
And hangeth the earth upon nothing.
He bindeth up the waters in his thick clouds;
And the cloud is not rent under them.
He holdeth back the face of his throne,
And spreadeth his cloud upon it.
He hath compassed the waters with bounds,   10
Until the day and night come to an end.
The pillars of heaven tremble
And are astonished at his reproof.
He divideth the sea with his power,
And by his understanding he smiteth through the
    proud.

By his spirit he hath garnished the heavens;
His hand hath formed the crooked serpent.
Lo, these are parts of his ways:
But how little a portion is heard of him?
But the thunder of his power who can understand?

27   Moreover Job continued his parable, and   1
said,

As God liveth, who hath taken away my
    judgment;
And the Almighty, who hath vexed my soul;
All the while my breath is in me,
And the spirit of God is in my nostrils;
My lips shall not speak wickedness,
Nor my tongue utter deceit.
God forbid that I should justify you: 5
Till I die I will not remove mine integrity from me.
My righteousness I hold fast, and will not let it go:
My heart shall not reproach me so long as I live.

. . . .

28   Surely there is a vein for the silver,   1
And a place for gold where they find it.
Iron is taken out of the earth,
And brass is molten out of the stone.
He setteth an end to darkness,
And searcheth out all perfection:
The stones of darkness, and the shadow of death.
The flood breaketh out from the inhabitant;
Even the waters forgotten of the foot:
They are dried up, they are gone away from men.
As for the earth, out of it cometh bread: 5
And under it is turned up as it were fire.
The stones of it are the place of sapphires:
And it hath dust of gold.
There is a path which no fowl knoweth,
And which the vulture's eye hath not seen:
The lion's whelps have not trodden it,
Nor the fierce lion passed by it.
He putteth forth his hand upon the rock;
He overturneth the mountains by the roots.

He cutteth out rivers among the rocks;   10
And his eye seeth every previous thing.
He bindeth the floods from overflowing;
And the thing that is hid bringeth he forth to light.

                          . . . .

Whence then cometh wisdom?   20
And where is the place of understanding?
Seeing it is hid from the eyes of all living,
And kept close from the fowls of the air.
Destruction and death say,
We have heard the fame thereof with our ears.
God understandeth the way thereof,
And he knoweth the place thereof.
For he looketh to the ends of the earth,
And seeth under the whole heaven;
To make the weight for the winds;   25
And he weigheth the waters by measure.
When he made a decree for the rain,
And a way for the lightning of the thunder:
Then did he see it, and declare it;
He prepared it, yea, and searched it out.
And unto man he said,
Behold, the fear of the Lord, that is wisdom;
And to depart from evil is understanding.

29   Moreover Job continued his parable, and   1
said,

Oh that I were as in months past,
As in the days when God preserved me;
When his candle shined upon my head,
And when by his light I walked through darkness;
As I was in the days of my youth,
When the secret of God was upon my tabernacle;
When the Almighty was yet with me,   5
When my children were about me;
When I washed my steps with butter,
And the rock poured me out rivers of oil;
When I went out to the gate through the city,
When I prepared my seat in the street!

                          . . . .

30   But now they that are younger than I have   1
      me in derision,
Whose fathers I would have disdained to have set
    with the dogs of my flock.

                    . . . .

        And now am I their song,
Yea, I am their byword.
They abhor me, they flee far from me,   10
And spare not to spit in my face.
Because he hath loosed my cord, and afflicted me,
They have also let loose the bridle before me.
Upon my right hand rise the youth;
They push away my feet,
And they raise up against me the ways of their de-
    struction.

                    . . . .

When I looked for good, then evil came unto me:
And when I waited for light, there came darkness.
My bowels boiled, and rested not:
The days of affliction prevented me.
I went mourning without the sun:
I stood up, and I cried in the congregation.
I am a brother to dragons,
And a companion to owls.
My skin is black upon me,   30
And my bones are burned with heat.
My harp also is turned to mourning,
And my organ into the voice of them that weep.

31   I made a covenant with mine eyes;   1
Why then should I think upon a maid?
For what portion of God is there from above?
And what inheritance of the Almighty from on
    high?
Is not destruction to the wicked?
And a strange punishment to the workers of iniq-
    uity?
Doth not he see my ways,
And count all my steps?

If I have walked with vanity,   5
Or if my foot hath hasted to deceit;
Let me be weighed in an even balance,
That God may know mine integrity.
If my step hath turned out of the way,
And mine heart walked after mine eyes,
And if any blot hath cleaved to mine hands;
Then let me sow, and let another eat;
Yea, let my offspring be rooted out.
If mine heart have been deceived by a woman,
Or if I have laid wait at my neighbour's door;
Then let my wife grind unto another,   10
And let others bow down upon her.
For this is an heinous crime;
Yea, it is an iniquity to be punished by the judges.
For it is a fire that consumeth to destruction,
And would root out all mine increase.
If I did despise the cause of my manservant or of
    my maidservant,
When they contended with me;
What then shall I do when God riseth up?
And when he visiteth, what shall I answer him?
Did not he that made me in the womb make him?   15
And did not one fashion us in the womb?

If I have withheld the poor from their desire,
Or have caused the eyes of the widow to fail;
Or have eaten my morsel myself alone,
And the fatherless hath not eaten thereof;
(For from my youth he was brought up with me,
    as with a father,
And I have guided her from my mother's womb;)
If I have seen any perish for want of clothing,
Or any poor without covering;
If his loins have not blessed me.   20
And if he were not warmed with the fleece of my
    sheep;
If I have lifted up my hand against the fatherless,
When I saw my help in the gate:
Then let mine arm fall from my shoulder blade,
And mine arm be broken from the bone.
For destruction from God was a terror to me,
And by reason of his highness I could not endure.

If I have made gold my hope,
Or have said to the fine gold, Thou art my confid-
ence;
If I rejoiced because my wealth was great, 25
And because mine hand had gotten much;
If I beheld the sun when it shined,
Or the moon walking in brightness;
And my heart hath been secretly enticed,
Or my mouth hath kissed my hand:
This also were an iniquity to be punished by the
judge:
For I should have denied the God that is above.

If I rejoiced at the destruction of him that
hated me,
Or lifted up myself when evil found him:
Neither have I suffered my mouth to sin 30
By wishing a curse to his soul.
If the men of my tabernacle said not,
Oh that we had of his flesh! we cannot be satis-
fied.
The stranger did not lodge in the street:
But I opened my doors to the traveller.
If I covered my transgressions as Adam,
By hiding mine iniquity in my bosom:
Did I fear a great multitude,
Or did the contempt of families terrify me,
That I kept silence, and went not out of the door?

Oh that one would hear me! 35
Behold, my desire is, that the Almighty would an-
swer me,
And that mine adversary had written a book.
Surely I would take it upon my shoulder,
And bind it as a crown to me.
I would declare unto him the number of my steps;
As a prince would I go near unto him.
If my land cry against me,
Or that the furrows likewise thereof complain;
If I have eaten the fruits thereof without money,
Or have caused the owners thereof to lose their
life:
Let thistles grow instead of wheat, 40

And cockle instead of barley.

The words of Job are ended.

. . . .

38   *The Lord Answered Job*

Then the LORD answered Job out of the whirl-   1
wind, and said,

Who is this that darkeneth counsel
By words without knowledge?
Gird up now thy loins like a man;
For I will demand of thee, and answer thou me.

Where wast thou when I laid the foundations
of the earth?
Declare, if thou hast understanding.
Who hath laid the measures thereof, if thou know-   5
est?
Or who hath stretched the line upon it?
Whereupon are the foundations thereof fastened?
Or who laid the corner stone thereof;
When the morning stars sang together,
And all the sons of God shouted for joy?

Or who shut up the sea with doors,
When it brake forth, as if it had issued out of the
womb?
When I made the cloud the garment thereof,
And thick darkness a swaddling band for it,
And brake up for it my decreed place,   10
And set bars and doors,
And said, Hitherto shalt thou come, but no fur-
ther:
And here shall thy proud waves be stayed?

Hast thou commanded the morning since thy
days;
And caused the dayspring to know his place;
That it might take hold of the ends of the earth,
That the wicked might be shaken out of it?
It is turned as clay to the seal;
And they stand as a garment.

And from the wicked their light is withholden,
And the high arm shall be broken.

Hast thou entered into the springs of the sea?
Or hast thou walked in the search of the depth?
Have the gates of death been opened unto thee?
Or has thou seen the doors of the shadow of
     death?
Hast thou perceived the breadth of the earth?
Declare if thou knowest it all.

Where is the way where light dwelleth?
And as for darkness, where is the place thereof,
That thou shouldest take it to the bound thereof,   20
And that thou shouldest know the paths to the
     house thereof?
Knowest thou it, because thou wast then born?
Or because the number of thy days is great?
Hast thou entered into the treasures of the snow?
Or hast thou seen the treasures of the hail,
Which I have reserved against the time of trouble,
Against the day of battle and war?
By what way is the light parted,
Which scattereth the east wind upon the earth?

Who hath divided a watercourse for the   25
     overflowing of waters,
Or a way for the lightning of thunder;
To cause it to rain on the earth, where no man is;
On the wilderness, wherein there is no man;
To satisfy the desolate and waste ground;
And to cause the bud of the tender herb to spring
     forth?
Hath the rain a father?
Or who hath begotten the drops of dew?
Out of whose womb came the ice?
And the hoary frost of heaven, who hath gendered
     it?
The waters are hid as with a stone,   30
And the face of the deep is frozen.

Canst thou bind the sweet influences of
     Pleiades,
Or loose the bands of Orion?

Canst thou bring forth Mazzaroth in his season?
Or canst thou guide Arcturus with his sons?
Knowest thou the ordinances of heaven?
Canst thou set the dominion thereof in the earth?

Canst thou lift up thy voice to the clouds,
That abundance of waters may cover thee?
Canst thou send lightnings, that they may go,   35
And say unto thee, Here we are?
Who hath put wisdom in the inward parts?
Or who hath given understanding to the heart?
Who can number the clouds in wisdom?
Or who can stay the bottles of heaven,
When the dust groweth into hardness,
And the clods cleave fast together?

Wilt thou hunt the prey for the lion?
Or fill the appetite of the young lions,
When they couch in their dens,   40
And abide in the covert to lie in wait?
Who provideth for the raven his food?
When his young ones cry unto God,
They wander for lack of meat.

39   Knowest thou the time when the wild goats   1
      of the rock bring forth?
Or canst thou mark when the hinds do calve?
Canst thou number the months that they fulfil?
Or knowest thou the time when they bring forth?
They bow themselves, they bring forth their young
      ones,
They cast out their sorrows.
Their young ones are in good liking, they grow up
      with corn;
They go forth, and return not unto them.

Who hath sent out the wild ass free?   5
Or who hath loosed the bands of the wild ass?
Whose house I have made the wilderness,
And the barren land his dwellings.
He scorneth the multitude of the city,
Neither regardeth he the crying of the driver.
The range of the mountains is his pasture,

And he searcheth after every green thing.
Will the unicorn be willing to serve thee,
Or abide by thy crib?
Canst thou bind the unicorn with his band in the   10
    furrow?
Or will he harrow the valleys after thee?
Wilt thou trust him, because his strength is great?
Or wilt thou leave thy labour to him?
Wilt thou believe him, that he will bring home thy
    seed,
And gather it into thy barn?

    Gavest thou the goodly wings unto the pea-
    cocks?
Or wings and feathers unto the ostrich?
Which leaveth her eggs in the earth,
And warmeth them in dust,
And forgetteth that the foot may crush them,   15
Or that the wild beast may break them.
She is hardened against her young ones, as though
    they were not hers:
Her labour is in vain without fear;
Because God hath deprived her of wisdom,
Neither hath he imparted to her understanding.
What time she lifteth up herself on high,
She scorneth the horse and his rider.

    Hast thou given the horse strength?
Hast thou clothed his neck with thunder?
Canst thou make him afraid as a grasshopper?   20
The glory of his nostrils is terrible.
He paweth in the valley, and rejoiceth in his
    strength:
He goeth on to meet the armed men.
He mocketh at fear, and is not affrighted;
Neither turneth he back from the sword.
The quiver rattleth against him,
The glittering spear and the shield.
He swalloweth the ground with fierceness and
    rage:
Neither believeth he that it is the sound of the
    trumpet.
He saith among the trumpets, Ha, ha;   25

And he smelleth the battle afar off,
The thunder of the captains, and the shouting.

Doth the hawk fly by thy wisdom,
And stretch her wings toward the south?
Doth the eagle mount up at thy command,
And make her nest on high?
She dwelleth and abideth on the rock,
Upon the crag of the rock, and the strong place.
From thence she seeketh the prey,
And her eyes behold afar off.
Her young ones also suck up blood: 30
And where the slain are, there is she.

40   Moreover the Lord answered Job, and said,

Shall he that contendeth with the Almighty   1
instruct him?
He that reproveth God, let him answer it.

Job's Reply

Then Job answered the Lord, and said,

Behold, I am vile; what shall I answer thee?
I will lay mine hand upon my mouth.
Once have I spoken; but I will not answer: 5
Yea, twice; but I will proceed no further.

The Lord's Answer

Then answered the Lord unto Job out of the
whirlwind, and said,

Gird up thy loins now like a man:
I will demand of thee, and declare thou unto me.
Wilt thou also disannul my judgment?
Wilt thou condemn me, that thou mayest be right-
eous?
Hast thou an arm like God?
Or canst thou thunder with a voice like him?

Deck thyself now with majesty and excellen-   10
cy;

And array thyself with glory and beauty.
Cast abroad the rage of thy wrath:
And behold every one that is proud, and abase
    him.
Look on every one that is proud, and bring him
    low;
And tread down the wicked in their place.
Hide them in the dust together;
And bind their faces in secret.
Then will I also confess unto thee
That thine own right hand can save thee.

     Behold now behemoth, which I made with   15
    thee;
He eateth grass as an ox.
Lo now, his strength is in his loins,
And his force is in the navel of his belly.
He moveth his tail like a cedar:
The sinews of his stones are wrapped together.
His bones are as strong pieces of brass;
His bones are like bars of iron.
He is the chief of the ways of God:
He that made him can make his sword to ap-
    proach unto him.
Surely the mountains bring him forth food,   20
Where all the beasts of the field play.
He lieth under the shady trees,
In the covert of the reed, and fens.
The shady trees cover him with their shadow;
The willows of the brook compass him about.
Behold, he drinketh up a river, and hasteth not:
He trusteth that he can draw up Jordan into his
    mouth.
He taketh it with his eyes:
His nose pierceth through snares.

41   Canst thou draw out leviathan with an hook?   1
Or his tongue with a cord which thou lettest down?
Canst thou put an hook into his nose?
Or bore his jaw through with a thorn?
Will he make many supplications unto thee?
Will he speak soft words unto thee?
Will he make a covenant with thee?
Wilt thou take him for a servant for ever?

Wilt thou play with him as with a bird?   5
Or wilt thou bind him for thy maidens?
Shall the companions make a banquet of him?
Shall they part him among the merchants?
Canst thou fill his skin with barbed irons?
Or his head with fish spears?
Lay thine hand upon him,
Remember the battle, do no more.
Behold, the hope of him is in vain:
Shall not one be cast down even at the sight of
      him?
None is so fierce that dare stir him up: 10
Who then is able to stand before me?
Who hath prevented me, that I should repay him?
Whatsoever is under the whole heaven is mine.

      I will not conceal his parts,
Nor his power, nor his comely proportion.
Who can discover the face of his garment?
Or who can come to him with his double bridle?
Who can open the doors of his face?
His teeth are terrible round about.
His scales are his pride,   15
Shut up together as with a close seal.
One is so near to another,
That no air can come between them.
They are joined one to another,
They stick together, that they cannot be sundered.
By his neesings a light doth shine,
And his eyes are like the eyelids of the morning.
Out of his mouth go burning lamps,
And sparks of fire leap out.
Out of his nostrils goeth smoke,   20
As out of a seething pot or caldron.
His breath kindleth coals,
And a flame goeth out of his mouth.
In his neck remaineth strength,
And sorrow is turned into joy before him.
The flakes of his flesh are joined together:
They are firm in themselves; they cannot be
      moved.
His heart is as firm as a stone;
Yea, as hard as a piece of the nether millstone.

When he raiseth up himself, the mighty are afraid: 25
By reason of breakings they purify themselves.
The sword of him that layeth at him cannot hold:
The spear, the dart, nor the habergeon.
He esteemeth iron as straw,
And brass as rotten wood.
The arrow cannot make him flee:
Slingstones are turned with him into stubble.
Darts are counted as stubble:
He laugheth at the shaking of a spear.
Sharp stones are under him: 30
He spreadeth sharp pointed things upon the mire.
He maketh the deep to boil like a pot:
He maketh the sea like a pot of ointment.
He maketh a path to shine after him;
One would think the deep to be hoary.
Upon earth there is not his like,
Who is made without fear.
He beholdeth all high things:
He is a king over all the children of pride.

42   *Job's Reply*

Then Job answered the LORD, and said,   1

I know that thou canst do every thing,
And that no thought can be withholden from thee.
Who is he that hideth counsel without knowledge?
Therefore have I uttered that I understood not;
Things too wonderful for me, which I knew not.
Hear, I beseech thee, and I will speak:
I will demand of thee, and declare thou unto me.
I have heard of thee by the hearing of the ear.   5
But now mine eye seeth thee.
Wherefore I abhor myself, and repent
In dust and ashes.

The Epilogue

And it was so, that after the LORD had spoken these words unto
Job, the LORD said to Eliphaz the Temanite, My wrath is kindled
against thee, and against thy two friends: for ye have not spoken of
me the thing that is right, as my servant Job hath. Therefore take unto

you now seven bullocks and seven rams, and go to my servant Job, and offer up for yourselves a burnt offering; and my servant Job shall pray for you: for him will I accept: lest I deal with you after your folly, in that ye have not spoken of me the thing which is right, like my servant Job. So Eliphaz the Temanite and Bildad the Shuhite and Zophar the Naamathite went, and did according as the LORD commanded them: the LORD also accepted Job. And the LORD turned the captivity of Job, when he prayed for his friends: also the LORD gave Job twice as much as he had before. Then came there unto him all his brethren, and all his sisters, and all they that had been of his acquaintance before, and did eat bread with him in his house: and they bemoaned him, and comforted him over all the evil that the LORD had brought upon him: every man also gave him a piece of money, and every one an earring of gold. So the LORD blessed the latter end of Job more than his beginning: for he had fourteen thousand sheep, and six thousand camels, and a thousand yoke of oxen, and a thousand she asses. He had also seven sons and three daughters. And he called the name of the first, Jemima; and the name of the second, Kezia; and the name of the third, Keren-happuch. And in all the land were no women found so fair as the daughters of Job: and their father gave them inheritance among their brethren. After this lived Job an hundred and forty years, and saw his sons, and his sons's sons, even four generations. So Job died, being old and full of days.

Questions on *The Book of Job*

A. For Close Reading

1. What do you learn about Job in 1: 1-5? What agreement is made between God and Satan (1: 8-12)? What then happens to Job? What is his response?

2. In Chap. 2, what new agreement is made between God and Satan (2: 4-6), and how does Job suffer as a result of it? What is the reaction of Job's wife? What is Job's reaction?

3. After Job breaks down and "cursed his day" in Chap. 3, he is answered by Eliphaz in Chaps. 4 and 5. Eliphaz argues the traditional belief that man suffers for his past sins. (Read carefully 4: 6-9,17). Suffering is not accidental (5: 6-7, 17-19). What examples does Eliphaz give that good people are rewarded and that evil people suffer?

4. Job responds in Chaps. 6 and 7. Note especially 6: 24-26 and 7: 16, 20-21. By the end of Chap. 7, what attitude has he taken toward suffering?
5. What argument is made by Bildad in Chap. 8? See especially 8: 2-6, 20. What response is made by Job? Note 9: 21-24, 9: 32-35, and 10: 6-7.
6. In Chap. 11, Zophar talks about the nature of wisdom. How does he define wisdom? What is Job's response this time?
7. In Chap. 18, Bildad argues that the evil will suffer. How do his metaphors reflect the lives that the evil have lived?
8. What is Job's response in Chap. 19? Read carefully the famous lines that end this chapter (19: 25-29).
9. Zophar goes on, in Chap. 20, to argue about the plight of the wicked. Why will they eventually suffer? What is Job's attitude toward what happens to the wicked? (Note especially 21: 7,17, 19-20, and 34.)
10. What, if anything, do you find in the third round of debates between Job and his "comforters" (Chaps. 22-28) that adds significantly to the argument?
11. In Chap. 31, Job contrasts the past and the present. What conclusions can you draw about what he considers a good life? What are his major examples?
12. The Lord answers Job "out of the whirlwind" (38-40: 2). As God defines his own power, what is he trying to prove to Job?
13. What is Job's final reaction? Did his question get answered? Why or why not?

B. For Writing and Discussion

1. So far as you are concerned, is there in *The Book of Job* any reconciling the suffering of an innocent man with the idea of a just God? Why or why not?
2. Many critics have argued that the Prologue (Chaps. 1 and 2) and the Epilogue (42:17) provide a convenient framework for the story but give it a soap-opera flavor that is inconsistent with the rest of Job's self-justifying debate with his accusers and God. Argue for or against the inclusion of these opening and closing sections.

Oedipus The King

(430 B. C.)

SOPHOCLES' *Oedipus the King* was first performed in the late fifth century B.C. in Athens, Greece during a religious festival in honor of Dionysus, the god of vegetation and wine. The festival, known as the Dionysia, was celebrated annually in the early spring and was highlighted by a series of dramatic contests held in a large outdoor theater. The play you are about to read (also called *Oedipus Rex* or *Oedipus Tyrannus)* was an entry in one such competition well over two thousand years ago.

The contests were held over a three-day period, during which three playwrights competed for the prize in tragedy, while three other writers contended for the award in comedy. Each morning, one of the three tragic playwrights had to present a *tetralogy* (group of four plays), consisting of three tragedies and a satyr play. (This last piece was a short burlesque performed by a chorus dressed like satyrs, mythological creatures that are part man and part goat.)

Each afternoon, one of the three comic playwrights presented a single comedy. Thus, a total of fifteen plays were performed during these annual dramatic "olympics": a feat that must have satisfied the most ardent Greek theatergoer.

At the end of the festival, prizes (first, second, and third) were awarded in each of the categories of tragedy and comedy. It is recorded that Sophocles (who wrote over a hundred plays, of which only seven are extant) had a brilliant record: 20 first prizes and many second prizes. It is ironic, however, that *Oedipus,* his most famous play, took only second place. One explanation could be the Greek practice of giving awards to tetralogies as a whole and not to single plays. In other words, Sophocles' dramatic gem may have been done in by three "bombs." Another, simpler reason may be that the winning playwright that year (whose plays no longer exist) was just too much, even for the great Sophocles.

The theater at Athens was quite different from our playhouse. For one thing, it was an *amphitheater,* a semicircular, outdoor arena with rising rows of marble benches terraced into a hillside. At some festivals, up to 14,000 Athenians sat from morning to evening watching the plays being acted in the performing area.

The major structural features of this area were the *orchestra* (a circular dancing floor used by the chorus), the *stage* (a platform on which the main actors performed), and the *stage building* (a roofed house often used as a palace or temple). The theater had neither curtains nor lights, and there were few if any props. Instead, the story was developed, the characters introduced, and the settings changed by means of the play's dialogue alone.

To signal to the spectators that the drama was about to begin, a trumpet sounded and the chorus filed out onto the dancing surface. Then the main actors appeared from the stage building, wearing, like the chorus, masks slightly larger than their faces. Though rooted in religious custom, this use of masks also permitted an actor to play more than one part, and since the number of actors was often limited, doubling up was necessary. Arranging themselves around the circular dancing floor, the members of the chorus danced and chanted in unison whenever the action of the drama required their response. The chorus filled several functions—now observer, now commentator, now actor.

The Greek play differed from ours in another very important sense: the audience was familiar with the plot before they saw it acted out. Athenian dramatists often used the myths of their people as subject matter for their plays, and since these stories had been handed down from father to son for many generations, one of the pleasures the audience experienced was that of recognition. The myths represented, in an exaggerated way, the history of the race. *Oedipus the King* is based on one of these myths, an outline of which follows.

An oracle prophesied that when a son was born to Laius, a king of ancient Thebes, and to Jocasta, his queen, the son would kill his father and marry his mother. In time a son was born, and Laius, in order to avoid the consequences of the prophecy, drove a metal pin through the infant's ankles and gave the child to a shepherd who was instructed to abandon him on Mt. Cithaeron where he would presumably perish. The child was saved when the shepherd, out of pity, handed him over to another shepherd who took the child to Corinth. Here he grew up, after being adopted by the childless Polybus and Merope, king and queen of Corinth. They named him Oedipus, from the Greek meaning "swollen foot." Years later Oedipus heard the prophecy from the Delphic oracle, and thinking himself the true son of Polybus and Merope, fled from Corinth to avoid the acts foretold for him. Ignorant of the agreement between the two shepherds, his real parents, Laius and Jocasta, assumed that their son was dead. After leaving Corinth, Oedipus was forced from the road at a point where three roads met and attacked by attendants of a chariot in which Laius was riding. Without knowledge of who they were, Oedipus killed Laius (the king of Thebes and his true father) and all but one of the attendants.

When Oedipus arrived at Thebes, the city was being ravaged by a monster called the Sphinx who would not relent until someone answered her riddle: What is it that has one voice, is two-footed, and also four-footed and three-footed, and when it travels on its greatest number of feet, goes most slowly. Oedipus' answer, "Man," solved the riddle: Man crawls on all fours as an infant, walks upright in maturity, and uses a cane in old age. Receiving the correct answer so vexed the Sphinx that she destroyed herself. As a reward for saving the city, Oedipus was offered the throne of Thebes and the hand of the queen, Jocasta, by Creon, her brother. After many years, during which he was a good king, a plague broke out in the city. At this point the play begins.

As we read *Oedipus the King,* our concern should focus on what use Sophocles made of the myth, how he transformed it into drama, and with what intention. To understand these factors is to get to the meaning of the play. Quite simply, what he did was to tell the old story in a new way. The play is organized around two main points, the discovery of truth and the fall of the hero—concepts common to all tragedy. However, in *Oedipus the King* both revelation and catastrophe occur at the same moment, each previous action and event leading by a cause-and-effect relationship to this climax.

Taking advantage of the fact that his audience was familiar with the myth, Sophocles based the structure of many scenes on dramatic irony, the contrast between what Oedipus is ignorant of at various times and what the audience knew full well, between Oedipus' faulty interpretation of a situation and the audience's clear foreknowledge. Since we are also acquainted with the myth, we are as aware of this ironic contrast as were the Athenians. When Oedipus curses the killer of Laius, we know that he had laid a curse on himself; when Oedipus searches for the killer, we know that he is really searching for himself. Such instances of dramatic irony become the pattern of the whole and, in their cumulative effect, create a tension which is relieved only when Oedipus *realizes* the frightful truth.

Sophocles made another major change in adapting the myth to dramatic art. He chose to begin the action very near the end of events, just before Oedipus' discovery of his identity. This fact forces us to reevaluate the reasons for Oedipus' suffering.

The play is not about guilt and punishment. If it were, the crimes of which Oedipus may be guilty would be included within the action of the play, not merely introduced as exposition. (And is sin possible without knowledge of wrongdoing?) By choosing to start his story near the conclusion of the myth, Sophocles shifted the emphasis: not guilt is involved but certainly suffering.

But why does Oedipus suffer? Once the play begins, Oedipus makes all the decisions which determine the outcome of the action. Even when he suspects the worst, his courage keeps him probing. The fact that the gods, represented by the prophecy and the plague, know his fate does not mean they control him. His are free choices, even at that dreadful moment when the Shepherd says, "Oh, God, here comes the dreadful truth. And I must speak." And Oedipus responds, "And I must hear it. But hear it I will."

The circumstances in which Oedipus finds himself at the beginning of the play carry the conditions of his doom. The prophecy indicates that the gods foresaw the future; the plague triggers the action. What Oedipus learns is that no man can be sure of the future; man's knowledge is partial. Beyond him there is always a mysterious design or purpose which he can never completely fathom. The play is about how Oedipus faces this timeless human dilemma.

If we interpret the play as a metaphor of life, we can see that forces buried deep in the past may often come back to trip people up at moments of their greatest prosperity. In this sense many literary critics have found that the play expresses theories popular in twentieth-century psychology. Forces that lie deep in our subconscious and in our past may come to the surface in moments of great tension. We may be blind to these influences in our everyday lives, but they are still there.

Another basic theme of the play, truth and ignorance, is reflected in the use of blindness and sight as motifs. When Oedipus has his sight, he cannot see the truth. Tiresias, who is blind, knows the truth. When Oedipus arrives at the truth, not through his eyes, but through his intelligence and insight, he blinds himself. In this way he asserts symbolically that what we can see may not be the truth.

The play, then, affirms that man suffers, that the past has a way of unpredictably reappearing, that truth is difficult to know, and that we should "call no man happy while he waits to see his last day, not until he has passed the border of life and death without suffering pain." Paradoxically, though Oedipus' agony is real, the most impressive quality of the play is not the suffering that he endures, but the courage with which he meets it in his commitment to truth. Blind, deprived of his children, intent on self-exile at the end, Oedipus still leaves us with an awesome sense of what man can be: dignified, unflinching, compassionate, great of soul.

Because man has never completely understood why he suffers, much of our literary heritage consists of efforts to explain why he does. One such answer is that given by Adam Parry who, in writing about *Oedipus the King,* said: "The play makes perfectly clear that in any meaningful moral sense, Oedipus is innocent. He does not suffer because he has a hot temper or because he doubts the validity of prophecy. He suffers because he is a man."

The Translation

Among other things, the translator, Bernard M. W. Knox, said the following in his introduction to The Pocket Library edition of the play: "This translation is an 'acting version.' It was made for actors, for a performance; in fact for the scenes from the play which are acted by the Stratford Shakespearean Festival Company of Canada in a series . . . filmed in color on the

Oedipus. . . . The stage directions all envisage a modern production, not a reconstruction of the original performance. I have taken the liberty of adding a few remarks of a directorial nature where I thought them necessary to bring out the meaning of the passage."

Oedipus The King

SOPHOCLES

Translator:
Bernard M. W. Knox

CHARACTERS
(*in order of appearance*)

OEDIPUS, *King of Thebes*
PRIEST OF ZEUS
CREON, *brother of Jocasta*
CHORUS *of Theban citizens*
TIRESIAS, *a blind prophet*
JOCASTA, *Queen of Thebes, wife and mother of Oedipus*
CORINTHIAN MESSENGER
SHEPHERD
PALACE MESSENGER
ANTIGONE *and* ISMENE, *daughters of Oedipus and Jocasta*

The background is the front wall of a building, with a double door in the center. Steps lead down from the door to stage level. In front of the steps, in the center, a square stone altar.

Enter, from the side, a procession of priests and citizens. They carry olive branches which have tufts of wool tied on them. They lay these branches on the altar, then sit on the ground in front of it. The door opens. Enter OEDIPUS.

OEDIPUS   My sons! Newest generation of this ancient city of Thebes! Why are you here? Why are you seated there at the altar, with these branches of supplication?°

The city is filled with the smoke of burning incense, with hymns to the healing god, with laments for the dead. I did not think it right, my children, to hear reports of this from others. Here I am, myself, world-famous Oedipus.

You, old man, speak up—you are the man to speak for the others. In what mood are you sitting there—in fear or resignation? You may

---

° **Branches of supplication:** The branches signify a request; they are removed when the request is granted.

63

count on me; I am ready to do anything to help. I would be insensitive to pain, if I felt no pity for my people seated here.

PRIEST   Oedipus, ruler of Thebes, you see us here at your altar, men of all ages—some not yet strong enough to fly far from the nest, others heavy with age, priests, of Zeus in my case, and these are picked men from the city's youth. The rest of the Thebans, carrying boughs like us, are sitting in the market place, at the two temples of Athena, and at the prophetic fire of Apollo near the river Ismenus.

You can see for yourself—the city is like a ship rolling dangerously; it has lost the power to right itself and raise its head up out of the waves of death. Thebes is dying. There is a blight on the crops of the land, on the ranging herds of cattle, on the still-born labor of our women. The fever-god swoops down on us, hateful plague, he hounds the city and empties the houses of Thebes. The black god of death is made rich with wailing and funeral laments.

It is not because we regard you as equal to the gods that we sit here in supplication, these children and I; in our judgment you are first of men, both in the normal crises of human life and in relations with the gods.

You came to us once and liberated our city, you freed us from the tribute which we paid that cruel singer, the Sphinx. You did this with no extra knowledge you got from us, you had no training for the task, but, so it is said and we believe, it was with divine support that you restored our city to life. And now, Oedipus, power to whom all men turn, we beg you, all of us here, in supplication—find some relief for us! Perhaps you have heard some divine voice, or have knowledge from some human source. You are a man of experience, the kind whose plans result in effective action. Noblest of men, we beg you, save this city. You must take thought for your reputation. Thebes now calls you its savior because of the energy you displayed once before. Let us not remember your reign as a time when we stood upright only to fall again. Set us firmly on our feet. You brought us good fortune then, with favorable signs from heaven—be now the equal of the man you were. You are king; if you are to rule Thebes, you must have an inhabited city, not a desert waste. A walled city or a ship abandoned, without men living together inside it, is nothing at all.

OEDIPUS   My children, I am filled with pity. I knew what you were longing for when you came here. I know only too well that you are all sick —but sick though you may be, there is not one of you as sick as I. *Your* pain torments each one of you, alone, by himself—but my spirit within me mourns for the city, and myself, and all of you. You see then, I was no dreamer you awoke from sleep. I have wept many tears, as you must know, and in my ceaseless reflection I have followed many paths of thought. My search has found one way to treat our disease—and I have acted already. I have sent Creon, my brother-in-law, to the prophetic oracle of Apollo,° to find out by what action or speech, if any, I may rescue Thebes. I am anxious now when I count the days since he left; I wonder what he is doing. He has been away longer than one would expect, longer than he should be. But when he comes, at that moment I would be a vile object if I did not do whatever the god prescribes.

PRIEST   Just as you say these words, these men have signaled to me to announce Creon's arrival.

(Enter CREON, from side.)

OEDIPUS   *(Turns to the altar)*   O King Apollo! May Creon bring us good fortune and rescue, bright as the expression I see on his face.

PRIEST   I guess that his news is joyful. For on his head is a crown of laurel° in bloom.

OEDIPUS   No more guessing—soon we shall know. For he is near enough to hear us now. *(Raising his voice)*   Lord Creon, what statement do you bring us from the god Apollo?

CREON   Good news. For, as I see it, even things hard to bear, if they should turn out right in the end, would be good fortune.

OEDIPUS   What exactly did the god say? *Your* words inspire neither confidence nor fear.

CREON   If you wish to hear my report in the presence of these people   *(points to priests)*   I am ready. Or shall we go inside?

OEDIPUS   Speak out, before all of us. The sorrows of my people here mean more to me than any fear I may have for my own life.

CREON   Very well. Here is what I was told by the god Apollo. He ordered us, in clear terms, to drive out the thing that defiles this land, which we, he says, have fed and cherished. We must not let it grow so far that it is beyond cure.

OEDIPUS   What is the nature of our misfortune? How are we to rid ourselves of it—by what rites?

CREON   Banishment—or repaying blood with blood. We must atone for a murder which brings this plague-storm on the city.

°   **Oracle of Apollo:** The temple at Delphi; Apollo was the god of music, poetry, and the healing arts.

°   **Crown of laurel:** The laurel wreath is traditionally the sign of victory or success.

OEDIPUS   Whose murder? Who is the man whose death Apollo lays to our charge?

CREON   The ruler of this land, my lord, was called Laius. That was before *you* took the helm of state.

OEDIPUS   I know—at least I have heard so. I never saw the man.

CREON   It is to *his* death that Apollo's command clearly refers. We must punish those who killed him—whoever they may be.

OEDIPUS   But where on earth are they? The track of this ancient guilt is hard to detect; how shall we find it now?

CREON   Here in Thebes, Apollo said. What is searched for can be caught. What is neglected escapes.

OEDIPUS   Where did Laius meet his death? In his palace, in the countryside, or on some foreign soil?

CREON   He left Thebes to consult the oracle, so he announced. But he never returned to his home.

OEDIPUS   And no messenger came back? No fellow traveler who saw what happened?

CREON   No, they were all killed—except for one, who ran away in terror. But he could give no clear account of what he saw—except one thing.

OEDIPUS   And what was that? One thing might be the clue to knowledge of many more—if we could get even a slight basis for hope.

CREON   Laius was killed, he said, not by one man, but by a strong and numerous band of robbers.

OEDIPUS   But how could a *robber* reach such a pitch of daring—to kill a king? Unless there had been words—and money—passed between him and someone here in Thebes.

CREON   We thought of that, too. But the death of Laius left us helpless and leaderless in our trouble—

OEDIPUS   Trouble? What kind of trouble could be big enough to prevent a full investigation? Your *king* had been killed.

CREON   The Sphinx with her riddling songs forced us to give up the mystery and think about more urgent matters.

OEDIPUS   But I will begin afresh. I will bring it all to light. You have done well, Creon, and Apollo has, too, to show this solicitude for the murdered man. Now you will have *me* on your side, as is only right. I shall be the defender of Thebes, and Apollo's champion, too. I shall rid us of this pollution, not for the sake of a distant relative, but for my own sake. For whoever killed Laius might decide to raise his hand against me. So, acting on behalf of Laius, I benefit myself, too.

    (To priests)   Quickly, my children, as fast as you can, stand up from the steps and take these branches of supplication off the altar.

    (To guards)   One of you summon the people of Thebes here.

I shall leave nothing undone. With God's help we shall prove fortunate—or fall.

PRIEST   My sons, stand up. *(The priests rise.)* King Oedipus has volunteered to do what we came to ask. May Apollo, who sent the message from his oracle, come as our savior, and put an end to the plague.

(The priests take the olive branches off the altar and exeunt to side. OEDIPUS goes back through the palace doors. Enter, from side, the CHORUS. They are fifteen dancers, representing old men. They stand for the people of Thebes, whom OEDIPUS has just summoned. They chant in unison the following lines, which, in the original Greek, make great use of solemn, traditional formulas of prayer to the gods.)

CHORUS   Sweet message of Zeus!° You have come from Apollo's golden temple to splendid Thebes, bringing us news. My fearful heart is stretched on the rack and shudders in terror.

Hail Apollo, Lord of Delos,° healer! I worship and revere you. What new form of atonement will you demand? Or will it be some ancient ceremony, repeated often as the seasons come round? Tell me, daughter of golden Hope, immortal Voice of Apollo.

First I call upon you, immortal Athena, daughter of Zeus. And on your sister Artemis, the protector of this land, who sits in glory on her throne in the market place. And I call on far-shooting Apollo, the archer. Trinity of Defenders against Death, appear to me! If ever in time past, when destruction threatened our city, you kept the flame of pain out of our borders, come now also.

There is no way to count the pains we suffer. All our people are sick. There is no sword of thought which will protect us. The fruits of our famous land do not ripen. Our women cannot ease their labor pains by giving birth. One after another you can see our people speed like winged birds, faster than irresistible fire, to the shore of evening, to death. The city is dying, the deaths cannot be counted. The children lie unburied, unmourned, spreading death. Wives and gray-haired mothers come from all over the city, wailing they come to the altar steps to pray for release from pain and sorrow. The hymn to the Healer flashes out, and with it, accompanied by flutes, the mourning for the dead. Golden daughter of Zeus, Athena, send help and bring us joy.

I pray that the raging War-god,° who now without shield and armor

---

°   **Zeus:** Father of Apollo, who spoke through his son.

°   **Delos:** Apollo was born on the island of Delos.

°   **War-god:** Ares, the Greek god of war.

hems me in with shouting and burns me, I pray that he may turn back and leave the borders of this land. Let him go to the great sea gulf of the Western ocean or north to the Thracian coasts which give no shelter from the sea. For now, what the night spares, he comes for by day.

Father Zeus, you that in majesty govern the blazing lightning, destroy him beneath your thunderbolt!

Apollo, king and protector! I pray for the arrows from your golden bow—let them be ranged on my side to help me. And with them the flaming torches of Artemis, with which she speeds along the Eastern mountains. And I invoke the god with the golden headdress, who gave this land his name, wine-faced Dionysus, who runs with the maddened girls—let him come to my side, shining with his blazing pine-torch, to fight the god who is without honor among all other gods.

(The CHORUS *stays on stage. Enter* OEDIPUS, *from the palace doors. He addresses the* CHORUS—*the people of Thebes.)*

OEDIPUS   You are praying. As for your prayers, if you are willing to hear and accept what I say now and so treat the disease, you will find rescue and relief from distress. I shall make a proclamation, speaking as one who has no connection with this affair, nor with the murder. Even if I had been here at the time, I could not have followed the track very far without some clue. As it is, I became a Theban citizen with you after it happened. So I now proclaim to all of you, citizens of Thebes: whoever among you knows by whose hand Laius son of Labdacus was killed, I order him to reveal the whole truth to me.

If he is afraid to speak up, I order him to speak even against himself, and so escape the indictment, for he will suffer no unpleasant consequence except exile; he can leave Thebes unharmed.

(Silence while OEDIPUS *waits for a reply.)*

Secondly, if anyone knows the identity of the murderer, and that he is a foreigner, from another land, let him speak up. I shall make it profitable for him, and he will have my gratitude, too.

(Pause.)

But if you keep silent—if someone among you refuses my offer, shielding some relative or friend, or himself—now, listen to what I intend to do in that case. That man, whoever he may be, I banish from this land where I sit on the throne and hold the power; no one shall take him in or speak to him. He is forbidden communion in prayers or offerings to the gods, or in holy water. Everyone is to expel him from their homes as if he were himself the source of infection which Apollo's oracle has just made known to me. That is how I fulfill my obligations as an ally to the god and to the murdered man. As for the murderer himself, I call down a curse on him, whether that unknown figure be one man or one among many. May he drag out an evil death-in-life in misery. And further, I pronounce a curse on myself if the murderer should, with my knowledge, share my house; in that case may I be subject to all the curses I have just called down on these people here. I order you all to obey these commands in full for my sake, for Apollo's sake, and for the sake of this land, withering away in famine, abandoned by heaven.

Even if this action had not been urged by the god, it was not proper for you to have left the matter unsolved—the death of a good man and a king. You should have investigated it. But now I am in command. I hold the office he once held, the wife who once was his is now mine, the mother of my children. Laius and I would be closely connected by children from the same wife, if his line had not met with disaster. But chance swooped down on his life. So I shall fight for him, as if he were my own father. I shall shrink from nothing in my search to find the murderer of Laius, of the royal line of Thebes, stretching back through Labdacus, Polydorus and Cadmus, to ancient Agenor. On those who do not co-operate with these measures I call down this curse in the gods' name: let no crop grow out of the earth for them, their wives bear no children. Rather let them be destroyed by the present plague, or something even worse. But to you people of Thebes who approve of my action I say this: May justice be our ally and all the gods be with us forever!

CHORUS   (*One member of the* CHORUS *speaks for them all.*)—You have put me under a curse, King, and under the threat of that curse I shall make my statement. I did not kill Laius and I am not in a position to say who did. This search to find the murderer should have been undertaken by Apollo who sent the message which began it.

OEDIPUS   What you say is just. But to compel the gods to act against their will—no man could do that.

CHORUS LEADER   Then let me make a second suggestion.

OEDIPUS   And a third, if you like—speak up.

CHORUS LEADER   The man who sees most eye to eye with Lord Apollo is Tiresias and from him you might learn most clearly the truth for which you are searching.

OEDIPUS   I did not leave *that* undone either. I have already sent for him, at Creon's suggestion. I have sent for him twice, in fact, and have been wondering for some time why he is not yet here.

CHORUS LEADER   Apart from what he will say, there is nothing but old, faint rumors.

OEDIPUS   What were they? I want to examine every single word.

CHORUS LEADER   Laius was killed, so they say, by some travelers.

OEDIPUS   I heard that, too. Where is the man who saw it?

CHORUS LEADER   If he has any trace of fear in him, he won't stand firm when he hears the curses you have called down on him.

OEDIPUS   If he didn't shrink from the action he won't be frightened by a word.

CHORUS LEADER   But here comes the one who will convict him. These men are bringing the holy prophet of the gods, the only man in whom truth is inborn.

(Enter TIRESIAS, *from the side. He has a boy to lead him, and is accompanied by guards.)*

OEDIPUS   Tiresias, you who understand all things—those which can be taught and those which may not be mentioned, things in the heavens and things which walk the earth! You cannot see, but you understand the city's distress, the disease from which it is suffering. You, my lord, are our shield against it, our savior, the only one we have. You may not have heard the news from the messengers. We sent to Apollo and he sent us back this answer: relief from this disease would come to us only if we discovered the identity of the murderers of Laius and then either killed them or banished them from Thebes. Do not begrudge us your knowledge—any voice from the birds° or any other way of prophecy you have. Save yourself and this city, save me, from all the infection caused by the dead man. We are in your hands. And the noblest of labors is for a man to help his fellow men with all he has and can do.

TIRESIAS   Wisdom is a dreadful thing when it brings no profit to its possessor. I knew all this well, but forgot. Otherwise I would never have come here.

OEDIPUS   What is the matter? Why this despairing mood?

TIRESIAS   Dismiss me, send me home. That will be the easiest way for both of us to bear our burden.

OEDIPUS   What you propose is unlawful—and unfriendly to this city which raised you. You are withholding information.

°   **Voice from the birds:** Prophets were thought to get knowledge of the future from the voices of birds.

TIRESIAS   I do not see that your talking is to the point. And I don't want the same thing to happen to me.

OEDIPUS   If you know something, in God's name, do not turn your back on us. Look. All of us here, on our knees, beseech you.

TIRESIAS   You are all ignorant. I will never reveal my dreadful secrets, or rather, yours.

OEDIPUS   What do you say? You know something? And will not speak? You intend to betray us, do you, and wreck the state?

TIRESIAS   I will not cause pain to myself or to you. Why do you question me? It is useless. You will get nothing from me.

OEDIPUS   You scoundrel! You would enrage a lifeless stone. Will nothing move you? Speak out and make an end of it.

TIRESIAS   You blame my temper, but you are not aware of one *you* live with.

OEDIPUS   *(To* CHORUS*)*   Who could control his anger listening to talk like this—these insults to Thebes?

TIRESIAS   What is to come will come, even if I shroud it in silence.

OEDIPUS   What is to come, *that* is what you are bound to tell *me*.

TIRESIAS   I will say no more. Do what you like—rage at me in the wildest anger you can muster.

OEDIPUS   I will. I am angry enough to speak out. I understand it all. Listen to me. I think that *you* helped to plan the murder of Laius— yes, and short of actually raising your hand against him you did it. If you weren't blind, I'd say that you alone struck him down.

TIRESIAS   Is that what you say? I charge you now to carry out the articles of the proclamation you made. From now on do not presume to speak to me or to any of these people. *You* are the murderer, *you* are the unholy defilement of this land.

OEDIPUS   Have you no shame? To start up such a story! Do you think you will get away with this?

TIRESIAS   Yes. The truth with all its strength is in me.

OEDIPUS   Who taught you this lesson? You didn't learn it from your prophet's trade.

TIRESIAS   *You* did. I was unwilling to speak but you drove me to it.

OEDIPUS   What was it you said? I want to understand it clearly.

TIRESIAS   Didn't you understand it the first time? Aren't you just trying to trip me up?

OEDIPUS   No, I did not grasp it fully. Repeat your statement.

TIRESIAS   I say that you are the murderer you are searching for.

OEDIPUS   Do you think you can say that twice and not pay for it?

TIRESIAS   Shall I say something more, to make you angrier still?

OEDIPUS   Say what you like. It will all be meaningless.

TIRESIAS   I say that without knowing it you are living in shameful intimacy with your nearest and dearest. You do not see the evil in which you live.

OEDIPUS   Do you think you can go on like this with impunity forever?

TIRESIAS   Yes, if the truth has power.

OEDIPUS   It has, except for you. You have no power or truth. You are blind, your ears and mind as well as eyes.

TIRESIAS   You are a pitiful figure. These reproaches you fling at me, all these people here will fling them at you—and before very long.

OEDIPUS   (Contemptuously)   You live your life in one continuous night of darkness. Neither I nor any other man that can see would do you any harm.

TIRESIAS   It is not destiny that I should fall through you. Apollo is enough for that. It is his concern.

OEDIPUS   Was it Creon, or you, that invented this story?

TIRESIAS   It is not Creon who harms you—you harm yourself.

OEDIPUS   Wealth, absolute power, skill surpassing skill in the competition of life—what envy is your reward! For the sake of this power which Thebes entrusted to me—I did not ask for it—to win this power faithful Creon, my friend from the beginning, sneaks up on me treacherously, longing to drive me out. He sets this intriguing magician on me, a lying quack, keen sighted for what he can make, but blind in prophecy.

(To TIRESIAS)   Tell me, when were you a true prophet? When the Sphinx chanted her riddle here, did you come forward to speak the word that would liberate the people of this town? That riddle was not for anyone who came along to answer—it called for prophetic insight. But you didn't come forward, you offered no answer told you by the birds or the gods. No. I came, know-nothing Oedipus, I stopped the Sphinx. I answered the riddle with my own intelligence—the birds had nothing to teach me. And now you try to drive me out, you think you will stand beside Creon's throne. I tell you, you will pay in tears for this witch-hunting—you and Creon, the man that organized this conspiracy. If you weren't an old man, you would already have realized, in suffering, what your schemes lead to.

CHORUS LEADER   If we may make a suggestion—both his words and yours, Oedipus, seem to have been spoken in anger. This sort of talk is not what we need—what we must think of is how to solve the problem set by the god's oracle.

TIRESIAS   King though you are, you must treat me as your equal in one respect—the right to reply. That is a power which belongs to me, too. I am not your servant, but Apollo's. I am not inscribed on the records as a dependent of Creon, with no right to speak in person. I can speak, and here is what I have to say. You have mocked at my blindness, but you, who have eyes, cannot see the evil in which you stand; you cannot see where you are living, nor with whom you share your house. Do you even know who your parents are? Without knowing it, you are the enemy of your own flesh and blood, the dead below and the living here above. The double-edged curse of your mother and father, moving on dread feet, shall one day drive you from this land. You see straight now but then you will see darkness. You will scream aloud on that day; there is no place which shall not hear you, no part of Mount Cithaeron here which will not ring in echo, on that day when you know the truth about your wedding, that evil harbor into which you sailed before a fair wind.

There is a multitude of other horrors which you do not even suspect, and they will equate you to yourself and to your own children. There! Now smear me and Creon with your accusations. There is no man alive whose ruin will be more pitiful than yours.

OEDIPUS   Enough! I won't listen to this sort of talk from you. Damn you! My curse on you! Get out of here, quickly. Away from this house, back to where you came from!

TIRESIAS   I would never have come here if you had not summoned me.

OEDIPUS   I didn't know that you were going to speak like a fool—or it would have been a long time before I summoned you to my palace.

TIRESIAS   I am what I am—a fool to you, so it seems, but the parents who brought you into the world thought me sensible enough. (TIRESIAS *turns to go.*)

OEDIPUS   Whom do you mean? Wait! Who is my father?

TIRESIAS   This present day will give you birth and death.

OEDIPUS   Everything you say is the same—riddles, obscurities.

TIRESIAS   Aren't you the best man alive at guessing riddles?

OEDIPUS   Insult me, go on—but that, you will find, is what makes me great.

TIRESIAS   Yet that good fortune was your destruction.

OEDIPUS   What does that matter, if I saved Thebes?

TIRESIAS   I will go, then. Boy, lead me away.

OEDIPUS   Yes, take him away. While you're here you are a hindrance, a nuisance; once out of the way you won't annoy me any more.

TIRESIAS   I am going. But first I will say what I came here to say. I have no fear of you. You cannot destroy me. Listen to me now. The man you are trying to find, with your threatening proclamations, the murderer of Laius, that man is here in Thebes. He is apparently an immigrant of foreign birth, but he will be revealed as a native-born Theban. He will take no pleasure in that revelation. Blind instead of seeing, beggar instead of rich, he will make his way to foreign soil, feeling his way with a stick. He will be revealed as brother and father of the children with whom he now lives, the son and husband of the woman who gave him birth, the murderer and marriage-partner of his father. Go think this out. And if you find that I am wrong, then say I have no skill in prophecy.

(Exit Tiresias *led by the boy to side.* Oedipus *goes back into the palace.)*

Chorus   Who is the man denounced by the prophetic voice from Delphi's cliffs—the man whose blood-stained hands committed a nameless crime? Now is the time for him to run, faster than storm-swift horses. In full armor Apollo son of Zeus leaps upon him, with the fire of the lightning. And in the murderer's track follow dreadful unfailing spirits of vengeance.

The word of Apollo has blazed out from snowy Parnassus° for all to see. Track down the unknown murderer by every means. He roams under cover of the wild forest, among caves and rocks, like a wild bull, wretched, cut off from mankind, his feet in pain. He turns his back on the prophecies delivered at the world's center, but they, alive forever, hover round him.

The wise prophet's words have brought me terror and confusion. I cannot agree with him, nor speak against him. I do not know what to say. I waver in hope and fear; I cannot see forward or back. What cause for quarrel was there between Oedipus and Laius? I never heard of one in time past; I know of none now.

I see no reason to attack the great fame of Oedipus in order to avenge the mysterious murder of Laius.

Zeus and Apollo, it is true, understand and know in full the events of man's life. But whether a mere man knows the truth—whether a human prophet knows more than I do—who is to be a fair judge of that? It is true that one man may be wiser than another. But I, for my part, will never join those who blame Oedipus, until I see these charges proved. We all saw how the Sphinx came against him—there his wisdom was proved. In that hour of danger he was the joy of Thebes. Remembering that day, my heart will never judge him guilty of evil action.

(Enter Creon, *from side.)*

Creon   Fellow citizens of Thebes, I am here in an angry mood. I hear that King Oedipus brings terrible charges against me. If, in the present

---

°   **Parnassus**: Mountain overlooking Delphi, sacred to Apollo.

dangerous situation, he thinks that I have injured him in any way, by word or deed, let me not live out the rest of my days with such a reputation. The damage done to me by such a report is no simple thing—it is the worst there is—to be called a traitor in the city, by all of you, by my friends.

CHORUS LEADER   This attack on you must have been forced out of him by anger; he lost control of himself.

CREON   Who told him that I advised Tiresias to make these false statements?

CHORUS LEADER   That's what was said—but I don't know what the intention was.

CREON   Were his eyes and mind unclouded when he made this charge against me?

CHORUS LEADER   I don't know. It is no use asking *me* about the actions of those who rule Thebes. Here is Oedipus. Look, he is coming out of the palace.

(Enter OEDIPUS, *from door.)*

OEDIPUS   *(To* CREON*)*   You! What are you doing here? Do you have the face to come to my palace—you who are convicted as my murderer, exposed as a robber attempting to steal my throne? In God's name, tell me, what did you take me for when you made this plot—a coward? Or a fool? Did you think I wouldn't notice this conspiracy of yours creeping up on me in the dark? That once I saw it, I wouldn't defend myself? Don't you see that your plan is foolish—to hunt for a crown without numbers or friends behind you? A crown is won by numbers and money.

CREON   I have a suggestion. You in your turn listen to a reply as long as your speech, and, after you have heard me, *then* judge me.

OEDIPUS   You are a clever speaker, but I am a slow learner—from *you.* I have found you an enemy and a burden to me.

CREON   Just one thing, just listen to what I say.

OEDIPUS   Just one thing, don't try to tell me you are not a traitor.

CREON   Listen, if you think stubbornness deprived of intelligence is a worth-while possession, you are out of your mind.

OEDIPUS   Listen, if you think you can injure a close relative and then not pay for it, you are out of your mind.

CREON   All right, that's fair. But at least explain to me what I am supposed to have done.

OEDIPUS   Did you or did you not persuade me that I ought to send fᵣ that "holy" prophet?

CREON   Yes, I did, and I am still of the same mind.

OEDIPUS   Well then, how long is it since Laius . . .   *(pauˢ*

CREON   Did what? I don't follow your drift.

OEDIPUS   Disappeared, vanished, violently murdered?

CREON   Many years ago; it is a long count back in time.

OEDIPUS   And at that time, was this prophet at his trade?

CREON   Yes, wise as he is now, and honored then as now.

OEDIPUS   Did he mention my name at that time?

CREON   No, at least not in my presence.

OEDIPUS   You investigated the murder of Laius, didn't you?

CREON   We did what we could, of course. But we learned nothing.

OEDIPUS   How was it that this wise prophet did not say all this *then?*

CREON   I don't know. And when I don't understand, *I* keep silent.

OEDIPUS   Here's something you *do* know, and could say, too, if you were a loyal man.

CREON   What do you mean? If I know, I will not refuse to answer.

OEDIPUS   Just this. If he had not come to an agreement with you, Tiresias would never have called the murder of Laius *my* work.

CREON   If that's what he says—you are the one to know. Now I claim my rights from you—answer my questions as I did yours just now.

OEDIPUS   Ask your questions. I shall not be proved a murderer.

CREON   You are married to my sister, are you not?

OEDIPUS   The answer to that question is yes.

CREON   And you rule Thebes jointly and equally with her?

OEDIPUS   She gets from me whatever she wants.

CREON   And I am on an equal basis with the two of you, isn't that right?

OEDIPUS   Yes, it is, and that fact shows what a disloyal friend you are.

CREON   No, not if you look at it rationally, as I am explaining it to you. Consider this point first—do you think anyone would prefer to be supreme ruler and live in fear rather than to sleep soundly at night and still have the same power as the king? I am not the man to long for royalty rather than royal power, and anyone who has any sense agrees with me. As it is now, I have everything I want from you, and nothing to fear; but if I were king, I would have to do many things I have no mind to. How could the throne seem more desirable to me than power and authority which bring me no trouble? I can see clearly—all I want is what is pleasant and profitable at the same time. As it is now, I am greeted by all, everyone salutes me, all those who want something from you play up to me—that's the key to success for them. What makes you think I would give up all this and accept what you have? No, a mind which sees things clearly, as I do, would never turn traitor. I have never been tempted by such an idea, and I would never have put up with anyone who took such action.

   You can test the truth of what I say. Go to Delphi and ask for the text of the oracle, to see if I gave you an accurate report. One thing more. If you find that I conspired with the prophet Tiresias, then condemn me to death, not by a single vote, but by a double, yours and mine both. But do not accuse me in isolation, on private, baseless fancy. It is not justice to make the mistake of taking bad men for good, or good for bad. To reject a good friend is the equivalent of throwing away one's own dear life—that's my opinion. Given time you will realize all this without fail: time alone reveals the just man—the unjust you can recognize in one short day.

CHORUS LEADER   That is good advice, my lord, for anyone who wants to avoid mistakes. Quick decisions are not the safest.

OEDIPUS   When a plotter moves against me in speed and secrecy, then I too must be quick to counterplot. If I take my time and wait, then his cause is won, and mine lost.

CREON   What do you want then? Surely you don't mean to banish me from Thebes?

OEDIPUS   Not at all. Death is what I want for you, not exile.

CREON   You give a clear example of what it is to feel hate and envy.

OEDIPUS   You don't believe me, eh? You won't give way?

CREON   No, for I can see you don't know what you are doing.

OEDIPUS   Looking after my own interests.

CREON   And what about mine?

OEDIPUS   You are a born traitor.

CREON   And you don't understand anything.

OEDIPUS   Whether I do or not—I am in power here.

CREON   Not if you rule badly.

OEDIPUS   *(To* CHORUS*)*   Listen to him, Thebes, my city.

CREON   My city, too, not yours alone.

CHORUS LEADER   Stop, my lords. Here comes Jocasta from the house, in the nick of time. With her help, you must compose this quarrel between you.

(Enter JOCASTA*, from door.)*

JOCASTA   Have you no sense, God help you, raising your voices in strife like this? Have you no sense of shame? The land is plague-stricken and you pursue private quarrels.   *(To* OEDIPUS*)*   You go into the house, and you, too, Creon, inside. Don't make so much trouble over some small annoyance.

CREON   Sister, your husband, Oedipus, claims the right to inflict dreadful punishments on me. He will choose between banishing me from my fatherland and killing me.

OEDIPUS   Exactly. Jocasta, I caught him in a treacherous plot against my life.

CREON   May I never enjoy life, but perish under a curse, if I have done to you any of the things you charge me with.

JOCASTA   In God's name, Oedipus, believe what he says. Show respect for the oath he swore by the gods—do it for my sake and the sake of these people here.

CHORUS   Listen to her, King Oedipus. Think over your decision, take her advice, I beg you.

OEDIPUS   What concession do you want me to make?

CHORUS   Creon was no fool before, and now his oath increases his stature. Respect him.

OEDIPUS   Do you know what you are asking?

CHORUS   Yes, I know.

OEDIPUS   Tell me what it means, then.

CHORUS   This man is your friend—he has sworn an oath—don't throw him out dishonored on the strength of hearsay alone.

OEDIPUS   Understand this. If that is what you are after, you want me to be killed or banished from this land.

CHORUS   No. By the sun, foremost of all the gods! May I perish miserably abandoned by man and God, if any such thought is in my mind. My heart is racked with pain for the dying land of Thebes—must you add new sorrows of your own making to those we already have?

OEDIPUS   Well then, let him go—even if it *does* lead to my death or inglorious banishment. It is *your* piteous speech that rouses my compassion—not what *he* says. As for him, I shall hate him, wherever he goes.

CREON   You show your sulky temper in giving way, just as you did in your ferocious anger. Natures like yours are hardest to bear for their owners—and justly so.

OEDIPUS   Get out, will you? Out!

CREON   I am going. I found you ignorant—but these men think I am right.

(Exit CREON *to side.)*

CHORUS   *(To* JOCASTA*)* Lady, why don't you get him into the house quickly?

JOCASTA   I will—when I have found out what happened here.

CHORUS   There was some ignorant talk based on hearsay and some hurt caused by injustice.

JOCASTA   On both sides?

CHORUS   Yes.

JOCASTA   And what did they say?

CHORUS   Enough, that is enough, it seems to me. I speak in the interests of the whole country. Let this matter lie where they left it.

OEDIPUS   You see where your good intentions have brought you. This is the result of turning aside and blunting the edge of my anger.

CHORUS   My king, I said it before, more than once—listen to me. I would be exposed as a madman, useless, brainless, if I were to turn my back on you. You found Thebes laboring in a sea of trouble, you righted her and set her on a fair course. All I wish now is that you should guide us as well as you did then.

JOCASTA   In God's name, explain to me, my lord—what was it made you so angry?

OEDIPUS   I will tell you. I have more respect for you than for these people here. Creon and his conspiracy against me, that's what made me angry.

JOCASTA   Tell me clearly, what was the quarrel between you?

OEDIPUS   He says that I am the murderer of Laius.

JOCASTA   On what evidence? His own knowledge, or hearsay?

OEDIPUS   Oh, he keeps his own lips clear of responsibility—he sent a swindling prophet in to speak for him.

JOCASTA   A prophet? In that case, rid your mind of your fear, and listen to me. I can teach you something. There is no human being born that is endowed with prophetic power. I can prove it to you—and in a few words.

A prophecy came to Laius once—I won't say from Apollo himself, but from his priests. It said that Laius was fated to die by the hand of his son, a son to be born to him and to me. Well, Laius, so the story goes, was killed by foreign robbers at a place where three highways meet. As for the son—three days after his birth Laius fastened his ankles together and had him cast away on the pathless mountains.

So, in this case, Apollo did not make the son kill his father or Laius die by his own son's hand, as he had feared. Yet these were the definite statements of the prophetic voices. Don't pay any attention to prophecies. If god seeks or needs anything, he will easily make it clear to us himself.

OEDIPUS   Jocasta, something I heard you say has disturbed me to the soul, unhinged my mind.

JOCASTA   What do you mean? What was it that alarmed you so?

OEDIPUS   I thought I heard you say that Laius was killed at a place where three highways meet.

JOCASTA   Yes, that's what the story was—and still is.

OEDIPUS   Where is the place where this thing happened?

JOCASTA   The country is called Phocis: two roads, one from Delphi and one from Daulia, come together and form one.

OEDIPUS   When did it happen? How long ago?

JOCASTA   We heard the news here in Thebes just before you appeared and became King.

OEDIPUS   O God, what have you planned to do to me?

JOCASTA   What is it, Oedipus, which haunts your spirit so?

OEDIPUS   No questions, not yet. Laius—tell me what he looked like, how old he was.

JOCASTA   He was a big man—his hair had just begun to turn white. And he had more or less the same build as you.

OEDIPUS   O God! I think I have just called down on myself a dreadful curse—not knowing what I did.

JOCASTA   What do you mean? To look at you makes me shudder, my lord.

OEDIPUS   I am dreadfully afraid the blind prophet could see. But tell me one more thing that will throw light on this.

JOCASTA   I am afraid. But ask your question; I will answer if I can.

OEDIPUS   Was Laius poorly attended, or did he have a big bodyguard, like a king?

JOCASTA   There were five men in his party. One of them was a herald. And there was one wagon—Laius was riding in it.

OEDIPUS   Oh, it is all clear as daylight now. Who was it told you all this at the time?

JOCASTA   A slave from the royal household. He was the only one who came back.

OEDIPUS   Is he by any chance in the palace now?

JOCASTA   No, he is not. When he came back and saw you ruling in place of Laius, he seized my hand and begged me to send him to work in the country, to the pastures, to the flocks, as far away as I could—out of sight of Thebes. And I sent him. Though he was a slave he deserved this favor from me—and much more.

OEDIPUS   Can I get him back here, in haste?

JOCASTA   It can be done. But why are you so intent on this?

OEDIPUS   I am afraid, Jocasta, that I have said too much—that's why I want to see this man.

JOCASTA   Well, he shall come. But I have a right, it seems to me, to know what it is that torments you so.

OEDIPUS   So you shall. Since I am so full of dreadful expectation, I shall hold nothing back from you. Who else should I speak to, who means more to me than you, in this time of trouble?

My father was Polybus, a Dorian, and my mother Merope, of Corinth. I was regarded as the greatest man in that city until something happened to me quite by chance, a strange thing, but not worth all the attention I paid it. A man at the banquet table, who had had too much to drink, told me, over his wine, that I was not the true son of my father. I was furious, but, hard though it was, I controlled my feelings, for that day at least. On the next day I went to my parents and questioned them. They were enraged against the man who had so taunted me. So I took comfort from their attitude, but still the thing tormented me—for the story spread far and wide. Without telling my parents, I set off on a journey to the oracle of Apollo, at Delphi. Apollo sent me away with my question unanswered but he foretold a dreadful, calamitous future for me—to lie with my mother and beget children men's eyes would not bear the sight of—and to be the killer of the father that gave me life.

When I heard that, I ran away. From that point on I measured the distance to the land of Corinth by the stars. I was running to a place where I would never see that shameful prophecy come true. On my way I came to the place in which you say this king, Laius, met his death.

I will tell you the truth, all of it. As I journeyed on I came near to this triple crossroad and there I was met by a herald and a man riding on a horse-drawn wagon, just as you described it. The driver, and the old man himself, tried to push me off the road. In anger I struck the driver as he tried to crowd me off. When the old man saw me coming past the wheels he aimed at my head with a two-pronged goad, and hit me. I paid him back in full, with interest: in no time at all he was hit by the stick I held in my hand and rolled backwards from the center of the wagon. I killed the whole lot of them.

Now, if this stranger had anything to do with Laius—is there a more unhappy man alive than I? Who could be more hateful to the gods than I am? No foreigner or citizen may take me into his house, no one can talk to me—everyone must expel me from his home. And the man who called down these curses on me was I myself, no one else. With these hands that killed him I defile the dead man's marriage bed. How can I deny that I am vile, utterly unclean? I must be banished from Thebes, and then I may not even see my own parents or set foot on my own fatherland—or else I am doomed to marry my own mother and kill my father Polybus, who brought me up and gave me life. I am the victim of some harsh divinity; what other explanation can there be?

Let it not happen, not that, I beg you, holy majesty of God, may I never see that day! May I disappear from among men without trace before I see such a stain of misfortune come upon me!

CHORUS LEADER   My lord, this makes us tremble. But do not despair—you have still to hear the story from the eye-witness.

OEDIPUS   That's right. That's my hope now, such as it is—to wait for the shepherd.

JOCASTA   Why all this urgency about his coming?

OEDIPUS   I'll tell you. If it turns out that he tells the same story as you —then I, at least, will be cleared of responsibility.

JOCASTA   What was so important in what you heard from me?

OEDIPUS   You said his story was that *several* robbers killed Laius. Well,
if he speaks of the same number as you—then I am not the killer. For
one could never be equal to many. But if he speaks of one man alone
—then clearly the balance tips towards me as the killer.

JOCASTA   You can be sure that his account was made public just as I
told it to you; he cannot go back on it, the whole city heard it, not I
alone. But, my lord, even if he should depart from his former account
in some particular, he still would never make the death of Laius what
it was supposed to be—for Apollo said clearly that Laius was to be
killed by my son. But that poor infant never killed Laius; it met its
own death first. So much for prophecy. For all it can say, I would not,
from now on, so much as look to right or left.

OEDIPUS   Yes, I agree. But all the same, that shepherd—send someone
to fetch him. Do it at once.

JOCASTA   I shall send immediately. And now let us go in. I would not do
anything except what pleases you.

(Exeunt OEDIPUS *and* JOCASTA *through doors.)*

CHORUS   *(Chanting in unison)*
May Destiny be with me always;
Let me observe reverence and purity
In word and deed.
Laws that stand above have been established—
Born in the upper air on high;
Their only father is heaven;
No mortal nature, no man gave them birth.
They never forget, or sleep.
In them God is great, and He does not grow old.

The despot is the child of violent pride,
Pride that vainly stuffs itself
With food unseasonably, unfit,
Climbs to the highest rim
And then plunges sheer down into defeat
Where its feet are of no use.
Yet I pray to God to spare that vigor
Which benefits the state.
God is my protector, on Him I shall never cease to call.
The man who goes his way
Overbearing in word and deed,
Who fears no justice,
Honors no temples of the gods—

May an evil destiny seize him
And punish his ill-starred pride.
How shall such a man defend his life
Against God's arrows?
If such deeds as this are honored,
Why should we join the sacred dance and worship?

I shall go no more in reverence to Delphi,
The holy center of the earth,
Nor to any temple in the world,
Unless these prophecies come true,
For all men to point at in wonder.
O Zeus, King of heaven, ruler of all,
If you deserve this name,
Do not let your everlasting power be deceived,
Do not forget.
The old prophecies about Laius are failing,
Men reject them now.
Apollo is without honor everywhere.
The gods are defeated.

(Enter JOCASTA, *with branches of olive.)*

JOCASTA   *(To* CHORUS)   Lords of Thebes, it occurred to me to come
to the temples of the gods bearing in my hands these branches and offerings of incense. For Oedipus is distracted with sorrows of all kinds.
He does not act like a man in control of his reason, judging the present by the past—he is at the mercy of anyone who speaks to him, especially one who speaks of terrors. I have given him advice, but it does
no good.   *(Facing the altar)*   So I come to you, Lord Apollo, for you
are closest to hand. I come in supplication with these emblems of prayer.
Deliver us, make us free and clear of defilement. We are all afraid, like
passengers on a ship who see their pilot crazed with fear.

(Enter from side CORINTHIAN MESSENGER.*)*

CORINTHIAN MESSENGER   *(To* CHORUS)   Strangers, can one of you tell
me—where is the palace of King Oedipus? Better still, if you know,
where is the king himself?
CHORUS LEADER   This is his palace, and he is inside, stranger. This lady
is his queen, his wife and mother of his children.
CORINTHIAN MESSENGER   Greetings to the noble wife of Oedipus! May
you and all your family be blessed forever.

JOCASTA   The same blessings on you, stranger, for your kind words. But tell us what you want. Why have you come? Have you some news for us?

CORINTHIAN MESSENGER   Good news for your house and your husband, lady.

JOCASTA   What news? Who sent you?

CORINTHIAN MESSENGER   I come from Corinth. My message will bring you joy—no doubt of that—but sorrow, too.

JOCASTA   What is it? How can it work both ways?

CORINTHIAN MESSENGER   The people of Corinth will make Oedipus their king, so I heard there.

JOCASTA   What? Is old Polybus no longer on the throne?

CORINTHIAN MESSENGER   No. He is dead and in his grave.

JOCASTA   What did you say? Polybus is dead? Dead?

CORINTHIAN MESSENGER   Condemn me to death if I am not telling the truth.

JOCASTA   *(To servant)*   You there, go in quickly and tell your master. O prophecies of the gods, where are you now?

Polybus was the man Oedipus feared he might kill—and so avoided him all this time. And now he's dead—a natural death, and not by the hand of Oedipus.

(Enter OEDIPUS, *from doors.)*

OEDIPUS   Jocasta, why did you send for me to come out here?

JOCASTA   Listen to what this man says, and see what has become of the holy prophecies of the gods.

OEDIPUS   Who is he? What does he have to say to me?

JOCASTA   He's from Corinth. He came to tell you that your father Polybus is dead and gone.

OEDIPUS   Is this true? Tell me yourself.

CORINTHIAN MESSENGER   If that's what you want to hear first, here it is, a plain statement: Polybus is dead and gone.

OEDIPUS   How? Killed by a traitor, or wasted by disease?

CORINTHIAN MESSENGER   He was old. It did not take much to put him to sleep.

OEDIPUS   By disease, then—that's how he died?

CORINTHIAN MESSENGER   Yes, that, and the length of years he had lived.

OEDIPUS   So! Why then, Jocasta, should we study Apollo's oracle, or gaze at the birds screaming over our heads—those prophets who announced that I would kill my father? He's dead, buried, below ground. And here I am in Thebes—I did not put hand to sword.

Perhaps he died from longing to see me again. That way, it could be said that I was the cause of his death. But there he lies, dead, taking with him all these prophecies I feared—they are worth nothing!

JOCASTA   Is that not what I told you?

OEDIPUS   It is. But I was led astray by fear.

JOCASTA   Now rid your heart of fear forever.

OEDIPUS   No, I must still fear—and who would not?—a marriage with my mother.

JOCASTA   Fear? Why should man fear? His life is governed by the operations of chance. Nothing can be clearly foreseen. The best way to live is by hit and miss, as best you can. Don't be afraid that you may marry your mother. Many a man before you, in dreams, has shared his mother's bed. But to live at ease one must attach no importance to such things.

OEDIPUS   All that you have said would be fine—if my mother were not still alive. But she is, and no matter how good a case you make, I am still a prey to fear.

JOCASTA   But your father's death—that much at least is a great blessing.

OEDIPUS   Yes, I see that. But my mother, as long as she is alive, fills me with fear.

CORINTHIAN MESSENGER   Who is this woman that inspires such fear in you?

OEDIPUS   Merope, old man, the wife of Polybus.

CORINTHIAN MESSENGER   And what is there about her which frightens you?

OEDIPUS   A dreadful prophecy sent by the gods.

CORINTHIAN MESSENGER   Can you tell me what it is? Or is it forbidden for others to know?

OEDIPUS   Yes, I can tell you. Apollo once announced that I am destined to mate with my mother, and shed my father's blood with my own hand. That is why for so many years I have lived far away from Corinth. It has turned out well—but still, there's nothing sweeter than the sight of one's parents.

CORINTHIAN MESSENGER   Is that it? It was in fear of this that you banished yourself from Corinth?

OEDIPUS   Yes. I did not want to be my father's murderer.

CORINTHIAN MESSENGER   My lord, I do not know why I have not already released you from that fear. I came here to bring you good news.

OEDIPUS   If you can do that, you will be handsomely rewarded.

CORINTHIAN MESSENGER   Yes, that was why I came, to bring you home to Corinth, and be rewarded for it.

OEDIPUS   I will never go to the city where my parents live.

CORINTHIAN MESSENGER   My son, it is clear that you don't know what you are doing.

OEDIPUS   What do you mean, old man? In God's name, explain yourself.

CORINTHIAN MESSENGER   You don't know what you are doing, if you are afraid to come home because of *them*.

OEDIPUS   I am afraid that Apollo's prophecy may come true.

CORINTHIAN MESSENGER   That you will be stained with guilt through your parents?

OEDIPUS   Yes, that's it, old man, that's the fear which pursues me always.

CORINTHIAN MESSENGER   In reality, you have nothing to fear.

OEDIPUS   Nothing? How, if I am the son of Polybus and Merope?

CORINTHIAN MESSENGER   Because Polybus was not related to you in any way.

OEDIPUS   What do you mean? Was Polybus not my father?

CORINTHIAN MESSENGER   No more than I am—he was as much your father as I.

OEDIPUS   How can my father be on the same level as you who are nothing to me?

CORINTHIAN MESSENGER   Because he was no more your father than I am.

OEDIPUS   Then why did he call me his son?

CORINTHIAN MESSENGER   He took you from my hands—I gave you to him.

OEDIPUS   Took me from your hands? Then how could he love me so much?

CORINTHIAN MESSENGER   He had been childless, that was why he loved you.

OEDIPUS   *You* gave me to him? Did you . . . buy me? or find me somewhere?

CORINTHIAN MESSENGER   I found you in the shady valleys of Mount Cithaeron.

OEDIPUS   What were you doing there?

CORINTHIAN MESSENGER   Watching over my flocks on the mountainside.

OEDIPUS   A shepherd, were you? A wandering day laborer?

CORINTHIAN MESSENGER   Yes, but at that moment I was your savior.

OEDIPUS   When you picked me up, was I in pain?

CORINTHIAN MESSENGER   Your ankles would bear witness on that point.

OEDIPUS   Oh, why do you speak of that old affliction?

CORINTHIAN MESSENGER   You had your ankles pinned together, and I freed you.

OEDIPUS   It is a dreadful mark of shame I have borne since childhood.

CORINTHIAN MESSENGER   From that misfortune comes the name which you still bear.

OEDIPUS   In God's name, who did it? My mother, or my father? Speak.

CORINTHIAN MESSENGER   I don't know. The one who gave you to me is the man to ask, not me.

OEDIPUS   You got me from someone else—you did not find me yourself?

CORINTHIAN MESSENGER   No. Another shepherd gave you to me.

OEDIPUS   Who was he? Do you know? Could you describe him?

CORINTHIAN MESSENGER   I think he belonged to the household of Laius.

OEDIPUS   You mean the man who was once king of this country?

CORINTHIAN MESSENGER   Yes. He was one of the shepherds of Laius.

OEDIPUS   Is he still alive? Can I talk to him?

CORINTHIAN MESSENGER   *(To* CHORUS*)*   You people who live here would know that better than I.

OEDIPUS   *(To* CHORUS*)*   Is there any one of you people here who knows this shepherd he mentioned? Has anyone seen him in the fields, or here in Thebes?

CHORUS LEADER   I think it is the same man from the fields you wanted to see before. But the queen here, Jocasta, could tell you that.

OEDIPUS   Jocasta, do you remember the man we sent for just now? Is *that* the man he is talking about?

JOCASTA   Why ask who he means? Don't pay any attention to him. Don't even think about what he said—it makes no sense.

OEDIPUS   What? With a clue like this? Give up the search? Fail to solve the mystery of my birth? Never!

JOCASTA   In God's name, if you place any value on your life, don't pursue the search. It is enough that *I* am sick to death.

OEDIPUS   *You* have nothing to be afraid of. Even if my mother turns out to be a slave, and I a slave for three generations back, *your* noble birth will not be called in question.

JOCASTA   Take my advice, I beg you—do not go on with it.

OEDIPUS   Nothing will move me. I *will* find out the whole truth.

JOCASTA   It is good advice I am giving you—I am thinking of you.

OEDIPUS   That "good advice" of yours is trying my patience.

JOCASTA   Ill-fated man. May you never find out who you are!

OEDIPUS   *(To attendants)*   One of you go and get that shepherd, bring him here. We will leave *her* to pride herself on her royal birth.

JOCASTA   Unfortunate! That is the only name I can call you by now. I shall not call your name again—ever!

(Exit JOCASTA *to palace. A long silence.)*

CHORUS   Why has the queen gone, Oedipus, why has she rushed away
in such wild grief? I am afraid that from this silence evil will burst out.

OEDIPUS   Burst out what will! I shall know my origin, mean though it
be. Jocasta perhaps—she is proud, *like* a woman—feels shame at the
low circumstances of my birth. But I count myself the son of Good
Chance, the giver of success—I shall not be dishonored. Chance is my
mother. My brothers are the months which have made me sometimes
small and sometimes great. Such is my lineage and I shall not betray
it. I will not give up the search for the truth about my birth.

(Exit OEDIPUS *to palace.)*

CHORUS   *(Chanting in unison)*
    If I am a true prophet
    And see clear in my mind,
    Tomorrow at the full moon
    Oedipus will honor Mount Cithaeron
    As his nurse and mother.
    Mount Cithaeron—our king's Theban birthplace!
    We shall celebrate it in dance and song—
    A place loved by our king.
    Lord Apollo, may this find favor in your sight.

    Who was it, Oedipus my son, who bore you?
    Which of the nymphs that live so long
    Was the bride of Pan the mountain god?
    Was your mother the bride of Apollo himself?
    He loves the upland pastures.
    Or was Hermes your father?
    Perhaps Dionysus who lives on the mountain peaks
    Received you as a welcome gift
    From one of the nymphs of Helicon,°
    His companions in sport.

(Enter from side the SHEPHERD, *accompanied by two guards. Enter*
OEDIPUS, *from doors.)*

OEDIPUS   I never met the man, but, if I may make a guess, I think this
man I see is the shepherd we have been looking for all this time. His

---

°   **Helicon:** A mountain near Thebes; the Chorus suggests that Oedipus is possibly the son of a nymph and a god.

age corresponds to that of the Corinthian here, and, in any case, the men bringing him are my servants, I recognize them.

   (To CHORUS LEADER*)* You have seen the shepherd before, you should know better than I.

CHORUS LEADER   Yes, I recognize him. He was in the household of Laius—a devoted servant, and a shepherd.

OEDIPUS   I question you first—you, the stranger from Corinth. Is this the man you spoke of?

CORINTHIAN MESSENGER   This is the man.

OEDIPUS   *(To* SHEPHERD*)* You, old man, come here. Look me in the face. Answer my questions. Were you a servant of Laius once?

SHEPHERD   I was. A slave. Not bought, though. I was born and reared in the palace.

OEDIPUS   What was your work? How did you earn your living?

SHEPHERD   For most of my life I have followed where the sheep flocks went.

OEDIPUS   And where did you graze your sheep most of the time?

SHEPHERD   Well, there was Mount Cithaeron, and all the country round it.

OEDIPUS   Do you know this man here? Did you ever see him before?

SHEPHERD   Which man do you mean? What would he be doing there?

OEDIPUS   This one, here. Did you ever come across him?

SHEPHERD   I can't say, right away. Give me time. I don't remember.

CORINTHIAN MESSENGER   No wonder he doesn't remember, master. He forgets, but I'll remind him, and make it clear. I am sure he knows very well how the two of us grazed our flocks on Cithaeron—he had two and I only one—we were together three whole summers, from spring until the rising of Arcturus in the fall. When winter came I used to herd my sheep back to their winter huts, and he took his back to the farms belonging to Laius. Do you remember any of this? Isn't that what happened?

SHEPHERD   What you say is true, but it was a long time ago.

CORINTHIAN MESSENGER   Well, then, tell me this. Do you remember giving me a child, a boy, for me to bring up as my own?

SHEPHERD   What are you talking about? Why do you ask that question?

CORINTHIAN MESSENGER   Oedipus here, my good man, Oedipus and that child are one and the same.

SHEPHERD   Damn you! Shut your mouth. Keep quiet!

OEDIPUS   Old man, don't you correct *him*. It is you and your tongue that need correction.

SHEPHERD   What have I done wrong, noble master?

OEDIPUS   You refuse to answer his question about the child.

SHEPHERD   That's because he does not know what he's talking about— he is just wasting your time.

OEDIPUS   If you won't speak willingly, we shall see if pain can make you speak.

(The guards seize the SHEPHERD.*)*

SHEPHERD   In God's name, don't! Don't torture me. I am an old man.

OEDIPUS   One of you twist his arms behind his back, quickly!

SHEPHERD   Oh, God, what for? What more do you want to know?

OEDIPUS   Did you give him the child he asked about?

SHEPHERD   Yes, I did. And I wish I had died that day.

OEDIPUS   You will die now, if you don't give an honest answer.

SHEPHERD   And if I speak, I shall be even worse off.

OEDIPUS   *(To guards)*   What? More delay?

SHEPHERD   No! No! I said it before—I gave him the child.

OEDIPUS   Where did *you* get it? Was it yours? Or did it belong to someone else?

SHEPHERD   It wasn't mine. Someone gave it to me.

OEDIPUS   Which of these Thebans here? From whose house did it come?

SHEPHERD   In God's name, master, don't ask any more questions.

OEIDPUS   You are a dead man if I have to ask you again.

SHEPHERD   It was a child born in the house of Laius.

OEDIPUS   Was it a slave? Or a member of the royal family?

SHEPHERD   Oh, God, here comes the dreadful truth. And I must speak.

OEDIPUS   And I must hear it. But hear it I will.

SHEPHERD   It was the son of Laius, so I was told. But the lady inside there, your wife, she is the one to tell you.

OEDIPUS   Did *she* give it to you?

SHEPHERD   Yes, my lord, she did.

OEDIPUS   For what purpose?

SHEPHERD   To destroy it.

OEDIPUS   Her own child?

SHEPHERD   She was afraid of dreadful prophecies.

OEDIPUS   What were they?

SHEPHERD   The child would kill its parents, that was the story.

OEDIPUS   Then why did you give it to this old man here?

SHEPHERD   In pity, master. I thought he would take it away to a foreign country—to the place he came from. If you are the man he says you are, you were born the most unfortunate of men.

OEDIPUS   O God! It has all come true. Light, let this be the last time I see you. I stand revealed—born in shame, married in shame, an unnatural murderer.

(Exit OEDIPUS *into palace. Exeunt others at sides.)*

Chorus

O generations of mortal men,
I add up the total of your lives
And find it equal to nothing.
What man wins more happiness
Than a mere appearance which quickly fades away?
With your example before me,
Your life, your destiny, miserable Oedipus, I call no man happy.

Oedipus outranged all others
And won complete prosperity and happiness.
He destroyed the Sphinx, that maiden
With curved claws and riddling songs,
And rose up like a towered wall against death—
Oedipus, savior of our city.
From that time on you were called King,
You were honored above all men,
Ruling over great Thebes.

And now—is there a man whose story is more pitiful?
His life is lived in merciless calamity and pain—
A complete reversal from his happy state.
O Oedipus, famous king,
You whom the same great harbor sheltered
As child and father both,
How could the furrows which your father plowed
Bear *you* in silence for so long?

Time, which sees all things, has found you out;
It sits in judgment on the unnatural marriage
Which was both begetter and begot.
O son of Laius,
I wish I had never seen you.
I weep, like a man wailing for the dead.
This is the truth:
You returned me to life once
And now you have closed my eyes in darkness.

(Enter a Palace Messenger.*)*

Palace Messenger   Citizens of Thebes, you who are most honored in
this city! What dreadful things you will see and hear! What a cry of

sorrow you will raise, if, as true Thebans, you have any feeling for the royal house. Not even the great rivers of Ister and Phasis° could wash this house clean of the horrors it hides within. And it will soon expose them to the light of day—horrors deliberately willed, not involuntary. Those calamities we inflict on ourselves are those which cause the most pain.

CHORUS LEADER   The horrors we knew about before were burden enough. What other dreadful news do you bring?

MESSENGER   Here is the thing quickest for me to say and you to hear. Jocasta, our queen, is dead.

CHORUS LEADER   Poor lady. From what cause?

MESSENGER   By her own hand. You are spared the worst of what has happened—you were not there to see it. But as far as my memory serves, you shall hear the full story of that unhappy woman's sufferings.

She came in through the door in a fury of passion and rushed straight towards her marriage bed, tearing at her hair with both hands. Into her bedroom she went, and slammed the doors behind her. She was calling the name of Laius, so long dead, remembering the child she bore to him so long ago—the child by whose hand Laius was to die, and leave her, its mother, to bear monstrous children to her own son. She wailed in mourning for her marriage, in which she had borne double offspring, a husband from her husband and children from her child. And after that—but I do not know exactly how she died. For Oedipus came bursting in, shouting, and so we could not watch Jocasta's suffering to the end; all of us looked at him as he ran to and fro. He rushed from one of us to the other, asking us to give him a sword, to tell him where he could find his wife—no, not his wife, but his mother, his mother and the mother of his children.

It must have been some supernatural being that showed the raving man where she was; it was not one of us. As if led by a guide he threw himself against the doors of her room with a terrible cry; he bent the bolts out of their sockets, and so forced his way into the room. And there we saw Jocasta, hanging, her neck caught in a swinging noose of rope. When Oedipus saw her he gave a deep dreadful cry of sorrow and loosened the rope round her neck. And when the poor woman was lying on the ground—then we saw the most dreadful sight of all. He ripped out the golden pins with which her clothes were fastened, raised them high above his head, and speared the pupils of his eyes. "You will not see," he said, "the horrors I have suffered and done. Be dark forever now—eyes that saw those you should never have seen, and failed to recognize those you longed to see." Murmuring words

---

°   **Ister and Phasis:** Ancient names for the Danube and Rion Rivers.

like these he raised his hands and struck his eyes again, and again. And each time the wounded eyes sent a stream of blood down his chin, no oozing flow but a dark shower of it, thick as a hailstorm.

These are the sorrows which have burst out and overwhelmed them both, man and wife alike. The wealth and happiness they once had was real while it lasted, but now—weeping, destruction, death, shame —name any shape of evil you will, they have them all.

CHORUS   And Oedipus—poor wretched Oedipus—has he now some rest from pain?

MESSENGER   He is shouting, "Open the doors, someone: show me to all the people of Thebes, my father's killer, my mother's"—I cannot repeat his unholy words. He speaks of banishing himself from Thebes, says he will not remain in his house under the curse which he himself pronounced. But he has no strength: he needs someone to guide his steps. The pain is more than he can bear.

But he will show you himself. The bolts of this door are opening. Now you will see a spectacle that even his enemies would pity.

(Enter OEDIPUS *from door, blind.)*

CHORUS   O suffering dreadful for mankind to see, most dreadful of all I ever saw. What madness came over you? What unearthly spirit, leaping farther than the mind can conceive, swooped down on your destiny? I pity you. I have many questions to ask you, much I wish to know; my eyes are drawn towards you—but I cannot bear to look. You fill me with horror.

OEDIPUS   Where am I going? Pity me! Where does my voice range to through the air? O spirit, what a leap you made!

CHORUS   To a point of dread, too far for men's ears and eyes.

OEDIPUS   Darkness, dark cloud all around me, enclosing me, unspeakable darkness, irresistible—you came to me on a wind that seemed favorable. Ah, I feel the stab of these sharp pains, and with it the memory of my sorrow.

CHORUS   In such torment it is no wonder that your pain and mourning should be double.

OEDIPUS   My friend! You are by my side still, you alone. You still stay by me, looking after the blind man. I know you are there. I am in the dark, but I can distinguish your voice clearly.

CHORUS   You have done a dreadful thing. How could you bring yourself to put out the light of your eyes? What superhuman power urged you on?

OEDIPUS   It was Apollo, friends, Apollo, who brought to fulfillment all my sufferings. But the hand that struck my eyes was mine and mine alone. What use had I for eyes? Nothing I could see would bring me joy.

CHORUS   It was just as you say.

OEDIPUS   What was there for me to look at, to speak to, to love? What joyful word can I expect to hear, my friends? Take me away, out of this country, quickly, take me away. I am lost, accursed, and hated by the gods beyond all other men.

CHORUS   I am moved to pity by your misfortunes and your understanding of them, too. I wish I had never known you!

OEDIPUS   A curse on the man who freed my feet from the cruel bonds on the mountain, who saved me and rescued me from death. He will get no thanks from me. I might have died then and there; but now I am a source of grief for myself and all who love me.

CHORUS   I wish it had turned out that way, too.

OEDIPUS   I would never have become my father's killer, never have been known to all men as my own mother's husband. Now I am godforsaken, the son of an accursed marriage, my own father's successor in the marriage bed. If there is any evil worse than the worst that a man can suffer—Oedipus has drawn it for his lot.

CHORUS   I cannot say you made the right decision. You would have been better dead than blind.

OEDIPUS   What I have done was the best thing to do. Don't read me any more lessons, don't give me any more advice. With what eyes could I have faced my father in the house of the dead, or my poor mother? I have done things to them both for which hanging is too small a punishment.

Do you think I longed to look at my children, born the way they were? No, not with these eyes of mine, never! Not this town either, its walls, its holy temples of the gods. From all of this I am cut off, I, the most nobly raised in Thebes, cut off by my own act. It was I who proclaimed that everyone should expel the impious man—the man the gods have now revealed as unholy—and the son of Laius. After I had exposed my own guilt—and what a guilt!—do you think I could have looked at my fellow citizens with steady eyes?

No, no! If there had been some way to block the source of hearing, I would not have held back: I would have isolated my wretched body completely, so as to see and hear nothing at all. If my mind could be put beyond reach of my miseries—that would be my pleasure.

O Cithaeron, why did you receive me? Why did you not take and kill me on the spot, so that I should never reveal my origin to mankind?

O Polybus, and Corinth, and the ancient house I thought was my father's—what a handsome heir you raised up in me, how rotten beneath the surface! For now I am exposed—evil and born in evil.

O three roads in the deep valley, you oak wood and you narrow pass where the three roads meet, you who soaked up my father's blood, spilled by my hand—do you remember me? Do you remember what I did there, and what I did when I came here?

O marriage, marriage! You gave me birth, and then bred up seed from the one you brought into the world. You made an incestuous breed of father, brother, son—bride, wife, mother—all the most shameful things known to man.

But I must not speak of things that should never have been done. Quickly, in God's name, hide me somewhere outside Thebes, kill me, throw me into the sea, where you will never see me again.

Come close to me. I am a man of sorrow, but take courage and touch me. Do not be afraid; do what I ask. The evil is mine; no one but me can bear its weight.

(Enter CREON, *from side, with attendants.)*

CHORUS LEADER   Here is Creon. He will listen to your request. Decision and action are up to him, now that he has taken your place as the sole ruler of Thebes.

OEDIPUS   What shall I say to him? What justification, what grounds for trust can I present? In everything I did to him before, I have been proved wrong.

CREON   I have not come to mock you, Oedipus, nor to reproach you for the wrong you did.

(To attendants)   If you have no respect for the feelings of human beings, at least show reverence for the sunlight which nourishes all men. Do not leave him there in full view, an object of dread and horror which appalls the holy rain and the daylight. Get him into the palace as fast as you can.

(The attendants move over to OEDIPUS, *and stand by him until the end of the scene.)*

Only his family should see the family shame; this public spectacle is indecent.

OEDIPUS   In God's name—since you have exceeded my hopes and come in so generous a spirit to one so low—do something for me. I ask it in your interest, not mine.

CREON   What is it you are so anxious to have me do?

OEDIPUS   Banish me from this country as fast as you can—to a place where no man can see me or speak to me.

CREON   You can be sure I would have done so already, but first I wanted to ask the god Apollo what should be done.

OEDIPUS   But his command was clear, every word of it; death for the unholy man, the father-killer.

CREON   That *is* what the oracle said. But all the same, in our situation, it is better to inquire what should be done.

OEDIPUS   Will you consult Apollo about anyone as miserable as I?

CREON   Yes, and this time, I take it, you will believe what the god says.

OEDIPUS   Yes. I command you—and beg you—the woman in the palace, see to her burial. She is your sister, you are the man to do this. As for me, do not condemn this city of my fathers to shelter me within its walls, but let me live on the mountain, on Cithaeron, forever linked with my name, the mountain which my mother and father while they still lived chose as my burial place. Let me die there where they tried to kill me.

And yet I know this—no disease or anything else will destroy me. Otherwise I would never have been saved from death in the first place. I was saved—for some strange and dreadful end.

Well, let my destiny go where it will. As for my children, do not concern yourself about the boys, Creon. They are men; and will always find a way to live, wherever they may be. But my two poor helpless girls, who were always at my table, who shared the same food I ate—take care of them for me.

What I wish for most is this. Let me touch them with these hands, as I weep for my sorrows. Please, my lord! Grant my prayer, generous man! If I could hold them I would think I had them with me, as I did when I could see.

(ANTIGONE *and* ISMENE *led in from the door by a nurse.*)

What's that? I hear something. Oh, God. It is my daughters, weeping. Creon took pity on me, and sent them to me, my dearest ones, my children. Am I right?

CREON   Yes, you are. I did this for you knowing the joy you always took in them, the joy you feel now.

OEDIPUS   Bless you for it! May you be rewarded for sending them. May God watch over you better than He did over me.

Children, where are you? Come here, come to these hands of mine, your brother's hands, the hands that intervened to make your father's once bright eyes so dim. Blind and thoughtless, I became your father, and your mother was my mother, too. I weep for you—see you I cannot—when I think of your future, the bitter life you will lead, the way men will treat you. What gatherings will you go to, what festivals, without returning home in tears, instead of taking part in the ceremonies?

And when you come to the age of marriage, who will take the risk, my daughters, and shoulder the burden of reproach which will be directed at my children—and yours? No reproach is missing. Your father killed his father. He sowed the field from which he himself had sprung, and begot you, his children, at the source of his own being. These are the reproaches you will hear. And who will marry you? There is no one who will do so, children; your destiny is clear—to waste away unmarried, childless.

Creon, you are the only father they have now, for we who brought them into the world are both of us destroyed. Do not abandon them to wander husbandless in poverty: they are your own flesh and blood. Do not make them equal to me and my miserable state, but pity them. They are children, they have no protector but you. Promise me this, noble Creon, touch me with your hand to confirm your promise.

And you, children—if you were old enough to understand, I would have much advice to give you. But as it is, I will tell you what to pray for. Pray that you may find a place where you are allowed to live, and for a life happier than your father's.

CREON   You have wept long enough. Now go inside the house.

OEDIPUS   I must obey, though it gives me no pleasure.

CREON   Yes, everything is good in its proper place and time.

OEDIPUS   I will go in then, but on one condition.

CREON   Tell me what it is. I am listening.

OEDIPUS   You must send me into exile—away from Thebes.

CREON   What you ask for is a gift only Apollo can grant.

OEDIPUS   But I am hateful to the gods above all men.

CREON   In that case, they will grant your request at once.

OEDIPUS   You consent, then?

CREON   It is not my habit to say what I don't mean.

OEDIPUS   Then take me away from here at once.

CREON   Come then, but let go of the children.

OEDIPUS   No, don't take them away from me.

CREON   Don't try to be master in everything. What you once won and held did not stay with you all your life long.

CHORUS°   Citizens who dwell in Thebes, look at Oedipus here, who knew the answer to the famous riddle and was a power in the land. On his good fortune all the citizens gazed with envy. Into what a stormy sea of dreadful trouble he has come now. Therefore we must call no

---

°   **Chorus:** This speech, for reasons too technical to discuss here, is considered by many authorities to be an addition to the play made by a later producer. The translator shares this opinion, but the lines are printed here for those who wish to use them.

man happy while he waits to see his last day, not until he has passed the border of life and death without suffering pain.

Questions on *Oedipus the King*

A. For Close Reading

1. At the beginning of the play, why are the citizens of Thebes calling on Oedipus? What do they ask of him? From the first speech of the Priest, what do we learn of Oedipus since he arrived in the city from Corinth?
2. What message from Apollo is brought by Creon? Read carefully his description of the murder of Laius.
3. What curse does Oedipus invoke upon the murderer?
4. What happens in the interview between Tiresias and Oedipus?
5. What is Oedipus' reaction to Tiresias' charge: ". . . *you* are the unholy defilement of this land"? What villainous motives does Oedipus ascribe to Creon and Tiresias?
6. Of what does Oedipus accuse Creon when they meet? Trace the pattern of the argument in this scene.
7. Find instances, in these first scenes, where Oedipus' unjustified attacks on others reflect his own inner thoughts rather than the facts at hand.
8. What additional information is supplied by the scene between Oedipus and Jocasta? How does Oedipus react to Jocasta's story about the murder of her former husband?
9. What reasons does Oedipus give for his having left Corinth? What account does he give of the incident at the crossroads? Why does Oedipus ask Jocasta to send for the shepherd?
10. Identify the turning point in the play, where the truth of his situation becomes clear to Oedipus.
11. The Chorus now comments on the relation of man to the gods and gives its ideas on religion and what constitutes undesirable human conduct. What are these ideas?
12. Tht next section of the play is concerned with the visit of the messenger from Corinth. What reaction does Oedipus have to the news of Polybus' death? By what steps are new truths revealed to Oedipus? Note Jocasta's long silence in this scene. Finally, what is her response? At what point does the truth strike her?
13. In the confrontation between the messenger and the shepherd, how is the link established between Oedipus' past and present life?
14. How does Oedipus react to his own suffering? Does he complain of injustice? Where does he put the blame?
15. What is the significance of Creon's last speech and that of the Chorus?

B. For Writing and Discussion

1. The play begins near the end of the myth. All the information about the past is provided by the various characters. Trace the stages by which the past is unveiled.

2. What is Oedipus' position at the beginning of the play? At the end? Point out all the differences you can see in his situation, in his personality, in his relations with other people, and in his attitude toward himself.

3. In an essay entitled "Sophocles' *Oedipus*" (from *Tragic Themes in Western Literature*), Bernard Knox makes the following observation: "Oedipus' problem is apparently simple: 'Who is the murderer of Laius?' but as he pursues the answer the question changes shape. It becomes a different problem: 'Who am I?' " Write a paper in which you prove the truth of this statement.

4. How much of Oedipus' downfall is caused by actions that he can control and how much by fate, actions that he cannot control? Give specific examples of each.

5. What evidence does the play give of Oedipus' qualities of suspicion, arrogance, and quick temper? Why does Sophocles stress these qualities?

6. After Oedipus has put out his own eyes, the Chorus says to him, "You would have been better dead than blind," and Oedipus replies: "What I have done was the best thing to do . . . don't give me any more advice." Why didn't Oedipus, like Jocasta, commit suicide and end his misery on earth?

7. Though we see less of Jocasta than we do of Oedipus, she is a fully drawn person in her own right and belongs among Sophocles' great portraits. What is she like? Cite specific scenes and lines to support your evaluation of her character. How does her character throw light on Oedipus'?

8. In a sense, Creon acts as a foil, or contrast, to Oedipus. What qualities does he possess that Oedipus does not? At several points he suggests that he is both wise and prudent. Is he justified in doing so? Explain by contrasting his behavior with that of Oedipus.

9. One of the controlling patterns of the play is dramatic irony: Oedipus makes statements that mean one thing to him but something quite different to the audience. Cite instances and show why the device is particularly appropriate for what Sophocles is saying about man's lot.

10. What functions does the Chorus perform in the play? Where does it comment on the action? Speak directly as a character would? Assist in characterizing any actor? In what ways does the Chorus contribute to the characterization of Oedipus? What is its attitude toward Oedipus (critical? sympathetic?) and what is his toward it?

11. "The major movement of the play is created by reversals; each action turns into its opposite." Write a paper demonstrating the truth of this statement.

12. One of the ideas being acted out in the play is the relation of the gods to man. At the beginning of the play Oedipus rules; at the end he says to Creon, "I must obey. . . ." Is the play about obedience? Is it about injus-

tice? Are the gods just to Oedipus? Is he just in his treatment of Tiresias? Of Creon? Of the shepherd?

13. Comment on the truth of the following statement: "Oedipus differs from others in that where they would withhold the truth, he wants to reveal it."

The Trial of Socrates (from the Apology and Crito)

(399 B. C.)

THE *Apology*[1] and *Crito* are two of the many Dialogues that make up a large portion of the writings of Plato, a Greek philosopher and one of the world's greatest minds. He was born in Athens in about 427 B.C., the son of a wealthy and politically important family. One of the most important moments of his life was his meeting with Socrates, the great teacher, around whom the brightest young men of Athens gathered in the agora, the public square, to discuss important questions. Socrates was an exciting figure, asking probing questions, bringing his students to an awareness of what it means to think. The Socratic question has become synonymous with a way of teaching a student to understand his own mind.

Each of Plato's Dialogues is a lesson on the meanings of the great words that define Western civilization, such words as *soul, friendship, courage, virtue, love,* and *logic.* The two Dialogues that follow, the *Apology* and *Crito,* are concerned with the trial and death of Socrates (399 B.C.). "There is nothing in any tragedy ancient or modern," says the great Greek scholar Benjamin Jowett,[2] "nothing in poetry or history (with one exception) like the last hours of Socrates in Plato." Plato's version of the trial is a fictionalized version of Socrates' final defense of himself. As far as we know, it seems to be a fair portrayal of what happened. It presents the image of a great man who refuses to compromise his principles to save his life.

Athens had only recently emerged from the Peloponnesian War, which marked the temporary breakdown of Athenian democracy. At the war's end, power was seized by "The Thirty," an oligarchy who ruled until democracy was re-established. In such times of stress, with so little belief in the power of the newly established democracy, the people of Athens demanded "loyalty" to the state. But the major characteristic of a democracy is that the state should be equally loyal to the citizens. At this moment in history Athens lost faith in herself and decided to silence criticism.

The procedure of a trial was such that the accusers made their charges before a body of the Assembly, those who governed Athens and made its laws. For the trial of Socrates 501 members of the Assembly acted as judges and jury. There seem to have been 280 votes against him.

The *Apology* is made up of Plato's version of Socrates' remarks at his trial. It is in three sections: The first tries to answer the charges; at its end

---

[1] As used here, the word "apology" means "defense."
[2] Translator of both dialogues in this text.

Socrates is voted guilty. In the second section, he considers what his punishment should be: a fine, exile, or death. He chooses the fine. After the second section, he is told that he must die, and the third section gives his reaction to that verdict.

In *Crito* the scene is Socrates' prison cell where his friends are urging that he escape. Socrates argues against this alternative. He is as loyal to his conscience as a modern conscientious objector, but he also has respect for the public conscience, the laws under which he has chosen to live his life. If he now disagrees with the mass of people, he chooses to die; he will not run away. He knows that a man who attacks the public conscience, who does not agree with the ways in which most people live, will get in trouble in whatever country he may choose to go to. He knows, too, that the state will have to live with the results of its actions.

When we think of Socrates, we think of questions. The dialogues are for the most part a series of questions and answers. His probing queries are aimed at discovering the truth about how man should live his life. If his opponent tried to answer a question, he was met with further questions: Can virtue be taught? Who is the most virtuous man in town? Are his sons virtuous? Such a man as Socrates will make enemies, but he can teach us much, especially if we consider his major question: How are we to live our lives?

Socrates lived from 470? to 399 B.C., strangely detached from other men, in a constant search for intellectual and moral qualities. Often forgetting to eat, he paid little attention to pleasure or pain. Truth, he felt, was inside men; by constant questioning, he could reveal some of it.

In the *Apology* and *Crito* we have the acting out of a tragedy. A man is pushed to a point where he may live or die, but either choice is destructive. To live, he must give some indication of changing his way of life, of being less a threat to the citizens of the state. But Socrates prefers to die in his own fashion than live in theirs. He prefers to obey God, rather than man, and feels that God intends that he should die.

This stubborn old man never let his fellow citizens rest in their vanity and ignorance. Because of him, they were forced to think more deeply about the meaning of human life, to think that luxury was not the end for which man was made. Virtue was, to Socrates, the knowledge of right living; all else was useless. Because he made people uncomfortable, he was forced to drink a cup of hemlock, a poison which has since become a symbol for all who dare to suffer for what they believe. Four hundred years before the birth of Christ, Socrates stated in *Crito* that one should not return evil for evil. Although the message is still valid, those who practice it may still die at the hands of the nonbelievers.

Apology

PLATO   *Translator:*
                                   Benjamin Jowett

PERSONS OF THE DIALOGUE: Socrates, Meletus

SCENE: IN THE COURT

Socrates speaks:

How you, O Athenians, have been affected by my accusers, I cannot tell; but I know that they almost made me forget who I was—so persuasively did they speak; and yet they have hardly uttered a word of truth. But of the many falsehoods told by them, there was one which quite amazed me—I mean when they said that you should be upon your guard and not allow yourselves to be deceived by the force of my eloquence. To say this, when they were certain to be detected as soon as I opened my lips and proved myself to be anything but a great speaker, did indeed appear to me most shameless—unless by the force of eloquence they mean the force of truth; for if such is their meaning, I admit that I am eloquent. But in how different a way from theirs! Well, as I was saying, they have scarcely spoken the truth at all; but from me you shall hear the whole truth—not, however, delivered after their manner in a set oration duly ornamented with words and phrases. No, by heaven! but I shall use the words and arguments which occur to me at the moment; for I am confident in the justice of my cause.° At my time of life I ought not to be appearing before you, O men of Athens, in the character of a juvenile orator—let no one expect it of me. And I must beg of you to grant me a favor:—If I defend myself in my accustomed manner, and you hear me using the words which I have been in the habit of using in the agora,° at the tables of the money-changers, or anywhere else, I would ask you not to be surprised, and not to interrupt me on this account. For I am more than seventy years of age, and appearing now for the first time in a court of law, I am quite a stranger to the language of the place; and therefore I would have you regard me as if I were really a stranger, whom you would excuse if he spoke in his native tongue, and after the fashion of his country. Am I making an unfair request of you? Never mind the

---

° Or, I am certain that I am right in taking this course. [Translator's note.]
° **Agora:** Market place.

manner, which may or may not be good; but think only of the truth of my words, and give heed to that. Let the speaker speak truly and the judge decide justly.

And first, I have to reply to the older charges and to my first accusers, and then I will go on to the later ones. For of old I have had many accusers, who have accused me falsely to you during many years; and I am more afraid of them than of Anytus° and his associates, who are dangerous, too, in their own way. But far more dangerous are the others, who began when you were children, and took possession of your minds with their falsehoods, telling of one Socrates, a wise man, who speculated about the heaven above, and searched into the earth beneath, and made the worse appear the better cause. The disseminators of this tale are the accusers whom I dread; for their hearers are apt to fancy that such inquirers do not believe in the existence of the gods. And they are many, and their charges against me are of ancient date, and they were made by them in the days when you were more impressible than you are now—in childhood, or it may have been in youth —and the cause when heard went by default, for there was none to answer. . . .

I will begin at the beginning, and ask what is the accusation which has given rise to the slander of me, and in fact has encouraged Meletus° to prefer this charge against me. Well, what do the slanderers say? They shall be my prosecutors, and I will sum up their words in an affidavit: "Socrates is an evildoer, and a curious person, who searches into things under the earth and in heaven, and he makes the worse appear the better cause; and he teaches the aforesaid doctrines to others." Such is the nature of the accusation: it is just what you have yourselves seen in the comedy of Aristophanes, who has introduced a man whom he calls Socrates, going about and saying that he walks in air, and talking a deal of nonsense concerning matters of which I do not pretend to know either much or little—not that I mean to speak disparagingly of any one who is a student of natural philosophy.° I should be very sorry if Meletus could bring so grave a charge against me. But the simple truth is, O Athenians, that I have nothing to do with physical speculations. Very many of those here present are witnesses to the truth of this, and to them I appeal. Speak then, you who have heard me, and tell your neighbors whether any of you have ever known me hold forth in few words or in many upon such matters. . . . You hear their answer. And from what they say of this part of the charge you will be able to judge of the truth of the rest.

As little foundation is there for the report that I am a teacher, and take

---

° **Anytus:** One of the three present "accusers."
° **Meletus:** Another accuser.
° **natural philosophy:** Study of the physical world.

money; this accusation has no more truth in it than the other. Although, if a man were really able to instruct mankind, to receive money for giving instruction would, in my opinion, be an honor to him. . . .

I dare say, Athenians, that someone among you will reply, "Yes, Socrates, but what is the origin of these accusations which are brought against you; there must have been something strange which you have been doing? All these rumors and this talk about you would never have arisen if you had been like other men: tell us, then, what is the cause of them, for we should be sorry to judge hastily of you." Now, I regard this as a fair challenge, and I will endeavor to explain to you the reason why I am called wise and have such an evil fame. Please to attend then. And although some of you may think that I am joking, I declare that I will tell you the entire truth. Men of Athens, this reputation of mine has come of a certain sort of wisdom which I possess. If you ask me what kind of wisdom, I reply, wisdom such as may perhaps be attained by man, for to that extent I am inclined to believe that I am wise; whereas the persons of whom I was speaking have a superhuman wisdom, which I may fail to describe, because I have it not myself; and he who says that I have, speaks falsely, and is taking away my character. And here, O men of Athens, I must beg you not to interrupt me, even if I seem to say something extravagant. For the word which I will speak is not mine. I will refer you to a witness who is worthy of credit; that witness shall be the God of Delphi°—he will tell you about my wisdom, if I have any, and of what sort it is. You must have known Chaerephon;° he was early a friend of mine, and also a friend of yours, for he shared in the recent exile° of the people, and returned with you. Well, Chaerephon, as you know, was very impetuous in all his doings, and he went to Delphi and boldly asked the oracle to tell him whether—as I was saying, I must beg you not to interrupt—he asked the oracle to tell him whether any one was wiser than I was, and the Pythian prophetess° answered, that there was no man wiser. Chaerephon is dead himself; but his brother, who is in court, will confirm the truth of what I am saying.

Why do I mention this? Because I am going to explain to you why I have such an evil name. When I heard the answer, I said to myself, What can the God mean? and what is the interpretation of his riddle? for I know that I have no wisdom, small or great. What then can he mean when he says

---

° **God of Delphi:** Apollo, whose temple was at Delphi. Men seeking answers about the future consulted the priestess of Apollo, whose replies were usually ambiguous.
° **Chaerephon:** A close friend of Socrates.
° **recent exile:** In 404 B.C. those who strongly favored democratic rule in Athens were forced into exile by the Thirty Tyrants, who had gained control of the city.
° **Pythian prophetess:** The priestess of Apollo.

that I am the wisest of men? And yet he is a god, and cannot lie; that would be against his nature. After long consideration, I thought of a method of trying the question. I reflected that if I could only find a man wiser than myself, then I might go to the god with a refutation in my hand. I should say to him, "Here is a man who is wiser than I am; but you said that I was the wisest." Accordingly I went to one who had the reputation of wisdom, and observed him—his name I need not mention; he was a politician whom I selected for examination—and the result was as follows: When I began to talk with him, I could not help thinking that he was not really wise, although he was thought wise by many, and still wiser by himself; and thereupon I tried to explain to him that he thought himself wise, but was not really wise; and the consequence was that he hated me, and his enmity was shared by several who were present and heard me. So I left him, saying to myself, as I went away: Well, although I do not suppose that either of us knows anything really beautiful and good, I am better off than he is—for he knows nothing, and thinks that he knows; I neither know nor think that I know. . . .

Then I went to one man after another, being not unconscious of the enmity which I provoked, and I lamented and feared this: but necessity was laid upon me—the word of God, I thought, ought to be considered first. And I said to myself, Go I must to all who appear to know, and find out the meaning of the oracle. And I swear to you, Athenians, by the dog° I swear! —for I must tell you the truth—the result of my mission was just this: I found that the men most in repute were all but the most foolish; and that others less esteemed were really wiser and better. I will tell you the tale of my wanderings and of the "Herculean" labors,° as I may call them, which I endured only to find at last the oracle irrefutable. After the politicians, I went to the poets: tragic, dithyrambic,° and all sorts. And there, I said to myself, you will be instantly detected; now you will find out that you are more ignorant than they are. Accordingly I took them some of the most elaborate passages in their own writings, and asked what was the meaning of them—thinking that they would teach me something. Will you believe me? I am almost ashamed to confess the truth, but I must say that there is hardly a person present who would not have talked better about their poetry than they did themselves. Then I knew that not by wisdom do poets write poetry, but by a sort of genius and inspiration; they are like diviners or soothsayers who also say many fine things, but do not understand the meaning of them. The poets appeared to me to be much in the same case; and I further ob-

---

°   **by the dog:** A mild oath.
°   **"Herculean" labors:** To gain immortality, Hercules had to perform twelve difficult and dangerous tasks.
°   **dithyrambic:** A dithyramb was a short poem in honor of Dionysus, the god of wine.

served that upon the strength of their poetry they believed themselves to be the wisest of men in other things in which they were not wise. So I departed, conceiving myself to be superior to them for the same reason that I was superior to the politicians.

At last I went to the artisans, I was conscious that I knew nothing at all, as I may say, and I was sure that they knew many fine things; and here I was not mistaken, for they did know many things of which I was ignorant, and in this they certainly were wiser than I was. But I observed that even the good artisans fell into the same error as the poets—because they were good workmen they thought that they also knew all sorts of high matters, and this defect in them overshadowed their wisdom; and therefore I asked myself on behalf of the oracle, whether I would like to be as I was, neither having their knowledge nor their ignorance, or like them in both; and I made answer to myself and to the oracle that I was better off as I was.

This inquisition has led to my having many enemies of the worst and most dangerous kind, and has given occasion also to many calumnies. And I am called wise, for my hearers always imagine that I myself possess the wisdom which I find wanting in others: but the truth is, O men of Athens, that God only is wise; and by his answer he intends to show that the wisdom of men is worth little or nothing; he is not speaking of Socrates; he is only using my name by way of illustration, as if he said, He, O men, is the wisest, who, like Socrates, knows that his wisdom is in truth worth nothing. And so I go about the world obedient to the god, and search and make inquiry into the wisdom of anyone, whether citizen or stranger, who appears to be wise; and if he is not wise, then in vindication of the oracle I show him that he is not wise; and my occupation quite absorbs me, and I have no time to give either to any public matter of interest or to any concern of my own, but I am in utter poverty by reason of my devotion to the god.

There is another thing: —young men of the richer classes, who have not much to do, come about me of their own accord; they like to hear the pretenders examined, and they often imitate me, and proceed to examine others; there are plenty of persons, as they quickly discover, who think that they know something, but really know little or nothing; and then those who are examined by them instead of being angry with themselves are angry with me: This confounded Socrates, they say; this villainous misleader of youth! —and then if somebody asks them, Why, what evil does he practice or teach? they do not know, and cannot tell; but in order that they may not appear to be at a loss, they repeat the ready-made charges which are used against all philosophers about teaching things up in the clouds and under the earth, and having no gods, and making the worse appear the better cause; for they do not like to confess that their pretense of knowledge has been detected—which is the truth; and as they are numerous and ambitious and energetic, and are drawn up in battle array and have persuasive tongues, they have filled your ears with their loud and inveterate calumnies. And this is the reason why my three accusers, Meletus and Anytus and Lycon,° have set upon me—Meletus, who has a quarrel with me on behalf of the poets; Anytus, on behalf of the craftsmen and politicians; Lycon, on behalf of the rhetoricians—and, as I said at the beginning, I cannot expect to get rid of such a mass of calumny all in a moment. And this, O men of Athens, is the truth and the whole truth; I have concealed nothing, I have dissembled nothing. And yet, I know that my plainness of speech makes them hate me, and what is their hatred but a proof that I am speaking the truth? Hence has arisen the prejudice against me; and this is the reason of it, as you will find out either in this or in any future inquiry.

I have said enough in my defense against the first class of my accusers; I turn to the second class. They are headed by Meletus, that good man and true lover of his country, as he calls himself. Against these, too, I must try to make a defense. Let their affidavit be read: it contains something of this kind: It says that Socrates is a doer of evil, who corrupts the youth, and who does not believe in the gods of the State, but has other new divinities of his own. Such is the charge; and now let us examine the particular counts. He says that I am a doer of evil, and corrupt the youth; but I say, O men of Athens, that Meletus is a doer of evil, in that he pretends to be in earnest when he is only in jest, and is so eager to bring men to trial from a pretended zeal and interest about matters in which he really never had the smallest interest. And the truth of this I will endeavor to prove to you.

Come hither, Meletus, and let me ask a question of you. You think a great deal about the improvement of youth?

Yes, I do.

Tell the judges, then, who is their improver; for you must know, as you have taken the pains to discover their corrupter, and are citing and accusing me before them. Speak, then, and tell the judges who their improver is. — Observe, Meletus, that you are silent, and have nothing to say. But is not this rather disgraceful, and a very considerable proof of what I was saying, that you have no interest in the matter? Speak up, friend, and tell us who their improver is.

The laws.

But that, my good sir, is not my meaning. I want to know who the person is, who, in the first place, knows the laws.

The judges, Socrates, who are present in court.

What, do you mean to say, Meletus, that they are able to instruct and improve youth?

Certainly they are.

°   **Meletus . . . Lycon:** Meletus was a poet, Anytus a politician and tanner, and Lycon an orator.

What, all of them, or some only and not others?

All of them.

By the goddess Hera° that is good news! There are plenty of improvers, then. And what do you say of the audience—do they improve them?

Yes, they do.

And the senators?

Yes, the senators improve them.

But perhaps the members of the assembly corrupt them?—or do they improve them?

They improve them.

Then every Athenian improves and elevates them; all with the exception of myself; and I alone am their corrupter? Is that what you affirm?

That is what I stoutly affirm. . . .

And when you accuse me of corrupting and deteriorating the youth, do you allege that I corrupt them intentionally or unintentionally?

Intentionally, I say. . . .

It will be very clear to you, Athenians, as I was saying, that Meletus has no care at all, great or small, about the matter. But still I should like to know, Meletus, in what I am affirmed to corrupt the young. I suppose you mean, as I infer from your indictment, that I teach them not to acknowledge the gods which the State acknowledges, but some other new divinities or spiritual agencies in their stead. These are the lessons by which I corrupt the youth, as you say.

Yes, that I say emphatically.

Then, by the gods, Meletus, of whom we are speaking, tell me and the court, in somewhat plainer terms, what you mean! For I do not as yet understand whether you affirm that I teach other men to acknowledge some gods, and therefore that I do believe in gods, and am not an entire atheist —this you do not lay to my charge—but only you say that they are not the same gods which the city recognizes—the charge is that they are different gods. Or, do you mean that I am an atheist simply, and a teacher of atheism?

I mean the latter—that you are a complete atheist. . . .

. . . I know only too well how many are the enmities which I have incurred, and this is what will be my destruction if I am destroyed—not Meletus, nor yet Anytus, but the envy and detraction of the world, which has been the death of many good men, and will probably be the death of many more; there is no danger of my being the last of them.

Some one will say: And are you not ashamed, Socrates, of a course of life which is likely to bring you to an untimely end? To him I may fairly answer: There you are mistaken: a man who is good for anything ought not to

---

° **Hera:** Wife of Zeus.

calculate the chance of living or dying; he ought only to consider whether in doing anything he is doing right or wrong—acting the part of a good man or of a bad. . . .

Strange, indeed, would be my conduct, O men of Athens, if I, who, when I was ordered by the generals whom you chose to command me at Potidaea and Amphipolis and Delium,° remained where they placed me, like any other man, facing death—if now, when, as I conceive and imagine, God orders me to fulfill the philosopher's mission of searching into myself and other men, I were to desert my post through fear of death, or any other fear; that would indeed be strange, and I might justly be arraigned in court for denying the existence of the gods, if I disobeyed the oracle because I was afraid of death, fancying that I was wise when I was not wise. For the fear of death is indeed the pretense of wisdom, and not real wisdom, being a pretense of knowing the unknown; and no one knows whether death, which men in their fear apprehend to be the greatest evil, may not be the greatest good. Is not this ignorance of a disgraceful sort, the ignorance which is the conceit that a man knows what he does not know? And in this respect only I believe myself to differ from men in general, and may perhaps claim to be wiser than they are—that whereas I know but little of the world below, I do not suppose that I know: but I do know that injustice and disobedience to a better, whether God or man, is evil and dishonorable, and I will never fear or avoid a possible good rather than a certain evil. . . . Men of Athens, I honor and love you; but I shall obey God rather than you, and while I have life and strength I shall never cease from the practice and teaching of philosophy, exhorting anyone whom I meet and saying to him after my manner: You, my friend—a citizen of the great and mighty and wise city of Athens —are you not ashamed of heaping up the greatest amount of money and honor and reputation, and caring so little about wisdom and truth and the greatest improvement of the soul, which you never regard or heed at all? . . . For I do nothing but go about persuading you all, old and young alike, not to take thought for your persons or your properties, but first and chiefly to care about the greatest improvement of the soul. I tell you that virtue is not given by money, but that from virtue comes money and every other good of man, public as well as private. This is my teaching, and if this is the doctrine which corrupts the youth, I am a mischievous person. But if any one says that this is not my teaching, he is speaking an untruth. Wherefore, O men of Athens, I say to you, do as Anytus bids or not as Anytus bids, and either acquit me or not; but whichever you do, understand that I shall never alter my ways, not even if I have to die many times.

. . . I would have you know, that if you kill such a one as I am, you

---

° **Potidaea . . . Delium:** Battles during the Peloponnesian war in which Socrates had fought.

will injure yourselves more than you will injure me. Nothing will injure me, not Meletus nor yet Anytus—they cannot, for a bad man is not permitted to injure a better than himself. I do not deny that Anytus may, perhaps, kill him, or drive him into exile, or deprive him of civil rights; and he may imagine, and others may imagine, that he is inflicting a great injury upon him: but there I do not agree. For the evil of doing as he is doing—the evil of unjustly taking away the life of another—is greater far.

And now, Athenians, I am not going to argue for my own sake, as you may think, but for yours, that you may not sin against the God by condemning me, who am his gift to you. For if you kill me you will not easily find a successor to me, who, if I may use such a ludicrous figure of speech, am a sort of gadfly, given to the State by God; and the State is a great and noble steed who is tardy in his motions owing to his very size, and requires to be stirred into life. I am that gadfly which God has attached to the State, and all day long and in all places am always fastening upon you, arousing and persuading and reproaching you. You will not easily find another like me, and therefore I would advise you to spare me. I dare say that you may feel out of temper (like a person who is suddenly awakened from sleep), and you think that you might easily strike me dead as Anytus advises, and then you would sleep on for the remainder of your lives, unless God in his care of you sent you another gadfly. When I say that I am given to you by God, the proof of my mission is this—if I had been like other men, I should not have neglected all my own concerns or patiently seen the neglect of them during all these years, and have been doing yours, coming to you individually like a father or elder brother, exhorting you to regard virtue; such conduct, I say, would be unlike human nature. If I had gained anything, or if my exhortations had been paid, there would have been some sense in my doing so; but now, as you will perceive, not even the impudence of my accusers dares to say that I have ever exacted or sought pay of anyone; of that they have no witness. And I have a sufficient witness to the truth of what I say—my poverty.

Someone may wonder why I go about in private giving advice and busying myself with the concerns of others, but do not venture to come forward in public and advise the State. I will tell you why. You have heard me speak at sundry times and in divers places of an oracle or sign which comes to me, and is the divinity which Meletus ridicules in the indictment. This sign, which is a kind of voice, first began to come to me when I was a child; it always forbids but never commands me to do anything which I am going to do. This is what deters me from being a politician. And rightly, as I think. For I am certain, O men of Athens, that if I had engaged in politics, I should have perished long ago, and done no good either to you or to myself. And do not be offended at my telling you the truth: for the truth is, that no man who goes to war with you or any other multitude, honestly striving against the many lawless and unrighteous deeds which are done in a state, will save his life; he who will fight for the right, if he would live even for a brief space, must have a private station and not a public one. . . .

Now, do you really imagine that I could have survived all these years, if I had led a public life, supposing that like a good man I had always maintained the right and had made justice, as I ought, the first thing? No, indeed, men of Athens, neither I nor any other man. But I have been always the same in all my actions, public as well as private, and never have I yielded any base compliance to those who are slanderously termed my disciples, or to any other. Not that I have any regular disciples. But if anyone likes to come and hear me while I am pursuing my mission, whether he be young or old, he is not excluded. Nor do I converse only with those who pay; but anyone, whether he be rich or poor, may ask and answer me and listen to my words; and whether he turns out to be a bad man or a good one, neither result can be justly imputed to me; for I never taught or professed to teach him anything. And if anyone says that he has ever learned or heard anything from me in private which all the world has not heard, let me tell you that he is lying.

But I shall be asked, Why do people delight in continually conversing with you? I have told you already, Athenians, the whole truth about this matter: they like to hear the cross-examination of the pretenders to wisdom; there is amusement in it. Now, this duty of cross-examining other men has been imposed upon me by God; and has been signified to me by oracles, visions, and in every way in which the will of divine power was ever intimated to anyone. This is true, O Athenians; or, if not true, would be soon refuted. If I am or have been corrupting the youth, those of them who are now grown up and have become sensible that I gave them bad advice in the days of their youth should come forward as accusers, and take their revenge; or if they do not like to come themselves, some of their relatives, fathers, brothers, or other kinsmen, should say what evil their families have suffered at my hands. Now is their time. Many of them I see in the court. . . .

Well, Athenians, this and the like of this is all the defense which I have to offer. Yet a word more. Perhaps there may be some one who is offended at me, when he calls to mind how he himself on a similar, or even a less serious occasion, prayed and entreated the judges with many tears, and how he produced his children in court, which was a moving spectacle, together with a host of relations and friends; whereas I, who am probably in danger of my life, will do none of these things. . . . And I say that these things ought not to be done by those of us who have a reputation; and if they are done, you ought not to permit them; you ought rather to show that you are far more disposed to condemn the man who gets up a doleful scene and makes the city ridiculous, than him who holds his peace.

. . . Do not then require me to do what I consider dishonorable and impious and wrong, especially now, when I am being tried for impiety on the indictment of Meletus. For if, O men of Athens, by force of persuasion and entreaty I could overpower your oaths, then I should be teaching you to believe that there are no gods, and in defending should simply convict myself of the charge of not believing in them. But that is not so—far otherwise. For I do believe that there are gods, and in a sense higher than that in which any of my accusers believe in them. And to you and to God I commit my cause, to be determined by you as is best for you and me.°

There are many reasons why I am not grieved, O men of Athens, at the vote of condemnation. I expected it, and am only surprised that the votes are so nearly equal; for I had thought that the majority against me would have been far larger; but now, had thirty votes gone over to the other side, I should have been acquitted. And I may say, I think, that I have escaped Meletus. . . .°

And so he proposes death as the penalty. And what shall I propose on my part, O men of Athens? Clearly that which is my due. And what is my due? What returns shall be made to the man who has never had the wit to be idle during his whole life; but has been careless of what the many care for—wealth, and family interests, and military offices, and speaking in the assembly, and magistracies, and plots, and parties. Reflecting that I was really too honest a man to be a politician and live, I did not go where I could do no good to you or to myself; but where I could do the greatest good privately to every one of you, thither I went, and sought to persuade every man among you that he must look to himself, and seek virtue and wisdom before he looks to his private interests, and look to the State before he looks to the interests of the State; and that this should be the order which he observes in all his actions. What shall be done to such an one? . . . What would be a reward suitable to a poor man who is your benefactor, and who desires leisure that he may instruct you? There can be no reward so fitting as maintenance in the Prytaneum,° O men of Athens, a reward which he deserves far more than the citizen who has won the prize at Olympia in the horse or chariot race, whether the chariots were drawn by two horses or by many. . . .

Perhaps you think that I am braving° you in what I am saying now, as

---

° At this point the jury is polled, and Socrates is found guilty by a vote of 280 to 221. The prosecution has proposed the death penalty; the defense has the right to offer an alternative.

° **I . . . Meletus:** That is, Meletus expected a far greater majority in favor of condemnation.

° **Prytaneum:** The meeting place of the Prytanes; also the place where distinguished individuals were honored and lodged.

° **braving:** Mocking.

in what I said before about the tears and prayers. But this is not so. I speak rather because I am convinced that I never intentionally wronged anyone, although I cannot convince you—the time has been too short; if there were a law at Athens, as there is in other cities, that a capital cause should not be decided in one day, then I believe that I should have convinced you. But I cannot in a moment refute great slanders; and, as I am convinced that I never wronged another, I will assuredly not wrong myself. I will not say to myself that I deserve any evil, or propose any penalty. Why should I? Because I am afraid of the penalty of death which Meletus proposes? When I do not know whether death is a good or an evil, why should I propose a penalty which would certainly be an evil? Shall I say imprisonment? And why should I live in prison, and be the slave of the magistrate of the year—of the Eleven?° Or shall the penalty be a fine, and imprisonment until the fine is paid? There is the same objection. I should have to lie in prison, for money I have none, and cannot pay. And if I say exile (and this may possibly be the penalty which you will affix), I must indeed be blinded by the love of life, if I am so irrational as to expect that when you, who are my own citizens, cannot endure my discourses and words, and have found them so grievous and odious that you will have no more of them, others are likely to endure me. No, indeed, men of Athens, that is not very likely. And what a life should I lead, at my age, wandering from city to city, ever changing my place of exile, and always being driven out! For I am quite sure that wherever I go, there, as here, the young men will flock to me; and if I drive them away, their elders will drive me out at their request; and if I let them come, their fathers and friends will drive me out for their sakes.

Someone will say: Yes, Socrates, but cannot you hold your tongue, and then you may go into a foreign city, and no one will interfere with you? Now, I have great difficulty in making you understand my answer to this. For if I tell you that to do as you say would be a disobedience to the God, and therefore that I cannot hold my tongue, you will not believe that I am serious; and if I say again that daily to discourse about virtue, and of those other things about which you hear me examining myself and others, is the greatest good of man, and that the unexamined life is not worth living, you are still less likely to believe me. Yet I say what is true, although a thing of which it is hard for me to persuade you. Also, I have never been accustomed to think that I deserve to suffer any harm. Had I money I might have estimated the offense at what I was able to pay, and not have been much the worse. But I have none, and therefore I must ask you to proportion the fine to my means. Well, perhaps I could afford a mina,° and therefore I

° **The Eleven:** The group of citizens in charge of prisons and executions.
° **Mina:** A mina (100 drachmae) was worth a considerable sum and was thought a reasonable ransom for a prisoner of war.

propose that penalty: Plato, Crito, Critobulus, and Apollodorus, my friends here, bid me say thirty minae, and they will be the sureties. Let thirty minae be the penalty; for which sum they will be ample security to you.°

Not much time will be gained, O Athenians, in return for the evil name which you will get from the detractors of the city, who will say that you killed Socrates, a wise man; for they will call me wise, even although I am not wise, when they want to reproach you. If you had waited a little while, your desire would have been fulfilled in the course of nature. For I am far advanced in years, as you may perceive, and not far from death. I am speaking now not to all of you, but only to those who have condemned me to death. And I have another thing to say to them: You think that I was convicted because I had no words of the sort which would have procured my acquittal—I mean, if I had thought fit to leave nothing undone or unsaid. Not so; the deficiency which led to my conviction was not of words—certainly not. But I had not the boldness or impudence or inclination to address you as you would have liked me to do, weeping and wailing and lamenting, and saying and doing many things which you have been accustomed to hear from others, and which, as I maintain, are unworthy of me. I thought at the time that I ought not to do anything common or mean when in danger: nor do I now repent of the style of my defense; I would rather die having spoken after my manner, than speak in your manner and live. For neither in war nor yet at law ought I or any man use every way of escaping death. Often in battle there can be no doubt that if a man will throw away his arms, and fall on his knees before his pursuers, he may escape death; and in other dangers there are other ways of escaping death, if a man is willing to say and do anything. The difficulty, my friends, is not to avoid death, but to avoid unrighteousness; for that runs faster than death. I am old and move slowly, and the slower runner has overtaken me, and my accusers are keen and quick, and the faster runner, who is unrighteousness, has overtaken them. And now I depart hence condemned by you to suffer the penalty of death—they too go their ways condemned by the truth to suffer the penalty of villainy and wrong; and I must abide by my award—let them abide by theirs. I suppose that these things may be regarded as fated—and I think that they are well.

And now, O men who have condemned me, I would fain prophesy to you; for I am about to die, and in the hour of death men are gifted with prophetic power. And I prophesy to you who are my murderers, that immediately after my departure punishment far heavier than you have inflicted on

---

°   Socrates' alternative penalty is rejected, and he is condemned to death.

me will surely await you. Me you have killed because you wanted to escape the accuser, and not to give an account of your lives. But that will not be as you suppose: far otherwise. For I say that there will be more accusers of you than there are now; accusers whom hitherto I have restrained: and as they are younger they will be more inconsiderate with you, and you will be more offended at them. If you think that by killing men you can prevent someone from censuring your evil lives, you are mistaken; that is not a way of escape which is either possible or honorable; the easiest and the noblest way is not to be disabling others, but to be improving yourselves. This is the prophecy which I utter before my departure to the judges who have condemned me. . . .

Wherefore, O judges, be of good cheer about death, and know of a certainty, that no evil can happen to a good man, either in life or after death. He and his are not neglected by the gods; nor has my own approaching end happened by mere chance. But I see clearly that the time had arrived when it was better for me to die and be released from trouble; wherefore the oracle gave no sign. For which reason, also, I am not angry with my condemners, or with my accusers; they have done me no harm, although they did not mean to do me any good; and for this I may gently blame them.

Still, I have a favor to ask of them. When my sons are grown up, I would ask you, O my friends, to punish them; and I would have you trouble them, as I have troubled you, if they seem to care about riches, or anything, more than about virtue; or if they pretend to be something when they are really nothing—then reprove them, as I have reproved you, for not caring about that for which they ought to care, and thinking that they are something when they are really nothing. And if you do this, both I and my sons will have received justice at your hands.

The hour of departure has arrived, and we go our ways—I to die, and you to live. Which is better God only knows.

Crito

PLATO

Translator:
Benjamin Jowett

PERSONS OF THE DIALOGUE: SOCRATES, CRITO

SCENE: THE PRISON OF SOCRATES

SOCRATES   Why have you come at this hour, Crito? It must be quite early?

CRITO   Yes, certainly.

SOCRATES   What is the exact time?

CRITO   The dawn is breaking.

SOCRATES   I wonder that the keeper of the prison would let you in.

CRITO   He knows me, because I often come, Socrates; moreover, I have done him a kindness.

SOCRATES   And are you only just arrived?

CRITO   No, I came some time ago.

SOCRATES   Then why did you sit and say nothing, instead of at once awakening me?

CRITO   I should not have liked myself, Socrates, to be in such great trouble and unrest as you are—indeed I should not: I have been watching with amazement your peaceful slumbers; and for that reason I did not awake you, because I wished to minimize the pain. I have always thought you to be of a happy disposition; but never did I see anything like the easy, tranquil manner in which you bear this calamity.

SOCRATES   Why, Crito, when a man has reached my age he ought not to be repining at the approach of death.

CRITO   And yet other old men find themselves in similar misfortunes, and age does not prevent them from repining.

SOCRATES   That is true. But you have not told me why you come at this early hour.

CRITO   I come to bring you a message which is sad and painful; not, as I believe, to yourself, but to all of us who are your friends, and saddest of all to me.

SOCRATES   What? Has the ship come from Delos, on the arrival of which I am to die?

CRITO   No, the ship has not actually arrived, but she will probably be here today, as persons who have come from Sunium tell me that they left her there; and therefore tomorrow, Socrates, will be the last day of your life.

SOCRATES   Very well, Crito; if such is the will of God, I am willing; but my belief is that there will be a delay of a day.

CRITO   Why do you think so?

SOCRATES   I will tell you. I am to die on the day after the arrival of the ship.

CRITO   Yes; that is what the authorities say.

SOCRATES   But I do not think that the ship will be here until tomorrow; this I infer from a vision which I had last night, or rather only just now, when you fortunately allowed me to sleep.

CRITO   And what was the nature of the vision?

SOCRATES   There appeared to me the likeness of a woman, fair and comely, clothed in bright raiment, who called to me and said: O Socrates, *"The third day hence to fertile Phthia shalt thou go."*°

CRITO   What a singular dream, Socrates!

SOCRATES   There can be no doubt about the meaning, Crito, I think.

CRITO   Yes; the meaning is only too clear. But, oh! my beloved Socrates, let me entreat you once more to take my advice and escape. For if you die I shall not only lose a friend who can never be replaced, but there is another evil: people who do not know you and me will believe that I might have saved you if I had been willing to give money, but that I did not care. Now, can there be a worse disgrace than this—that I should be thought to value money more than the life of a friend? For the many will not be persuaded that I wanted you to escape, and that you refused.

SOCRATES   But why, my dear Crito, should we care about the opinion of the many? Good men, and they are the only persons who are worth considering, will think of these things truly as they occurred.

CRITO   But you see, Socrates, that the opinion of the many must be regarded, for what is now happening shows that they can do the greatest evil to any one who has lost their good opinion.

SOCRATES   I only wish it were so, Crito; and that the many could do the greatest evil; for then they would also be able to do the greatest good —and what a fine thing this would be! But in reality they can do neither; for they cannot make a man either wise or foolish; and whatever they do is the result of chance.

CRITO   Well, I will not dispute with you; but please to tell me, Socrates, whether you are not acting out of regard to me and your other friends: are you not afraid that if you escape from prison we may get into trouble with the informers for having stolen you away, and lose either the whole or a great part of our property; or that even a worse evil may

---

°   Homer, *Iliad*, ix. 363. [Translator's note]

happen to us? Now, if you fear on our account, be at ease; for in order to save you, we ought surely to run this, or even a greater risk; be persuaded, then, and do as I say.

SOCRATES   Yes, Crito, that is one fear which you mention, but by no means the only one.

CRITO   Fear not—there are persons who are willing to get you out of prison at no great cost; and as for the informers, they are far from being exorbitant in their demands—a little money will satisfy them. . . . men will love you in other places to which you may go, and not in Athens only; there are friends of mine in Thessaly,° if you like to go to them, who will value and protect you, and no Thessalian will give you any trouble. Nor can I think that you are at all justified, Socrates, in betraying your own life when you might be saved; in acting thus you are playing into the hands of your enemies, who are hurrying on your destruction. And further I should say that you are deserting your own children; for you might bring them up and educate them; instead of which you go away and leave them, and they will have to take their chance; and if they do not meet with the usual fate of orphans, there will be small thanks to you. No man should bring children into the world who is unwilling to persevere to the end in their nurture and education. . . .

SOCRATES   Dear Crito, your zeal is invaluable, if a right one; but if wrong, the greater the zeal the greater the danger; and therefore we ought to consider whether I shall or shall not do as you say. For I am and always have been one of those natures who must be guided by reason, whatever the reason may be which upon reflection appears to me to be the best; and now that this chance has befallen me, I cannot repudiate my own words: the principles which I have hitherto honored and revered I still honor, and unless we can at once find other and better principles, I am certain not to agree with you; no, not even if the power of the multitude could inflict many more imprisonments, confiscations, deaths, frightening us like children with hobgoblin terrors. . . . Tell me, then, whether I am right in saying that some opinions, and the opinions of some men only, are to be valued, and that other opinions, and the opinions of other men, are not to be valued. I ask you whether I was right in maintaining this?

CRITO   Certainly.

SOCRATES   The good are to be regarded, and not the bad?

CRITO   Yes.

SOCRATES   And the opinions of the wise are good, and the opinions of the unwise are evil?

CRITO   Certainly. . . .

°   **Thessaly:** Region in Greece north of Athens.

SOCRATES   Very good; and is not this true, Crito, of other things which we need not separately enumerate? In questions of just and unjust, fair and foul, good and evil, which are the subjects of our present consultation, ought we to follow the opinion of the many and to fear them; or the opinion of the one man who has understanding? ought we not to fear and reverence him more than all the rest of the world; and if we desert him shall we not destroy and injure that principle in us which may be assumed to be improved by justice and deteriorated by injustice—there is such a principle?

CRITO   Certainly there is, Socrates. . . .

SOCRATES   Then, my friend, we must not regard what the many say of us: but what he, the one man who has understanding of just and unjust, will say, and what the truth will say. And therefore you begin in error when you advise that we should regard the opinion of the many about just and unjust, good and evil, honorable and dishonorable. — "Well," someone will say, "But the many can kill us."

CRITO   Yes, Socrates; that will clearly be the answer.

SOCRATES   And it is true: but still I find with surprise that the old argument is unshaken as ever. And I should like to know whether I may say the same of another proposition—that not life, but a good life, is to be chiefly valued?

CRITO   Yes, that also remains unshaken.

SOCRATES   And a good life is equivalent to a just and honorable one— that holds also?

CRITO   Yes, it does.

SOCRATES   From these premises I proceed to argue the question whether I ought or ought not to try to escape without the consent of the Athenians: and if I am clearly right in escaping, then I will make the attempt; but if not, I will abstain. The other considerations which you mention, of money and loss of character and the duty of educating one's children, are, I fear, only the doctrines of the multitude, who would be as ready to restore people to life, if they were able, as they are to put them to death—and with as little reason. But now, since the argument has thus far prevailed, the only question which remains to be considered is, whether we shall do rightly either in escaping or in suffering others to aid in our escape and paying them in money and thanks, or whether in reality we shall not do rightly; and if the latter, then death or any other calamity which may ensue on my remaining here must not be allowed to enter into the calculation. . . . in spite of the opinion of the many, and in spite of consequences whether better or worse, shall we insist on the truth of what was then said, that injustice is always an evil and dishonor to him who acts unjustly? Shall we say so or not?

CRITO   Yes.

SOCRATES   Then we must do no wrong?

CRITO   Certainly not.

SOCRATES   Nor when injured injure in return, as the many imagine; for we must injure no one at all?

CRITO   Clearly not.

SOCRATES   Again, Crito, may we do evil?

CRITO   Surely not, Socrates.

SOCRATES   And what of doing evil in return for evil, which is the morality of the many—is that just or not?

CRITO   Not just.

SOCRATES   For doing evil to another is the same as injuring him?

CRITO   Very true.

SOCRATES   Then we ought not to retaliate or render evil for evil to anyone, whatever evil we may have suffered from him. . . . I will go on to the next point, which may be put in the form of a question: —Ought a man to do what he admits to be right, or ought he to betray the right?

CRITO   He ought to do what he thinks right.

SOCRATES   But if this is true, what is the application? In leaving the prison against the will of the Athenians, do I wrong any? or rather do I not wrong those whom I ought least to wrong? Do I not desert the principles which were acknowledged by us to be just—what do you say?

CRITO   I cannot tell, Socrates; for I do not know.

SOCRATES   Then consider the matter in this way:—Imagine that I am about to play truant (you may call the proceeding by any name which you like), and the laws and the government come and interrogate me: "Tell us, Socrates," they say, "what are you about? are you not going by an act of yours to overturn us—the laws, and the whole state, as far as in you lies? Do you imagine that a state can subsist and not be overthrown, in which the decisions of law have no power, but are set aside and trampled upon by individuals?" What will be our answer, Crito, to these and the like words? Anyone, and especially a rhetorician, will have a good deal to say on behalf of the law which requires a sentence to be carried out. He will argue that this law should not be set aside; and shall we reply, "Yes; but the state has injured us and given an unjust sentence." Suppose I say that?

CRITO   Very good, Socrates.

SOCRATES   "And was that our agreement with you?" the law would answer; "or were you to abide by the sentence of the state?" And if I were to express my astonishment at their words, the law would probably add: "Answer, Socrates, instead of opening your eyes—you are in the habit of asking and answering questions. Tell us, —What complaint have you to make against us which justifies you in attempting to destroy us and the state? In the first place did we not bring you into existence? Your father married your mother by our aid and begat you. Say whether you have any objection to urge against those of us who regulate marriage?" None, I should reply. "Or against those of us who after birth regulate the nurture and education of children, in which you also were trained? Were not the laws, which have the charge of education, right in commanding your father to train you in music and gymnastic?" Right, I should reply. "Well, then, since you were brought into the world and nurtured and educated by us, can you deny in the first place that you are our child and slave, as your fathers were before you? And if this is true, you are not on equal terms with us; nor can you think that you have a right to do to us what we are doing to you. Would you have any right to strike or revile or do any other evil to your father or your master, if you had one, because you have been struck or reviled by him, or received some other evil at his hands?—you would not say this? And because we think right to destroy you, do you think that you have any right to destroy us in return, and your country as far as in you lies? Will you, O professor of true virtue, pretend that you are justified in this? Has a philosopher like you failed to discover that our country is more to be valued and higher and holier far than mother or father or any ancestor, and more to be regarded in the eyes of the gods and of men of understanding? also to be soothed, and gently and reverently entreated when angry, even more than a father, and either to be persuaded, or if not persuaded, to be obeyed? And when we are punished by her, whether with imprisonment or stripes, the punishment is to be endured in silence; and if she lead us to wounds or death in battle, thither we follow as is right, neither may anyone yield or retreat or leave his rank, but whether in battle or in a court of law, or in any other place, he must do what his city and his country order him; or he must change their view of what is just: and if he may do no violence to his father or mother, much less may he do violence to his country." What answer shall we make to this, Crito? Do the laws speak truly, or do they not?

CRITO   I think that they do.

SOCRATES   Then the laws will say: "Consider, Socrates, if we are speaking truly that in your present attempt you are going to do us an injury. For, having brought you into the world, and nurtured and educated you, and given you and every other citizen a share in every good which we had to give, we further proclaim to any Athenian by the liberty which we allow him, that if he does not like us when he has become of age and has seen the ways of the city, and made our acquaintance, he may go where he pleases and take his goods with him. None of us laws will forbid him or interfere with him. Anyone who does not like us and the city, and who wants to emigrate to a colony or to any other city, may go where he likes, retaining his property. But he who has experience of the manner in which we order justice and administer the State, and still remains, has entered into an implied contract that he will do as we command him. And he who disobeys us is, as we maintain, thrice wrong; first, because in disobeying us he is disobeying his parents; secondly, because we are the authors of his education; thirdly, because he has made an agreement with us that he will duly obey our commands; and he neither obeys them nor convinces us that our commands are unjust; and we do not rudely impose them, but give him the alternative of obeying or convincing us; —that is what we offer, and he does neither. . . . Moreover, you might in the course of the trial, if you had liked, have fixed the penalty at banishment; the State which refuses to let you go now would have let you go then. But you pretended that you preferred death to exile, and that you were not unwilling to die. And now you have forgotten these fine sentiments, and pay no respect to us, the laws, of whom you are the destroyer; and are doing what only a miserable slave would do, running away and turning your back upon the compacts and agreements which you made as a citizen. And, first of all, answer this very question: Are we right in saying that you agreed to be governed according to us in deed, and not in word only? Is that true or not?" How shall we answer, Crito? Must we not assent?

CRITO   We cannot help it, Socrates.

SOCRATES   Then will they not say: "You, Socrates, are breaking the covenants and agreements which you made with us at your leisure, not in any haste or under any compulsion or deception, but after you have had seventy years to think of them, during which time you were at liberty to leave the city, if we were not to your mind, or if our covenants appeared to you to be unfair. . . .

"For just consider, if you transgress and err in this sort of way, what good will you do either to yourself or to your friends? That your friends will be driven into exile and deprived of citizenship, or will lose their property, is tolerably certain; and you yourself, if you fly to one of the neighboring cities, as, for example, Thebes or Megara, both of which are well governed, will come to them as an enemy, Socrates, and their government will be against you, and all patriotic citizens will cast an evil eye upon you as a subverter of the laws, and you will confirm in the minds of the judges the justice of their own condemnation of you. For he who is a corrupter of the laws is more than likely to be a corrupter of the young and foolish portion of mankind. Will you then flee from well-ordered cities and virtuous men? and is existence worth having on these terms? Or will you go to them without shame, and talk to them, Socrates? And what will you say to them? What you say here about virtue and justice and institutions and laws being the best things among men? Would that be decent of you? Surely not. . . .

"Listen, then, Socrates, to us who have brought you up. Think not of life and children first, and of justice afterwards, but of justice first, that you may be justified before the princes of the world below. For neither will you nor any that belong to you be happier or holier or juster in this life, or happier in another, if you do as Crito bids. Now you depart in innocence, a sufferer and not a doer of evil; a victim, not of the laws but of men. But if you go forth, returning evil for evil and injury for injury, breaking the covenants and agreements which you have made with us, and wronging those whom you ought least of all to wrong, that is to say, yourself, your friends, your country, and us, we shall be angry with you while you live, and our brethren, the laws in the world below, will receive you as an enemy; for they will know that you have done your best to destroy us. Listen, then, to us and not to Crito.

This, dear Crito, is the voice which I seem to hear murmuring in my ears, like the sound of the flute in the ears of the mystic; that voice, I say, is humming in my ears, and prevents me from hearing any other. And I know that anything more which you may say will be vain. Yet speak, if you have anything to say.

CRITO   I have nothing to say, Socrates.

SOCRATES   Leave me then, Crito, to fulfill the will of God, and to follow whither he leads.

Questions on *The Trial of Socrates*

A.   For Close Reading of the Apology

1. What do your learn in this dialogue of Socrates' past life and character? Why is he unpopular?
2. As Socrates begins his speech, he mentions the charges brought by "my first accusers." What are those charges?
3. Why does he think that those who are most dangerous are those "who began when you were children, and took possession of your minds with their falsehoods"? Why are such people "most difficult to deal with"?
4. Socrates then turns to the charges now being brought against him ("I will begin at the beginning. . . ."). What charges are brought in the affidavit? Put them in your own words.
5. Socrates then goes on to talk about the nature of wisdom. The oracle had said "that there was no man wiser" than Socrates. The latter then goes on

to say, "What can the God mean . . . when he says that I am the wisest of men?" What conclusion does he reach about what wisdom is?

6. Why, according to Socrates, are his three accusers, Meletus, Anytus, and Lycon, bringing charges against him?

7. Socrates next turns to defending himself by questioning Meletus. What answers are given to the charges?

8. When Socrates says, ". . . I would have you know, that if you kill such one as I am, you will injure yourselves more than you will injure me," what does he mean by the statement? What is meant by his phrase, "I am that gadfly which God has attached to the state"?

9. One of the key words in this dialogue is *corrupt*. What does the word mean as it is used here?

10. When the vote of condemnation is taken, Socrates must propose a punishment for himself. What attitude does he take toward exile? What does he mean by the statement, "the unexamined life is not worth living"?

11. When Socrates is finally sentenced, what attitude does he take toward death? What does he mean by the statement, "Me you have killed because you wanted to escape the accuser, and not to give an account of your lives." What does he hope for his sons?

B.   For Close Reading of Crito

1. Why does Crito want Socrates to escape? What are his arguments? What are Socrates' answers to these arguments?

2. What does Socrates conclude about the relation of man to the state?

3. Would Socrates agree with the Declaration of Independence? Would he agree with Stephen Decatur's toast: "Our country! . . . may she always be in the right, but our country, right or wrong"?

4. How can society be improved if, as Socrates says, a good man cannot survive in public life?

5. What does he mean by the following statements: (1) "Then we ought not to retaliate or render evil for evil to anyone, whatever evil we may have suffered from him." (2) "Now you depart in innocence, a sufferer and not a doer of evil; a victim, not of the laws but of men."

6. What is Socrates' definition of good and of evil?

7. Was the verdict just? Was Socrates guilty? Of what?

C.   For Writing and Discussion

1. Aristotle said that a tragic action must have a beginning, a middle, and an end. By this he meant that we should discover the causes, see the tragic action, and know the outcome. Write a paper summarizing what happens in *The Trial of Socrates,* showing how we come to understand the beginning, the middle, and the end.

2. In *Job* and *Oedipus,* as well as in *The Trial of Socrates,* the tragic action begins when the leading actor has his back to the wall; he is in a desperate

situation. He must act; yet, because of the kind of person he is, the actions available to him will not save him. Some things he cannot do. Write a paper showing how these ideas are true of Socrates.

3. In tragedy the death of the hero has some effect on those who live in his own world and on those who live after him. What effect might the death of Socrates have? Do you know any historical figures who have acted at all like Socrates? Do you know ordinary men who have? Discuss in some detail.

Hamlet

SHAKESPEARE
(1601)

FOR an actor Hamlet is the greatest part he can ever play. His challenge is to make up his mind on what kind of man he takes Hamlet to be and then offer a consistent interpretation of the character. The words of a play are like the notes of a piece of music. The actor, like the musician, must give them sound. If we knew how Shakespeare had intended his lines to be spoken, with what tones, what pauses, what gestures, some of the mystery of the play would disappear. How, for example, should Hamlet speak to Ophelia when he says, "Get thee to a nunnery"? How should his mother say, "As kill a king?" If we knew the intended sound, we could better understand the meaning. The actor must resolve for himself the ambiguities in the play, supplying meaning by the way he speaks his lines. Some actors have played Hamlet as a moody introvert, incapable of action until it is forced on him. Some have interpreted him as a man of action, first making sure that he is right and then forging ahead.

The person who sits down to read Hamlet must live with the ambiguities. He can never be exactly sure what it all means, and he need not worry too much about that. What he must do is see the kinds of questions that are raised. Critics make reputations by telling us how to read the play. Then, other critics point out how wrong those interpretations are. But every good reading raises new questions, and it is by raising good questions that we become better readers.

The ambiguity resides chiefly in the character of Hamlet himself. What kind of person is he? His murdered father's ghost calls for Hamlet to revenge the crime. Why does Hamlet hesitate? Is he restrained by circumstances over which he has no control? Or are his difficulties internal ones? Does he prefer thought to action? Does he accept the idea of revenge? Does he lack nerve? Has the shock of his mother's actions paralyzed his ability to act? Is he too noble to kill until his own life is in danger? Above all, why can Hamlet not carry out his father's injunction until the last scene of the play?

What is Hamlet's relation to the other characters? He says he loves Ophelia, yet is the cause of her madness and death. Does his feeling toward her change during the course of the play? When does Hamlet definitely know that Claudius is a murderer? Certainly he does not accept the word of the Ghost. Why did Hamlet arrange the killing of Rosencrantz and Guildenstern, his former friends? What is his relationship with his mother? Answers to such questions can seldom be definite, but only a close reading of the text can give us any clues at all.

The structure of the play is built largely on contrasts: good characters with bad, the search for truth with the attempt to hide it, what characters want and what they get. The contrast that includes all others is the contrast of appearance and reality; things are never what they seem. As each personnage is introduced, we get an idea about him only to have it reversed when we see him in another scene.

One of Hamlet's first speeches, in answer to his mother, begins: "Seems, madam? Nay, it is. I know not 'seems'." For the rest of the play he tries to separate "what seems" from "what is," as do many of those about him. Every major character becomes a player acting a part, and spying becomes a recurrent motif. Scene after scene resolves itself as a play-within-a-play, with a hidden audience trying to separate what seems from what is. Hamlet pretends madness and is spied on by others to learn the source of that affliction. At the actual play-within-the-play Horatio and Hamlet spy on the King. Later, Hamlet listens in on the King at prayer. Polonius hides to eavesdrop on Hamlet's scene with his mother.

When we move away from the specific happenings of the play, we can make out its tragic elements. Hamlet is subjected to a series of circumstances within which he must act. Like all great tragic characters, he does act. He cannot accept the conditions of life in which he finds himself. He cannot be merely swept along by outside circumstances. The quality of any man is thus seen to be defined by what he does when his world is breaking up, when he is pushed to the limits of human endurance.

And again, like other great figures in tragedy, Hamlet must act alone. His friend Horatio is merely a sounding board, Shakespeare's device for letting Hamlet talk. Before the play begins, Hamlet is separated from his father, the older Hamlet, by death and from his mother by her "o'erhasty marriage"; within the play, he is separated from Ophelia by her obedience to her father. The play begins as the father's ghost appears with information that shatters Hamlet's view of the world. None of the old ways of looking at things will work any longer; he is confronted with the mystery of human suffering.

Hamlet's consequent actions define who he is. He cannot submit to evil and fights back against the forces that would impel him to accept it. As in other great tragedies we see here the acting out of an answer to the question: What is man? The fact that the answer is not made clear is no fault of the play. The mystery lies in the complexity of man's mind—if we push hard enough to search for real answers.

Good men have always lived with the understanding that there is evil and suffering in the world. What differentiates men is their acceptance or rejection of the position in which they find themselves. As Hamlet wrestles with his problems, we all see ourselves metaphorically reflected in the great mirror that the play sets up—a mirror in which, to an extent, we can judge our own tolerance of evil.

As indicated in the Preface, the text of *Hamlet* is not included in this book. Any complete text may be used, but we recommend the one in the Hayden Shakespeare series edited by Maynard Mack and Robert W. Boynton. All references in the following questions to specific lines of the play are based on the line numbering of the Hayden text but are further identified by reproducing the opening words of the passage involved to facilitate identification.

Questions on *Hamlet*

A. For Close Reading

ACT I, SCENE I

1. What information are we given in this opening scene?
2. What major questions are asked?
3. What is the mood of the scene? In suggesting it, consider the setting, both in time and place.
4. How do the various characters react to the appearance of the ghost? What possible reasons are given for its appearance?

SCENE II

5. What matters of business does the King take up as the court scene opens?
6. What do we learn of Hamlet, particularly his relationship with the other characters?
7. Rephrase in your own words Hamlet's soliloquy (lines 131–161) beginning "O that this too too solid flesh would melt. . . ."
8. Remember that Hamlet has no idea when we meet him that his father has been murdered. Why, then, does he say, "How weary, stale, flat, and unprofitable/ Seem to me all the uses of this world"?
9. What is Hamlet's reaction to the news of his father's ghost?
10. What have you learned so far about the positions of the three young men: Fortinbras, Laertes, and Hamlet?

SCENE III

11. Why do Laertes and Polonius advise Ophelia to have nothing to do with Hamlet? What do you think might be the effect of this warning on Hamlet's state of mind?

12. In what ways are the first three scenes alike? How are they variations on the theme of threat? Who is threatening whom in each instance? What are the various reactions to the threats?

SCENE IV

13. What do we learn of the behavior of the King's court?
14. Summarize Hamlet's comment beginning at line 25, "So oft it chances. . . ." What is he saying here about the cause of tragedy?
15. What is the significance of the first lines in Hamlet's next speech (lines 42–48, beginning "Angels and ministers. . . .")?

SCENE V

16. What significant information about Claudius and Gertrude does the Ghost reveal? What does the Ghost ask of Hamlet?
17. Why are Hamlet's words, "Haste me to know't. . . ." (lines 33–35), ironic?
18. What is the significance of Hamlet's "antic disposition" speech (lines 185–196)?
19. What is the significance of Hamlet's statement in lines 204–205, beginning "The time is out of joint"?
20. What have you learned in Act I about each of the leading characters: Hamlet, Claudius, Gertrude, Polonius, Laertes, Ophelia, and Horatio?
21. What major conflicts have now developed in the play? What characters have been set in opposition to one another?

ACT II, SCENE I

22. Describe what happened during Hamlet's visit to Ophelia (lines 84–109). What might be Hamlet's purpose in making this visit? How is he dressed?
23. In the last part of Scene i and the first part of Scene ii, we get the views of others on Hamlet's behavior. Summarize them.
24. One of the main themes developed so far is the mistrust that the characters have for one another. Show how this element of mistrust is at work among the major characters.
25. What does each major character see as his or her main problem so far in the play?

SCENE II

26. Why did the king send for Rosencrantz and Guildenstern?
27. What is the King's reaction to the various theories on what is bothering Hamlet?
28. In some interpretations of *Hamlet* (supplied by actors), Hamlet enters at line 172 ("Here in the lobby. . .") and overhears the speech of Polonius. How would this entrance influence the later scene between Hamlet and Ophelia?
29. What is the significance of the line (229), "These tedious old fools!"?
30. In this scene we learn something of Hamlet's normal interests and behavior. From his conversation with Rosencrantz and Guildenstern and the players, draw conclusions as to what those interests would be. Note the places that determine your judgment.

31. At this point in the play what is Hamlet's conception of man (line 309 on, beginning "What a piece of work is a man"?)
32. What is the significance of Hamlet's words beginning "I am but mad north-north-west" (lines 378–379)?
33. What is Hamlet's opinion of himself? Read the soliloquy at the end of the scene as you think he would say it.
34. What is Hamlet's plan? Why is he making it?

ACT III, SCENE I

35. What problem is stated at the beginning of the scene?
36. What causes the King's outburst starting at line 55, "O, 'tis too true"? Notice that this is the first hint (apart from the Ghost's revelation) of his guilt. What function does the speech serve in the play? What scene does it foreshadow?
37. Paraphrase Hamlet's soliloquy, "To be, or not to be. . . ," beginning at line 62.
38. The actor's problem in this scene is to establish the point at which Hamlet gets angry. Some actors begin with Hamlet's first words to Ophelia, some with line 110 ("Ha, ha! Are you honest?"), some with line 139 ("Let the doors. . ."). For each of these three interpretations point out what might be the cause of his anger in each instance.
39. What would have been the effect on the King had he heard the three lines beginning at line 154, "I say we will have no moe marriage. . . ."?
40. After Hamlet's exit, at line 157, Ophelia gives us a characterization of what Hamlet was like before the play began; read it carefully. What is he like now?
41. How does the King react to what he has seen (line 170 on, "Love? his affections do not that way tend. . . .")?
42. How does Polonius react? What does he propose?

SCENE II

43. In lines 71 ("There is a play to-night. . . .") to 83 Hamlet explains his plan. Put it in your own words.
44. The play-within-the-play begins at line 132. What connection do you see between the action portrayed therein and the action of the play itself as we have seen it so far?
45. Why does Hamlet call the play "The Mousetrap"?
46. What causes the action described at line 256, "The King rises"?
47. What questions does Hamlet put to Horatio? What does Hamlet now know?
48. Judging by Hamlet's speech in lines 374–385 (beginning " 'Tis now the very witching time of night. . ."), what change has taken place in him?

SCENE III

49. In his first speech, what plan does the King announce for dealing with Hamlet? Why has he made it?
50. Paraphrase the King's soliloquy, line 39 on: "O, my offense is rank. . . ." What does it reveal of his character?

51. Why did Hamlet not kill the King when he came upon him (line 76)?

SCENE IV

52. In line 11, Hamlet should accent the word "my." What effect does this have on the meaning of the dialogue?

53. In what different tones of voice could Gertrude say, "As kill a king?" What would each interpretation show about the Queen's situation in the play? How do you think that she should say the line?

54. In line 60 Hamlet shows "this picture" of his father in a locket that he wears around his neck, and "this," the picture of Claudius, worn by his mother. Paraphrase the speech (lines 60–95).

55. What is the purpose of the Ghost's visit? What does Gertrude see during this scene? What judgment had the Ghost originally passed on Gertrude (see I,v,88–92)?

56. How does the Ghost's visit affect Hamlet?

57. In what manner should Hamlet say, "Good night, mother"? Why?

ACT IV, SCENE I

58. What is the significance of lines 14–16, "It had been so with us . . ."?

SCENE II

59. What further do we learn of Hamlet's character in this scene?

SCENE III

60. What information does Claudius give to the audience in lines 63–73?

SCENE IV

61. What situation inspires Hamlet's soliloquy in this scene? Paraphrase the soliloquy.

SCENE V

62. What do we learn here of Ophelia's predicament?

63. What parallel do you see between Laertes' situation and Hamlet's? How does Laertes propose to handle his?

64. Paraphrase the King's speech, lines 125–132, beginning "What is the cause, Laertes . . . ."

SCENE VI

65. What information are we given in this scene?

SCENE VII

66. How does the King make his peace with Laertes?

67. What two reasons does the King give to Laertes for not moving directly against Hamlet?

68. What is the King's plan for getting rid of Hamlet (lines 140–152)?

69. Read aloud the speeches on Ophelia's death (line 177 on).

ACT V, SCENE I

70. Much of this scene deals with the futility of human action. How does Hamlet express this idea?
71. What general comments on the meaning of death are acted out in the graveyard scene?

SCENE II

72. What does Hamlet mean by lines 10-11, "There's a divinity. . ."?
73. How does Hamlet justify the killing of Rosencrantz and Guildenstern to Horatio?
74. Does Hamlet's speech (line 218 on, beginning "Give me your pardon, sir. . . .") show any change in him?
75. How does each major character die in the duel scene?

B. For Writing and Discussion

1. By the end of Act I, how has Shakespeare described the world in which Hamlet must act? What contrasts have been built up between what situations seem to be and what they really are?
2. Like *Oedipus the King, Hamlet* begins with a corrupt state in need of a savior. What is the nature of the corruption in Denmark? What duty is asked of the savior?
3. One of the major motifs of the play is spying. In scene after scene someone spies on someone else. Cite specific instances throughout the play.
4. From one point of view *Hamlet* is a detective story: A murderer must be discovered. By what steps is the mystery unravelled?
5. How is Hamlet understood by those about him: Gertrude, Polonius, Laertes, Horatio, Claudius, Ophelia? Take any one character and show what he knows of Hamlet and how that knowledge changes as the play progresses.
6. Hamlet is told by the Ghost to revenge his "unnatural" murder. Trace Hamlet's attempts to do so. What delays him, his own will or outside circumstances? When he finally gets his revenge, in Act V, how is the situation different from what it was at the end of Act I?
7. Why does Hamlet hesitate? Is he really after revenge? Does he accept the Ghost's demand for revenge? Does he know whether Claudius is really guilty? Does he delay only because he never had a chance to kill the King? Does he mention revenge in his dying speech?
8. Is Hamlet a man of indecision or is he an impetuous man of action? It is possible to support either of these points of view by selecting some details and overlooking others. Try debating the question.
9. Shakespeare uses soliloquies to show what his leading characters really think. If you judge only by the soliloquies, why does Hamlet delay in acting? Do his reasons change at different points in the play?
10. How many of Hamlet's actions are forced on him by what other people do?

11. What evidence can you find to support the argument that Hamlet falls from a state of innocence into the knowledge of evil and that the shock of this knowledge paralyzes his ability to act?

12. Laertes is in a position that parallels that of Hamlet: a father murdered and revenge called for. How does Laertes handle his problem? How do his actions throw light on Hamlet's failure to act?

13. Trace the parallels between the social disorder revealed by Laertes' rebellion and the mental disorder of Ophelia. Develop your ideas in terms of what causes each and what is the result of each.

14. How does the subplot reflect the main plot; that is, how is the plight of the family of Polonius-Laertes-Ophelia similar and dissimilar to that of the family of Claudius-Hamlet-Gertrude?

15. The play is built on a contrast between the corrupters (Claudius, Polonius, Gertrude) and the corrupted (Laertes, Ophelia, Hamlet). What is the nature of the corruption in the first three? How does it affect the second group?

16. When Laertes, as he is dying, says, "The King, the King's to blame," he certainly refers to the particular plot in which he was involved. Is Shakespeare also commenting here on the cause of the whole tragic movement of the play?

17. One of the basic themes of Hamlet is the failure of love. Where and why do the normal relationships of love break down?

18. Poison has a literal role in the play (it kills five people), and it also has a metaphoric role (the state is poisoned). What is the nature of the metaphoric poisoning?

19. What similarities or differences do you see between Hamlet and Oedipus in terms of the complications in which they find themselves and the ways in which they go about solving them. What use is made of minor characters in each play?

Hedda Gabler

(1890)

HENRIK Ibsen, a Norwegian playwright who lived from 1828 to 1906, was a superb craftsman and dramatic poet who thought of the theater as an instrument for reform. He centered most of his plays on the conflicts within and between men in the society of his time and saw himself as a judge of that society. In the dedication to one of his books he wrote:

> To *live*—is to war with fiends
> That infest the brain and heart;
> To *write*—is to summon one's self,
> And play the judge's part.

In *Hedda Gabler* he was a harsh judge. Hedda is a neurotic woman with little sense of what is real in life. Her husband does not interest her; he merely supports her. She feels herself an aristocrat among bourgeois dolts. She allows her "heroic" ideals no flesh and blood reality. Since she cannot involve herself in life, it bores her. With no useful outlet for her energy, she turns it to destructive purposes and finds an antidote for her boredom in trying to manipulate the lives of others.

This play differs from the earlier tragedies in this book in several major ways. It is written in a realistic mode; there are no prophecies or ghosts here, only real people living in the everyday world. The leading character is not the "man of high estate" (Aristotle's term for the tragic hero), the king or prince on whom the security of the state depends. Hedda Gabler could be the woman-next-door. Consequently the fall of the hero does not have the "magnitude" (Aristotle again) of those of the earlier plays. The consequences of Hedda's fall do not seem to extend beyond her immediate circle. But such is the nature of the egalitarian world we live in that Hedda's fall does have a "democratic magnitude," as it were, especially if she is seen as the embodiment of the evil of indifference and the failure of love.

Several recurring symbols underscore the theme. One recalls the Biblical story of Samson and Delilah (Judges 16). When Delilah cut off Samson's hair, thus depriving him of his strength, she carried out a symbolic act that appears repeatedly in myth and legend. Hedda refers often to Mrs. Elvsted's hair, and the symbol is woven into the structure of the play. For another, the pistols that Hedda inherited from her father represent not only her old life as a general's daughter, but also her method of getting and losing power. There is also the symbolic use of light and dark. Hedda shuts out the sun early in the play, and from then on the action takes place mainly at night. The primary act of the play is focused on the artificial light of the fire: "Now I am burning your child, Thea!"

The basic structure of the play, as in *Oedipus the King,* is built on irony. Aristotle pointed out that reversal, or irony, is "the change of an action into its opposite": what is expected is not what happens. Hedda has her triumphs, but each turns into a mockery of what she had wanted.

Ibsen is considered the father of modern drama and the first major playwright to deal forthrightly and successfully with serious social issues. Even though *Hedda Gabler* was written in 1890, it speaks directly to modern man, whose most important problems are a reflection of the dehumanizing insensitivity and self-centeredness of contemporary life.

Hedda Gabler

HENRIK IBSEN   *Translators:*
                          Edmund Gosse and William Archer

CHARACTERS

GEORGE TESMAN
HEDDA TESMAN, *his wife*
MISS JULIANA TESMAN, *his aunt*
MRS. ELVSTED
JUDGE BRACK
EILERT LÖVBORG
BERTA, *servant at the Tesmans'*

SCENE: TESMAN'S VILLA, IN THE WEST END OF CHRIS-
TIANIA, NORWAY

ACT I

*A spacious, handsome, and tastefully furnished drawing-room, deco-
rated in dark colors. In the back, a wide doorway with curtains drawn
back, leading into a smaller room decorated in the same style as the
drawing-room. In the right-hand wall of the front room, a folding door
leading out to the hall. In the opposite wall, on the left, a glass door,
also with curtains drawn back. Through the panes can be seen part of
a veranda outside, and trees covered with autumn foliage. An oval table, with a cover on it, and surrounded by chairs, stands well forward.
In front, by the wall on the right, a wide stove of dark porcelain, a
high-backed armchair, a cushioned footrest, and two footstools. A settee, with a small round table in front of it, fills the upper right-hand
corner. In front, on the left, a little way from the wall, a sofa. Further
back than the glass door, a piano. On either side of the doorway at the
back a what-not with terra-cotta and majolica ornaments. —Against
the back wall of the inner room a sofa, with a table, and one or two
chairs. Over the sofa hangs the portrait of a handsome elderly man in
a general's uniform. Over the table a hanging lamp, with an opal glass
shade. —A number of bouquets are arranged about the drawing*

room, in vases and glasses. Others lie upon the tables. The floors in both rooms are covered with thick carpets. —Morning light. The sun shines in through the glass door.

MISS JULIANA TESMAN, *with her bonnet on and carrying a parasol, comes in from the hall, followed by* BERTA, *who carries a bouquet wrapped in paper.* MISS TESMAN *is a comely and pleasant-looking lady of about sixty-five. She is nicely but simply dressed in a grey walking-costume.* BERTA *is a middle-aged woman of plain and rather countryfied appearance.*

MISS TESMAN   *(Stops close to the door, listens, and says softly)*   Upon my word, I don't believe they are stirring yet!

BERTA   *(Also softly)*   I told you so, Miss. Remember how late the steamboat got in last night. And then, when they got home! —good Lord, what a lot the young mistress had to unpack before she could get to bed.

MISS TESMAN   Well well—let them have their sleep out. But let us see that they get a good breath of the fresh morning air when they do appear.   *(She goes to the glass door and throws it open.)*

BERTA   *(Beside the table, at a loss what to do with the bouquet in her hand)*   I declare there isn't a bit of room left. I think I'll put it down here, Miss.   *(She places it on the piano.)*

MISS TESMAN   So you've got a new mistress now, my dear Berta. Heaven knows it was a wrench to me to part with you.

BERTA   *(On the point of weeping)*   And do you think it wasn't hard for me too, Miss? After all the blessed years I've been with you and Miss Rina.°

MISS TESMAN   We must make the best of it, Berta. There was nothing else to be done. George can't do without you, you see—he absolutely can't. He has had you to look after him ever since he was a little boy.

BERTA   Ah but, Miss Julia, I can't help thinking of Miss Rina lying helpless at home there, poor thing. And with only that new girl too! She'll never learn to take proper care of an invalid.

MISS TESMAN   Oh, I shall manage to train her. And of course, you know, I shall take most of it upon myself. You needn't be uneasy about my poor sister, my dear Berta.

BERTA   Well, but there's another thing, Miss. I'm so mortally afraid I shan't be able to suit the young mistress.

MISS TESMAN   Oh well—just at first there may be one or two things—

BERTA   Most like she'll be terrible grand in her ways.

°   **Rina:** Pronounced *Reena.*

MISS TESMAN   Well, you can't wonder at that—General Gabler's daughter! Think of the sort of life she was accustomed to in her father's time. Don't you remember how we used to see her riding down the road along with the General? In that long black habit—and with feathers in her hat?

BERTA   Yes indeed—I remember well enough!—But, good Lord, I should never have dreamt in those days that she and Master George would make a match of it.

MISS TESMAN   Nor I.—But by-the-bye, Berta—while I think of it: in future you mustn't say Master George. You must say Dr. Tesman.

BERTA   Yes, the young mistress spoke of that too—last night—the moment they set foot in the house. Is it true then, Miss?

MISS TESMAN   Yes, indeed it is. Only think, Berta—some foreign university has made him a doctor—while he has been abroad, you understand. I hadn't heard a word about it, until he told me himself upon the pier.

BERTA   Well well, he's clever enough for anything, he is. But I didn't think he'd have gone in for doctoring people too.

MISS TESMAN   No no, it's not that sort of doctor he is. *(Nods significantly)* But let me tell you, we may have to call him something still grander before long.

BERTA   You don't say so! What can that be, Miss?

MISS TESMAN   *(Smiling)* H'm—wouldn't you like to know! *(With emotion)* Ah, dear dear—if my poor brother could only look up from his grave now, and see what his little boy has grown into *(Looks around)* But bless me, Berta—why have you done this? Taken the chintz covers off all the furniture?

BERTA   The mistress told me to. She can't abide covers on the chairs, she says.

MISS TESMAN   Are they going to make this their everyday sitting-room then?

BERTA   Yes, that's what I understood—from the mistress. Master George —the doctor—he said nothing.

GEORGE TESMAN *comes from the right into the inner room, humming to himself, and carrying an unstrapped empty portmanteau. He is a middle-sized, young-looking man of thirty-three, rather stout, with a round, open, cheerful face, fair hair and beard. He wears spectacles, and is somewhat carelessly dressed in comfortable indoor clothes.*

MISS TESMAN   Good morning, good morning, George.

TESMAN   *(In the doorway between the rooms)* Aunt Julia! Dear Aunt

Julia! *(Goes up to her and shakes hands warmly)* Come all this way—so early! Eh?

MISS TESMAN   Why, of course I had to come and see how you were getting on.

TESMAN   In spite of your having had no proper night's rest?

MISS TESMAN   Oh, that makes no difference to me.

TESMAN   Well, I suppose you got home all right from the pier? Eh?

MISS TESMAN   Yes, quite safely, thank goodness. Judge Brack was good enough to see me right to my door.

TESMAN   We were so sorry we couldn't give you a seat in the carriage. But you saw what a pile of boxes Hedda had to bring with her.

MISS TESMAN   Yes, she had certainly plenty of boxes.

BERTA   *(To* TESMAN*)* Shall I go in and see if there's anything I can do for the mistress?

TESMAN   No thank you, Berta—you needn't. She said she would ring if she wanted anything.

BERTA   *(Going towards the right)* Very well.

TESMAN   But look here—take this portmanteau with you.

BERTA   *(Taking it)* I'll put it in the attic. *(She goes out by the hall door.)*

TESMAN   Fancy, Auntie—I had the whole of that portmanteau chock full of copies of documents. You wouldn't believe how much I have picked up from all the archives I have been examining—curious old details that no one has had any idea of—

MISS TESMAN   Yes, you don't seem to have wasted your time on your wedding trip, George.

TESMAN   No, that I haven't. But do take off your bonnet, Auntie. Look here! Let me untie the strings—eh?

MISS TESMAN   *(While he does so)* Well well—this is just as if you were still at home with us.

TESMAN   *(With the bonnet in his hand, looks at it from all sides)* Why, what a gorgeous bonnet you've been investing in!

MISS TESMAN   I bought it on Hedda's account.

TESMAN   On Hedda's account? Eh?

MISS TESMAN   Yes, so that Hedda needn't be ashamed of me if we happened to go out together.

TESMAN   *(Patting her cheek)* You always think of everything, Aunt Julia. *(Lays the bonnet on a chair beside the table)* And now, look here—suppose we sit comfortably on the sofa and have a little chat, till Hedda comes. *(They seat themselves. She places her parasol in the corner of the sofa.)*

MISS TESMAN   *(Takes both his hands and looks at him)* What a delight it is to have you again, as large as life, before my very eyes, George! My George—my poor brother's own boy!

TESMAN   And it's a delight for me, too, to see you again, Aunt Julia! You, who have been father and mother in one to me.

MISS TESMAN   Oh yes, I know you will always keep a place in your heart for your old aunts.

TESMAN   And what about Aunt Rina? No improvement—eh?

MISS TESMAN   Oh no—we can scarcely look for any improvement in her case, poor thing. There she lies, helpless, as she has lain for all these years. But heaven grant I may not lose her yet awhile! For if I did, I don't know what I should make of my life, George—especially now that I haven't you to look after any more.

TESMAN   *(Patting her back)*   There there there—!

MISS TESMAN   *(Suddenly changing her tone)*   And to think that here are you a married man, George!—And that you should be the one to carry off Hedda Gabler—the beautiful Hedda Gabler! Only think of it—she, that was so beset with admirers!

TESMAN   *(Hums a little and smiles complacently)*   Yes, I fancy I have several good friends about town who would like to stand in my shoes —eh?

MISS TESMAN   And then this fine long wedding tour you have had! More than five—nearly six months—

TESMAN   Well, for me it has been a sort of tour of research as well. I have had to do so much grubbing among old records—and to read no end of books too, Auntie.

MISS TESMAN   Oh yes, I suppose so. *(More confidentially, and lowering her voice a little)*   But listen now, George,—have you nothing—nothing special to tell me?

TESMAN   As to our journey?

MISS TESMAN   Yes.

TESMAN   No, I don't know of anything except what I have told you in my letters. I had a doctor's degree conferred on me—but that I told you yesterday.

MISS TESMAN   Yes, yes, you did. But what I mean is—haven't you any —any—expectations—?

TESMAN   Expectations?

MISS TESMAN   Why you know, George—I'm your old auntie!

TESMAN   Why, of course I have expectations.

MISS TESMAN   Ah!

TESMAN   I have every expectation of being a professor one of these days.

MISS TESMAN   Oh yes, a professor—

TESMAN   Indeed, I may say I am certain of it. But my dear Auntie— you know all about that already!

MISS TESMAN   *(Laughing to herself)*   Yes, of course I do. You are quite right there. *(Changing the subject)*   But we were talking about your journey. It must have cost a great deal of money, George?

TESMAN   Well, you see—my handsome traveling scholarship went a good way.

MISS TESMAN   But I can't understand how you can have made it go far enough for two.

TESMAN   No, that's not so easy to understand—eh?

MISS TESMAN   And especially travelling with a lady—they tell me that makes it ever so much more expensive.

TESMAN   Yes, of course—it makes it a little more expensive. But Hedda had to have this trip, Auntie! She really had to. Nothing else would have done.

MISS TESMAN   No no, I suppose not. A wedding tour seems to be quite indispensable nowadays.—But tell me now—have you gone thoroughly over the house yet?

TESMAN   Yes, you may be sure I have. I have been afoot ever since daylight.

MISS TESMAN   And what do you think of it all?

TESMAN   I'm delighted! Quite delighted! Only I can't think what we are to do with the two empty rooms between this inner parlor and Hedda's bedroom.

MISS TESMAN   *(Laughing)* Oh my dear George, I daresay you may find some use for them—in the course of time.

TESMAN   Why of course you are quite right, Aunt Julia! You mean as my library increases—eh?

MISS TESMAN   Yes, quite so, my dear boy. It was your library I was thinking of.

TESMAN   I am specially pleased on Hedda's account. Often and often, before we were engaged, she said that she would never care to live anywhere but in Secretary Falk's villa.°

MISS TESMAN   Yes, it was lucky that this very house should come into the market, just after you had started.

TESMAN   Yes, Aunt Julia, the luck was on our side, wasn't it—eh?

MISS TESMAN   But the expense, my dear George! You will find it very expensive, all this.

TESMAN   *(Looks at her, a little cast down)* Yes, I suppose I shall, Aunt!

MISS TESMAN   Oh, frightfully!

TESMAN   How much do you think? In round numbers?—Eh?

MISS TESMAN   Oh, I can't even guess until all the accounts come in.

°   **Secretary Fauk's villa:** In the original, "Statsrådinde Falks villa"—showing that it had belonged to the widow of a cabinet minister.

TESMAN   Well, fortunately, Judge Brack has secured the most favorable terms for me,—so he said in a letter to Hedda.

MISS TESMAN   Yes, don't be uneasy, my dear boy.—Besides, I have given security for the furniture and all the carpets.

TESMAN   Security? You? My dear Aunt Julia—what sort of security could you give?

MISS TESMAN   I have given a mortgage on our annuity.

TESMAN   *(Jumps up)*   What! On your—and Aunt Rina's annuity!

MISS TESMAN   Yes, I knew of no other plan, you see.

TESMAN   *(Placing himself before her)*   Have you gone out of your senses, Auntie! Your annuity—it's all that you and Aunt Rina have to live upon.

MISS TESMAN   Well well—don't get so excited about it. It's only a matter of form you know—Judge Brack assured me of that. It was he that was kind enough to arrange the whole affair for me. A mere matter of form, he said.

TESMAN   Yes, that may be all very well. But nevertheless—

MISS TESMAN   You will have your own salary to depend upon now. And, good heavens, even if we did have to pay up a little—! To eke things out a bit at the start—! Why, it would be nothing but a pleasure to us.

TESMAN   Oh Auntie—will you never be tired of making sacrifices for me!

MISS TESMAN   *(Rises and lays her hand on his shoulders)*   Have I any other happiness in this world except to smooth your way for you, my dear boy? You, who have had neither father nor mother to depend on. And now we have reached the goal, George! Things have looked black enough for us, sometimes; but, thank heaven, now you have nothing to fear.

TESMAN   Yes, it is really marvelous how everything has turned out for the best.

MISS TESMAN   And the people who opposed you—who wanted to bar the way for you—now you have them at your feet. They have fallen, George. Your most dangerous rival—his fall was the worst.—And now he has to lie on the bed he has made for himself—poor misguided creature.

TESMAN   Have you heard anything of Eilert? Since I went away, I mean.

MISS TESMAN   Only that he is said to have published a new book.

TESMAN   What! Eilert Lövborg! Recently—eh?

MISS TESMAN   Yes, so they say. Heaven knows whether it can be worth anything! Ah, when your new book appears—that will be another story, George! What is it to be about?

TESMAN   It will deal with the domestic industries of Brabant during the Middle Ages.

MISS TESMAN   Fancy—to be able to write on such a subject as that!

TESMAN   However, it may be some time before the book is ready. I have all these collections to arrange first, you see.

MISS TESMAN   Yes, collecting and arranging—no one can beat you at that. There you are my poor brother's own son.

TESMAN   I am looking forward eagerly to setting to work at it; especially now that I have my own delightful home to work in.

MISS TESMAN   And, most of all, now that you have got the wife of your heart, my dear George.

TESMAN   *(Embracing her)* Oh yes, yes, Aunt Julia! Hedda—she is the best part of it all! *(Looks towards the doorway)* I believe I hear her coming—eh?

HEDDA *enters from the left through the inner room. She is a woman of nine-and-twenty. Her face and figure show refinement and distinction. Her complexion is pale and opaque. Her steel-grey eyes express a cold, unruffled repose. Her hair is of an agreeable medium brown, but not particularly abundant. She is dressed in a tasteful, somewhat loose-fitting morning gown.*

MISS TESMAN   *(Going to meet* HEDDA*)* Good morning, my dear Hedda! good morning, and a hearty welcome.

HEDDA   *(Holds out her hand)* Good morning, dear Miss Tesman! So early a call! That is kind of you.

MISS TESMAN   *(With some embarrassment)* Well—has the bride slept well in her new home?

HEDDA   Oh yes, thanks. Passably.

TESMAN   *(Laughing)* Passably! Come, that's good, Hedda! You were sleeping like a stone when I got up.

HEDDA   Fortunately. Of course one has always to accustom one's self to new surroundings, Miss Tesman—little by little. *(Looking towards the left)* Oh—there the servant has gone and opened the veranda door, and let in a whole flood of sunshine.

MISS TESMAN   *(Going towards the door)* Well, then we will shut it.

HEDDA   No no, not that! Tesman, please draw the curtains. That will give a softer light.

TESMAN   *(At the door)* All right—all right.—There now, Hedda, now you have both shade and fresh air.

HEDDA   Yes, fresh air we certainly must have, with all these stacks of flowers—. But—won't you sit down, Miss Tesman?

MISS TESMAN   No, thank you. Now that I have seen that everything is all right here—thank heaven!—I must be getting home again. My sister is lying longing for me, poor thing.

TESMAN   Give her my very best love, Auntie; and say I shall look in and see her later in the day.

MISS TESMAN   Yes, yes, I'll be sure to tell her. But by-the-bye, George — *(feeling in her dress pocket)* —I had almost forgotten—I have something for you here.

TESMAN   What is it, Auntie? Eh?

MISS TESMAN   *(Produces a flat parcel wrapped in newspaper and hands it to him)* Look here, dear boy.

TESMAN   *(Opening the parcel)* Well, I declare! — Have you really saved them for me, Aunt Julia! Hedda! isn't this touching—eh?

HEDDA   *(Beside the whatnot on the right)* Well, what is it?

TESMAN   My old morning-shoes! My slippers.

HEDDA   Indeed. I remember you often spoke of them while we were abroad.

TESMAN   Yes, I missed them terribly. *(Goes up to her)* Now you shall see them, Hedda!

HEDDA   *(Going towards the stove)* Thanks, I really don't care about it.

TESMAN   *(Following her)* Only think—ill as she was, Aunt Rina embroidered these for me. Oh you can't think how many associations cling to them.

HEDDA   *(At the table)* Scarcely for me.

MISS TESMAN   Of course not for Hedda, George.

TESMAN   Well, but now that she belongs to the family, I thought—

HEDDA   *(Interrupting)* We shall never get on with this servant, Tesman.

MISS TESMAN   Not get on with Berta?

TESMAN   Why, dear, what puts that in your head? Eh?

HEDDA   *(Pointing)* Look there! She has left her old bonnet lying about on a chair.

TESMAN   *(In consternation, drops the slippers on the floor)* Why, Hedda—

HEDDA   Just fancy, if any one should come in and see it!

TESMAN   But Hedda—that's Aunt Julia's bonnet.

HEDDA   Is it!

MISS TESMAN   *(Taking up the bonnet)* Yes, indeed it's mine. And, what's more, it's not old, Madam Hedda.

HEDDA   I really did not look closely at it, Miss Tesman.

MISS TESMAN   *(Trying on the bonnet)* Let me tell you it's the first time I have worn it—the very first time.

TESMAN   And a very nice bonnet it is too—quite a beauty!

MISS TESMAN   Oh, it's no such great thing, George. *(Looks around her)* My parasol—? Ah, here. *(Takes it)* For this is mine too— *(mutters)* —not Berta's.

TESMAN   A new bonnet and a new parasol! Only think, Hedda!

HEDDA   Very handsome indeed.

TESMAN   Yes, isn't it? Eh? But Auntie, take a good look at Hedda before you go! See how handsome she is!

MISS TESMAN   Oh, my dear boy, there's nothing new in that. Hedda was always lovely. *(She nods and goes towards the right)*

TESMAN   *(Following)* Yes, but have you noticed what splendid condition she is in? How she has filled out on the journey?

HEDDA   *(Crossing the room)* Oh, do be quiet—!

MISS TESMAN   *(Who has stopped and turned)* Filled out?

TESMAN   Of course you don't notice it so much now that she has that dress on. But I, who can see—

HEDDA   *(At the glass door, impatiently)* Oh, you can't see anything.

TESMAN   It must be the mountain air in the Tyrol—

HEDDA   *(Curtly, interrupting)* I am exactly as I was when I started.

TESMAN   So you insist; but I'm quite certain you are not. Don't you agree with me, Auntie?

MISS TESMAN   *(Who has been gazing at her with folded hands)* Hedda is lovely—lovely—lovely. *(Goes up to her, takes her head between both hands, draws it downwards, and kisses her hair)* God bless and preserve Hedda Tesman—for George's sake.

HEDDA   *(Gently freeing herself)* Oh—! Let me go.

MISS TESMAN   *(In quiet emotion)* I shall not let a day pass without coming to see you.

TESMAN   No you won't, will you, Auntie? Eh?

MISS TESMAN   Good-bye—good-bye!

She goes out by the hall door. TESMAN accompanies her. The door remains half open. TESMAN can be heard repeating his message to Aunt Rina and his thanks for the slippers.

In the meantime, HEDDA walks about the room, raising her arms and clenching her hands as if in desperation. Then she flings back the curtains from the glass door, and stands there looking out.

Presently TESMAN returns and closes the door behind him.

TESMAN   *(Picks up the slippers from the floor)* What are you looking at, Hedda?

HEDDA   *(Once more calm and mistress of herself)* I am only looking at the leaves. They are so yellow—so withered.

TESMAN   *(Wraps up the slippers and lays them on the table)* Well you see, we are well into September now.

HEDDA   *(Again restless)* Yes, to think of it!—Already in—in September.

TESMAN   Don't you think Aunt Julia's manner was strange, dear? Almost solemn? Can you imagine what was the matter with her? Eh?

HEDDA   I scarcely know her, you see. Is she not often like that?

TESMAN   No, not as she was today.

HEDDA   *(Leaving the glass door)* Do you think she was annoyed about the bonnet?

TESMAN   Oh, scarcely at all. Perhaps a little, just at the moment—

HEDDA   But what an idea, to pitch her bonnet about in the drawing room! No one does that sort of thing.

TESMAN   Well you may be sure Aunt Julia won't do it again.

HEDDA   In any case, I shall manage to make my peace with her.

TESMAN   Yes, my dear, good Hedda, if you only would.

HEDDA   When you call this afternoon, you might invite her to spend the evening here.

TESMAN   Yes, that I will. And there's one thing more you could do that would delight her heart.

HEDDA   What is it?

TESMAN   If you could only prevail on yourself to say *du*° to her. For my sake, Hedda? Eh?

HEDDA   No no, Tesman—you really mustn't ask that of me. I have told you so already. I shall try to call her "Aunt"; and you must be satisfied with that.

TESMAN   Well well. Only I think now that you belong to the family, you—

HEDDA   H'm—I can't in the least see why— *(She goes up towards the middle doorway)*

TESMAN   *(After a pause)* Is there anything the matter with you, Hedda? Eh?

HEDDA   I'm only looking at my old piano. It doesn't go at all well with all the other things.

TESMAN   The first time I draw my salary, we'll see about exchanging it.

HEDDA   No, no—no exchanging. I don't want to part with it. Suppose we put it there in the inner room, and then get another here in its place. When it's convenient, I mean.

TESMAN   *(A little taken aback)* Yes—of course we could do that.

HEDDA   *(Takes up the bouquet from the piano)* These flowers were not here last night when we arrived.

TESMAN   Aunt Julia must have brought them for you.

HEDDA   *(Examining the bouquet)* A visiting card. *(Takes it out and*

° **Du:** Tesman means, "If you could persuade yourself to *tutoyer* her"—that is, to use the familiar form of "you." The familiar form in English, no longer in use, is "thou."

reads) "Shall return later in the day." Can you guess whose card it is?

TESMAN   No. Whose? Eh?

HEDDA   The name is "Mrs. Elvsted."

TESMAN   Is it really? Sheriff Elvsted's wife? Miss Rysing that was.

HEDDA   Exactly. The girl with the irritating hair, that she was always showing off. An old flame of yours I've been told.

TESMAN   *(Laughing)* Oh, that didn't last long; and it was before I knew you, Hedda. But fancy her being in town!

HEDDA   It's odd that she should call upon us. I have scarcely seen her since we left school.

TESMAN   I haven't seen her either for—heaven knows how long. I wonder how she can endure to live in such an out-of-the way hole—eh?

HEDDA   *(After a moment's thought, says suddenly)* Tell me, Tesman —isn't it somewhere near there that he—that—Eilert Lövborg is living?

TESMAN   Yes, he is somewhere in that part of the country.

BERTA *enters by the hall door.*

BERTA   That lady, ma'am, that brought some flowers a little while ago, is here again. *(Pointing)* The flowers you have in your hand, ma'am.

HEDDA   Ah, is she? Well, please show her in.

BERTA *opens the door for* MRS. ELVSTED, *and goes out herself. —* MRS. ELVSTED *is a woman of fragile figure, with pretty, soft features. Her eyes are light blue, large, round, and somewhat prominent, with a startled, inquiring expression. Her hair is remarkably light, almost flaxen, and unusually abundant and wavy. She is a couple of years younger than* HEDDA. *She wears a dark visiting dress, tasteful, but not quite in the latest fashion.*

HEDDA   *(Receives her warmly)* How do you do, my dear Mrs. Elvsted? It's delightful to see you again.

MRS. ELVSTED   *(Nervously, struggling for self-control)* Yes, it's a very long time since we met.

TESMAN   *(Gives her his hand)* And we too—eh?

HEDDA   Thanks for your lovely flowers—

MRS. ELVSTED   Oh, not at all—. I would have come straight here yesterday afternoon; but I heard that you were away—

TESMAN   Have you just come to town? Eh?

MRS. ELVSTED   I arrived yesterday, about midday. Oh, I was quite in despair when I heard that you were not at home.

HEDDA   In despair! How so?

TESMAN   Why, my dear Mrs. Rysing—I mean Mrs. Elvsted—

HEDDA   I hope that you are not in any trouble?

MRS. ELVSTED   Yes, I am. And I don't know another living creature here that I can turn to.

HEDDA   *(Laying the bouquet on the table)*   Come—let us sit here on the sofa—

MRS. ELVSTED   Oh, I am too restless to sit down.

HEDDA   Oh no, you're not. Come here. *(She draws* MRS. ELVSTED *down upon the sofa and sits at her side.)*

TESMAN   Well? What is it, Mrs. Elvsted—?

HEDDA   Has anything particular happened to you at home?

MRS. ELVSTED   Yes—and no. Oh—I am so anxious you should not misunderstand me—

HEDDA   Then your best plan is to tell us the whole story, Mrs. Elvsted.

TESMAN   I suppose that's what you have come for—eh?

MRS. ELVSTED   Yes, yes—of course it is. Well then, I must tell you—if you don't already know—that Eilert Lövborg is in town, too.

HEDDA   Lövborg—!

TESMAN   What! Has Eilert Lövborg come back? Fancy that, Hedda!

HEDDA   Well well—I hear it.

MRS. ELVSTED   He has been here a week already. Just fancy—a whole week! In this terrible town, alone! With so many temptations on all sides.

HEDDA   But, my dear Mrs. Elvsted—how does he concern you so much?

MRS. ELVSTED   *(Looks at her with a startled air, and says rapidly)*   He was the children's tutor.

HEDDA   Your children's?

MRS. ELVSTED   My husband's. I have none.

HEDDA   Your stepchildren's, then?

MRS. ELVSTED   Yes.

TESMAN   *(Somewhat hesitatingly)*   Then was he—I don't know how to express it—was he—regular enough in his habits to be fit for the post? Eh?

MRS. ELVSTED   For the last two years his conduct has been irreproachable.

TESMAN   Has it indeed? Fancy that, Hedda!

HEDDA   I hear it.

MRS. ELVSTED   Perfectly irreproachable, I assure you! In every respect. But all the same—now that I know he is here—in this great town— and with a large sum of money in his hands—I can't help being in mortal fear for him.

TESMAN   Why did he not remain where he was? With you and your husband? Eh?

MRS. ELVSTED   After his book was published he was too restless and unsettled to remain with us.

TESMAN   Yes, by-the-bye, Aunt Julia told me he had published a new book.

MRS. ELVSTED   Yes, a big book, dealing with the march of civilization —in broad outline, as it were. It came out about a fortnight ago. And since it has sold so well, and been so much read—and made such a sensation—

TESMAN   Has it indeed? It must be something he has had lying by since his better days.

MRS. ELVSTED   Long ago, you mean?

TESMAN   Yes.

MRS. ELVSTED   No, he has written it all since he has been with us— within the last year.

TESMAN   Isn't that good news, Hedda? Think of that.

MRS. ELVSTED   Ah yes, if only it would last!

HEDDA   Have you seen him here in town?

MRS. ELVSTED   No, not yet. I have had the greatest difficulty in finding out his address. But this morning I discovered it at last.

HEDDA   *(Looks searchingly at her)*   Do you know, it seems to me a little odd of your husband—h'm—

MRE. ELVSTED   *(Starting nervously)*   Of my husband! What?

HEDDA   That he should send you to town on such an errand—that he does not come himself and look after his friend.

MRS. ELVSTED   Oh no, no—my husband has no time. And besides, I—I had some shopping to do.

HEDDA   *(With a slight smile)*   Ah, that is a different matter.

MRS. ELVSTED   *(Rising quickly and uneasily)*   And now I beg and implore you, Mr. Tesman—receive Eilert Lövborg kindly if he comes to you! And that he is sure to do. You see you were such great friends in the old days. And then you are interested in the same studies—the same branch of science—so far as I can understand.

TESMAN   We used to be, at any rate.

MRS. ELVSTED   That is why I beg so earnestly that you—you too—will keep a sharp eye upon him. Oh, you will promise me that, Mr. Tesman—won't you?

TESMAN   With the greatest of pleasure, Mrs. Rysing—

HEDDA   Elvsted.

TESMAN   I assure you I shall do all I possibly can for Eilert. You may rely upon me.

MRS. ELVSTED   Oh, how very, very kind of you! *(Presses his hands)* Thanks, thanks, thanks! *(Frightened)* You see, my husband is so very fond of him!

HEDDA   *(Rising)*   You ought to write to him, Tesman. Perhaps he may not care to come to you of his own accord.

TESMAN   Well, perhaps it would be the right thing to do, Hedda? Eh?

HEDDA   And the sooner the better. Why not at once?

MRS. ELVSTED   *(Imploringly)*   Oh, if you only would!

TESMAN   I'll write this moment. Have you his address, Mrs.—Mrs. Elvsted.

MRS. ELVSTED   Yes. *(Takes a slip of paper from her pocket, and hands it to him)*   Here it is.

TESMAN   Good, good. Then I'll go in— *(Looks about him)*   By-the-bye,—my slippers? Oh, here.   *(Takes the packet, and is about to go)*

HEDDA   Be sure you write him a cordial, friendly letter. And a good long one too.

TESMAN   Yes, I will.

MRS. ELVSTED   But please, please don't say a word to show that I suggested it.

TESMAN   No, how could you think I would? Eh?   *(He goes out to the right, through the inner room.)*

HEDDA   *(Goes up to* MRS. ELVSTED, *smiles, and says in a low voice)*   There! We have killed two birds with one stone.

MRS. ELVSTED   What do you mean?

HEDDA   Could you not see that I wanted him to go?

MRS. ELVSTED   Yes, to write the letter—

HEDDA   And that I might speak to you alone.

MRS. ELVSTED   *(Confused)*   About the same thing?

HEDDA   Precisely.

MRS. ELVSTED   *(Apprehensively)*   But there is nothing more Mrs. Tesman! Absolutely nothing!

HEDDA   Oh yes, but there is. There is a great deal more—I can see that. Sit here—and we'll have a cosy, confidential chat.   *(She forces* MRS. ELVSTED *to sit in the easy-chair beside the stove, and seats herself on one of the footstools.)*

MRS. ELVSTED   *(Anxiously, looking at her watch)*   But, my dear Mrs. Tesman—I was really on the point of going.

HEDDA   Oh, you can't be in such a hurry. —Well? Now tell me something about your life at home.

MRS. ELVSTED   Oh, that is just what I care least to speak about.

HEDDA   But to me, dear—? Why, weren't we schoolfellows?

MRS. ELVSTED   Yes, but you were in the class above me. Oh, how dreadfully afraid of you I was then!

HEDDA   Afraid of me?

MRS. ELVSTED   Yes, dreadfully. For when we met on the stairs you used always to pull my hair.

HEDDA   Did I, really?

MRS. ELVSTED   Yes, and once you said you would burn it off my head.

HEDDA   Oh that was all nonsense, of course.

MRS. ELVSTED   Yes, but I was so silly in those days.—And since then, too—we have drifted so far—far apart from each other. Our circles have been so entirely different.

HEDDA   Well then, we must try to drift together again. Now listen! At school we said *du* to each other; and we called each other by our Christian names—

MRS. ELVSTED   No, I am sure you must be mistaken.

HEDDA   No, not at all! I can remember quite distinctly. So now we are going to renew our old friendship. *(Draws the footstool closer to* MRS. ELVSTED*)* There now! *(Kisses her cheek)* You must say *du* to me and call me Hedda.

MRS. ELVSTED   *(Presses and pats her hands)* Oh, how good and kind you are! I am not used to such kindness.

HEDDA   There, there, there! And I shall say *du* to you as in the old days, and call you my dear Thora.°

MRS. ELVSTED   My name is Thea.°

HEDDA   Why, of course! I meant Thea. *(Looks at her compassionately)* So you are not accustomed to goodness and kindness, Thea? Not in your own home?

MRS. ELVSTED   Oh, if I only had a home! But I haven't any; I have never had a home.

HEDDA   *(Looks at her for a moment)* I almost suspected as much.

MRS. ELVSTED   *(Gazing helplessly before her)* Yes—yes—yes.

HEDDA   I don't quite remember—was it not as housekeeper that you first went to Mr. Elvsted's?

MRS. ELVSTED   I really went as governess. But his wife—his late wife —was an invalid,—and rarely left her room. So I had to look after the housekeeping as well.

HEDDA   And then—at last—you became mistress of the house.

MRS. ELVSTED   *(Sadly)* Yes, I did.

HEDDA   Let me see—about how long ago was that?

MRS. ELVSTED   My marriage?

HEDDA   Yes.

MRS. ELVSTED   Five years ago.

HEDDA   To be sure; it must be that.

MRS. ELVSTED   Oh those five years—! Or at all events the last two or three of them! Oh, if you° could only imagine—

HEDDA   *(Giving her a little slap on the hand)* De? Fie, Thea!

MRS. ELVSTED   Yes, yes, I will try—Well, if—you could only imagine and understand—

°   **Thora:** Pronounced "Tora."
°   **Thea:** Pronounced "Taya."
°   **You:** Mrs. Elvsted here uses the formal pronoun *De*, whereupon Hedda rebukes her. In her next speech Mrs. Elvsted says *du*.

HEDDA   *(Lightly)*   Eilert Lövborg has been in your neighborhood about three years, hasn't he?

MRS. ELVSTED   *(Looks at her doubtfully)*   Eilert Lövborg? Yes—he has.

HEDDA   Had you known him before, in town here?

MRS. ELVSTED   Scarcely at all. I mean—I knew him by name of course.

HEDDA   But you saw a good deal of him in the country?

MRS. ELVSTED   Yes, he came to us every day. You see, he gave the children lessons; for in the long run I couldn't manage it all myself.

HEDDA   No, that's clear.—And your husband—? I suppose he is often away from home?

MRS. ELVSTED   Yes. Being sheriff, you know, he has to travel about a good deal in his district.

HEDDA   *(Leaning against the arm of the chair)*   Thea—my poor, sweet Thea—now you must tell me everything—exactly as it stands.

MRS. ELVSTED   Well then, you must question me.

HEDDA   What sort of a man is your husband, Thea? I mean—you know —in everyday life. Is he kind to you?

MRS. ELVSTED   *(Evasively)*   I am sure he means well in everything.

HEDDA   I should think he must be altogether too old for you. There is at least twenty years' difference between you, is there not?

MRS. ELVSTED   *(Irritably)*   Yes, that is true, too. Everything about him is repellent to me! We have not a thought in common. We have no single point of sympathy—he and I.

HEDDA   But is he not fond of you all the same? In his own way?

MRS. ELVSTED   Oh I really don't know. I think he regards me simply as a useful property. And then it doesn't cost much to keep me. I am not expensive.

HEDDA   That is stupid of you.

MRS. ELVSTED   *(Shakes her head)*   It cannot be otherwise—not with him. I don't think he really cares for anyone but himself—and perhaps a little for the children.

HEDDA   And for Eilert Lövberg, Thea.

MRS. ELVSTED   *(Looking at her)*   For Eilert Lövborg? What puts that into your head?

HEDDA   Well, my dear—I should say, when he sends you after him all the way to town—   *(Smiling almost imperceptibly)*   And besides, you said so yourself, to Tesman.

MRS. ELVSTED   *(With a little nervous twitch)*   Did I? Yes, I suppose I did.   *(Vehemently, but not loudly)*   No—I may just as well make a clean breast of it at once! For it must all come out in any case.

HEDDA   Why, My dear Thea—?

MRS. ELVSTED   Well, to make a long story short: My husband did not know that I was coming.

HEDDA   What! Your husband didn't know it!

MRS. ELVSTED   No, of course not. For that matter, he was away from home himself—he was traveling. Oh, I could bear it no longer, Hedda! I couldn't indeed—so utterly alone as I should have been in the future.

HEDDA   Well? And then?

MRS. ELVSTED   So I put together some of my things—what I needed most—as quietly as possible. And then I left the house.

HEDDA   Without a word?

MRS. ELVSTED   Yes—and took the train straight to town.

HEDDA   Why, my dear, good Thea—to think of you daring to do it!

MRS. ELVSTED   *(Rises and moves about the room)*   What else could I possibly do?

HEDDA   But what do you think your husband will say when you go home again?

MRS. ELVSTED   *(At the table, looks at her)*   Back to him?

HEDDA   Of course.

MRS. ELVSTED   I shall never go back to him again.

HEDDA   *(Rising and going towards her)*   Then you have left your home—for good and all?

MRS. ELVSTED   Yes. There was nothing else to be done.

HEDDA   But then—to take flight so openly.

MRS. ELVSTED   Oh, it's impossible to keep things of that sort secret.

HEDDA   But what do you think people will say of you, Thea?

MRS. ELVSTED   They may say what they like, for aught *I* care. *(Seats herself wearily and sadly on the sofa)*   I have done nothing but what I had to do.

HEDDA   *(After a short silence)*   And what are your plans now? What do you think of doing?

MRS. ELVSTED   I don't know yet. I only know this, that I must live here, where Eilert Lövborg is—if I am to live at all.

HEDDA   *(Takes a chair from the table, seats herself beside her, and strokes her hands)*   My dear Thea—how did this—this friendship— between you and Eilert Lövborg come about?

MRS. ELVSTED   Oh it grew up gradually. I gained a sort of influence over him.

HEDDA   Indeed?

MRS. ELVSTED   He gave up his old habits. Not because I asked him to, for I never dared do that. But of course he saw how repulsive they were to me; and so he dropped them.

HEDDA   *(Concealing an involuntary smile of scorn)*   Then you have reclaimed him—as the saying goes—my little Thea.

MRS. ELVSTED   So he says himself, at any rate. And he, on his side, has made a real human being of me—taught me to think, and to understand so many things.

HEDDA   Did he give you lessons too, then?

MRS. ELVSTED   No, not exactly lessons. But he talked to me—talked about such an infinity of things. And then came the lovely, happy time when I began to share in his work—when he allowed me to help him!

HEDDA   Oh he did, did he?

MRS. ELVSTED   Yes! He never wrote anything without my assistance.

HEDDA   You were two good comrades, in fact?

MRS. ELVSTED   *(Eagerly)*   Comrades! Yes, fancy, Hedda—that is the very word he used!—Oh, I ought to feel perfectly happy; and yet I cannot; for I don't know how long it will last.

HEDDA   Are you no surer of him than that?

MRS. ELVSTED   *(Gloomily)*   A woman's shadow stands between Eilert Lövberg and me.

HEDDA   *(Looks at her anxiously)*   Who can that be?

MRS. ELVSTED   I don't know. Someone he knew in his—in his past. Someone he has never been able wholly to forget.

HEDDA   What has he told you—about this?

MRS. ELVSTED   He has only once—quite vaguely—alluded to it.

HEDDA   Well! And what did he say?

MRS. ELVSTED   He said that when they parted, she threatened to shoot him with a pistol.

HEDDA   *(With cold composure)*   Oh nonsense! No one does that sort of thing here.

MRS. ELVSTED   No. And that is why I think it must have been that red-haired singing-woman whom he once—

HEDDA   Yes, very likely.

MRS. ELVSTED   For I remember they used to say of her that she carried loaded firearms.

HEDDA   Oh—then of course it must have been she.

MRS. ELVSTED   *(Wringing her hands)*   And now just fancy, Hedda—I hear that this singing-woman—that she is in town again! Oh, I don't know what to do—

HEDDA   *(Glancing towards the inner room)*   Hush! Here comes Tesman. *(Rises and whispers)*   Thea—all this must remain between you and me.

MRS. ELVSTED   *(Springing up)*   Oh yes—yes! For heaven's sake—

GEORGE TESMAN, *with a letter in his hand, comes from the right through the inner room.*

TESMAN   There now—the epistle is finished.

HEDDA   That's right. And now Mrs. Elvsted is just going. Wait a moment—I'll go with you to the garden gate.

TESMAN   Do you think Berta could post the letter, Hedda dear?

HEDDA   *(Takes it)*   I will tell her to.

BERTA *enters from the hall.*

BERTA   Judge Brack wishes to know if Mrs. Tesman will receive him.
HEDDA   Yes, ask Judge Brack to come in. And look here—put this letter
in the post.
BERTA   *(Taking the letter)*   Yes, ma'am.

She opens the door for JUDGE BRACK *and goes out herself.* BRACK *is a
man of forty-five; thick set, but well-built and elastic in his movements.
His face is roundish with an aristocratic profile. His hair is short, still
almost black, and carefully dressed. His eyes are lively and sparkling.
His eyebrows thick. His moustaches are also thick, with short-cut ends.
He wears a well-cut walking suit, a little too youthful for his age. He
uses an eyeglass, which he now and then lets drop.*

JUDGE BRACK   *(With his hat in his hand, bowing)*   May one venture to
call so early in the day?
HEDDA   Of course one may.
TESMAN   *(Presses   his   hand)*   You   are   welcome   at   any
time.   *(Introducing him)*   Judge Brack—Miss Rysing—
HEDDA   Oh—!
BRACK   *(Bowing)*   Ah—delighted—
HEDDA   *(Looks at him and laughs)*   It's nice to have a look at you by
daylight, Judge!
BRACK   Do you find me—altered?
HEDDA   A little younger, I think.
BRACK   Thank you so much.
TESMAN   But what do you think of Hedda—eh? Doesn't she look flour-
ishing? She has actually—
HEDDA   Oh, do leave me alone. You haven't thanked Judge Brack for
all the trouble he has taken—
BRACK   Oh, nonsense—it was a pleasure to me—
HEDDA   Yes, you are a friend indeed. But here stands Thea all impati-
ence to be off—so *au revoir* Judge. I shall be back again presently.

Mutual salutations. MRS. ELVSTED *and* HEDDA *go out by the hall
door.*

BRACK   Well—is your wife tolerably satisfied—
TESMAN   Yes, we can't thank you sufficiently. Of course she talks of a
little rearrangement here and there; and one or two things are still
wanting. We shall have to buy some additional trifles.

BRACK   Indeed!

TESMAN   But we won't trouble you about these things. Hedda says she herself will look after what is wanting—Shan't we sit down? Eh?

BRACK   Thanks, for a moment. *(Seats himself beside the table)* There is something I wanted to speak to you about, my dear Tesman.

TESMAN   Indeed? Ah, I understand! *(Seating himself)* I suppose it's the serious part of the frolic that is coming now. Eh?

BRACK   Oh, the money question is not so very pressing; though, for that matter, I wish we had gone a little more economically to work.

TESMAN   But that would never have done, you know! Think of Hedda, my dear fellow! You, who know her so well—. I couldn't possibly ask her to put up with a shabby style of living!

BRACK   No, no—that is just the difficulty.

TESMAN   And then—fortunately—it can't be long before I receive my appointment.

BRACK   Well, you see—such things are often apt to hang fire for a time.

TESMAN   Have you heard anything definite? Eh?

BRACK   Nothing exactly definite—. *(Interrupting himself)* But by-the-bye—I have one piece of news for you.

TESMAN   Well?

BRACK   Your old friend, Eilert Lövborg, has returned to town.

TESMAN   I know that already.

BRACK   Indeed! How did you learn it?

TESMAN   From that lady who went out with Hedda.

BRACK   Really? What was her name? I didn't quite catch it.

TESMAN   Mrs. Elvsted.

BRACK   Aha—Sheriff Elvsted's wife? Of course—he has been living up in their regions.

TESMAN   And fancy—I'm delighted to hear that he is quite a reformed character!

BRACK   So they say.

TESMAN   And then he has published a new book—eh?

BRACK   Yes, indeed he has.

TESMAN   And I hear it has made some sensation!

BRACK   Quite an unusual sensation.

TESMAN   Fancy—isn't that good news! A man of such extraordinary talents—. I felt so grieved to think that he had gone irretrievably to ruin.

BRACK   That was what everybody thought.

TESMAN   But I cannot imagine what he will take to now! How in the world will he be able to make his living? Eh?

During the last words, HEDDA *has entered by the hall door.*

HEDDA   *(To* BRACK, *laughing with a touch of scorn)*   Tesman is for ever worrying about how people are to make their living.

TESMAN   Well you see, dear—we were talking about poor Eilert Lövborg.

HEDDA   *(Glancing at him rapidly)*   Oh, indeed?   *(Seats herself in the armchair beside the stove and asks indifferently)*   What is the matter with him?

TESMAN   Well—no doubt he has run through all his property long ago; and he can scarcely write a new book every year—eh? So I really can't see what is to become of him.

BRACK   Perhaps I can give you some information on that point.

TESMAN   Indeed!

BRACK   You must remember that his relations have a good deal of influence.

TESMAN   Oh, his relations, unfortunately, have entirely washed their hands of him.

BRACK   At one time they called him the hope of the family.

TESMAN   At one time, yes! But he has put an end to all that.

HEDDA   Who knows?   *(With a slight smile)*   I hear they have reclaimed him up at Sheriff Elvsted's—

BRACK   And then this book that he has published—

TESMAN   Well well, I hope to goodness they may find something for him to do. I have just written to him. I asked him to come and see us this evening, Hedda dear.

BRACK   But my dear fellow, you are booked for my bachelors' party this evening. You promised on the pier last night.

HEDDA   Had you forgotten, Tesman?

TESMAN   Yes, I had utterly forgotten.

BRACK   But it doesn't matter, for you may be sure he won't come.

TESMAN   What makes you think that? Eh?

BRACK   *(With a little hesitation, rising and resting his hands on the back of his chair)*   My dear Tesman—and you too, Mrs. Tesman—I think I ought not to keep you in the dark about something that—that—

TESMAN   That concerns Eilert—?

BRACK   Both you and him.

TESMAN   Well, my dear Judge, out with it.

BRACK   You must be prepared to find your appointment deferred longer than you desired or expected.

TESMAN   *(Jumping up uneasily)*   Is there some hitch about it? Eh?

BRACK   The nomination may perhaps be made conditional on the result of a competition—

TESMAN   Competition! Think of that, Hedda!

HEDDA   *(Leans further back in the chair)*   Aha—aha!

TESMAN   But who can my competitor be? Surely not—?

BRACK   Yes, precisely—Eilert Lövborg.

TESMAN   *(Clasping his hands)*   No, no—it's quite inconceivable! Quite impossible! Eh?

BRACK   H'm—that is what it may come to, all the same.

TESMAN   Well but, Judge Brack—it would show the most incredible lack of consideration for me. *(Gesticulates with his arms)*   For—just think—I'm a married man! We have married on the strength of these prospects, Hedda and I; and run deep into debt; and borrowed money from Aunt Julia too. Good heavens, they had as good as promised me the appointment. Eh?

BRACK   Well, well, well—no doubt you will get it in the end; only after a contest.

HEDDA   *(Immovable in her armchair)*   Fancy, Tesman, there will be a sort of sporting interest in that.

TESMAN   Why, my dearest Hedda, how can you be so indifferent about it.

HEDDA   *(As before)*   I am not at all indifferent. I am most eager to see who wins.

BRACK   In any case, Mrs. Tesman, it is best that you should know how matters stand. I mean—before you set about the little purchases I hear you are threatening.

HEDDA   This can make no difference.

BRACK   Indeed! Then I have no more to say. Goodbye! *(To* TESMAN*)*   I shall look in on my way back from my afternoon walk, and take you home with me.

TESMAN   Oh yes, yes—your news has quite upset me.

HEDDA   *(Reclining, holds out her hand)*   Good-bye, Judge; and be sure you call in the afternoon.

BRACK   Many thanks. Good-bye, good-bye!

TESMAN   *(Accompanying him to the door)*   Good-bye my dear Judge! You must really excuse me—

JUDGE BRACK *goes out by the hall door.*

TESMAN   *(Crosses the room)*   Oh Hedda—one should never rush into adventures. Eh?

HEDDA   *(Looks at him, smiling)*   Do you do that?

TESMAN   Yes, dear—there is no denying—it was adventurous to go and marry and set up a house upon mere expectations.

HEDDA   Perhaps you are right there.

TESMAN   Well—at all events, we have our delightful home, Hedda! Fancy, the home we both dreamed of—the home we were in love with, I may almost say. Eh?

HEDDA   *(Rising slowly and wearily)* It was part of our compact that we were to go into society—to keep open house.

TESMAN   Yes, if you only knew how I had been looking forward to it! Fancy—to see you as hostess—in a select circle! Eh? Well, well, well —for the present we shall have to get on without society, Hedda— only to invite Aunt Julia now and then.—Oh, I intended you to lead such an utterly different life, dear—!

HEDDA   Of course I cannot have my man in livery just yet.

TESMAN   Oh no, unfortunately. It would be out of the question for us to keep a footman, you know.

HEDDA   And the saddle-horse I was to have had—

TESMAN   *(Aghast)* The saddle-horse!

HEDDA   —I suppose I must not think of that now.

TESMAN   Good heavens, no!—that's as clear as daylight

HEDDA   *(Goes up the room)* Well, I shall have one thing at least to kill time with in the meanwhile.

TESMAN   *(Beaming)* Oh thank heaven for that! What is it, Hedda? Eh?

HEDDA   *(In the middle doorway, looks at him with covert scorn)* My pistols, George.

TESMAN   *(In alarm)* Your pistols!

HEDDA   *(With cold eyes)* General Gabler's pistols. *(She goes out through the inner room, to the left)*

TESMAN   *(Rushes up to the middle doorway and calls after her)* No, for heaven's sake, Hedda darling—don't touch those dangerous things! For my sake, Hedda! Eh?

ACT II

The room at the TESMANS' *as in Act I, except that the piano has been removed, and an elegant little writing table with bookshelves put in its place. A smaller table stands near the sofa on the left. Most of the bouquets have been taken away.* MRS. ELVSTED'S *bouquet is upon the large table in front. —It is afternoon.*

HEDDA, *dressed to receive callers, is alone in the room. She stands by the open glass door, loading a revolver. The fellow to it lies in an open pistol case on the writing table.*

HEDDA   *(Looks down the garden, and calls)* So you are here again, Judge!

BRACK   *(Is heard calling from a distance)* As you see, Mrs. Tesman!

HEDDA   *(Raises the pistol and points)* Now I'll shoot you, Judge Brack!

BRACK   *(Calling unseen)* No, no, no! Don't stand aiming at me!

HEDDA   This is what comes of sneaking in by the back way.° *(She fires)*

BRACK   *(Near)* Are you out of your senses—?

HEDDA   Dear me—did I happen to hit you?

BRACK   *(Still outside)* I wish you would let these pranks alone!

HEDDA   Come in then, Judge.

JUDGE BRACK, *dressed as though for a men's party, enters by the glass door. He carries a light overcoat over his arm.*

BRACK   What the deuce—haven't you tired of that sport, yet? What are you shooting at?

HEDDA   Oh, I am only firing in the air.

BRACK   *(Gently takes the pistol out of her hand)* Allow me, madam! *(Looks at it)* Ah—I know this pistol well! *(Looks around)* Where is the case? Ah, here it is. *(Lays the pistol in it, and shuts it)* Now we won't play at that game any more today.

HEDDA   Then what in heaven's name would you have me do with myself?

BRACK   Have you had no visitors?

HEDDA   *(Closing the glass door)* Not one. I suppose all our set are still out of town.

BRACK   And is Tesman not at home either?

HEDDA   *(At the writing table, putting the pistol case in a drawer which she shuts)* No. He rushed off to his aunt's directly after lunch; he didn't expect you so early.

BRACK   H'm—how stupid of me not to have thought of that!

HEDDA   *(Turning her head to look at him)* Why stupid?

BRACK   Because if I had thought of it I should have come a little—earlier.

HEDDA   *(Crossing the room)* Then you would have found no one to receive you; for I have been in my room changing my dress ever since lunch.

BRACK   And is there no sort of little chink that we could hold a parley through?

HEDDA   You have forgotten to arrange one.

BRACK   That was another piece of stupidity.

HEDDA   Well, we must just settle down here—and wait. Tesman is not likely to be back for some time yet.

°   **back way:** *"Bagveje"* means "back ways" and "underhand courses."

BRACK   Never mind; I shall not be impatient.

HEDDA *seats herself in the corner of the sofa.* BRACK *lays his overcoat over the back of the nearest chair, and sits down, but keeps his hat in his hand. A short silence. They look at each other.*

HEDDA   Well?

BRACK   *(In the same tone)*   Well?

HEDDA   I spoke first.

BRACK   *(Bending a little forward)*   Come, let us have a cosy little chat, Mrs. Hedda.°

HEDDA   *(Leaning further back in the sofa)*   Does it not seem like a whole eternity since our last talk? Of course I don't count those few words yesterday evening and this morning.

BRACK   You mean since our last confidential talk? Our last *tête-à-tête?*

HEDDA   Well yes—since you put it so.

BRACK   Not a day has passed but I have wished that you were home again.

HEDDA   And I have done nothing but wish the same thing.

BRACK   You? Really, Mrs. Hedda? And I thought you had been enjoying your tour so much!

HEDDA   Oh yes, you may be sure of that!

BRACK   But Tesman's letters spoke of nothing but happiness.

HEDDA   Oh, Tesman. You see, he thinks nothing so delightful as grubbing in libraries and making copies of old parchments, or whatever you call them.

BRACK   *(With a spice of malice)*   Well, that is his vocation in life—or part of it at any rate.

HEDDA   Yes, of course; and no doubt when it's your vocation—. But *I!* Oh, my dear Mr. Brack, how mortally bored I have been.

BRACK   *(Sympathetically)*   Do you really say so? In downright earnest?

HEDDA   Yes, you can surely understand it—! To go for six whole months without meeting a soul that knew anything of our circle, or could talk about the things we are interested in.

BRACK   Yes, yes—I too should feel that a deprivation.

HEDDA   And then, what I found most intolerable of all—

BRACK   Well?

°   **Mrs. Hedda:** As this form of address is contrary to English usage, and as the note of familiarity would be lacking in "Mrs. Tesman," Brack may, in stage representation, say "Miss Hedda," thus ignoring her marriage and reverting to the form of address no doubt customary between them of old.

HEDDA   —was being everlastingly in the company of—one and the same person—

BRACK   *(With a nod of assent)*   Morning, noon, and night, yes—at all possible times and seasons.

HEDDA   I said "everlastingly."

BRACK   Just so. But I should have thought, with our excellent Tesman, one could—

HEDDA   Tesman is—a specialist, my dear Judge.

BRACK   Undeniably.

HEDDA   And specialists are not at all amusing to travel with. Not in the long run at any rate.

BRACK   Not even—the specialist one happens to love?

HEDDA   Faugh—don't use that sickening word!

BRACK   *(Taken aback)*   What do you say, Mrs. Hedda?

HEDDA   *(Half laughing, half irritated)*   You should just try it! To hear of nothing but the history of civilisation, morning, noon, and night—

BRACK   Everlastingly.

HEDDA   Yes yes yes! And then all this about the domestic industry of the middle ages—! That's the most disgusting part of it!

BRACK   *(Looks searchingly at her)*   But tell me—in that case, how am I to understand your—? H'm—

HEDDA   My accepting George Tesman, you mean?

BRACK   Well, let us put it so.

HEDDA   Good heavens, do you see anything so wonderful in that?

BRACK   Yes and no—Mrs. Hedda.

HEDDA   I had positively danced myself tired, my dear Judge. My day was done—   *(With a slight shudder)*   Oh no—I won't say that; nor think it either!

BRACK   You have assuredly no reason to.

HEDDA   Oh, reasons—   *(Watching him closely)*   And George Tesman —after all, you must admit that he is correctness itself.

BRACK   His correctness and respectability are beyond all question.

HEDDA   And I don't see anything absolutely ridiculous about him.—Do you?

BRACK   Ridiculous? No—no—I shouldn't exactly say so—

HEDDA   Well—and his powers of research, at all events, are untiring.—I see no reason why he should not one day come to the front, after all.

BRACK   *(Looks at her hesitatingly)*   I thought that you, like everyone else, expected him to attain the highest distinction.

HEDDA   *(With an expression of fatigue)*   Yes, so I did.—And then, since he was bent, at all hazards, on being allowed to provide for me —I really don't know why I should not have accepted his offer?

BRACK   No—if you look at it in that light—

HEDDA   It was more than my other adorers were prepared to do for me, my dear Judge.

BRACK   (*Laughing*) Well, I can't answer for all the rest; but as for myself, you know quite well that I have always entertained a—a certain respect for the marriage tie—for marriage as an institution, Mrs. Hedda.

HEDDA   (*Jestingly*) Oh, I assure you I have never cherished any hopes with respect to you.

BRACK   All I require is a pleasant and intimate interior, where I can make myself useful in every way, and am free to come and go as—as a trusted friend—

HEDDA   Of the master of the house, do you mean?

BRACK   (*Bowing*) Frankly—of the mistress first of all; but of course of the master too, in the second place. Such a triangular friendship—if I may call it so—is really a great convenience for all parties, let me tell you.

HEDDA   Yes, I have many a time longed for someone to make a third on our travels. Oh—those railway carriage *tête-à-têtes*—!

BRACK   Fortunately your wedding journey is over now.

HEDDA   (*Shaking her head*) Not by a long—long way. I have only arrived at a station on the line.

BRACK   Well, then the passengers jump out and move about a little, Mrs. Hedda.

HEDDA   I never jump out.

BRACK   Really?

HEDDA   No—because there is always some one standing by to—

BRACK   (*Laughing*) To look at your ankles, do you mean?

HEDDA   Precisely.

BRACK   Well but, dear me—

HEDDA   (*With a gesture of repulsion*) I won't have it. I would rather keep my seat where I happen to be—and continue the *tête-à-tête*.

BRACK   But suppose a third person were to jump in and join the couple.

HEDDA   Ah—that is quite another matter!

BRACK   A trusted, sympathetic friend—

HEDDA   —with a fund of conversation on all sorts of lively topics—

BRACK   —and not the least bit of a specialist!

HEDDA   (*With an audible sigh*) Yes, that would be a relief indeed.

BRACK   (*Hears the front door open, and glances in that direction*) The triangle is completed.

HEDDA   (*Half aloud*) And on goes the train.

GEORGE TESMAN, *in a grey walking suit, with a soft felt hat, enters from the hall. He has a number of unbound books under his arm and in his pockets.*

TESMAN *(Goes up to the table beside the corner settee)* Ouf—what a load for a warm day—all these books. *(Lays them on the table)* I'm positively perspiring, Hedda. Hallo—are you there already, my dear Judge? Eh? Berta didn't tell me.

BRACK *(Rising)* I came in through the garden.

HEDDA What books have you got there?

TESMAN *(Stands looking them through)* Some new books on my special subjects—quite indispensable to me.

HEDDA Your special subjects?

BRACK Yes, books on his special subjects, Mrs. Tesman.

BRACK *and* HEDDA *exchange a confidential smile.*

HEDDA Do you need still more books on your special subjects?

TESMAN Yes, my dear Hedda, one can never have too many of them. Of course one must keep up with all that is written and published.

HEDDA Yes, I suppose one must.

TESMAN *(Searching among his books)* And look here—I have got hold of Eilert Lövborg's new book too. *(Offering it to her)* Perhaps you would like to glance through it, Hedda? Eh?

HEDDA No, thank you. Or rather—afterwards perhaps.

TESMAN I looked into it a little on the way home.

BRACK Well, what do you think of it—as a specialist?

TESMAN I think it shows quite remarkable soundness of judgment. He never wrote like that before. *(Putting the books together)* Now I shall take all these into my study. I'm longing to cut the leaves—! And then I must change my clothes. *(To* BRACK) I suppose we needn't start just yet? Eh?

BRACK Oh, dear no—there is not the slightest hurry.

TESMAN Well then, I will take my time. *(Is going with his books, but stops in the doorway and turns)* By-the-bye, Hedda—Aunt Julia is not coming this evening.

HEDDA Not coming? Is it that affair of the bonnet that keeps her away?

TESMAN Oh, not at all. How could you think such a thing of Aunt Julia? Just fancy—! The fact is, Aunt Rina is very ill.

HEDDA She always is.

TESMAN Yes, but today she is much worse than usual, poor dear.

HEDDA Oh, then it's only natural that her sister should remain with her. I must bear my disappointment.

TESMAN And you can't imagine, dear, how delighted Aunt Julia seemed to be—because you had come home looking so flourishing!

HEDDA *(Half aloud, rising)* Oh, those everlasting Aunts!

TESMAN What?

HEDDA *(Going to the glass door)* Nothing.

TESMAN   Oh, all right. *(He goes through the inner room, out to the right)*

BRACK   What bonnet were you talking about?

HEDDA   Oh, it was a little episode with Miss Tesman this morning. She had laid down her bonnet on the chair there— *(Looks at him and smiles)* —and I pretended to think it was the servant's.

BRACK   *(Shaking his head)* Now my dear Mrs. Hedda, how could you do such a thing? To that excellent old lady, too!

HEDDA   *(Nervously crossing the room)* Well, you see—these impulses come over me all of a sudden; and I cannot resist them. *(Throws herself down in the easy chair by the stove)* Oh, I don't know how to explain it.

BRACK   *(Behind the easy chair)* You are not really happy—that is at the bottom of it.

HEDDA   *(Looking straight before her)* I know of no reason why I should be—happy. Perhaps you can give me one?

BRACK   Well—amongst other things, because you have got exactly the home you had set your heart on.

HEDDA   *(Looks up at him and laughs)* Do you too believe in that legend?

BRACK   Is there nothing in it, then?

HEDDA   Oh yes, there is something in it.

BRACK   Well?

HEDDA   There is this in it, that I made use of Tesman to see me home from evening parties last summer—

BRACK   I, unfortunately, had to go quite a different way.

HEDDA   That's true. I know you were going a different way last summer.

BRACK   *(Laughing)* Oh fie, Mrs. Hedda! Well then—you and Tesman—?

HEDDA   Well, we happened to pass here one evening; Tesman, poor fellow, was writhing in the agony of having to find conversation; so I took pity on the learned man—

BRACK   *(Smiles doubtfully)* You took pity? H'm—

HEDDA   Yes, I really did. And so—to help him out of his torment—I happened to say, in pure thoughtlessness, that I should like to live in this villa.

BRACK   No more than that?

HEDDA   Not that evening.

BRACK   But afterwards?

HEDDA   Yes, my thoughtlessness had consequences, my dear Judge.

BRACK   Unfortunately that too often happens, Mrs. Hedda.

HEDDA   Thanks! So you see it was this enthusiasm for Secretary Falk's villa that first constituted a bond of sympathy between George Tesman and me. From that came our engagement and our marriage, and our wedding journey, and all the rest of it. Well, well, my dear Judge—as you make your bed so you must lie, I could almost say.

BRACK   This is exquisite! And you really cared not a rap about it all the time?

HEDDA   No, heaven knows I didn't.

BRACK   But now? Now that we have made it so homelike for you?

HEDDA   Uh—the rooms all seem to smell of lavender and dried rose-leaves.—But perhaps it's Aunt Julia that has brought that scent with her.

BRACK   *(Laughing)*   No, I think it must be a legacy from the late Mrs. Secretary Falk.

HEDDA   Yes, there is an odor of mortality about it. It reminds me of a bouquet—the day after the ball. *(Clasps her hands behind her head, leans back in her chair and looks at him)*   Oh, my dear Judge—you cannot imagine how horribly I shall bore myself here.

BRACK   Why should not you, too, find some sort of vocation in life, Mrs. Hedda?

HEDDA   A vocation—that should attract me?

BRACK   If possible, of course.

HEDDA   Heaven knows what sort of a vocation that could be. I often wonder whether—   *(Breaking off)*   But that would never do either.

BRACK   Who can tell? Let me hear what it is.

HEDDA   Whether I might not get Tesman to go into politics, I mean.

BRACK   *(Laughing)*   Tesman? No really now, political life is not the thing for him—not at all in his line.

HEDDA   No, I daresay not. —But if I could get him into it all the same?

BRACK   Why—what satisfaction could you find in that? If he is not fitted for that sort of thing, why should you want to drive him into it?

HEDDA   Because I am bored, I tell you! *(After a pause)*   So you think it quite out of the question that Tesman should ever get into the ministry?

BRACK   H'm—you see, my dear Mrs. Hedda—to get into the ministry, he would have to be a tolerably rich man.

HEDDA   *(Rising impatiently)*   Yes, there we have it! It is this genteel poverty I have managed to drop into—! *(Crosses the room)*   That is what makes life so pitiable! So utterly ludicrous!—For that's what it is.

BRACK   Now I should say the fault lay elsewhere.

HEDDA   Where, then?

BRACK   You have never gone through any really stimulating experience.

HEDDA   Anything serious, you mean?

BRACK   Yes, you may call it so. But now you may perhaps have one in store.

HEDDA   *(Tossing her head)*   Oh, you're thinking of the annoyances about this wretched professorship! But that must be Tesman's own affair. I assure you I shall not waste a thought upon it.

BRACK   No, no. I daresay not. But suppose now that what people call— in elegant language—a solemn responsibility were to come upon you? *(Smiling)*   A new responsiblity, Mrs. Hedda?

HEDDA   *(Angrily)*   Be quiet! Nothing of that sort will ever happen!

BRACK   *(Warily)*   We will speak of this again a year hence—at the very outside.

HEDDA   *(Curtly)*   I have no turn for anything of the sort, Judge Brack. No responsibilities for me!

BRACK   Are you so unlike the generality of women as to have no turn for duties which—?

HEDDA   *(Beside the glass door)*   Oh, be quiet, I tell you! —I often think there is only one thing in the world I have any turn for.

BRACK   *(Drawing near to her)*   And what is that, if I may ask?

HEDDA   *(Stands looking out)*   Boring myself to death. Now you know it.   *(Turns, looks towards the inner room, and laughs)*   Yes, as I thought! Here comes the Professor.

BRACK   *(Softly, in a tone of warning)*   Come, come, come, Mrs. Hedda!

GEORGE TESMAN, *dressed for the party, with his gloves and hat in his hand, enters from the right through the inner room.*

TESMAN   Hedda, has no message come from Eilert Lövborg? Eh?

HEDDA   No.

TESMAN   Then you'll see he'll be here presently.

BRACK   Do you really think he will come?

TESMAN   Yes, I am almost sure of it. For what you were telling us this morning must have been a mere floating rumour.

BRACK   You think so?

TESMAN   At any rate, Aunt Julia said she did not believe for a moment that he would ever stand in my way again. Fancy that!

BRACK   Well then, that's all right.

TESMAN   *(Placing his hat and gloves on a chair on the right)*   Yes, but you must really let me wait for him as long as possible.

BRACK   We have plenty of time yet. None of my guests will arrive before seven or half-past.

TESMAN   Then meanwhile we can keep Hedda company, and see what happens. Eh?

HEDDA   *(Placing BRACK's hat and overcoat upon the corner setee)*   And at the worst Mr. Lövborg can remain here with me.

BRACK   *(Offering to take his things)*   Oh, allow me, Mrs. Tesman! —What do you mean by "at the worst"?

HEDDA   If he won't go with you and Tesman.

TESMAN   *(Looks dubiously at her)*   But, Hedda dear—do you think it would quite do for him to remain with you? Eh? Remember, Aunt Julia can't come.

HEDDA   No, but Mrs. Elvsted is coming. We three can have a cup of tea together.

TESMAN   Oh yes, that will be all right.

BRACK   *(Smiling)*   And that would perhaps be the safest plan for him.

HEDDA   Why so?

BRACK   Well, you know, Mrs. Tesman, how you used to gird° at my little bachelor parties. You declared they were adapted only for men of the strictest principles.

HEDDA   But no doubt Mr. Lövborg's principles are strict enough now. A converted sinner—

BERTA *appears at the hall door.*

BERTA   There's a gentleman asking if you are at home, ma'am—

HEDDA   Well, show him in.

TESMAN   *(Softly)*   I'm sure it is he! Fancy that!

EILERT LÖVBORG *enters from the hall. He is slim and lean; of the same age as* TESMAN, *but looks older and somewhat worn-out. His hair and beard are of a blackish brown, his face long and pale, but with patches of color on the cheekbones. He is dressed in a well-cut black visiting suit, quite new. He has dark gloves and a silk hat. He stops near the door, and makes a rapid bow, seeming somewhat embarrassed.*

TESMAN   *(Goes up to him and shakes him warmly by the hand)*   Well, my dear Eilert—so at last we meet again!

EILERT LÖVBORG   *(Speaks in a subdued voice)*   Thanks for your letter, Tesman. *(Approaching* HEDDA*)*   Will you too shake hands with me, Mrs. Tesman?

HEDDA   *(Taking his hand)*   I am glad to see you, Mr. Lövborg. *(With a motion of her hand)*   I don't know whether you two gentlemen—?

LÖVBORG   *(Bowing slightly)*   Judge Brack, I think.

BRACK   *(Doing likewise)*   Oh yes—in the old days—

TESMAN   *(To* LÖVBORG, *with hands on his shoulders)*   And now you must make yourself entirely at home, Eilert! Mustn't he, Hedda?— For I hear you are going to settle in town again? Eh?

°   **gird:** Sneer, gibe.

LÖVBORG   Yes, I am.

TESMAN   Quite right, quite right. Let me tell you, I have got hold of your new book; but I haven't had time to read it yet.

LÖVBORG   You may spare yourself the trouble.

TESMAN   Why so?

LÖVBORG   Because there is very little in it.

TESMAN   Just fancy—how can you say so?

BRACK   But it has been very much praised, I hear.

LÖVBORG   That was what I wanted; so I put nothing into the book but what everyone would agree with.

BRACK   Very wise of you.

TESMAN   Well but, my dear Eilert—!

LÖVBORG   For now I mean to win myself a position again—to make a fresh start.

TESMAN   *(A little embarrassed)*   Ah, that is what you wish to do? Eh?

LÖVBORG   *(Smiling, lays down his hat, and draws a packet, wrapped in paper, from his coat pocket)*   But when this one appears, George Tesman, you will have to read it. For this is the real book—the book I have put my true self into.

TESMAN   Indeed? And what is it?

LÖVBORG   It is the continuation.

TESMAN   The continuation? Of what?

LÖVBORG   Of the book.

TESMAN   Of the new book?

LÖVBORG   Of course.

TESMAN   Why, my dear Eilert—does it not come down to our own days?

LÖVBORG   Yes, it does; and this one deals with the future.

TESMAN   With the future! But, good heavens, we know nothing of the future!

LÖVBORG   No; but there is a thing or two to be said about it all the same. *(Opens the packet)*   Look here—

TESMAN   Why, that's not your handwriting.

LÖVBORG   I dictated it. *(Turning over the pages)*   It falls into two sections. The first deals with the civilizing forces of the future. And here is the second— *(running through the pages towards the end)* —forecasting the probable line of development.

TESMAN   How odd now! I should never have thought of writing anything of that sort.

HEDDA   *(At the glass door, drumming on the pane)*   H'm—. I daresay not.

LÖVBORG   *(Replacing the manuscript in its paper and laying the packet on the table)*   I brought it, thinking I might read you a little of it this evening.

TESMAN   That was very good of you, Eilert. But this evening—? *(Looking at* BRACK*)*   I don't quite see how we can manage it—

LÖVBORG   Well then, some other time. There is no hurry.

BRACK   I must tell you, Mr. Lövborg—there is a little gathering at my house this evening—mainly in honor of Tesman, you know—

LÖVBORG   *(Looking for his hat)*   Oh—then I won't detain you—

BRACK   No, but listen—will you not do me the favor of joining us?

LÖVBORG   *(Curtly and decidedly)*   No, I can't—thank you very much.

BRACK   Oh, nonsense—do! We shall be quite a select little circle. And I assure you we shall have a "lively time," as Mrs. Hed—as Mrs. Tesman says.

LÖVBORG   I have no doubt of it. But nevertheless—

BRACK   And then you might bring your manuscript with you, and read it to Tesman at my house. I could give you a room to yourselves.

TESMAN   Yes, think of that, Eilert—why shouldn't you? Eh?

HEDDA   *(Interposing)*   But, Tesman, if Mr. Lövborg would really rather not! I am sure Mr. Lövborg is much more inclined to remain here and have supper with me.

LÖVBORG   *(Looking at her)*   With you, Mrs. Tesman?

HEDDA   And with Mrs. Elvsted.

LÖVBORG   Ah— *(Lightly)*   I saw her for a moment this morning.

HEDDA   Did you? Well, she is coming this evening. So you see you are almost bound to remain, Mr. Lövborg, or she will have no one to see her home.

LÖVBORG   That's true. Many thanks, Mrs. Tesman—in that case I will remain.

HEDDA   Then I have one or two orders to give the servant—

She goes to the hall door and rings. BERTA *enters.* HEDDA *talks to her in a whisper, and points towards the inner room.* BERTA *nods and goes out again.*

TESMAN   *(At the same time, to* LÖVBORG*)*   Tell me, Eilert—is it this new subject—the future—that you are going to lecture about?

LÖVBORG   Yes.

TESMAN   They told me at the bookseller's that you are going to deliver a course of lectures this autumn.

LÖVBORG   That is my intention. I hope you won't take it ill, Tesman.

TESMAN   Oh no, not in the least! But—?

LÖVBORG   I can quite understand that it must be disagreeable to you.

TESMAN   *(Cast down)*   Oh, I can't expect you, out of consideration for me, to—

LÖVBORG   But I shall wait till you have received your appointment.

TESMAN   Will you wait? Yes but—yes but—are you not going to compete with me? Eh?

LÖVBORG   No; it is only the moral victory I care for.

TESMAN   Why, bless me—then Aunt Julia was right after all! Oh yes —I knew it! Hedda! Just fancy—Eilert Lövborg is not going to stand in our way!

HEDDA   *(Curtly)*   Our way? Pray leave me out of the question.

She goes up towards the inner room, where BERTA *is placing a tray with decanters and glasses on the table.* HEDDA *nods approval, and comes forward again.* BERTA *goes out.*

TESMAN   *(At the same time)*   And you, Judge Brack—what do you say to this? Eh?

BRACK   Well, I say that a moral victory—h'm—may be all very fine—

TESMAN   Yes, certainly. But all the same—

HEDDA   *(Looking at* TESMAN *with a cold smile)*   You stand there looking as if you were thunderstruck—

TESMAN   Yes—so I am—I almost think—

BRACK   Don't you see, Mrs. Tesman, a thunderstorm has just passed over?

HEDDA   *(Pointing towards the inner room)*   Will you not take a glass of cold punch, gentlemen?

BRACK   *(Looking at his watch)*   A stirrup-cup? Yes, it wouldn't come amiss.

TESMAN   A capital idea, Hedda! Just the thing! Now that the weight has been taken off my mind—

HEDDA   Will you not join them, Mr. Lövborg?

LÖVBORG   *(With a gesture of refusal)*   No, thank you. Nothing for me.

BRACK   Why bless me—cold punch is surely not poison.

LÖVBORG   Perhaps not for everyone.

HEDDA   I will keep Mr. Lövborg company in the meantime.

TESMAN   Yes, yes, Hedda dear, do.

He and BRACK *go into the inner room, seat themselves, drink punch, smoke cigarettes, and carry on a lively conversation during what follows.* EILERT LÖVBORG *remains standing beside the stove.* HEDDA *goes to the writing table.*

HEDDA   *(Raising her voice a little)*   Do you care to look at some photographs, Mr. Lövborg? You know Tesman and I made a tour in the Tyrol on our way home?

She takes up an album, and places it on the table beside the sofa, in the further corner of which she seats herself. EILERT LÖVBORG *approaches, stops, and looks at her. Then he takes a chair and seats himself to her left, with his back towards the inner room.*

HEDDA   *(Opening the album)*   Do you see this range of mountains, Mr. Lövborg? It's the Ortler group. Tesman has written the name underneath. Here it is: "The Ortler group near Meran."

LÖVBORG   *(Who has never taken his eyes off her, says softly and slowly)* Hedda—Gabler!

HEDDA   *(Glancing hastily at him)*   Ah! Hush!

LÖVBORG   *(Repeats softly)*   Hedda Gabler!

HEDDA   *(Looking at the album)*   That was my name in the old days— when we two knew each other.

LÖVBORG   And I must teach myself never to say Hedda Gabler again— never, as long as I live.

HEDDA   *(Still turning over the pages)*   Yes, you must. And I think you ought to practice in time. The sooner the better, I should say.

LÖVBORG   *(In a tone of indignation)*   Hedda Gabler married? And married to—George Tesman!

HEDDA   Yes—so the world goes.

LÖVBORG   Oh, Hedda, Hedda—how could you° throw yourself away!

HEDDA   *(Looks sharply at him)*   What? I can't allow this!

LÖVBORG   What do you mean?

TESMAN *comes into the room and goes towards the sofa.*

HEDDA   *(Hears him coming and says in an indifferent tone)*   And this is a view from the Val d'Ampezzo, Mr. Lövborg. Just look at these peaks!   *(Looks affectionately up at* TESMAN*)*   What's the name of these curious peaks, dear?

TESMAN   Let me see. Oh, those are the Dolomites.

HEDDA   Yes, that's it! —Those are the Dolomites, Mr. Lövborg.

TESMAN   Hedda dear, —I only wanted to ask whether I shouldn't bring you a little punch after all? For yourself at any rate—eh?

HEDDA   Yes, do, please; and perhaps a few biscuits.

TESMAN   No cigarettes?

HEDDA   No.

TESMAN   Very well.

He goes into the inner room and out to the right. BRACK *sits in the inner room, and keeps an eye from time to time on* HEDDA *and* LÖVBORG.

°   **You:** He uses the familiar *du.*

LÖVBORG   *(Softly, as before)*   Answer me, Hedda—how could you go and do this?

HEDDA   *(Apparently absorbed in the album)*   If you continue to say *du* to me I won't talk to you.

LÖVBORG   May I not say *du* even when we are alone?

HEDDA   No. You may think it; but you mustn't say it.

LÖVBORG   Ah, I understand. It is an offense against George Tesman, whom you°—love.

HEDDA   *(Glances at him and smiles)*   Love? What an idea!

LÖVBORG   You don't love him then!

HEDDA   But I won't hear of any sort of unfaithfulness! Remember that.

LÖVBORG   Hedda—answer me one thing—

HEDDA   Hush!

TESMAN *enters with a small tray from the inner room.*

TESMAN   Here you are! Isn't this tempting? *(He puts the tray on the table)*

HEDDA   Why do you bring it yourself?

TESMAN   *(Filling the glasses)*   Because I think it's such fun to wait upon you, Hedda.

HEDDA   But you have poured out two glasses. Mr. Lövborg said he wouldn't have any—

TESMAN   No, but Mrs. Elvsted will soon be here, won't she?

HEDDA   Yes, by-the-bye—Mrs. Elvsted—

TESMAN   Had you forgotten her? Eh?

HEDDA   We were so absorbed in these photographs. *(Shows him a picture)*   Do you remember this little village?

TESMAN   Oh, it's that one just below the Brenner Pass. It was there we passed the night—

HEDDA   —and met that lively party of tourists.

TESMAN   Yes, that was the place. Fancy—if we could only have had you with us, Eilert! Eh?

He returns to the inner room and sits beside BRACK.

LÖVBORG   Answer me this one thing, Hedda—

HEDDA   Well?

LÖVBORG   Was there no love in your friendship for me either? Not a spark—not a tinge of love in it?

HEDDA   I wonder if there was? To me it seems as though we were two

---

°   **You:** From this point onward Lövborg uses the formal *De.*

good comrades—two thoroughly intimate friends. *(Smilingly)* You especially were frankness itself.

LÖVBORG   It was you that made me so.

HEDDA   As I look back upon it all, I think there was really something beautiful, something fascinating—something daring—in—in that secret intimacy—that comradeship which no living creature so much as dreamed of.

LÖVBORG   Yes, yes, Hedda! Was there not? —When I used to come to your father's in the afternoon—and the General sat over at the window reading his papers—with his back towards us—

HEDDA   And we two on the corner sofa—

LÖVBORG   Always with the same illustrated paper before us—

HEDDA   For want of an album, yes.

LÖVBORG   Yes, Hedda, and when I made my confessions to you—told you about myself, things that at that time no one else knew! There I would sit and tell you of my escapades—my days and nights of devilment. Oh, Hedda—what was the power in you that forced me to confess these things?

HEDDA   Do you think it was any power in me?

LÖVBORG   How else can I explain it? And all those—those roundabout questions you used to put to me—

HEDDA   Which you understood so particularly well—

LÖVBORG   How could you sit and question me like that? Question me quite frankly—

HEDDA   In roundabout terms, please observe.

LÖVBORG   Yes, but frankly nevertheless. Cross-question me about—all that sort of thing?

HEDDA   And how could you answer, Mr. Lövborg?

LÖVBORG   Yes, that is just what I can't understand—in looking back upon it. But tell me now, Hedda—was there not love at the bottom of our friendship? On your side, did you not feel as though you might purge my stains away—if I made you my confessor? Was it not so?

HEDDA   No, not quite.

LÖVBORG   What was your motive, then?

HEDDA   Do you think it quite incomprehensible that a young girl—when it can be done—without any one knowing—

LÖVBORG   Well?

HEDDA   —should be glad to have a peep, now and then, into a world which—

LÖVBORG   Which—?

HEDDA   —which she is forbidden to know anything about?

LÖVBORG   So that was it?

HEDDA   Partly. Partly—I almost think.

LÖVBORG   Comradeship in the thirst for life. But why should not that, at any rate, have continued?

HEDDA   The fault was yours.

LÖVBORG   It was you that broke with me.

HEDDA   Yes, when our friendship threatened to develop into something more serious. Shame upon you, Eilert Lövborg! How could you think of wronging your—your frank comrade?

LÖVBORG   *(Clenching his hands)*   Oh, why did you not carry out your threat? Why did you not shoot me down?

HEDDA   Because I have such a dread of scandal.

LÖVBORG   Yes, Hedda, you are a coward at heart.

HEDDA   A terrible coward. *(Changing her tone)*   But it was a lucky thing for you. And now you have found ample consolation at the Elvsteds'.

LÖVBORG   I know what Thea has confided to you.

HEDDA   And perhaps you have confided to her something about us?

LÖVBORG   Not a word. She is too stupid to understand anything of that sort.

HEDDA   Stupid?

LÖVBORG   She is stupid about matters of that sort.

HEDDA   And I am cowardly. *(Bends over towards him, without looking him in the face, and says more softly)*   But now I will confide something to you.

LÖVBORG   *(Eagerly)*   Well?

HEDDA   The fact that I dared not shoot you down—

LÖVBORG   Yes!

HEDDA   —that was not my most arrant cowardice—that evening.

LÖVBORG   *(Looks at her a moment, understands, and whispers passionately)*   Oh, Hedda! Hedda Gabler! Now I begin to see a hidden reason beneath our comradeship! You° and I—! After all, then, it was your craving for life—

HEDDA   *(Softly, with a sharp glance)*   Take care! Believe nothing of the sort!

Twilight has begun to fall. The hall door is opened from without by BERTA.

HEDDA   *(Closes the album with a bang and calls smilingly)*   Ah, at last! My darling Thea —come along!

°   **You:** In this speech he once more says *du.* Hedda addresses him throughout as *De.*

MRS. ELVSTED *enters from the hall. She is in evening dress. The door is closed behind her.*

HEDDA   *(On the sofa, stretches out her arms towards her)*   My sweet Thea—you can't think how I have been longing for you!

MRS. ELVSTED, *in passing, exchanges slight salutations with the gentlemen in the inner room, then goes up to the table and gives* HEDDA *her hand.* EILERT LÖVBORG *has risen. He and* MRS. ELVSTED *greet each other with a silent nod.*

MRS. ELVSTED   Ought I to go in and talk to your husband for a moment?

HEDDA   Oh, not at all. Leave those two alone. They will soon be going.

MRS. ELVSTED   Are they going out?

HEDDA   Yes, to a supper party.

MRS. ELVSTED   *(Quickly, to* LÖVBORG*)*   Not you?

LÖVBORG   No.

HEDDA   Mr. Lövborg remains with us.

MRS. ELVSTED   *(Takes a chair and is about to seat herself at his side)*   Oh, how nice it is here!

HEDDA   No, thank you, my little Thea! Not there! You'll be good enough to come over here to me. I will sit between you.

MRS. ELVSTED   Yes, just as you please.

She goes round the table and seats herself on the sofa on HEDDA'S *right.* LÖVBORG *reseats himself on his chair.*

LÖVBORG   *(After a short pause, to* HEDDA*)*   Is not she lovely to look at?

HEDDA   *(Lightly stroking her hair)*   Only to look at?

LÖVBORG   Yes. For we two—she and I—we are two real comrades. We have absolute faith in each other; so we can sit and talk with perfect frankness—

HEDDA   Not round about, Mr. Lövborg?

LÖVBORG   Well—

MRS. ELVSTED   *(Softly clinging close to* HEDDA*)*   Oh, how happy I am, Hedda! For, only think, he says I have inspired him too.

HEDDA   *(Looks at her with a smile)*   Ah! Does he say that, dear?

LÖVBORG   And then she is so brave, Mrs. Tesman!

MRS. ELVSTED   Good heavens—am I brave?

LÖVBORG   Exceedingly—where your comrade is concerned.

HEDDA   Ah yes—courage! If one only had that!

LÖVBORG   What then? What do you mean?

HEDDA   Then life would perhaps be liveable, after all.   *(With a sudden change of tone)*   But now, my dearest Thea, you really must have a glass of cold punch.

MRS. ELVSTED   No, thanks—I never take anything of that kind.

HEDDA   Well then, you, Mr. Lövborg.

LÖVBORG   Nor I, thank you.

MRS. ELVSTED   No, he doesn't either.

HEDDA   *(Looks fixedly at him)*   But if I say you shall?

LÖVBORG   It would be no use.

HEDDA   *(Laughing)*   Then I, poor creature, have no sort of power over you?

LÖVBORG   Not in that respect.

HEDDA   But seriously, I think you ought to—for your own sake.

MRS. ELVSTED   Why, Hedda—!

LÖVBORG   How so?

HEDDA   Or rather on account of other people.

LÖVBORG   Indeed?

HEDDA   Otherwise people might be apt to suspect that—in your heart of hearts—you did not feel quite secure—quite confident in yourself.

MRS. ELVSTED   *(Softly)*   Oh please, Hedda—.

LÖVBORG   People may suspect what they like—for the present.

MRS. ELVSTED   *(Joyfully)*   Yes, let them!

HEDDA   I saw it plainly in Judge Brack's face a moment ago.

LÖVBORG   What did you see?

HEDDA   His contemptuous smile, when you dared not go with them into the inner room.

LÖVBORG   Dared not? Of course I preferred to stop here and talk to you.

MRS. ELVSTED   What could be more natural, Hedda?

HEDDA   But the Judge could not guess that. And I saw, too, the way he smiled and glanced at Tesman when you dared not accept his invitation to this wretched little supper party of his.

LÖVBORG   Dared not! Do you say I dared not?

HEDDA   *I* don't say so. But that was how Judge Brack understood it.

LÖVBORG   Well, let him.

HEDDA   Then you are not going with them?

LÖVBORG   I will stay here with you and Thea.

MRS. ELVSTED   Yes, Hedda—how can you doubt that?

HEDDA   *(Smiles and nods approvingly to* LÖVBORG)   Firm as a rock! Faithful to your principles, now and forever! Ah, that is how a man should be! *(Turns to* MRS. ELVSTED *and caresses her)*   Well now, what did I tell you, when you came to us this morning in such a state of distraction—

LÖVBORG   *(Surprised)*   Distraction!

MRS. ELVSTED   *(Terrified)*   Hedda—oh Hedda—!

HEDDA   You can see for yourself! You haven't the slightest reason to be in such mortal terror—   *(Interrupting herself)*   There! Now we can all three enjoy ourselves!

LÖVBORG   *(Who has given a start)*   Ah—what is all this, Mrs. Tesman?

MRS. ELVSTED   Oh my God, Hedda! What are you saying? What are you doing?

HEDDA   Don't get excited! That horrid Judge Brack is sitting watching you.

LÖVBORG   So she was in mortal terror! On my account!

MRS. ELVSTED   *(Softly and piteously)*   Oh, Hedda—now you have ruined everything!

LÖVBORG   *(Looks fixedly at her for a moment. His face is distorted.)*   So that was my comrade's frank confidence in me?

MRS. ELVSTED   *(Imploringly)*   Oh, my dearest friend—only let me tell you—

LÖVBORG   *(Takes one of the glasses of punch, raises it to his lips, and says in a low, husky voice)*   Your health, Thea!   *(He empties the glass, puts it down, and takes the second.)*

MRS. ELVSTED   *(Softly)*   Oh, Hedda, Hedda—how could you do this?

HEDDA   *I* do it? *I*? Are you crazy?

LÖVBORG   Here's to your health too, Mrs. Tesman. Thanks for the truth. Hurrah for the truth!   *(He empties the glass and is about to refill it.)*

HEDDA   *(Lays her hand on his arm)*   Come, come—no more for the present. Remember you are going out to supper.

MRS. ELVSTED   No, no, no!

HEDDA   Hush! They are sitting watching you.

LÖVBORG   *(Putting down the glass)*   Now, Thea—tell me the truth—

MRS. ELVSTED   Yes.

LÖVBORG   Did your husband know that you had come after me?

MRS. ELVSTED   *(Wringing her hands)*   Oh, Hedda—do you hear what he is asking?

LÖVBORG   Was it arranged between you and him that you were to come to town and look after me? Perhaps it was the Sheriff himself that urged you to come? Aha, my dear—no doubt he wanted my help in his office! Or was it at the card table that he missed me?

MRS. ELVSTED   *(Softly, in agony)*   Oh, Lövborg, Lövborg—!

LÖVBORG   *(Seizes a glass and is on the point of filling it)*   Here's a glass for the old Sheriff too!

HEDDA   *(Preventing him)*   No more just now. Remember, you have to read your manuscript to Tesman.

LÖVBORG   *(Calmly, putting down the glass)*   It was stupid of me, all this, Thea—to take it in this way, I mean. Don't be angry with me, my dear, dear comrade. You shall see—both you and the others—that if I was fallen once—now I have risen again! Thanks to you, Thea.

MRS. ELVSTED   *(Radiant with joy)*   Oh, heaven be praised—!

BRACK *has in the meantime looked at his watch. He and* TESMAN *rise and come into the drawing room.*

BRACK   *(Takes his hat and overcoat)*   Well, Mrs. Tesman, our time has come.

HEDDA   I suppose it has.

LÖVBORG   *(Rising)*   Mine too, Judge Brack.

MRS. ELVSTED   *(Softly and imploringly)*   Oh, Lövborg, don't do it!

HEDDA   *(Pinching her arm)*   They can hear you!

MRS. ELVSTED   *(With a suppressed shriek)*   Ow!

LÖVBORG   *(To* BRACK)   You were good enough to invite me.

BRACK   Well, are you coming after all?

LÖVBORG   Yes, many thanks.

BRACK   I'm delighted—

LÖVBORG   *(To* TESMAN, *putting the parcel of M.S. in his pocket)*   I should like to show you one or two things before I send it to the printers.

TESMAN   Fancy—that will be delightful. But, Hedda dear, how is Mrs. Elvsted to get home? Eh?

HEDDA   Oh, that can be managed somehow.

LÖVBORG   *(Looking towards the ladies)*   Mrs. Elvsted? Of course, I'll come again and fetch her. *(Approaching)*   At ten or thereabouts, Mrs. Tesman? Will that do?

HEDDA   Certainly. That will do capitally.

TESMAN   Well, then, that's all right. But you must not expect me so early, Hedda.

HEDDA   Oh, you may stop as long—as long as ever you please.

MRS. ELVSTED   *(Trying to conceal her anxiety)*   Well then, Mr. Lövborg—I shall remain here until you come.

LÖVBORG   *(With his hat in his hand)*   Pray do, Mrs. Elvsted.

BRACK   And now off goes the excursion train, gentlemen! I hope we shall have a lively time, as a certain fair lady puts it.

HEDDA   Ah, if only the fair lady could be present unseen—!

BRACK   Why unseen?

HEDDA   In order to hear a little of your liveliness at first hand, Judge Brack.

BRACK   *(Laughing)*   I should not advise the fair lady to try it.

TESMAN   *(Also laughing)*   Come, you're a nice one, Hedda! Fancy that!

BRACK   Well, good-bye, good-bye, ladies.

LÖVBORG   *(Bowing)* About ten o'clock, then.

BRACK, LÖVBORG, and TESMAN go out by the hall door. At the same time, BERTA enters from the inner room with a lighted lamp, which she places on the drawing room table; she goes out by the way she came.

MRS. ELVSTED   *(Who has risen and is wandering restlessly about the room)* Hedda—Hedda—what will come of all this?

HEDDA   At ten o'clock—he will be here. I can see him already—with vine leaves in his hair—flushed and fearless—

MRS. ELVSTED   Oh, I hope he may.

HEDDA   And then, you see—then he will have regained control over himself. Then he will be a free man for all his days.

MRS. ELVSTED   Oh God! —if he would only come as you see him now!

HEDDA   He will come as I see him—so, and not otherwise! *(Rises and approaches* THEA) You may doubt him as long as you please; *I* believe in him. And now we will try—

MRS. ELVSTED   You have some hidden motive in this, Hedda!

HEDDA   Yes, I have. I want for once in my life to have power to mould a human destiny.

MRS. ELVSTED   Have you not the power?

HEDDA   I have not—and have never had it.

MRS. ELVSTED   Not your husband's?

HEDDA   Do you think that is worth the trouble? Oh, if you could only understand how poor I am. And fate has made you so rich! *(Clasps her passionately in her arms)* I think I must burn your hair off, after all.

MRS. ELVSTED   Let me go! Let me go! I am afraid of you, Hedda!

BERTA   *(In the middle doorway)* Tea is laid in the dining room, ma'am.

HEDDA   Very well. We are coming.

MRS. ELVSTED   No, no, no! I would rather go home alone! At once!

HEDDA   Nonsense! First you shall have a cup of tea, you little stupid. And then—at ten o'clock—Eilert Lövborg will be here—with vine leaves in his hair.

She drags MRS. ELVSTED *almost by force towards the middle doorway.*

ACT III

The room at the TESMANS'. *The curtains are drawn over the middle doorway, and also over the glass door. The lamp, half turned down, and with a shade over it, is burning on the table. In the stove, the door of which stands open, there has been a fire, which is nearly burnt out.*

MRS. ELVSTED, *wrapped in a large shawl, and with her feet upon a foot rest sits close to the stove, sunk back in the arm chair.* HEDDA, *fully dressed, lies sleeping upon the sofa, with a sofa blanket over her.*

MRS. ELVSTED   *(After a pause, suddenly sits up in her chair and listens eagerly. Then she sinks back again wearily, moaning to herself.)*   Not yet! —Oh God—oh God—not yet!

BERTA *slips cautiously in by the hall door. She has a letter in her hand.*

MRS. ELVSTED   *(Turns and whispers eagerly)*   Well—has any one come?
BERTA   *(Softly)*   Yes, a girl has just brought this letter.
MRS. ELVSTED   *(Quickly, holding out her hand)*   A letter! Give it to me!
BERTA   No, it's for Dr. Tesman, ma'am.
MRS. ELVSTED   Oh, indeed.
BERTA   It was Miss Tesman's servant that brought it. I'll lay it here on the table.
MRS. ELVSTED   Yes, do.
BERTA   *(Laying down the letter)*   I think I had better put out the lamp. It's smoking.
MRS. ELVSTED   Yes, put it out. It must soon be daylight now.
BERTA   *(Putting out the lamp)*   It is daylight already, ma'am.
MRS. ELVSTED   Yes, broad day! And no one come back yet—!
BERTA   Lord bless you, ma'am—I guessed how it would be.
MRS. ELVSTED   You guessed?
BERTA   Yes, when I saw that a certain person had come back to town —and that he went off with them. For we've heard enough about the gentleman before now.
MRS. ELVSTED   Don't speak so loud. You will waken Mrs. Tesman.
BERTA   *(Looks towards the sofa and sighs)*   No, no—let her sleep, poor thing. Shan't I put some wood on the fire?
MRS. ELVSTED   Thanks, not for me.
BERTA   Oh, very well. *(She goes softly out by the hall door.)*
HEDDA   *(Is wakened by the shutting of the door, and looks up)*   What's that—?

MRS. ELVSTED   It was only the servant—

HEDDA   *(Looking about her)*   Oh, we're here—! Yes, now I remember. *(Sits erect upon the sofa, stretches herself, and rubs her eyes)*   What time is it, Thea?

MRS. ELVSTED   *(Looks at her watch)*   It's past seven.

HEDDA   When did Tesman come home?

MRS. ELVSTED   He has not come.

HEDDA   Not come home yet?

MRS. ELVSTED   *(Rising)*   No one has come.

HEDDA   Think of our watching and waiting here till four in the morning—

MRS. ELVSTED   *(Wringing her hands)*   And how I watched and waited for him!

HEDDA   *(Yawns, and says with her hand before her mouth)*   Well well —we might have spared ourselves the trouble.

MRS. ELVSTED   Did you get a little sleep?

HEDDA   Oh yes; I believe I have slept pretty well. Have you not?

MRS. ELVSTED   Not for a moment. I couldn't, Hedda! —not to save my life.

HEDDA   *(Rises and goes towards her)*   There there there! There's nothing to be so alarmed about. I understand quite well what has happened.

MRS. ELVSTED   Well, what do you think? Won't you tell me?

HEDDA   Why, of course it has been a very late affair at Judge Brack's—

MRS. ELVSTED   Yes, yes—that is clear enough. But all the same—

HEDDA   And then, you see, Tesman hasn't cared to come home and ring us up in the middle of the night. *(Laughing)*   Perhaps he wasn't inclined to show himself either—immediately after a jollification.

MRS. ELVSTED   But in that case—where can he have gone?

HEDDA   Of course he has gone to his Aunts' and slept there. They have his old room ready for him.

MRS. ELVSTED   No, he can't be with them; for a letter has just come for him from Miss Tesman. There it lies.

HEDDA   Indeed? *(Looks at the address)*   Why yes, it's addressed in Aunt Julia's own hand. Well then, he has remained at Judge Brack's. And as for Eilert Lövborg—he is sitting, with vine leaves in his hair, reading his manuscript.

MRS. ELVSTED   Oh Hedda, you are just saying things you don't believe a bit.

HEDDA   You really are a little blockhead, Thea.

MRS. ELVSTED   Oh yes, I suppose I am.

HEDDA   And how mortally tired you look.

MRS. ELVSTED   Yes, I am mortally tired.

HEDDA   Well then, you must do as I tell you. You must go into my room and lie down for a little while.

MRS. ELVSTED   Oh no, no—I shouldn't be able to sleep.

HEDDA   I am sure you would.

MRS. ELVSTED   Well, but your husband is certain to come soon now; and then I want to know at once—

HEDDA   I shall take care to let you know when he comes.

MRS. ELVSTED   Do you promise me, Hedda?

HEDDA   Yes, rely upon me. Just you go in and have a sleep in the meantime.

MRS. ELVSTED   Thanks; then I'll try to. *(She goes off through the inner room.)*

HEDDA *goes up to the glass door and draws back the curtains. The broad daylight streams into the room. Then she takes a little hand glass from the writing table, looks at herself in it, and arranges her hair. Next she goes to the hall door and presses the bell-button.*
    BERTA *presently appears at the hall door.*

BERTA   Did you want anything, ma'am?

HEDDA   Yes; you must put some more wood in the stove. I am shivering.

BERTA   Bless me—I'll make up the fire at once.   *(She rakes the embers together and lays a piece of wood upon them; then stops and listens.)*   That was a ring at the front door, ma'am.

HEDDA   Then go to the door. I will look after the fire.

BERTA   It'll soon burn up.   *(She goes out by the hall door.)*

HEDDA *kneels on the foot rest and lays some more pieces of wood in the stove.*
    After a short pause, GEORGE TESMAN *enters from the hall. He looks tired and rather serious. He steals on tiptoe towards the middle doorway and is about to slip through the curtains.*

HEDDA   *(At the stove, without looking up)*   Good morning.

TESMAN   *(Turns)* Hedda! *(Approaching her)* Good heavens—are you up so early? Eh?

HEDDA   Yes, I am up very early this morning.

TESMAN   And I never doubted you were still sound asleep. Fancy that, Hedda!

HEDDA   Don't speak so loud. Mrs. Elvsted is resting in my room.

TESMAN   Has Mrs. Elvsted been here all night?

HEDDA   Yes, since no one came to fetch her.

TESMAN   Ah, to be sure.

HEDDA   *(Closes the door of the stove and rises)*   Well, did you enjoy yourself at Judge Brack's?

TESMAN   Have you been anxious about me? Eh?

HEDDA   No, I should never think of being anxious. But I asked if you had enjoyed yourself.

TESMAN   Oh yes, —for once in a way. Especially the beginning of the evening; for then Eilert read me part of his book. We arrived more than an hour too early—fancy that! And Brack had all sorts of arrangements to make—so Eilert read to me.

HEDDA   *(Seating herself by the table on the right)*   Well? Tell me, then—

TESMAN   *(Sitting on a footstool near the stove)*   Oh Hedda, you can't conceive what a book that is going to be! I believe it is one of the most remarkable things that have ever been written. Fancy that!

HEDDA   Yes, yes; I don't care about that—

TESMAN   I must make a confession to you, Hedda. When he had finished reading—a horrid feeling came over me.

HEDDA   A horrid feeling?

TESMAN   I felt jealous of Eilert for having had it in him to write such a book. Only think, Hedda!

HEDDA   Yes, yes, I am thinking!

TESMAN   And then how pitiful to think that he—with all his gifts—should be irreclaimable, after all.

HEDDA   I suppose you mean that he has more courage than the rest?

TESMAN   No, not at all—I mean that he is incapable of taking his pleasures in moderation.

HEDDA   And what came of it all—in the end?

TESMAN   Well, to tell the truth, I think it might best be described as an orgy, Hedda.

HEDDA   Had he vine leaves in his hair?

TESMAN   Vine leaves? No, I saw nothing of the sort. But he made a long, rambling speech in honor of the woman who had inspired him in his work—that was the phrase he used.

HEDDA   Did he name her?

TESMAN   No, he didn't; but I can't help thinking he meant Mrs. Elvsted. You may be sure he did.

HEDDA   Well—where did you part from him?

TESMAN   On the way to town. We broke up—the last of us at any rate —all together; and Brack came with us to get a breath of fresh air. And then, you see, we agreed to take Eilert home; for he had had far more than was good for him.

HEDDA   I daresay.

TESMAN   But now comes the strange part of it, Hedda; or, I should rather say, the melancholy part of it. I declare I am almost ashamed—on Eilert's account—to tell you—

HEDDA   Oh, go on—!

TESMAN   Well, as we were getting near town, you see, I happened to drop a little behind the others. Only for a minute or two—fancy that!

HEDDA   Yes yes yes, but—?

TESMAN   And then, as I hurried after them—what do you think I found by the wayside? Eh?

HEDDA   Oh, how should I know!

TESMAN   You mustn't speak of it to a soul, Hedda! Do you hear! Promise me, for Eilert's sake. *(Draws a parcel, wrapped in paper, from his coat pocket)*   Fancy, dear—I found this.

HEDDA   Is not that the parcel he had with him yesterday?

TESMAN   Yes, it is the whole of his precious, irreplaceable manuscript! And he had gone and lost it, and knew nothing about it. Only fancy, Hedda! So deplorably—

HEDDA   But why did you not give him back the parcel at once?

TESMAN   I didn't dare to—in the state he was then in—

HEDDA   Did you not tell any of the others that you had found it?

TESMAN   Oh, far from it! You can surely understand that, for Eilert's sake, I wouldn't do that.

HEDDA   So no one knows that Eilert Lövborg's manuscript is in your possession?

TESMAN   No. And no one must know it.

HEDDA   Then what did you say to him afterwards?

TESMAN   I didn't talk to him again at all; for when we got in among the streets, he and two or three of the others gave us the slip and disappeared. Fancy that!

HEDDA   Indeed! They must have taken him home then.

TESMAN   Yes, so it would appear. And Brack, too, left us.

HEDDA   And what have you been doing with yourself since?

TESMAN   Well, I and some of the others went home with one of the party, a jolly fellow, and took our morning coffee with him; or perhaps I should rather call it our night coffee—eh? But now, when I have rested a little, and given Eilert, poor fellow, time to have his sleep out, I must take this back to him.

HEDDA   *(Holds out her hand for the packet)*   No—don't give it to him! Not in such a hurry, I mean. Let me read it first.

TESMAN   No, my dearest Hedda, I mustn't, I really mustn't.

HEDDA   You must not?

TESMAN   No—for you can imagine what a state of despair he will be in when he wakens and misses the manuscript. He has no copy of it, you must know! He told me so.

HEDDA   *(Looking searchingly at him)*   Can such a thing not be reproduced? Written over again?

TESMAN   No, I don't think that would be possible. For the inspiration, you see—

HEDDA   Yes, yes—I suppose it depends on that—   *(Lightly)*   But, by-the-bye—here is a letter for you.

TESMAN   Fancy—!

HEDDA   *(Handing it to him)*   It came early this morning.

TESMAN   It's from Aunt Julia! What can it be? *(He lays the packet on the other footstool, opens the letter, runs his eye through it, and jumps up.)*   Oh, Hedda,—she says that poor Aunt Rina is dying!

HEDDA   Well, we were prepared for that.

TESMAN   And that if I want to see her again, I must make haste. I'll run in to them at once.

HEDDA   *(Suppressing a smile)*   Will you run?

TESMAN   Oh, my dearest Hedda—if you could only make up your mind to come with me! Just think!

HEDDA   *(Rises and says wearily, repelling the idea)*   No, no, don't ask me. I will not look upon sickness and death. I loathe all sorts of ugliness.

TESMAN   Well, well, then—! *(Bustling around)*   My hat—? My overcoat—? Oh, in the hall—. I do hope I mayn't come too late, Hedda! Eh?

HEDDA   Oh, if you run—

BERTA *appears at the hall door.*

BERTA   Judge Brack is at the door, and wishes to know if he may come in.

TESMAN   At this time! No, I can't possibly see him.

HEDDA   But I can. *(To BERTA)*   Ask Judge Brack to come in.

BERTA *goes out.*

HEDDA   *(Quickly, whispering)*   The parcel, Tesman! *(She snatches it up from the stool.)*

TESMAN   Yes, give it to me!

HEDDA   No, no, I will keep it till you come back.

She goes to the writing table and places it in the bookcase. TESMAN *stands in a flurry of haste, and cannot get his gloves on.*
   JUDGE BRACK *enters from the hall.*

HEDDA   *(Nodding to him)*   You are an early bird, I must say.

BRACK   Yes, don't you think so? *(To TESMAN)*   Are you on the move, too?

TESMAN   Yes, I must rush off to my aunts'. Fancy—the invalid one is lying at death's door, poor creature.

BRACK   Dear me, is she indeed? Then on no account let me detain you. At such a critical moment—

TESMAN   Yes, I must really rush— Good-bye! Good-bye! *(He hastens out by the hall door.)*

HEDDA   *(Approaching)* You seem to have made a particularly lively night of it at your rooms, Judge Brack.

BRACK   I assure you I have not had my clothes off, Mrs. Hedda.

HEDDA   Not you, either?

BRACK   No, as you may see. But what has Tesman been telling you of the night's adventures?

HEDDA   Oh, some tiresome story. Only that they went and had coffee somewhere or other.

BRACK   I have heard about that coffee party already. Eilert Lövborg was not with them, I fancy?

HEDDA   No, they had taken him home before that.

BRACK   Tesman too?

HEDDA   No, but some of the others, he said.

BRACK   *(Smiling)* George Tesman is really an ingenuous creature, Mrs. Hedda.

HEDDA   Yes, heaven knows he is. Then is there something behind all this?

BRACK   Yes, perhaps there may be.

HEDDA   Well then, sit down, my dear Judge, and tell your story in comfort. *(She seats herself to the left of the table.* BRACK *sits near her, at the long side of the table.)*

HEDDA   Now then?

BRACK   I had special reasons for keeping track of my guests—or rather of some of my guests—last night.

HEDDA   Of Eilert Lövborg among the rest, perhaps?

BRACK   Frankly—yes.

HEDDA   Now you make me really curious—

BRACK   Do you know where he and one or two of the others finished the night, Mrs. Hedda?

HEDDA   If it is not quite unmentionable, tell me.

BRACK   Oh no, it's not at all unmentionable. Well, they put in an appearance at a particularly animated soirée.

HEDDA   Of the lively kind?

BRACK   Of the very liveliest—

HEDDA   Tell me more of this, Judge Brack—

BRACK   Lövborg, as well as the others, had been invited in advance. I knew all about it. But he had declined the invitation; for now, as you know, he has become a new man.

HEDDA   Up at the Elvsteds', yes. But he went after all, then?

BRACK   Well, you see, Mrs. Hedda—unhappily the spirit moved him at my rooms last evening—

HEDDA   Yes, I hear he found inspiration.

BRACK   Pretty violent inspiration. Well, I fancy that altered his purpose; for we menfolk are unfortunately not always so firm in our principles as we ought to be.

HEDDA   Oh, I am sure you are an exception, Judge Brack. But as to Lövborg—?

BRACK   To make a long story short—he landed at last in Mademoiselle Diana's rooms.

HEDDA   Mademoiselle Diana's?

BRACK   It was Mademoiselle Diana that was giving the soirée, to a select circle of her admirers and her lady friends.

HEDDA   Is she a red-haired woman?

BRACK   Precisely.

HEDDA   A sort of a—singer?

BRACK   Oh yes—in her leisure moments. And moreover a mighty huntress—of men—Mrs. Hedda. You have no doubt heard of her. Eilert Lövborg was one of her most enthusiastic protectors—in the days of his glory.

HEDDA   And how did all this end?

BRACK   Far from amicably, it appears. After a most tender meeting, they seem to have come to blows—

HEDDA   Lövborg and she?

BRACK   Yes. He accused her or her friends of having robbed him. He declared that his pocket-book had disappeared—and other things as well. In short, he seems to have made a furious disturbance.

HEDDA   And what came of it all?

BRACK   It came to a general scrimmage, in which the ladies as well as the gentlemen took part. Fortunately the police at last appeared on the scene.

HEDDA   The police too?

BRACK   Yes. I fancy it will prove a costly frolic for Eilert Lövborg, crazy being that he is.

HEDDA   How so?

BRACK   He seems to have made a violent resistance—to have hit one of the constables on the head and torn the coat off his back. So they had to march him off to the police station with the rest.

HEDDA   How have you learnt all this?

BRACK   From the police themselves.

HEDDA   *(Gazing straight before her)* So that is what happened. Then he had no vine leaves in his hair.

BRACK   Vine leaves, Mrs. Hedda?

HEDDA   *(Changing her tone)* But tell me now, Judge—what is your real reason for tracking out Eilert Lövborg's movements so carefully?

BRACK   In the first place, it could not be entirely indifferent to me if it should appear in the police court that he came straight from my house.

HEDDA   Will the matter come into court then?

BRACK   Of course. However, I should scarcely have troubled so much about that. But I thought that, as a friend of the family, it was my duty to supply you and Tesman with a full account of his nocturnal exploits.

HEDDA   Why so, Judge Brack?

BRACK   Why, because I have a shrewd suspicion that he intends to use you as a sort of blind.

HEDDA   Oh, how can you think such a thing!

BRACK   Good heavens, Mrs. Hedda—we have eyes in our head. Mark my words! This Mrs. Elvsted will be in no hurry to leave town again.

HEDDA   Well, even if there should be anything between them, I suppose there are plenty of other places where they could meet.

BRACK   Not a single home. Henceforth, as before, every respectable house will be closed against Eilert Lövborg.

HEDDA   And so ought mine to be, you mean?

BRACK   Yes. I confess it would be more than painful to me if this personage were to be made free of your house. How superfluous, how intrusive he would be, if he were to force his way into—

HEDDA   —into the triangle?

BRACK   Precisely. It would simply mean that I should find myself homeless.

HEDDA   *(Looks at him with a smile)*   So you want to be the one cock in the basket—that is your aim.

BRACK   *(Nods slowly and lowers his voice)*   Yes, that is my aim. And for that I will fight—with every weapon I can command.

HEDDA   *(Her smile vanishing)*   I see you are a dangerous person—when it comes to the point.

BRACK   Do you think so?

HEDDA   I am beginning to think so. And I am exceedingly glad to think—that you have no sort of hold over me.

BRACK   *(Laughing equivocally)*   Well, well, Mrs. Hedda—perhaps you are right there. If I had, who knows what I might be capable of?

HEDDA   Come, come now, Judge Brack! That sounds almost like a threat.

BRACK   *(Rising)*   Oh, not at all! The triangle, you know, ought, if possible, to be spontaneously constructed.

HEDDA   There I agree with you.

BRACK   Well, now I have said all I had to say; and I had better be getting back to town. Good-bye, Mrs. Hedda. *(He goes towards the glass door.)*

HEDDA   *(Rising)*   Are you going through the garden?
BRACK   Yes, it's a short cut for me.
HEDDA   And then it is a back way, too.
BRACK   Quite so. I have no objection to back ways. They may be piquant enough at times.
HEDDA   When there is ball practice going on, you mean?
BRACK   *(In the doorway, laughing to her)*   Oh, people don't shoot their tame poultry, I fancy.
HEDDA   *(Also laughing)*   Oh no, when there is only one cock in the basket—

They exchange laughing nods of farewell. He goes. She closes the door behind him.

   HEDDA, *who has become quite serious, stands for a moment looking out. Presently she goes and peeps through the curtain over the middle doorway. Then she goes to the writing table, takes* LÖVBORG'S *packet out of the bookcase, and is on the point of looking through its contents.* BERTA *is heard speaking loudly in the hall.* HEDDA *turns and listens. Then she hastily locks up the packet in the drawer, and lays the key on the inkstand.*

   EILERT LÖVBORG, *with his greatcoat on and his hat in his hand, tears open the hall door. He looks somewhat confused and irritated.*

LÖVBORG   *(Looking towards the hall)*   And I tell you I must and will come in! There!   *(He closes the door, turns, sees* HEDDA, *at once regains his self-control, and bows.)*
HEDDA   *(At the writing table)*   Well, Mr. Lövborg, this is rather a late hour to call for Thea.
LÖVBORG   You mean rather an early hour to call on you. Pray pardon me.
HEDDA   How do you know that she is still here?
LÖVBORG   They told me at her lodgings that she had been out all night.
HEDDA   *(Going to the oval table)*   Did you notice anything about the people of the house when they said that?
LÖVBORG   *(Looks inquiringly at her)*   Notice anything about them?
HEDDA   I mean, did they seem to think it odd?
LÖVBORG   *(Suddenly understanding)*   Oh yes, of course! I am dragging her down with me! However, I didn't notice anything. —I suppose Tesman is not up yet?
HEDDA   No—I think not—
LÖVBORG   When did he come home?
HEDDA   Very late.
LÖVBORG   Did he tell you anything?

HEDDA   Yes, I gathered that you had had an exceedingly jolly evening at Judge Brack's.

LÖVBORG   Nothing more?

HEDDA   I don't think so. However, I was so dreadfully sleepy—

MRS. ELVSTED *enters through the curtains of the middle doorway.*

MRS. ELVSTED   *(Going towards him)*   Ah, Lövborg! At last—!

LÖVBORG   Yes, at last. And too late!

MRS. ELVSTED   *(Looks anxiously at him)*   What is too late?

LÖVBORG   Everything is too late now. It is all over with me.

MRS. ELVSTED   Oh no, no—don't say that!

LÖVBORG   You will say the same when you hear—

MRS. ELVSTED   I won't hear anything!

HEDDA   Perhaps you would prefer to talk to her alone! If so, I will leave you.

LÖVBORG   No, stay—you too. I beg you to stay.

MRS. ELVSTED   Yes, but I won't hear anything, I tell you.

LÖVBORG   It is not last night's adventures that I want to talk about.

MRS. ELVSTED   What is it then—?

LÖVBORG   I want to say that now our ways must part.

MRS. ELVSTED   Part!

HEDDA   *(Involuntarily)*   I knew it!

LÖVBORG   You can be of no more service to me, Thea.

MRS. ELVSTED   How can you stand there and say that! No more service to you! Am I not to help you now, as before? Are we not to go on working together?

LÖVBORG   Henceforward I shall do no work.

MRS. ELVSTED   *(Despairingly)*   Then what am I to do with my life?

LÖVBORG   You must try to live your life as if you had never known me.

MRS. ELVSTED   But you know I cannot do that!

LÖVBORG   Try if you cannot, Thea. You must go home again—

MRS. ELVSTED   *(In vehement protest)*   Never in this world! Where you are, there will I be also! I will not let myself be driven away like this! I will remain here! I will be with you when the book appears.

HEDDA   *(Half aloud, in suspense)*   Ah yes—the book!

LÖVBORG   *(Looks at her)*   My book and Thea's; for that is what it is.

MRS. ELVSTED   Yes, I feel that it is. And that is why I have a right to be with you when it appears! I will see with my own eyes how respect and honor pour in upon you afresh. And the happiness—the happiness—oh, I must share it with you!

LÖVBORG   Thea—our book will never appear.

HEDDA   Ah!

MRS. ELVSTED   Never appear!

LÖVBORG   Can never appear.

MRS. ELVSTED   *(In agonized foreboding)*   Lövborg—what have you done with the manuscript?

HEDDA   *(Looks anxiously at him)*   Yes, the manuscript—?

MRS. ELVSTED   Where is it?

LÖVBORG   Oh Thea—don't ask me about it!

MRS. ELVSTED   Yes, yes, I will know. I demand to be told at once.

LÖVBORG   The manuscript—. Well then—I have torn the manuscript into a thousand pieces.

MRS. ELVSTED   *(Shrieks)*   Oh no, no—!

HEDDA   *(Involuntarily)*   But that's not—

LÖVBORG   *(Looks at her)*   Not true, you think?

HEDDA   *(Collecting herself)*   Oh well, of course—since you say so. But it sounded so improbable—

LÖVBORG   It is true, all the same.

MRS. ELVSTED   *(Wringing her hands)*   Oh God—oh God, Hedda —torn his own work to pieces!

LÖVBORG   I have torn my own life to pieces. So why should I not tear my life-work too—?

MRS. ELVSTED   And you did this last night?

LÖVBORG   Yes, I tell you! Tore it into a thousand pieces—and scattered them on the fiord—far out. There there is cool sea water at any rate —let them drift upon it—drift with the current and the wind. And then presently they will sink—deeper and deeper—as I shall, Thea.

MRS. ELVSTED   Do you know, Lövborg, that what you have done with the book—I shall think of it to my dying day as though you had killed a little child.

LÖVBORG   Yes, you are right. It is a sort of child murder.

MRS. ELVSTED   How could you, then—! Did not the child belong to me too?

HEDDA   *(Almost inaudibly)*   Ah, the child—

MRS. ELVSTED   *(Breathing heavily)*   It is all over then. Well well, now I will go, Hedda.

HEDDA   But you are not going away from town?

MRS. ELVSTED   Oh, I don't know what I shall do. I see nothing but darkness before me.   *(She goes out by the hall door.)*

HEDDA   *(Stands waiting for a moment)*   So you are not going to see her home, Mr. Lövborg?

LÖVBORG   I? Through the streets? Would you have people see her walking with me?

HEDDA   Of course I don't know what else may have happened last night. But is it so utterly irretrievable?

LÖVBORG   It will not end with last night—I know that perfectly well. And the thing is that now I have no taste for that sort of life either. I won't begin it anew. She has broken my courage and my power of braving life out.

HEDDA   *(Looking straight before her)*   So that pretty little fool has had her fingers in a man's destiny.   *(Looks at him)*   But all the same, how could you treat her so heartlessly.

LÖVBORG   Oh, don't say that it was heartless!

HEDDA   To go and destroy what has filled her whole soul for months and years! You do not call that heartless!

LÖVBORG   To you I can tell the truth, Hedda.

HEDDA   The truth?

LÖVBORG   First promise me—give me your word—that what I now confide to you Thea shall never know.

HEDDA   I give you my word.

LÖVBORG   Good. Then let me tell you that what I said just now was untrue.

HEDDA   About the manuscript?

LÖVBORG   Yes. I have not torn it to pieces—nor thrown it into the fiord.

HEDDA   No, no—. But—where is it then?

LÖVBORG   I have destroyed it none the less—utterly destroyed it, Hedda!

HEDDA   I don't understand.

LÖVBORG   Thea said that what I had done seemed to her like a child murder.

HEDDA   Yes, so she said.

LÖVBORG   But to kill his child—that is not the worst thing a father can do to it.

HEDDA   Not the worst?

LÖVBORG   No. I wanted to spare Thea from hearing the worst.

HEDDA   Then what is the worst?

LÖVBORG   Suppose now, Hedda, that a man—in the small hours of the morning—came home to his child's mother after a night of riot and debauchery, and said: "Listen—I have been here and there—in this place and in that. And I have taken our child with me—to this place and to that. And I have lost the child—utterly lost it. The devil knows into what hands it may have fallen—who may have had their clutches on it."

HEDDA   Well—but when all is said and done, you know—this was only a book—

LÖVBORG   Thea's pure soul was in that book.

HEDDA   Yes, so I understand.

LÖVBORG   And you can understand, too, that for her and me together no future is possible.

HEDDA   What path do you mean to take then?

Lövborg   None. I will only try to make an end of it all—the sooner the better.

Hedda   *(A step nearer him)* Eilert Lövborg—listen to me. —Will you not try to—to do it beautifully?

Lövborg   Beautifully? *(Smiling)* With vine leaves in my hair, as you used to dream in the old days—?

Hedda   —No, no. I have lost my faith in the vine leaves. But beautifully nevertheless! For once in a way! —Good-bye! You must go now— and do not come here any more.

Lövborg   Good-bye, Mrs. Tesman. And give George Tesman my love. *(He is on the point of going.)*

Hedda   No, wait! I must give you a memento to take with you. *(She goes to the writing table and opens the drawer and the pistol case; then returns to* Lövborg *with one of the pistols.)*

Lövborg   *(Looks at her)* This? Is this the memento?

Hedda   *(Nodding slowly)* Do you recognize it? It was aimed at you once.

Lövborg   You should have used it then.

Hedda   Take it—and do you use it now.

Lövborg   *(Puts the pistol in his breast pocket)* Thanks!

Hedda   And beautifully, Eilert Lövborg. Promise me that!

Lövborg   Good-bye, Hedda Gabler. *(He goes out by the hall door.)*

Hedda *listens for a moment at the door. Then she goes up to the writing table, takes out the packet of manuscript, peeps under the cover, draws a few of the sheets half out, and looks at them. Next she goes over and seats herself in the armchair beside the stove, with the packet in her lap. Presently she opens the stove door, and then the packet.*

Hedda   *(Throws one of the quires into the fire and whispers to herself)* Now I am burning your child, Thea!—Burning it, curly-locks! *(Throwing one or two more quires into the stove)* Your child and Eilert Lövborg's. *(Throws the rest in)* I am burning—I am burning your child.

ACT IV

The same rooms at the Tesmans'. *It is evening. The drawing room is in darkness. The back room is lighted by the hanging lamp over the table. The curtains over the glass door are drawn close.*

HEDDA, *dressed in black, walks to and fro in the dark room. Then she goes into the back room and disappears for a moment to the left. She is heard to strike a few chords on the piano. Presently she comes in sight again, and returns to the drawing room.*

BERTA *enters from the right, through the inner room, with a lighted lamp, which she places on the table in front of the corner settee in the drawing room. Her eyes are red with weeping, and she has black ribbons in her cap. She goes quietly and circumspectly out to the right.* HEDDA *goes up to the glass door, lifts the curtain a little aside, and looks out into the darkness.*

Shortly afterwards, MISS TESMAN, *in mourning, with a bonnet and veil on, comes in from the hall.* HEDDA *goes towards her and holds out her hand.*

MISS TESMAN   Yes, Hedda, here I am, in mourning and forlorn; for now my poor sister has at last found peace.

HEDDA   I have heard the news already, as you see. Tesman sent me a card.

MISS TESMAN   Yes, he promised me he would. But nevertheless I thought that to Hedda—here in the house of life—I ought myself to bring the tidings of death.

HEDDA   That was very kind of you.

MISS TESMAN   Ah, Rina ought not to have left us just now. This is not the time for Hedda's house to be a house of mourning.

HEDDA   *(Changing the subject)*   She died quite peacefully, did she not, Miss Tesman?

MISS TESMAN   Oh, her end was so calm, so beautiful. And then she had the unspeakable happiness of seeing George once more—and bidding him good-bye. —Has he not come home yet?

HEDDA   No. He wrote that he might be detained. But won't you sit down?

MISS TESMAN   No thank you, my dear, dear Hedda. I should like to, but I have so much to do. I must prepare my dear one for her rest as well as I can. She shall go to her grave looking her best.

HEDDA   Can I not help you in any way?

MISS TESMAN   Oh, you must not think of it! Hedda Tesman must have no hand in such mournful work. Nor let her thoughts dwell on it either —not at this time.

HEDDA   One is not always mistress of one's thoughts—

MISS TESMAN   *(Continuing)*   Ah yes, it is the way of the world. At home we shall be sewing a shroud; and here there will soon be sewing too, I suppose—but of another sort, thank God!

GEORGE TESMAN *enters by the hall door.*

HEDDA   Ah, you have come at last!

TESMAN   You here, Aunt Julia? With Hedda? Fancy that!

MISS TESMAN   I was just going, my dear boy. Well, have you done all you promised?

TESMAN   No; I'm really afraid I have forgotten half of it. I must come to you again tomorrow. Today my brain is all in a whirl. I can't keep my thoughts together.

MISS TESMAN   Why, my dear George, you mustn't take it in this way.

TESMAN   Mustn't—? How do you mean?

MISS TESMAN   Even in your sorrow you must rejoice, as I do—rejoice that she is at rest.

TESMAN   Oh yes, yes—you are thinking of Aunt Rina.

HEDDA   You will feel lonely now, Miss Tesman.

MISS TESMAN   Just at first, yes. But that will not last very long, I hope. I daresay I shall soon find an occupant for poor Rina's little room.

TESMAN   Indeed? Who do you think will take it? Eh?

MISS TESMAN   Oh, there's always some poor invalid or other in want of nursing, unfortunately.

HEDDA   Would you really take such a burden upon you again?

MISS TESMAN   A burden! Heaven forgive you, child—it has been no burden to me.

HEDDA   But suppose you had a total stranger on your hands—

MISS TESMAN   Oh, one soon makes friends with sick folk; and it's such an absolute necessity for me to have someone to live for. Well, heaven be praised, there may soon be something in this house, too, to keep an old aunt busy.

HEDDA   Oh, don't trouble about anything here.

TESMAN   Yes, just fancy what a nice time we three might have together, if—

HEDDA   If—?

TESMAN   *(Uneasily)* Oh, nothing. It will all come right. Let us hope so —eh?

MISS TESMAN   Well, well, I daresay you two want to talk to each other. *(Smiling)* And perhaps Hedda may have something to tell you too, George. Good-bye! I must go home to Rina. *(Turning at the door)* How strange it is to think that now Rina is with me and with my poor brother as well!

TESMAN   Yes, fancy that, Aunt Julia! Eh? (MISS TESMAN *goes out by the hall door.)*

HEDDA   *(Follows* TESMAN *coldly and searchingly with her eyes)* I almost believe your Aunt Rina's death affects you more than it does your Aunt Julia.

TESMAN   Oh, it's not that alone. It's Eilert I am so terribly uneasy about.

HEDDA   *(Quickly)* Is there anything new about him?

TESMAN   I looked in at his rooms this afternoon, intending to tell him the manuscript was in safe keeping.

HEDDA   Well, did you not find him?

TESMAN   No. He wasn't at home. But afterwards I met Mrs. Elvsted, and she told me that he had been here early this morning.

HEDDA   Yes, directly after you had gone.

TESMAN   And he said that he had torn his manuscript to pieces—eh?

HEDDA   Yes, so he declared.

TESMAN   Why, good heavens, he must have been completely out of his mind! And I suppose you thought it best not to give it back to him, Hedda?

HEDDA   No, he did not get it.

TESMAN   But of course you told him that we had it?

HEDDA   No. *(Quickly)* Did you tell Mrs. Elvsted?

TESMAN   No; I thought I had better not. But you ought to have told him. Fancy, if, in desperation, he should go and do himself some injury! Let me have the manuscript, Hedda! I will take it to him at once. Where is it?

HEDDA   *(Cold and immovable, leaning on the arm chair)* I have not got it.

TESMAN   Have not got it? What in the world do you mean?

HEDDA   I have burnt it—every line of it.

TESMAN   *(With a violent movement of terror)* Burnt! Burnt Eilert's manuscript!

HEDDA   Don't scream so. The servant might hear you.

TESMAN   Burnt! Why, good God—! No, no, no! It's impossible!

HEDDA   It is so, nevertheless.

TESMAN   Do you know what you have done, Hedda? It's unlawful appropriation of lost property. Fancy that! Just ask Judge Brack, and he'll tell you what it is.

HEDDA   I advise you not to speak of it—either to judge Brack, or to any one else.

TESMAN   But how could you do anything so unheard-of? What put it into your head? What possessed you? Answer me that—eh?

HEDDA   *(Suppressing an almost imperceptible smile)* I did it for your sake, George.

TESMAN   For my sake!

HEDDA   This morning, when you told me about what he had read to you—

TESMAN   Yes yes—what then?

HEDDA   You acknowledged that you envied him his work.

TESMAN   Oh, of course I didn't mean that literally.

HEDDA   No matter—I could not bear the idea that any one should throw you into the shade.

TESMAN   *(In an outburst of mingled doubt and joy)*   Hedda! Oh, is this true? But—but—I never knew you show your love like that before. Fancy that!

HEDDA   Well, I may as well tell you that—just at this time— *(Impatiently, breaking off)*   No, no; you can ask Aunt Julia. She will tell you, fast enough.

TESMAN   Oh, I almost think I understand you, Hedda!   *(Clasps his hands together)*   Great heavens! do you really mean it! Eh?

HEDDA   Don't shout so. The servant might hear.

TESMAN   *(Laughing in irrepressible glee)*   The servant! Why, how absurd you are, Hedda. It's only my old Berta! Why, I'll tell Berta myself.

HEDDA   *(Clenching her hands together in desperation)*   Oh, it is killing me—it is killing me, all this!

TESMAN   What is, Hedda? Eh?

HEDDA   *(Coldly controlling herself)*   All this—absurdity—George.

TESMAN   Absurdity! Do you see anything absurd in my being overjoyed at the news! But after all—perhaps I had better not say anything to Berta.

HEDDA   Oh—why not that too?

TESMAN   No, no, not yet! But I must certainly tell Aunt Julia. And then that you have begun to call me George too! Fancy that! Oh, Aunt Julia will be so happy—so happy!

HEDDA   When she hears that I have burnt Eilert Lövborg's manuscript —for your sake?

TESMAN   No, by-the-bye—that affair of the manuscript—of course nobody must know about that. But that you love me so much, Hedda— Aunt Julia must really share my joy in that! I wonder, now, whether this sort of thing is usual in young wives? Eh?

HEDDA   I think you had better ask Aunt Julia that question too.

TESMAN   I will indeed, some time or other.   *(Looks uneasy and downcast again)*   And yet the manuscript—the manuscript! Good God! it is terrible to think what will become of poor Eilert now.

MRS. ELVSTED, *dressed as in the first Act, with hat and cloak, enters by the hall door.*

MRS. ELVSTED   *(Greets them hurriedly and says in evident agitation)*   Oh, dear Hedda, forgive my coming again.

HEDDA   What is the matter with you, Thea?

TESMAN   Something about Eilert Lövborg again—eh?

MRS. ELVSTED   Yes! I am dreadfully afraid some misfortune has happened to him.

HEDDA   *(Seizes her arm)*   Ah —do you think so!

TESMAN   Why, good Lord—what makes you think that, Mrs. Elvsted?

MRS. ELVSTED   I heard them talking of him at my boarding-house—just as I came in. Oh, the most incredible rumors are afloat about him to-day.

TESMAN   Yes, fancy, so I heard too! And I can bear witness that he went straight home to bed last night. Fancy that!

HEDDA   Well, what did they say at the boarding-house?

MRS. ELVSTED   Oh, I couldn't make out anything clearly. Either they knew nothing definite, or else—. They stopped talking when they saw me; and I did not dare to ask.

TESMAN   *(Moving about uneasily)*   We must hope—we must hope that you misunderstood them, Mrs. Elvsted.

MRS. ELVSTED   No, no; I am sure it was of him they were talking. And I heard something about the hospital or—

TESMAN   The hospital?

HEDDA   No—surely that cannot be!

MRS. ELVSTED   Oh, I was in such mortal terror! I went to his lodgings and asked for him there.

HEDDA   You could make up your mind to that, Thea!

MRS. ELVSTED   What else could I do? I really could bear the suspense no longer.

TESMAN   But you didn't find him either—eh?

MRS. ELVSTED   No. And the people knew nothing about him. He hadn't been home since yesterday afternoon, they said.

TESMAN   Yesterday! Fancy, how could they say that?

MRS. ELVSTED   Oh, I am sure something terrible must have happened to him.

TESMAN   Hedda dear—how would it be if I were to go and make inquiries—?

HEDDA   No, no—don't you mix yourself up in this affair.

JUDGE BRACK, *with his hat in his hand, enters by the hall door, which* BERTA *opens, and closes behind him. He looks grave and bows in silence.*

TESMAN   Oh, is that you, my dear Judge? Eh?

BRACK   Yes. It was imperative I should see you this evening.

TESMAN   I can see you have heard the news about Aunt Rina?

BRACK   Yes, that among other things.

TESMAN   Isn't it sad—eh?

BRACK   Well, my dear Tesman, that depends on how you look at it.

TESMAN   *(Looks doubtfully at him)*   Has anything else happened?

BRACK   Yes.

HEDDA   *(In suspense)*   Anything sad, Judge Brack?

BRACK   That, too, depends on how you look at it, Mrs. Tesman.

MRS. ELVSTED   *(Unable to restrain her anxiety)*   Oh! it is something about Eilert Lövborg!

BRACK   *(With a glance at her)*   What makes you think that, Madam? Perhaps you have already heard something—?

MRS. ELVSTED   *(In confusion)*   No, nothing at all, but—

TESMAN   Oh, for heaven's sake, tell us!

BRACK   *(Shrugging his shoulders)*   Well, I regret to say Eilert Lövborg has been taken to the hospital. He is lying at the point of death.

MRS. ELVSTED   *(Shrieks)*   Oh God! oh God—!

TESMAN   To the hospital! And at the point of death.

HEDDA   *(Involuntarily)*   So soon then—

MRS. ELVSTED   *(Wailing)*   And we parted in anger, Hedda!

HEDDA   *(Whispers)*   Thea—Thea—be careful!

MRS. ELVSTED   *(Not heeding her)*   I must go to him! I must see him alive!

BRACK   It is useless, Madam. No one will be admitted.

MRS. ELVSTED   Oh, at least tell me what has happened to him? What is it?

TESMAN   You don't mean to say that he has himself—Eh?

HEDDA   Yes, I am sure he has.

TESMAN   Hedda, how can you—?

BRACK   *(Keeping his eyes fixed upon her)*   Unfortunately you have guessed quite correctly, Mrs. Tesman.

MRS. ELVSTED   Oh, how horrible!

TESMAN   Himself, then! Fancy that!

HEDDA   Shot himself!

BRACK   Rightly guessed again, Mrs. Tesman.

MRS. ELVSTED   *(With an effort at self-control)*   When did it happen, Mr. Brack?

BRACK   This afternoon—between three and four.

TESMAN   But, good Lord, where did he do it? Eh?

BRACK   *(With some hesitation)*   Where? Well—I suppose at his lodgings.

MRS. ELVSTED   No, that cannot be; for I was there between six and seven.

BRACK   Well then, somewhere else. I don't know exactly. I only know that he was found—. He had shot himself—in the breast.

MRS. ELVSTED   Oh. How terrible! That he should die like that!

HEDDA   *(To BRACK)*   Was it in the breast?

BRACK   Yes—as I told you.

HEDDA   Not in the temple?

BRACK   In the breast, Mrs. Tesman.

HEDDA   Well, well—the breast is a good place, too.

BRACK   How do you mean, Mrs. Tesman?

HEDDA   *(Evasively)* Oh, nothing—nothing.

TESMAN   And the wound is dangerous, you say—eh?

BRACK   Absolutely mortal. The end has probably come by this time.

MRS. ELVSTED   Yes, yes, I feel it. The end! The end! Oh, Hedda—!

TESMAN   But tell me, how have you learnt all this?

BRACK   *(Curtly)* Through one of the police. A man I had some business with.

HEDDA   *(In a clear voice)* At last a deed worth doing!

TESMAN   *(Terrified)* Good heavens, Hedda! What are you saying?

HEDDA   I say there is beauty in this.

BRACK   H'm, Mrs. Tesman—

TESMAN   Beauty! Fancy that!

MRS. ELVSTED   Oh, Hedda, how can you talk of beauty in such an act!

HEDDA   Eilert Lövborg has himself made up his account with life. He has had the courage to do—the one right thing.

MRS. ELVSTED   No, you must never think that was how it happened! It must have been in delirium that he did it.

TESMAN   In despair!

HEDDA   That he did not. I am certain of that.

MRS. ELVSTED   Yes, yes! In delirium! Just as when he tore up our manuscript.

BRACK   *(Starting)* The manuscript? Has he torn that up?

MRS. ELVSTED   Yes, last night.

TESMAN   *(Whispers softly)* Oh, Hedda, we shall never get over this.

BRACK   H'm, very extraordinary.

TESMAN   *(Moving about the room)* To think of Eilert going out of the world in this way! And not leaving behind him the book that would have immortalized his name—

MRS. ELVSTED   Oh, if only it could be put together again!

TESMAN   Yes, if it only could! I don't know what I would not give—

MRS. ELVSTED   Perhaps it can, Mr. Tesman.

TESMAN   What do you mean?

MRS. ELVSTED   *(Searches in the pocket of her dress)* Look here. I have kept all the loose notes he used to dictate from.

HEDDA   *(A step forward)* Ah—!

TESMAN   You have kept them, Mrs. Elvsted! Eh?

MRS. ELVSTED   Yes, I have them here. I put them in my pocket when I left home. Here they still are—

TESMAN   Oh, do let me see them!

MRS. ELVSTED   *(Hands him a bundle of papers)* But they are in such disorder—all mixed up.

TESMAN   Fancy, if we could make something out of them, after all! Perhaps if we two put our heads together—

MRS. ELVSTED   Oh yes, at least let us try—

TESMAN   We will manage it! We must! I will dedicate my life to this task.

HEDDA   You, George? Your life?

TESMAN   Yes, or rather all the time I can spare. My own collections must wait in the meantime. Hedda—you understand, eh? I owe this to Eilert's memory.

HEDDA   Perhaps.

TESMAN   And so, my dear Mrs. Elvsted, we will give our whole minds to it. There is no use in brooding over what can't be undone—eh? We must try to control our grief as much as possible, and—

MRS. ELVSTED   Yes, yes, Mr. Tesman, I will do the best I can.

TESMAN   Well then, come here. I can't rest until we have looked through the notes. Where shall we sit? Here? No, in there, in the back room. Excuse me, my dear Judge. Come with me, Mrs. Elvsted.

MRS. ELVSTED   Oh, if only it were possible!

TESMAN *and* MRS. ELVSTED *go into the back room. She takes off her hat and cloak. They both sit at the table under the hanging lamp, and are soon deep in an eager examination of the papers.* HEDDA *crosses to the stove and sits in the arm chair. Presently* BRACK *goes up to her.*

HEDDA   *(In a low voice)*   Oh, what a sense of freedom it gives one, this act of Eilert Lövborg's.

BRACK   Freedom, Mrs. Hedda? Well, of course, it is a release for him—

HEDDA   I mean for me. It gives me a sense of freedom to know that a deed of deliberate courage is still possible in this world—a deed of spontaneous beauty.

BRACK   *(Smiling)*   H'm—my dear Mrs. Hedda—

HEDDA   Oh, I know what you are going to say. For you are a kind of specialist too, like—you know!

BRACK   *(Looking hard at her)*   Eilert Lövborg was more to you than perhaps you are willing to admit to yourself. Am I wrong?

HEDDA   I don't answer such questions. I only know that Eilert Lövborg has had the courage to live his life after his own fashion. And then— the last great act, with its beauty! Ah! that he should have the will and the strength to turn away from the banquet of life—so early.

BRACK   I am sorry, Mrs. Hedda, —but I fear I must dispel an amiable illusion.

HEDDA   Illusion?

BRACK   Which could not have lasted long in any case.

HEDDA   What do you mean?

BRACK   Eilert Lövborg did not shoot himself—voluntarily.

HEDDA   Not voluntarily?

BRACK   No. The thing did not happen exactly as I told it.

HEDDA   *(In suspense)*   Have you concealed something? What is it?

BRACK   For poor Mrs. Elvsted's sake I idealized the facts a little.

HEDDA   What are the facts?

BRACK   First, that he is already dead.

HEDDA   At the hospital?

BRACK   Yes—without regaining consciousness.

HEDDA   What more have you concealed?

BRACK   This—the event did not happen at his lodgings.

HEDDA   Oh, that can make no difference.

BRACK   Perhaps it may. For I must tell you—Eilert Lövborg was found shot in—in Mademoiselle Diana's boudoir.

HEDDA   *(Makes a motion as if to rise, but sinks back again)*   That is impossible, Judge Brack! He cannot have been there again today.

BRACK   He was there this afternoon. He went there, he said, to demand the return of something which they had taken from him. Talked wildly about a lost child—

HEDDA   Ah—so that was why—

BRACK   I thought probably he meant his manuscript; but now I hear he destroyed that himself. So I suppose it must have been his pocketbook.

HEDDA   Yes, no doubt. And there—there he was found?

BRACK   Yes, there. With a pistol in his breast pocket, discharged. The ball had lodged in a vital part.

HEDDA   In the breast—yes.

BRACK   No—in the bowels.

HEDDA   *(Looks up at him with an expression of loathing)*   That too! Oh, what curse is it that makes everything I touch turn ludicrous and mean?

BRACK   There is one point more, Mrs. Hedda—another disagreeable feature in the affair.

HEDDA   And what is that?

BRACK   The pistol he carried—

HEDDA   *(Breathless)*   Well? What of it?

BRACK   He must have stolen it.

HEDDA   *(Leaps up)*   Stolen it! That is not true! He did not steal it!

BRACK   No other explanation is possible. He must have stolen it—. Hush!

TESMAN *and* MRS. ELVSTED *have risen from the table in the back room, and come into the drawing room.*

TESMAN   *(With the papers in both his hands)*   Hedda dear, it is almost impossible to see under that lamp. Think of that!

HEDDA   Yes, I am thinking.
TESMAN   Would you mind our sitting at your writing table—eh?
HEDDA   If you like. *(Quickly)* No, wait! Let me clear it first!
TESMAN   Oh, you needn't trouble, Hedda. There is plenty of room.
HEDDA   No, no, let me clear it, I say! I will take these things in and put
them on the piano. There!

*She has drawn out an object, covered with sheet music, from under
the bookcase, places several other pieces of music upon it, and carries
the whole into the inner room, to the left.* TESMAN *lays the scraps of
paper on the writing table, and moves the lamp there from the corner
table. He and* MRS. ELVSTED *sit down and proceed with their work.*
HEDDA *returns.*

HEDDA   *(Behind* MRS. ELVSTED'S *chair, gently ruffling her hair)* Well,
my sweet Thea, —how goes it with Eilert Lövborg's monument?
MRS. ELVSTED   *(Looks dispiritedly up at her)* Oh, it will be terribly
hard to put in order.
TESMAN   We must manage it. I am determined. And arranging other
people's papers is just the work for me.

HEDDA *goes over to the stove, and seats herself on one of the footstools.* BRACK *stands over her, leaning on the arm chair.*

HEDDA   *(Whispers)* What did you say about the pistol?
BRACK   *(Softly)* That he must have stolen it.
HEDDA   Why stolen it?
BRACK   Because every other explanation ought to be impossible, Mrs.
Hedda.
HEDDA   Indeed?
BRACK   *(Glances at her)* Of course, Eilert Lövborg was here this morn-
ing. Was he not?
HEDDA   Yes.
BRACK   Were you alone with him?
HEDDA   Part of the time.
BRACK   Did you not leave the room while he was here?
HEDDA   No.
BRACK   Try to recollect. Were you not out of the room a moment?
HEDDA   Yes, perhaps just a moment—out in the hall.
BRACK   And where was your pistol case during that time?
HEDDA   I had it locked up in—
BRACK   Well, Mrs. Hedda?
HEDDA   The case stood there on the writing table.

BRACK   Have you looked since, to see whether both the pistols are there?

HEDDA   No.

BRACK   Well, you need not. I saw the pistol found in Lövborg's pocket, and I knew it at once as the one I had seen yesterday—and before, too.

HEDDA   Have you it with you?

BRACK   No; the police have it.

HEDDA   What will the police do with it?

BRACK   Search till they find the owner.

HEDDA   Do you think they will succeed?

BRACK   *(Bends over her and whispers)*   No, Hedda Gabler—not so long as I say nothing.

HEDDA   *(Looks frightened at him)*   And if you do not say nothing, — what then?

BRACK   *(Shrugs his shoulders)*   There is always the possibility that the pistol was stolen.

HEDDA   *(Firmly)*   Death rather than that.

BRACK   *(Smiling)*   People say such things—but they don't do them.

HEDDA   *(Without replying)*   And supposing the pistol was not stolen, and the owner is discovered? What then?

BRACK   Well, Hedda—then comes the scandal.

HEDDA   The scandal!

BRACK   Yes, the scandal—of which you are so mortally afraid. You will, of course, be brought before the court—both you and Mademoiselle Diana. She will have to explain how the thing happened—whether it was an accidental shot or murder. Did the pistol go off as he was trying to take it out of his pocket to threaten her with? Or did she tear the pistol out of his hand, shoot him, and push it back into his pocket? That would be quite like her; for she is an able-bodied young person, this same Mademoiselle Diana.

HEDDA   But *I* have nothing to do with all this repulsive business.

BRACK   No. But you will have to answer the question: Why did you give Eilert Lövborg the pistol? And what conclusions will people draw from the fact that you did give it to him?

HEDDA   *(Lets her head sink)*   That is true. I did not think of that.

BRACK   Well, fortunately, there is no danger, so long as I say nothing.

HEDDA   *(Looks up at him)*   So I am in your power, Judge Brack. You have me at your beck and call from this time forward.

BRACK   *(Whispers softly)*   Dearest Hedda—believe me—I shall not abuse my advantage.

HEDDA   I am in your power none the less. Subject to your will and your demands. A slave, a slave then!   *(Rises impetuously)*   No, I cannot endure the thought of that! Never!

BRACK *(Looks half-mockingly at her)* People generally get used to the inevitable.

HEDDA *(Returns his look)* Yes, perhaps. *(She crosses to the writing table. Suppressing an involuntary smile, she imitates* TESMAN'S *intonations.)* Well? Are you getting on, George? Eh?

TESMAN Heaven knows, dear. In any case it will be the work of months.

HEDDA *(As before)* Fancy that! *(Passes her hands softly through* MRS. ELVSTED'S *hair)* Doesn't it seem strange to you, Thea? Here are you sitting with Tesman—just as you used to sit with Eilert Lövborg?

MRS. ELVSTED Ah, if I could only inspire your husband in the same way!

HEDDA Oh, that will come too—in time.

TESMAN Yes, do you know, Hedda—I really think I begin to feel something of the sort. But won't you go and sit with Brack again?

HEDDA Is there nothing I can do to help you two?

TESMAN No, nothing in the world. *(Turning his head)* I trust to you to keep Hedda company, my dear Brack.

BRACK *(With a glance at* HEDDA) With the very greatest of pleasure.

HEDDA Thanks. But I am tired this evening. I will go in and lie down a little on the sofa.

TESMAN Yes, do dear—eh?

HEDDA *goes into the back room and draws the curtains. A short pause. Suddenly she is heard playing a wild dance on the piano.*

MRS. ELVSTED *(Starts from her chair)* Oh—what is that?

TESMAN *(Runs to the doorway)* Why, my dearest Hedda—don't play dance music tonight! Just think of Aunt Rina! And of Eilert too!

HEDDA *(Puts her head out between the curtains)* And of Aunt Julia. And of all the rest of them. —After this, I will be quiet. *(Closes the curtains again.)*

TESMAN *(At the writing table)* It's not good for her to see us at this distressing work. I'll tell you what, Mrs. Elvsted —you shall take the empty room at Aunt Julia's, and then I will come over in the evenings, and we can sit and work there—eh?

HEDDA *(In the inner room)* I hear what you are saying, Tesman. But how am *I* to get through the evenings out here?

TESMAN *(Turning over the papers)* Oh, I daresay Judge Brack will be so kind as to look in now and then, even though I am out.

BRACK *(In the arm chair, calls out gaily)* Every blessëd evening, with all the pleasure in life, Mrs. Tesman! We shall get on capitally together, we two!

HEDDA   *(Speaking loud and clear)*   Yes, don't you flatter yourself we
will, Judge Brack? Now that you are the one cock in the basket—

A shot is heard within. TESMAN, MRS. ELVSTED, *and* BRACK *leap to
their feet.*

TESMAN   Oh, now she is playing with those pistols again.

He throws back the curtains and runs in, followed by MRS. ELVSTED.
HEDDA *lies stretched on the sofa, lifeless. Confusion and cries.* BERTA
enters in alarm from the right.

TESMAN   *(Shrieks to* BRACK)   Shot herself! Shot herself in the temple!
Fancy that!
BRACK   *(Half-fainting in the arm chair)*   Good God!—people don't do
such things.

Questions on *Hedda Gabler*

A. For Close Reading

ACT I

1. What do we learn about the situation at the opening of the play before
    Hedda enters? What people are introduced? Why are they where they are?
    What are they like?
2. What characteristics does Hedda display when we first get to know her?
    In the scene about the bonnet, how would Hedda say, "Is it!"? How
    would you support your reading of this line? In what ways is Hedda con-
    trasted with Miss Tesman?
3. After Miss Tesman leaves, what reason does Mrs. Elvsted give for coming
    on the scene? What is her relationship with her husband? With Eilert
    Lövborg?
4. When Judge Brack enters, what news does he bring? What is George's
    reaction to the news? What is Hedda's?
5. Trace through the first act the various repeated motifs: George's appoint-
    ment, his financial situation, the books written by George and by Lövborg,
    the pistols, Hedda's boredom. Where is each motif introduced? How is
    each developed?
6. What relationships do you see between the various grouping of char-

acters: between Miss Tesman and George, between George and Hedda, between Lövborg and Mrs. Elvsted, between Hedda and Lövborg? How does each relationship affect the other?

7. At the end of Act I we have learned of Hedda's many dissatisfactions with her current situation. What are these dissatisfactions as she sees them? Do you, as observer, see them any differently? Explain.

ACT II

8. In the scene between Hedda and Brack what else do we learn about the honeymoon? What reasons does Hedda give for having married George? What do we learn of Brack's character? Just before George enters, Brack says, "The triangle is completed." What does he mean?

9. Why does Hedda consider persuading George to go into politics? What does Brack mean by saying, "But suppose . . . a solemn responsibility were to come upon you"? Where has the same idea been mentioned earlier?

10. In what ways does Ibsen arrange for Hedda to be alone with Lövborg? Why did Lövborg refuse to drink the punch?

11. During this scene what else do we learn of the relationship between Hedda and Lövborg. When had they last seen one another?

12. When Mrs. Elvsted enters, Hedda says that Brack and Tesman are going to a supper-party, and Mrs. Elvsted "quickly" responds, according to the stage direction, "Not you?" What is the significance of the word, "quickly"? Which word would she emphasize in saying, "Not you?" Why?

13. Mrs. Elvsted decides to sit next to Lövborg. Hedda says, "You'll be good enough to come over here to me. I will sit between you." In what way is this action a symbolic one? How, in other words, does it reflect what is going on in the play?

14. After Lövborg has declined the punch, Hedda manipulates things so that he finally takes some. How does she do this? In what ways are her remark, "But if I say you shall!?," and somewhat later her use of the words "dare" and "distraction" significant? How does this scene reflect on Lövborg's previous statement about his relationship with Mrs. Elvsted that they have "absolute faith in each other."

15. Trace Hedda's treatment of Mrs. Elvsted in this act. Read carefully the last scene between the two when they have been left alone by the men. What is symbolized by the expression, "vine leaves in his hair"?

ACT III

16. At the beginning of the act, how has the author indicated a passage of time from the previous scene? What is the mood of the opening scene? Before Tesman enters, what contrasts are built up between Hedda and Mrs. Elvsted?

17. When Tesman describes Lövborg's book as "one of the most remarkable things that have ever been written," Hedda replies, "Yes, yes; I don't care about that—." Compare her reaction with Tesman's.

18. When Tesman and Hedda discuss the lost manuscript, what attitude does each take toward it?

19. Why does Ibsen introduce at this point in the play the information that Aunt Rina is dying? What dramatic function does it serve?

20. Hedda learns from Brack the story of the preceding evening. From Hedda's point of view what irony is involved in the story, what difference between what she expected and what actually happened?

21. After Brack leaves, Hedda picks up Lövborg's manuscript. How does this action relate to what we learned in the previous scene (Brack's story).

22. Why did Hedda destroy the manuscript? Trace all of the references to it in establishing your proof for what you say. What symbolic act is she carrying out?

ACT IV

23. What does Miss Tesman mean by saying, ". . . and here there will be some sewing too, I suppose—but of another sort, thank God!" What is Miss Tesman's reaction to the death of Aunt Rina? What is Hedda's reaction? Just before Miss Tesman leaves, Hedda interrupts her husband by repeating his "If—?" How would she say it? What does she mean?

24. When George asks Hedda to explain her burning of the manuscript, she says, *"suppressing an almost imperceptible smile":* "I did it for your sake, George." What should her reply mean to the reader? What does George take it to mean? What does the stage direction add to the meaning of the line? Is it needed to indicate how the line should be spoken? Why or why not? Later, Hedda says, ". . . you can ask Aunt Julia. She will tell you fast enough." Why does this remark so elate George?

25. When Mrs. Elvsted enters and says of Lövborg, "Yes! I am dreadfully afraid some misfortune has happened to him," Hedda replies, "Ah,—do you think so?" How should Hedda's line be spoken? Support your answer.

26. After she learns of Lövborg's attempt at suicide, Hedda says, "At last a deed worth doing!" What does she mean by that remark? What irony do you find in the contrast between Brack's first explanation of Lövborg's suicide and his second telling of it to Hedda?

27. What is the significance of the discussion between Hedda and Brack about the pistols? What does he know? What is he guessing?

28. Why did Hedda shoot herself? The answer is not a simple one; it grows partly out of her relationships with Tesman, Brack, Lövborg, and Mrs. Elvsted. How is each of them in some way related to her suicide?

B. Questions For Writing and Discussion

1. How much of the interpretation of the play depends on the author's stage directions? In your answer show how different the play would be if the stage directions were not there.

2. At the end of Act I the pistols are introduced. Trace the various references to them throughout the play. How do they help tie the plot together?

3. Discuss Ibsen's handling of time and place in the play considering the fact that the entire action is compressed into thirty-six hours and that the set-

ting does not change. What major scenes are omitted, that is, merely described instead of acted out? If you were directing this play in a motion picture version (where a change of setting is no problem), would you have any of the off-stage scenes performed? Why? Why not?

4. *Hedda Gabler* is continually pointed out as a model for good playwriting. One reason is the skill with which Ibsen brings characters onto the stage or gets them off, each arrival and departure having its own dramatic justification. Trace the ways in which characters are brought together or separated.

5. Do the actions of the play just happen, or are they principally caused by the character traits of the participants?

6. Describe the conflicts between the various characters. In your answer indicate what each wants and what each gets.

7. What information are we given about Hedda's life before the action of the play begins?

8. As you look back at the whole play, why do you think that Hedda married George Tesman?

9. One of the major motifs (or themes) that runs through the play is that when Hedda plans or expects something to happen in one way, it actually occurs in a contradictory way. She says at one point, "Oh, what curse is it that makes everything I touch turn ludicrous and mean?" Explain the major reversals in the play and show why they are ironic.

10. Discuss Hedda's relationships with the other characters and show how her self-centeredness prevents all of these relationships from being satisfactory.

11. Trace through the play the contest between Hedda and Mrs. Elvsted in their attempts to control the destiny of a man.

12. Trace the way in which Ibsen uses Lövborg's manuscript in the play. In the first part of your answer indicate exactly what happens to it (including all references). Then go on to show how each character reacts to it each time it is mentioned. Finally, discuss the symbolic meaning of the manuscript (why, for example, both Hedda and Lövborg refer to it as a "child").

13. In what ways was Tesman responsible for the burning of the manuscript? In your answer trace carefully his actions and thoughts between the time he found the manuscript and the time it was burned. Could he have acted differently from the way he did? Why or why not?

14. One of the major patterns of the play is the ways in which the other characters are compared with Hedda. In what ways are the following characters like or unlike Hedda: Aunt Julia, Tesman, Brack, Mrs. Elvsted, and Lövborg? Be sure to point out how each acts in situations that resemble those in which Hedda finds herself.

15. In what ways could the following statement of Hedda's be considered the theme of the play: "I want for once in my life to have power to mold a human destiny"?

16. There might be some doubt about whether this play is a tragedy, since tragedy demands that we feel sympathy toward the leading character or characters. And sympathy usually rises from the belief that to some extent they are victims of fate. Argue for or against the assertion that Hedda deserves sympathy.

17. One critic, speaking of the way that Hedda's role should be acted, said, "Unless Hedda is able to convince people, to charm them, to inspire confidence in them—before proceeding to destroy them—there is no play." Show how Hedda charms each major character before proceeding to destroy him or her.

An Enemy of the People

IBSEN

(1882)

THE tones of anger and derisive humor that dominate Ibsen's *An Enemy of the People,* as they dominate *Hedda Gabler,* reflect the author's personality. Ibsen had much in common with Doctor Stockman, the hero of this play, since he too put great value on individuality and the need for society to honor and foster individualism.

As with *Hedda Gabler, An Enemy of the People* can be called a social tragedy, since there is a dual emphasis on the individual and the society that molds him. Yet there are vital parallels with earlier tragedies. In *An Enemy of the People,* as in *Oedipus the King,* a source of contagion (pollution of the Baths) begins the action, and that pollution is found to be metaphorically in the minds of the community as well. The problem for the hero is the cleansing of society, literally and spiritually. As in the other plays, appearances are contrasted with reality; people are not what they seem. Ibsen is concerned with their inner lives, the motives that make them what they are. Like earlier heroes, moreover, Doctor Stockmann pursues the truth relentlessly, and in so doing becomes an isolated man in his own world.

The effect of the play is propagandistic as well as tragic. Ibsen had harsh things to say about his countrymen: about their government, their press, and their values. Often he seems to be speaking directly to his audience through his characters. As he said in a letter (September 9, 1882): "Doctor Stockmann and I got on excellently together; we agree on so many subjects. But the Doctor is a more muddle-headed person than I am, and he has, moreover, several other characteristics for the sake of which people will stand hearing a good many things from him which they might perhaps not have taken in such very good part had they been said by me."

Questions on *An Enemy of the People*

A. For Close Reading

ACT I

1. The play opens with some minor characters on stage. What do you learn about each? What information do they give us about Dr. Stockmann?

213

2. When Stockmann enters, what more do we learn of him? What contrasts are developed between him and his brother?

3. In what way is suspense introduced by references to the article and the postman?

4. What ideas are represented by Petra?

5. Trace the references to the Baths. During the first act of the play, what attitude is taken toward them by each character?

6. What does Dr. Stockmann expect will be the result of his discovery?

ACT II

7. What attitude is initially taken toward the revelation of the truth about the Baths by Morten Kiil, Hovstad, Aslaksen, and the Mayor? What reason does each give for his own stand? How does each response affect Dr. Stockmann?

8. Why does the act end with a discussion of Stockmann's family?

ACT III

9. What attitude does Hovstad now take toward the revelation? What is beginning to bother Aslaksen? How is his reference to Dr. Stockmann as a "friend of society" ironic?

10. After Stockmann leaves the newspaper office for the first time, in what ways is the theme of money introduced? What uses of money are discussed?

12. What is the purpose of the scene between Petra and Hovstad? What point of view does each represent concerning the function of a newspaper? What foreshadowing is going on here?

13. By what comments does the Mayor get Aslaksen on his side? By what steps is each character persuaded to change his mind?

14. In what symbolic way are the Mayor's cap and stick used? At what point does Stockmann lay them aside? Why?

15. What pressures make Stockmann's position more desperate?

ACT IV

16. What information are we given, before the meeting, by the various men in the audience and by other minor characters?

17. How does the Mayor manage to control in advance what will happen at the meeting?

18. Aslaksen is still talking of "moderation." What meaning for the term does he himself act out in the play?

19. How has Hovstad changed from our first view of him?

20. What does the drunk represent? In what ways is his behavior like or unlike that of the rest of the audience?

21. What is the major argument of Stockmann's speech? What evidence does he offer to prove it? Is what he says supported by the action of the play? What kind of government is he calling for?

22. What is the source of the bitterness and gossip as the meeting ends?

23. Stockmann asks Horster whether there is room on his boat for passage "to the New World." Will he find his kind of government there?

ACT V

24. How does the pressure mount on Stockmann, his family, and Horster?
25. In what ways do people question Stockmann's motives for attacking the Baths?
26. What opportunities are offered to Stockmann for making peace with the community?
27. What does Stockmann mean by saying at the end, "the strongest man in the world is the man who stands alone"?

B. For Writing and Discussion

1. In what way is contrast the basic pattern of the play? Point out contrasts set up between characters, within scenes, and in ideas.
2. Trace the shifting attitudes of Mrs. Stockmann toward her husband's position. What in each case makes her change her attitude?
3. "Each character in this play represents an idea." Choose one character and show how this statement is borne out.
4. To what extent do you agree or disagree with the following statement? "Ibsen's characters, in this play, do not seem real, because they are mere mouthpieces for what the playwright wants to say."
5. One of the recurring motifs of the play is misinterpretation—the way that the other characters ascribe to Stockmann motives that he does not have. In doing this, they show more about themselves than about Stockmann. Trace through the play the points at which his motives are misinterpreted.
6. What forces work against Stockmann's taking action? What drives him to act?
7. One critic says of the play, ". . . too sudden a revelation of the social lie creates as many problems as it solves." Does Stockmann make "too sudden a revelation"? Given the conditions and the people of the play and their reasons for acting, would it have made any difference if he had proceeded with caution?
8. The action of the play helps spell out Ibsen's own interpretations of a series of key words that recur again and again. Judging by what is said and done, how does Ibsen define "truth," "public opinion," "free press," "self-government," "duty," "freedom," "enemy," "poison," and "majority"?
9. What irony do you find in the title, *An Enemy of the People?*
10. Would Dr. Stockmann agree with Ralph Waldo Emerson's statement that "Whoso would be a man must be a nonconformist"? Why or why not?
11. How much of Stockmann's downfall is caused by his own character; how much by the character of other people; how much by fate? How much, especially, by what has happened before the play began?
12. In his argument for Stockmann and against the people does Ibsen present a fair case? Or does he slant his argument to get the effect that he wants? How does he get our sympathies on the side of the doctor?
13. Judging by this play, does Ibsen believe in democratic government? Cite reasons for your positions.

14. One of the important problems of tragedy is not whether the hero succeeds or fails but whether he acts and for what reasons. Why does Stockmann decide to stay? What effect does his suffering have in the world of the play? Does the doctor ever consider the consequences of his discovery on the life of the town? Should he? Does the question have more than two sides?

15. If the majority is always wrong, does it follow that the minority is always right? Which minority?

Heart of Darkness

JOSEPH CONRAD
(1902)

HEART OF DARKNESS is the story of a journey up the Congo narrated almost
entirely by a seaman named Marlow who turns "fresh-water sailor for a
bit." His mission is to relieve a Company agent who lives deep in the interi-
or of Africa. That man at the far end of the river is Kurtz, a trader in ivory,
who is characterized by others before we meet him as "an exceptional man,"
"a prodigy," "a universal genius." In part, the narrative is about the effect
of Africa on this "remarkable man" who had once written in a pamphlet,
"By the simple exercise of our will we can exert a power for good practically unbounded," yet is corrupted by his experience and dies crying out,
"The horror! The horror!"

But primarily the book is about the effect of the experience on Marlow, for whom the journey involves moving from a civilized world to a bar-
baric one, from illusion to reality, from ignorance of himself to self-knowl-
edge. In this sense the novel is an account of a voyage of discovery. Both
Kurtz and Marlow learn something they had not known before. They discover what it means to be a man and what happens if primitive instincts are
not controlled by the restraints of reason and compassion.

Like all great literature the book has many levels of meaning. It is also
about European colonialism and the exploitation of Africa in the late nine-
teenth century. "All Europe," we are told, "contributed to the making of
Kurtz." He is a symbolic figure. The search of his "Company," always re-
ferred to in this general way, for ivory gives a universality to the story; it
symbolizes any search with similar unscrupulous means and ends. Many Eu-
ropeans went into Africa solely with the idea of making money and with little or no regard for the welfare of the natives. Unquestionably, Conrad is
saying that such unconscionable greed is corrupting. Submission to it reveals
the ever-present darkness in the heart of all mankind.

Though Europe's financial involvment with Africa, especially in terms
of the slave trade, dates back to at least the fifteenth century, a more general
interest in the continent did not come about until David Livingstone, a Scot-
tish missionary, was reported lost there in 1868, somewhere in the vicinity
of Lake Tanganyika. The next year, realizing the news value of the story,
James Gordon Bennett, Jr., managing editor of the *New York Herald,* hired
Henry Morton Stanley, an American journalist, to go to the Congo and find
Livingstone. After searching for 236 days, Stanley found Livingstone on
November 10, 1871 and uttered his famous greeting, "Doctor Livingstone, I

presume." For this exploit Stanley became world-famous. A later expedition of his from Zanzibar to the mouth of the Congo marked the further opening of Africa to exploitation, especially by the Belgians under King Leopold II. Subsequently, Stanley became disillusioned with the colonial administration of the Belgians in Africa and said in a letter to the *London Times* in 1890 that "self-control is more indispensable than gunpowder" and called for "heartfelt sympathy for the natives with whom one has to deal."

Conrad certainly shared this opinion. In 1890 he made his own journey into the heart of Africa, up the Congo River. He tells us in *Last Essays* that as a boy he put his finger on the middle of a map of Africa and declared that he would go there. When he did get there, as acting captain of a steamboat, he became melancholy over "the distasteful knowledge of the vilest scramble for loot that ever disfigured the history of human conscience and geographical exploration." (In *Heart of Darkness,* Marlow is also fascinated by the idea of Africa, especially by the "mighty big river," and experiences the same revulsion after he arrives.) At the head of the river Conrad picked up a company trader (as Marlow does), and this trader became a model for Kurtz. Like Kurtz, he died on the return trip. Conrad's wife, in a 1930 letter, said that her husband returned from the Congo a "disillusioned and bitter man," and that the trip had a profound effect on the remainder of his life.

It is one thing to live an experience and quite another to put it into a novel. In translating his Congo venture into the art that informs *Heart of Darkness,* Conrad went far beyond the mere telling of a story. He created a complex tale, even a mystery, in the sense that all great tragedies are mysteries, and consequently not all the questions we may have about the book can be answered.

Marlow, through whose consciousness most of the story is told, stands between the reader and Kurtz. What we can know of Kurtz is kept some distance from us; we are allowed into Marlow's mind but not into Kurtz's, except as we can infer his thoughts from his actions and words. Marlow, then, is the central character in the story.

Essentially, there are three main settings for the narrative. The first is a cruising yawl anchored in the Thames, near London, a center of civilized society, where Marlow and his friends wait for the turn of the tide. The second main setting is what is called the Central Station, two hundred miles above the mouth of the Congo, though the river is never named. Here is the middle ground, where the insensitive can survive, saved by "no learning and no intelligence" and symbolized by "the manager." Although a brutal evil is apparent here, it is seen only by those who have not yet yielded to greed and intrigue. At the last major setting, the Inner Station near the source of the river, is Kurtz, a man who acts out all the possible evils but is nevertheless perfectly capable of recognizing what he does. These settings are all symbolic clues to the meaning of the tale.

Literary symbols, and Conrad uses many of them, are a way of compressing several ideas in a short space. A writer speaks symbolically when he uses concrete objects, people, actions, natural phenomena, or dialogue to represent more than their literal meaning. Thus, a symbol stands for a complex of meanings communicated indirectly. When Conrad says that the river resembles "an immense snake uncoiled," he speaks merely metaphorically, comparing the shape of the river, as seen on a map, to the shape of a snake. He also brings to mind all the associations with snakes that we may have, including possibly a recollection of the story of the Garden of Eden, with which Conrad's story has some obvious parallels. But *repeated* metaphors take on wider meanings and become symbols. Notice the emphasis on "repeated." We come back to the river time and again in this story, and to the things associated with it: the shore, the fog, the difference between life on the shore and life on the water.

Actually, both rivers that take part in the story are used symbolically. At the outset we are told that the Thames stands for the way to wealth and conquest: "Hunters for gold or pursuers of fame, they all had gone out on that stream, bearing the sword, and often the torch, messengers of the might within the land, bearers of a spark from the sacred fire." To a certain extent, the Congo is the way to truth, through darkness. It also seems evident that while Marlow remains on the water, he is safe. The land is the place of corruption. All of these ideas rush into any interpretation of the river, Conrad's central symbol.

In addition to the symbols already mentioned, it is obvious that the title itself has symbolic connotations. Literally, it refers to the "Dark Continent," as Stanley called it, to the darkness of the landscape and to the darkness in which much of the story takes place. Often the term is associated with ignorance. The white man thinks that he is bringing civilization into the darkness, but as we follow Marlow on his journey up the river we learn otherwise; we see the irony based on what seems to be and what actually is, the difference between expectation and fulfillment. Marlow goes into the darkness and finds that the white man's claims of being superior are not true, that what is called civilization is a veneer that cracks under pressure. Ordinarily, light and dark symbolize good and evil, or truth and falsehood. In Conrad we get no such clearcut distinction. Intentionally, the symbolism is manipulated to suggest the shadowy complexity of human life. When looked at in this way, the title has several implications, some of which are clearly ironic.

Though in everyday life there are symbols (such as the cross, the flag, the sword) upon the significance of which we can more or less generally agree, it should be apparent that literary symbols are more complex and derive their meaning from the special context in which they appear. No one reader can be expected to perceive all the symbolic implications in any great piece of writing, but it is better to make the effort than to ignore them. A writer turns to symbols because they are a means of suggesting the abstract and intangible and because they bear an organic relationship to the material with which he is dealing. They grow *from* his subject matter; they are not superimposed upon it. In Conrad, symbolism is a technique for conveying a multiplicity of meanings. It is not a simple way of writing, but it is an effective one.

Questions on *Heart of Darkness*

A. For Close Reading

1. The first speaker, who begins the story, recounts the history of the Thames River. What episodes does he mention? What does Marlow remember of the past in his own second speech? What attitudes is each taking toward man in general?

2. As Marlow commences his tale, he comments on the motive which had impelled him to go to the "mighty big river," the Congo. Define this motive. What attitudes are expressed about his intentions by his aunt; by the Company head (the "great man himself"); by the doctor? How does Marlow react to each attitude?

3. On his trip toward the Company's first station, how does Marlow respond to the evidences of colonialism? Consider his descriptions of the coast, the native boatmen, the man-of-war, the "enemies."

4. When Marlow finally arrives at the Company's station, what does he see? How does he feel about what he sees? What irony does he find in the situation? From the evidence presented here, what conclusions can you draw about the Company's business methods?

5. The next stage in Marlow's journey is the "two-hundred-mile tramp" to the Central Station. What is the symbolic function of the "white companion" who keeps fainting? Marlow says, of the manager, "Perhaps there was nothing within him." What evidence does he offer for this judgment?

6. Almost at once Marlow goes to work repairing the steamboat, turning his back on the station. As he puts it, "In that way only it seemed to me I could keep my hold on the redeeming facts of life." On what kinds of things is he turning his back? What might he mean by "the redeeming facts of life"?

7. Section I of the story ends with a long discussion of rivets. How are they used symbolically here? Note particularly the line, ". . . and rivets were really what Mr. Kurtz wanted, if he had only known it."

8. On the trip up the river what contrast in behavior does Marlow observe be-

tween the cannibals and the pilgrims, especially in terms of "restraint," a continually recurring word? What restrains each group?

9. After the attack on the boat, Marlow discourses at length about Kurtz. What further do we learn of Kurtz? How are his gifts contrasted with his conduct? What had he been like before Africa and ivory-gathering? What changes had taken place in him since his arrival?

10. What do we learn about the Russian, the "harlequin," as Marlow calls him? How is he like—and unlike—Kurtz and Marlow? What additional information about Kurtz do we get from the Russian?

11. Describe Kurtz's station. What does its appearance show about how he has been living?

12. After Kurtz escapes from the boat, what judgment does Marlow make about him when they meet in the jungle?

13. Describe the death of Kurtz. Was he afraid to die?

14. Near the end of the book "the spectacled man," "Kurtz's cousin," and a "journalist" call on Marlow. What does each want? What does each get? What statements do they make about Kurtz's talents?

15. In the final confrontation between Marlow and the girl, Kurtz's "Intended," what irony do you find?

B. For Writing and Discussion

1. Reread Marlow's description of the Romans, noting especially the phrase, "fascination of the abomination." In what respect is his journey like theirs? How does the quoted phrase apply to Kurtz?

2. In the next paragraph Marlow says, "What saves us is efficiency—the devotion to efficiency." Later in the paragraph, speaking of the Romans again, he adds, "They grabbed what they could get for the sake of what was to be got. It was just robbery with violence, aggravated murder on a great scale, and men going at it blind—as is very proper for those who tackle a darkness. The conquest of the earth, which mostly means the taking it away from those who have a different complexion or slightly flatter noses than ourselves, is not a pretty thing when you look into it too much." To what extent do these sentences express a basic theme of the book? How does the story act out a meaning for these words?

3. Now look at Marlow's first statement, "And this also has been one of the dark places of the earth." When he says "has been," does he mean it still is? Or that things are better now? This question is really asking about the effect on Marlow of his whole experience in the Congo.

4. At one point Marlow says, "The mind of men is capable of anything—because everything is in it, all the past as well as all the future." And later, "He must meet that truth with his own true stuff—with his own inborn strength. Principles? Principles won't do. Acquisitions, clothes, pretty rags —rags that would fly off at the first good shake. No; you want a deliberate belief." Do these words point up any difference between Marlow and Kurtz?

5. The fog that holds up the expedition on the edge of Kurtz's station seems to mark the moment at which we go from appearance into reality. The quotation of the previous question speaks of "clothes, pretty rags—rags that would fly off at the first good shake." After the fog clears, Marlow throws overboard a pair of new shoes. What might the shoes symbolize? Remember that he later gives some old shoes to the Russian and that Kurtz's letters are tied with a shoelace. Do you see any symbolic pattern here? How does it relate to the significance of the story?

6. Instead of letting us see and hear Kurtz, Conrad has Marlow summarize his impressions of Kurtz:

    > You should have heard him say, "My ivory." Oh yes, I heard him. "My Intended, my ivory, my station, my river, my—" everything belonged to him. It made me hold my breath in expectation of hearing the wilderness burst into a prodigious peal of laughter that would shake the fixed stars in their places. Everything belonged to him—but that was a trifle. The thing was to know what he belonged to, how many powers of darkness claimed him for their own. That was the reflection that made you creepy all over. It was impossible—it was not good for one either—trying to imagine. He had taken a high seat amongst the devils of the land—I mean literally. You can't understand. How could you?—with solid pavement under your feet, surrounded by kind neighbors ready to cheer you or to fall on you, stepping delicately between the butcher and the policeman, in the holy terror of scandal and gallows and lunatic asylums—how can you imagine what particular region of the first ages a man's untrammelled feet may take him into by the way of solitude—utter solitude without a policeman—by the way of silence—utter silence, where no warning voice of a kind neighbor can be heard whispering of public opinion? These little things make all the great difference. When they are gone you must fall back upon your own innate strength, upon your own capacity for faithfulness.

    What is symbolized by the ivory; by the policeman; by the "warning voice of a kind neighbor"? What is meant by "faithfulness"? To what has Kurtz given his faith? To what has Marlow pledged his?

7. Continuing the description, Marlow speaks of the report that Kurtz had written. What is ironic about the name of the society for which Kurtz had written it? How do its content and style add to the portrayal of Kurtz? Why, at the end of the story, does Marlow tear off the postscript before giving the pamphlet to the journalist?

8. What judgment does the manager pass on Kurtz as the latter is dying? On Marlow? Comment on the significance of the repeated word, "unsound."

9. What are the functions of the various women in the story: Marlow's aunt? The knitting women in the Company office? The barbarian woman? Kurtz's "Intended"? Are any of them alike in any way? Compare the gesture made by the girl in the last scene, "She put out her arms as if after a retreating figure," with the last movement of the barbarian woman. Why does Marlow make this link?

10. In the last scene why does Marlow lie to the girl? Is he merely affirming the judgment he made on women in speaking of his aunt: "It's queer how out of touch with truth women are. They live in a world of their own, and there had never been anything like it, and never can be. It is too beautiful altogether, and if they were to set it up it would go to pieces before the first sunset. Some confounded fact we men have been living contentedly with ever since the day of creation would start up and knock the whole thing over"? (This judgment was confirmed in remarks made about the "Intended": "They—the women I mean—are out of it—should be out of it. We must help them to stay in that beautiful world of their own, lest ours gets worse.") Or does he lie for some other reason?

11. The novel begins and ends with descriptions of the Thames and of Marlow. Judging by the nature of these scenes, what effect has the experience, his voyage into darkness, had on him?

12. Marlow refers several times to the journey as a dream. What qualities of the narrative are particularly dreamlike?

13. Conrad chose to tell most of his story through the eyes of Marlow. How would the story have been different if it had been told by Kurtz; by the Russian; by the manager? Consider what each would see and know about Kurtz, and by what code of values each would be judging.

14. By limiting what we can know of Kurtz, Conrad keeps the focus of the story on Marlow. Support the idea that the story is principally about Marlow, not about Kurtz.

15. Conrad divides his story into three sections. Suggest titles (and defend your suggestions) for these divisions that would indicate specifically what each of the three is about.

Beyond the Horizon

(1919)

THE American theater as a serious art form began in the summer of 1916 when the Provincetown Playhouse on Cape Cod, Massachusetts, performed Eugene O'Neill's first one-act play, *Bound East for Cardiff.* Like so many of his later plays, this one was partly autobiographical. It dealt with the incident of a dying sailor aboard a freighter, an incident that O'Neill had been party to as a seaman in his own youth. He early proved himself to be one of those rare persons who have not only had wide experience with people and places but also the talent to make literature out of it.

He was born to the theater and lived for the theater. Son of an actor, an actor himself, an experimenter in theater forms, he gave substance and leadership to American drama over two decades of prolific production. Even in the seclusion of the last twenty years of his life, his influence remained strong.

His most typical play, the one that best represents his many interests, is probably *Beyond the Horizon.* It reveals the same brooding, tragic mood that suffuses his other plays, the same probing into the mystery of why man must suffer. We meet Robert Mayo at the moment he is about to make the tragic decision that will determine his future. Perhaps, as critics have pointed ed out, he wills his own future by making a free choice, but fate is also present in the circumstances that surround his choice: the marginal nature of the farm, his own health, Andy's sudden decision, Ruth's personality, his father's death. Other men have made similar choices in different circumstances and not been destroyed as a result. Perhaps Ruth, like the witches in *Macbeth,* is merely a personification of fate. Would Robert have made a good sailor? Was there really something for him out there "beyond the horizon"? Or is he merely a dreamer, always thinking that things are better somewhere else?

At any rate, O'Neill asked the questions that all tragic writers have asked: What gives meaning to life? Why do people suffer? To what extent can man control his destiny? His answers are different from those of other playwrights in this book. Robert's choice is not clearly motivated; he is not challenging fate, as is Oedipus. He does not go through the long challenge to action that drives Hamlet. He hardly acts at all; choices are forced on him by others. He does not fight fate; he accepts it. Death comes to him not as a moment of triumph, as it does to Oedipus and to Hamlet, but rather as a release from life. As Robert is dying, he says, "Look! Isn't it beautiful beyond the hills? I can hear the old voices calling me to come. And this time I'm going!" O'Neill seems to be saying that if men deny their talents and try to find substitutes, they may be doomed.

Robert Mayo is the prototype of the twentieth-century American tragic character. He is a common man who fails by choosing a life that he is not suited for. He acts not according to his conscience, as does Oedipus, but rather against his conscience. He knows what he should do but puts other things first. As he sums up life, in talking with Andy (Act III, Scene 1), he says, "I've been wondering what the great change was in you. You—a farmer—to gamble in a wheat pit with scraps of paper. There's a spiritual significance in that picture, Andy. I'm a failure, and Ruth's another—but we can both justly lay some of the blame for our stumbling on God. But you're the deepest-dyed failure of the three, Andy. You've spent eight years running away from yourself. Do you see what I mean? You used to be a creator when you loved the farm. You and life were in harmonious partnership." And later he adds, "Only through contact with suffering, Andy, will you—awaken."

The tragic fall in the play seems inevitable from the first. Aristotle pointed out that a requisite of great tragedy is that the individual has to have a chance of winning. Then out of his battle against circumstances, we get a sense of terror: If a strong man cannot win, what about us? But in *Beyond the Horizon*, Robert never seems to have a chance, and we are left at best with a sense of pity. If the measure of a man is how he faces the tragic moment, how do we measure Robert Mayo?

O'Neill's plays have a way of ending in the frustration of his characters, and perhaps he himself felt the same way about his own life. But at his death in 1953 he was America's greatest and most honored playwright, a three-time winner of the Pulitzer Prize (1920, 1922, 1928) and then, in 1936, of the Nobel Prize.

Beyond the Horizon

EUGENE O'NEILL

CHARACTERS

JAMES MAYO, *a farmer*
KATE MAYO, *his wife*
CAPTAIN DICK SCOTT, *of the bark* Sunda, *her brother*
ANDREW MAYO ⎱ *sons of James Mayo*
ROBERT MAYO ⎰
RUTH ATKINS
MRS. ATKINS, *her widowed mother*
MARY
BEN, *a farm hand*
DOCTOR FAWCETT

ACT I

SCENE I

A section of country highway. The road runs diagonally from the left, forward, to the right, rear, and can be seen in the distance winding toward the horizon like a pale ribbon between the low, rolling hills with their freshly plowed fields clearly divided from each other, checkerboard fashion, by the lines of stone walls and rough snake fences.

The forward triangle cut off by the road is a section of a field from the dark earth of which myriad bright-green blades of fall-sown rye are sprouting. A straggling line of piled rocks, too low to be called a wall, separates this field from the road.

To the rear of the road is a ditch with a sloping, grassy bank on the far side. From the center of this an old, gnarled apple tree, just budding into leaf, strains its twisted branches heavenwards, black against the pallor of distance. A snake fence sidles from left to right along the top of the bank, passing beneath the apple tree.

The hushed twilight of a day in May is just beginning. The horizon hills are still rimmed by a faint line of flame, and the sky above them glows with the crimson flush of the sunset. This fades gradually as the action of the scene progresses.

226

At the rise of the curtain, ROBERT MAYO *is discovered sitting on the fence. He is a tall, slender young man of twenty-three. There is a touch of the poet about him expressed in his high forehead and wide, dark eyes. His features are delicate and refined, leaning to weakness in the mouth and chin. He is dressed in gray corduroy trousers pushed into high laced boots, and a blue flannel shirt with a bright colored tie. He is reading a book by the fading sunset light. He shuts this, keeping a finger in to mark the place, and turns his head toward the horizon, gazing out over the fields and hills. His lips move as if he were reciting something to himself.*

His brother ANDREW *comes along the road from the right, returning from his work in the fields. He is twenty-seven years old, an opposite type to* ROBERT—*husky, sun-bronzed, handsome in a large-featured, manly fashion—a son of the soil, intelligent in a shrewd way, but with nothing of the intellectual about him. He wears overalls, leather boots, a gray flannel shirt open at the neck, and a soft, mud-stained hat pushed back on his head. He stops to talk to* ROBERT, *leaning on the hoe he carries.*

ANDREW   *(Seeing* ROBERT *has not noticed his presence—in a loud shout)* Hey there! *(*ROBERT *turns with a start. Seeing who it is, he smiles.)* Gosh, you do take the prize for daydreaming! And I see you've toted one of the old books along with you. *(He crosses the ditch and sits on the fence near his brother.)* What is it this time—poetry, I'll bet. *(He reaches for the book.)* Let me see.

ROBERT   *(Handing it to him rather reluctantly)* Look out you don't get it full of dirt.

ANDREW   *(Glancing at his hands)* That isn't dirt—it's good clean earth. *(He turns over the pages. His eyes read something and he gives an exclamation of disgust.)* Hump! *(With a provoking grin at his brother he reads aloud in a doleful, sing-song voice.)* "I have loved wind and light and the bright sea. But holy and most sacred night, not as I love and have loved thee." *(He hands the book back.)* Here! Take it and bury it. I suppose it's that year in college gave you a liking for that kind of stuff. I'm darn glad I stopped at high school, or maybe I'd been crazy too. *(He grins and slaps* ROBERT *on the back affectionately.)* Imagine me reading poetry and plowing at the same time! The team'd run away, I'll bet.

ROBERT   *(Laughing)* Or picture me plowing.

ANDREW   You should have gone back to college last fall, like I know you wanted to. You're fitted for that sort of thing—just as I ain't.

ROBERT   You know why I didn't go back, Andy. Pa didn't like the idea, even if he didn't say so; and I know he wanted the money to use improving the farm. And besides, I'm not keen on being a student, just because you see me reading books all the time. What I want to do now is keep on moving so that I won't take root in any one place.

ANDREW   Well, the trip you're leaving on tomorrow will keep you moving all right. *(At this mention of the trip they both fall silent. There is a pause. Finally* ANDREW *goes on, awkwardly, attempting to speak casually)* Uncle says you'll be gone three years.

ROBERT   About that, he figures.

ANDREW   *(Moodily)* That's a long time.

ROBERT   No so long when you come to consider it. You know the *Sunda* sails around the Horn for Yokohama first, and that's a long voyage on a sailing ship; and if we go to any of the other places Uncle Dick mentions—India, or Australia, or South Africa, or South America—they'll be long voyages, too.

ANDREW   You can have all those foreign parts for all of me. *(After a pause)* Ma's going to miss you a lot, Rob.

ROBERT   Yes—and I'll miss her.

ANDREW   And Pa ain't feeling none too happy to have you go—though he's been trying not to show it.

ROBERT   I can see how he feels.

ANDREW   And you can bet that I'm not giving any cheers about it. *(He puts one hand on the fence near* ROBERT.)

ROBERT   *(Putting one hand on top of* ANDREW's *with a gesture almost of shyness)* I know that, too, Andy.

ANDREW   I'll miss you as much as anybody, I guess. You see, you and I ain't like most brothers—always fighting and separated a lot of the time, while we've always been together—just the two of us. It's different with us. That's why it hits so hard, I guess.

ROBERT   *(With feeling)* It's just as hard for me, Andy—believe that! I hate to leave you and the old folks—but—I feel I've got to. There's something calling me— *(He points to the horizon.)* Oh, I can't just explain it to you, Andy.

ANDREW   No need to, Rob. *(Angry at himself)* Hell! You want to go—that's all there is to it; and I wouldn't have you miss this chance for the world.

ROBERT   It's fine of you to feel that way, Andy.

ANDREW   Huh! I'd be a nice son-of-a-gun if I didn't, wouldn't I? When I know how you need this sea trip to make a new man of you—in the body, I mean—and give you your full health back.

ROBERT   *(A trifle impatiently)* All of you seem to keep harping on my health. You were so used to seeing me lying around the house in the old days that you never will get over the notion that I'm a chronic invalid. You don't realize how I've bucked up in the past few years. If I had no other excuse for going on Uncle Dick's ship but just my health, I'd stay right here and start in plowing.

ANDREW   Can't be done. Farming ain't your nature. There's all the difference shown in just the way us two feel about the farm. You—well,
you like the home part of it, I expect; but as a place to work and grow
things, you hate it. Ain't that right?

ROBERT   Yes, I suppose it is. For you it's different. You're a Mayo
through and through. You're wedded to the soil. You're as much a
product of it as an ear of corn is, or a tree. Father is the same. This
farm is his life-work, and he's happy in knowing that another Mayo,
inspired by the same love, will take up the work where he leaves off. I
can understand your attitude, and Pa's; and I think it's wonderful and
sincere. But I—well, I'm not made that way.

ANDREW   No, you ain't; but when it comes to understanding, I guess I
realize that you've got your own angle of looking at things.

ROBERT   *(Musingly)* I wonder if you do, really.

ANDREW   *(Confidently)* Sure I do. You've seen a bit of the world,
enough to make the farm seem small, and you've got the itch to see it
all.

ROBERT   It's more than that, Andy.

ANDREW   Oh, of course. I know you're going to learn navigation, and
all about a ship, so's you can be an officer. That's natural, too. There's
fair pay in it, I expect, when you consider that you've always got a
home and grub thrown in; and if you're set on traveling, you can go
anywhere you're a mind to without paying fare.

ROBERT   *(With a smile that is half sad)* It's more than that, Andy.

ANDREW   Sure it is. There's always a chance of a good thing coming
your way in some of those foreign ports or other. I've heard there are
great opportunities for a young fellow with his eyes open in some of
those new countries that are just being opened up. *(Jovially)* I'll
bet that's what you've been turning over in your mind under all your
quietness! *(He slaps his brother on the back with a laugh.)* Well,
if you get to be a millionaire all of a sudden, call 'round once in a
while and I'll pass the plate to you. We could use a lot of money right
here on the farm without hurting it any.

ROBERT   *(Forced to laugh)* I've never considered that practical side
of it for a minute, Andy.

ANDREW   Well, you ought to.

ROBERT   No, I oughtn't. *(Pointing to the horizon—dreamily)* Supposing I was to tell you that it's just Beauty that's calling me,
the beauty of the far off and unknown, the mystery and spell
of the East which lures me in the books I've read, the need of the freedom of great wide spaces, the joy of wandering on and on—in quest
of the secret which is hidden over there, beyond the horizon? Suppose
I told you that was the one and only reason for my going?

ANDREW   I should say you were nutty.

ROBERT   *(Frowning)* Don't, Andy. I'm serious.

ANDREW   Then you might as well stay here, because we've got all you're looking for right on this farm. There's wide space enough, Lord knows; and you can have all the sea you want by walking a mile down to the beach; and there's plenty of horizon to look at, and beauty enough for anyone, except in the winter. *(He grins.)* As for the mystery and spell, I haven't met 'em yet, but they're probably lying around somewheres. I'll have you understand this is a first class farm with all the fixings. *(He laughs.)*

ROBERT   *(Joining in the laughter in spite of himself)* It's no use talking to you, you chump!

ANDREW   You'd better not say anything to Uncle Dick about spells and things when you're on the ship. He'll likely chuck you overboard for a Jonah. *(He jumps down from fence.)* I'd better run along. I've got to wash up some as long as Ruth's Ma is coming over for supper.

ROBERT   *(Pointedly—almost bitterly)* And Ruth.

ANDREW   *(Confused—looking everywhere except at* ROBERT—*trying to appear unconcerned)* Yes, Ruth'll be staying too. Well, I better hustle, I guess, and— *(He steps over the ditch to the road while he is talking.)*

ROBERT   *(Who appears to be fighting some strong inward emotion— impulsively)* Wait a minute, Andy! *(He jumps down from the fence.)* There is something I want to— *(He stops abruptly, biting his lips, his face coloring.)*

ANDREW   *(Facing him; half-defiantly)* Yes?

ROBERT   *(Confusedly)* No— never mind— it doesn't matter, it was nothing.

ANDREW   *(After a pause, during which he stares fixedly at* ROBERT'S *averted face)* Maybe I can guess— what you were going to say— but I guess you're right not to talk about it. *(He pulls* ROBERT'S *hand from his side and grips it tensely; the two brothers stand looking into each other's eyes for a minute.)* We can't help those things, Rob. *(He turns away, suddenly releasing* ROBERT'S *hand.)* You'll be coming along shortly, won't you?

ROBERT   *(Dully)* Yes.

ANDREW   See you later, then. *(He walks off down the road to the left.* ROBERT *stares after him for a moment; then climbs to the fence rail again, and looks out over the hills, an expression of deep grief on his face. After a moment or so,* RUTH *enters hurriedly from the left. She is a healthy, blonde, out-of-door girl of twenty, with a graceful, slender figure. Her face, though inclined to roundness, is undeniably pretty, its large eyes of a deep blue set off strikingly by the sun-bronzed complexion. Her small, regular features are marked by a certain strength—an underlying, stubborn fixity of purpose hidden in the*

*frankly-appealing charm of her fresh youthfulness. She wears a simple
white dress but no hat).*

RUTH   *(Seeing him)* Hello, Rob!

ROBERT   *(Startled)* Hello, Ruth!

RUTH   *(Jumps the ditch and perches on the fence beside him)* I was
looking for you.

ROBERT   *(Pointedly)* Andy just left here.

RUTH   I know. I met him on the road a second ago. He told me you
were here. *(Tenderly playful)* I wasn't looking for Andy, Smarty,
if that's what you mean. I was looking for *you.*

ROBERT   Because I'm going away tomorrow?

RUTH   Because your mother was anxious to have you come home and
asked me to look for you. I just wheeled Ma over to your house.

ROBERT   *(Perfunctorily)* How is your mother?

RUTH   *(A shadow coming over her face)* She's about the same. She
never seems to get any better or any worse. Oh, Rob, I do wish she'd
try to make the best of things that can't be helped.

ROBERT   Has she been nagging at you again?

RUTH   *(Nods her head, and then breaks forth rebelliously)* She never
stops nagging. No matter what I do for her she finds fault. If only Pa
was still living— *(She stops as if ashamed of her outburst.)* I suppose I shouldn't complain this way. *(She sighs.)* Poor Ma, Lord
knows it's hard enough for her. I suppose it's natural to be cross when
you're not able ever to walk a step. Oh, I'd like to be going away some
place—like you!

ROBERT   It's hard to stay—and equally hard to go, sometimes.

RUTH   There! If I'm not the stupid body! I swore I wasn't going to
speak about your trip—until after you'd gone; and there I go, first
thing!

ROBERT   Why didn't you want to speak of it?

RUTH   Because I didn't want to spoil this last night you're here. Oh,
Rob, I'm going to—we're all going to miss you so awfully. Your
mother is going around looking as if she'd burst out crying any minute. You ought to know how I feel. Andy and you and I—why it
seems as if we'd always been together.

ROBERT   *(With a wry attempt at a smile)* You and Andy will still
have each other. It'll be harder for me without anyone.

RUTH   But you'll have new sights and new people to take your mind off;
while we'll be here with the old, familiar place to remind us every
minute of the day. It's a shame you're going—just at this time, in
spring, when everything is getting so nice. *(With a sigh)* I oughtn't
to talk that way when I know going's the best thing for you. You're
bound to find all sorts of opportunities to get on, your father says.

ROBERT   *(Heatedly)* I don't give a damn about that! I wouldn't take a voyage across the road for the best opportunity in the world of the kind Pa thinks of. *(He smiles at his own irritation.)* Excuse me, Ruth, for getting worked up over it; but Andy gave me an overdose of the practical considerations.

RUTH   *(Slowly, puzzled)* Well, then, if it isn't— *(With sudden intensity)* Oh, Rob, *why* do you want to go?

ROBERT   *(Turning to her quickly, in surprise—slowly)* Why do you ask that, Ruth?

RUTH   *(Dropping her eyes before his searching glance)* Because— *(Lamely)* It seems such a shame.

ROBERT   *(Insistently)* Why?

RUTH   Oh, because— everything.

ROBERT   I could hardly back out now, even if I wanted to. And I'll be forgotten before you know it.

RUTH   *(Indignantly)* You won't! I'll never forget— *(She stops and turns away to hide her confusion.)*

ROBERT   *(Softly)* Will you promise me that?

RUTH   *(Evasively)* Of course. It's mean of you to think that any of us would forget so easily.

ROBERT   *(Disappointedly)* Oh!

RUTH   *(With an attempt at lightness)* But you haven't told me your reason for leaving yet.

ROBERT   *(Moodily)* I doubt if you'll understand. It's difficult to explain, even to myself. Either you feel it, or you don't. I can remember being conscious of it first when I was only a kid—you haven't forgotten what a sickly specimen I was then, in those days, have you?

RUTH   *(With a shudder)* Let's not think about them.

ROBERT   You'll have to, to understand. Well, in those days, when Ma was fixing meals, she used to get me out of the way by pushing my chair to the west window and telling me to look out and be quiet. That wasn't hard. I guess I was always quiet.

RUTH   *(Compassionately)* Yes, you always were—and you suffering so much, too!

ROBERT   *(Musingly)* So I used to stare out over the fields to the hills, out there— *(he points to the horizon)*   and somehow after a time I'd forget any pain I was in, and start dreaming. I knew the sea was over beyond those hills—the folks had told me—and I used to wonder what the sea was like, and try to form a picture of it in my mind. *(With a smile)* There was all the mystery in the world to me then about that—far-off sea—and there still is! It called to me then just as it does now. *(After a slight pause)* And other times my eyes would follow this road, winding off into the distance, toward the hills, as if it, too, was searching for the sea. And I'd promise myself that when I grew up and was strong, I'd follow that road, and it and I would find the sea together. *(With a smile)* You see, my making this trip is only keeping that promise of long ago.

RUTH   *(Charmed by his low, musical voice telling the dreams of his childhood)* Yes, I see.

ROBERT   Those were the only happy moments of my life then, dreaming there at the window. I liked to be all alone—those times. I got to know all the different kinds of sunsets by heart. And all those sunsets took place over there— *(he points)* beyond the horizon. So gradually I came to believe that all the wonders of the world happened on the other side of those hills. There was the home of the good fairies who performed beautiful miracles. I believed in fairies then. *(With a smile)* Perhaps I still do believe in them. Anyway, in those days they were real enough, and sometimes I could actually hear them calling to me to come out and play with them, dance with them down the road in the dusk in a game of hide-and-seek to find out where the sun was hiding himself. They sang their little songs to me, songs that told of all the wonderful things they had in their home on the other side of the hills; and they promised to show me all of them, if I'd only come, come! But I couldn't come then, and I used to cry sometimes and Ma would think I was in pain. *(He breaks off suddenly with a laugh.)* That's why I'm going now, I suppose. For I can still hear them calling. But the horizon is as far away and as luring as ever. *(He turns to her—softly)* Do you understand now, Ruth?

RUTH   *(Spellbound, in a whisper)* Yes.

ROBERT   You feel it then?

RUTH   Yes, yes, I do! *(Unconsciously she snuggles close against his side. His arm steals about her as if he were not aware of the action.)* Oh, Rob, how could I help feeling it? You tell things so beautifully!

ROBERT   *(Suddenly realizing that his arm is around her, and that her head is resting on his shoulder, he gently takes his arm away. RUTH, brought back to herself, is overcome with confusion.)* So now you know why I'm going. It's for that reason—that and one other.

RUTH   You've another? Then you must tell me that, too.

ROBERT   *(Looking at her searchingly. She drops her eyes before his gaze.)* I wonder if I ought to! You'll promise not to be angry—whatever it is?

RUTH   *(Softly, her face still averted)* Yes, I promise.

ROBERT   *(Simply)* I love you. That's the other reason.

RUTH   *(Hiding her face in her hands)* Oh, Rob!

ROBERT   I wasn't going to tell you, but I feel I have to. It can't matter now that I'm going so far away, and for so long—perhaps forever. I've loved you all these years, but the realization never came 'til I agreed to go away with Uncle Dick. Then I thought of leaving you, and the pain of that thought revealed to me in a flash—that I loved you, had loved you as long as I could remember. *(He gently pulls one of* RUTH's *hands away from her face.)* You mustn't mind my telling you this, Ruth. I realize how impossible it all is—and I understand; for the revelation of my own love seemed to open my eyes to the love of others. I saw Andy's love for you—and I knew that you must love him.

RUTH   *(Breaking out stormily)* I don't! I don't love Andy! I don't! *(*ROBERT *stares at her in stupid astonishment.* RUTH *weeps hysterically.)* Whatever—put such a fool notion into—into your head? *(She suddenly throws her arms about his neck and hides her head on his shoulder)* Oh, Rob! Don't go away! Please! You mustn't, now! You can't! I won't let you! It'd break my—my heart!

ROBERT   *(The expression of stupid bewilderment giving way to one of overwhelming joy. He presses her close to him—slowly and tenderly.)* Do you mean that—that you love me?

RUTH   *(Sobbing)* Yes, yes— of course I do— what d'you s'pose? *(She lifts her head and looks into his eyes with a tremulous smile.)* You stupid thing! *(He kisses her.)* I've loved you right along.

ROBERT   *(Mystified)* But you and Andy were always together!

RUTH   Because you never seemed to want to go any place with me. You were always reading an old book, and not paying any attention to me. I was too proud to let you see I cared because I thought the year you had away to college had made you stuck-up, and you thought yourself too educated to waste any time on me.

ROBERT   *(Kissing her)* And I was thinking— *(With a laugh)* What fools we've both been!

RUTH   *(Overcome by a sudden fear)* You won't go away on the trip, will you, Rob? You'll tell them you can't go on account of me, won't you? You can't go now! You can't!

ROBERT   *(Bewildered)* Perhaps—you can come too.

RUTH   Oh, Rob, don't be so foolish. You know I can't. Who'd take care of ma? Don't you see I couldn't go—on her account? *(She clings to him imploringly.)* Please don't go—not now. Tell them you've decided not to. They won't mind. I know your mother and father'll be glad. They'll all be. They don't want you to go so far away from them. Please, Rob! We'll be so happy here together where it's natural and we know things. Please tell me you won't go!

ROBERT   *(Face to face with a definite, final decision, he betrays the conflict going on within him.)* But—Ruth—I—Uncle Dick—

RUTH   He won't mind when he knows it's for your happiness to stay. How could he? *(As* ROBERT *remains silent she burst into sobs again.)* Oh, Rob! And you said—you loved me!

ROBERT   *(Conquered by this appeal—an irrevocable decision in his voice)* I won't go, Ruth. I promise you. There! Don't cry! *(He presses her to him, stroking her hair tenderly. After a pause he speaks with happy hopefulness.)* Perhaps after all Andy was right—righter than he knew—when he said I could find all the things I was seeking for here, at home on the farm. I think love must have been the secret —the secret that called to me from over the world's rim—the secret beyond every horizon; and when I did not come, it came to me. *(He clasps* RUTH *to him fiercely)* Oh, Ruth, our love is sweeter than any distant dream! *(He kisses her passionately and steps to the ground, lifting* RUTH *in his arms and carrying her to the road where he puts her down.)*

RUTH   *(With a happy laugh)* My, but you're strong!

ROBERT   Come! We'll go and tell them at once.

RUTH   *(Dismayed)* Oh, no, don't, Rob, not 'til after I've gone. There'd be bound to be such a scene with them all together.

ROBERT   *(Kissing her—gayly)* As you like—little Miss Common Sense!

RUTH   Let's go, then. *(She takes his hand, and they start to go off left.* ROBERT *suddenly stops and turns as though for a last look at the hills and the dying sunset flush.)*

ROBERT   *(Looking upward and pointing)* See! The first star. *(He bends down and kisses her tenderly.)* Our star!

RUTH   *(In a soft murmur)* Yes. Our very own star. *(They stand for a moment looking up at it, their arms around each other. Then* RUTH *takes his hand again and starts to lead him away.)* Come, Rob, let's go. *(His eyes are fixed again on the horizon as he half turns to follow her.* RUTH *urges.)* We'll be late for supper, Rob.

ROBERT   *(Shakes his head impatiently, as though he were throwing off some disturbing thought—with a laugh)* All right. We'll run then. Come on! *(They run off laughing as The Curtain Falls.)*

SCENE II

The sitting room of the Mayo farm house about nine o'clock the same night. On the left, two windows looking out on the fields. Against the wall between the windows, an old-fashioned walnut desk. In the left corner, rear, a sideboard with a mirror. In the rear wall to the right of the sideboard, a window looking out on the road. Next to the window a door leading out into the yard. Farther right, a black horse-hair sofa, and another door opening on a bedroom. In the corner, a straight-backed chair. In the right wall, near the middle, an open doorway leading to the kitchen. Farther forward a double-heater stove with coal scuttle, etc. In the center of the newly carpeted floor, an oak dining-room table with a red cover. In the center of the table, a large oil reading lamp. Four chairs, three rockers with crocheted tidies on their backs, and one straight-backed, are placed about the table. The walls are papered a dark red with a scrolly-figured pattern.

Everything in the room is clean, well-kept, and in its exact place, yet there is no suggestion of primness about the whole. Rather the at-mosphere is one of the orderly comfort of a simple, hard-earned pros-perity, enjoyed and maintained by the family as a unit.

JAMES MAYO, his wife, her brother, CAPTAIN DICK SCOTT, and AN-DREW are discovered. MAYO is his son ANDREW over again in body and face—an ANDREW sixty-five years old with a short, square, white beard. MRS. MAYO is a slight, round-faced, rather prim-looking wom-an of fifty-five who had once been a school teacher. The labors of a farmer's wife have bent but not broken her, and she retains a certain refinement of movement and expression foreign to the MAYO part of the family. Whatever of resemblance ROBERT has to his parents may be traced to her. Her brother, the CAPTAIN, is short and stocky, with a weather-beaten, jovial face and a white mustache—a typical old salt, loud of voice and given to gesture. He is fifty-eight years old.

JAMES MAYO sits in front of the table. He wears spectacles, and a farm journal which he has been reading lies in his lap. THE CAPTAIN leans forward from a chair in the rear, his hands on the table in front of him. ANDREW is tilted back on the straight-backed chair to the left, his chin sunk forward on his chest, staring at the carpet, preoccupied and frowning.

As the Curtain rises the CAPTAIN is just finishing the relation of some sea episode. The others are pretending an interest which is belied by the absent-minded expressions on their faces.

THE CAPTAIN   *(Chuckling)*   And that mission woman, she hails me on the dock as I was acomin' ashore, and she says—with her silly face all screwed up serious as judgment—"Captain," she says, "would you be so kind as to tell me where the sea-gulls sleeps at nights?" Blow me if them warn't her exact words! *(He slaps the table with the palm of his hands and laughs loudly. The others force smiles.)*   Ain't that just like a fool woman's question? And I looks at her serious as I could, "Ma'm," says I, "I couldn't rightly answer that question. I ain't never seed a sea-gull in his bunk yet. The next time I hears one snorin'," I says, "I'll make a note of where he's turned in, and write you a letter 'bout it." And then she calls me a fool real spiteful and tacks away from me quick. *(He laughs again uproariously.)*   So I got rid of her that way. *(The others smile but immediately relapse into expressions of gloom again.)*

MRS. MAYO   *(Absent-mindedly—feeling that she has to say something)*
But when it comes to that, where *do* sea-gulls sleep, Dick?

SCOTT   *(Slapping the table)*   Ho! Ho! Listen to her, James. 'Nother
one! Well, if that don't beat all hell—'scuse me for cussin', Kate.

MAYO   *(With a twinkle in his eyes)*   They unhitch their wings, Katey,
and spreads 'em out on a wave for a bed.

SCOTT   And then they tells the fish to whistle to 'em when it's time to
turn out. Ho! Ho!

MRS. MAYO   *(With a forced smile)*   You men folks are too smart to
live, aren't you?   *(She resumes her knitting:* MAYO *pretends to read
his paper;* ANDREW *stares at the floor.)*

SCOTT   *(Looks from one to the other of them with a puzzled air. Finally
he is unable to bear the thick silence a minute longer, and blurts
out:)*   You folks look as if you was settin' up with a corpse.   *(With
exaggerated concern)*   God A'mighty, there ain't anyone dead, be
there?

MAYO   *(Sharply)*   Don't play the dunce, Dick! You know as well as we
do there ain't no great cause to be feelin' chipper.

SCOTT   *(Argumentatively)*   And there ain't no cause to be wearin'
mourning, either, I can make out.

MRS. MAYO   *(Indignantly)*   How can you talk that way, Dick Scott, when
you're taking our Robbie away from us, in the middle of the night,
you might say, just to get on that old boat of yours on time! I think
you might wait until morning when he's had his breakfast.

SCOTT   *(Appealing to the others hopelessly)*   Ain't that a woman's way
o' seein' things for you? God A'mighty, Kate, I can't give orders to the
tide that it's got to be high just when it suits me to have it. I ain't gettin' no fun out o' missin' sleep and leavin' here at six bells
myself.   *(Protestingly)*   And the *Sunda* ain't an old ship—leastways,
not very old—and she's good's she ever was.

MRS. MAYO   *(Her lips trembling)*   I wish Robbie weren't going.

MAYO   *(Looking at her over his glasses—consolingly)*   There, Katey!

MRS. MAYO   *(Rebelliously)*   Well, I *do* wish he wasn't!

SCOTT   You shouldn't be taking it so hard, 's far as I kin see. This vige'll
make a man of him. I'll see to it he learns how to navigate, 'n' study
for a mate's c'tificate right off—and it'll give him a trade for the rest
of his life, if he wants to travel.

MRS. MAYO   But I don't want him to travel all his life. You've got to see
he comes home when this trip is over. Then he'll be all well, and he'll
want to—to marry—   (ANDREW *sits forward in his chair with an ab-
rupt movement)*   —and settle down right here.   *(She stares down at
the knitting in her lap—after a pause)*   I never realized how hard it
was going to be for me to have Robbie go—or I wouldn't have considered it a minute.

SCOTT   It ain't no good goin' on that way, Kate, now it's all settled.

MRS. MAYO   *(On the verge of tears)*   It's all right for *you* to talk. You've never had any children. You don't know what it means to be parted from them—and Robbie my youngest, too.   (ANDREW *frowns and fidgets in his chair.)*

ANDREW   *(Suddenly turning to them)*   There's one thing none of you seem to take into consideration—that Rob wants to go. He's dead set on it. He's been dreaming over this trip ever since it was first talked about. It wouldn't be fair to him not to have him go.   *(A sudden uneasiness seems to strike him.)*   At least, not if he still feels the same way about it he did when he was talking to me this evening.

MAYO   *(With an air of decision)*   Andy's right, Katey. That ends all argyment, you can see that.   *(Looking at his big silver watch)*   Wonder what's happened to Robert? He's been gone long enough to wheel the widder to home, certain. He can't be out dreamin' at the stars his last night.

MRS. MAYO   *(A bit reproachfully)*   Why didn't you wheel Mrs. Atkins back tonight, Andy? You usually do when she and Ruth come over.

ANDREW   *(Avoiding her eyes)*   I thought maybe Robert wanted to tonight. He offered to go right away when they were leaving.

MRS. MAYO   He only wanted to be polite.

ANDREW   *(Gets to his feet)*   Well, he'll be right back, I guess.   *(He turns to his father.)*   Guess I'll go take a look at the black cow, Pa—see if she's ailing any.

MAYO   Yes—better had, son.   (ANDREW *goes into the kitchen on the right.)*

SCOTT   *(As he goes out—in a low tone)*   There's the boy that would make a good, strong sea-farin' man—if he'd a mind to.

MAYO   *(Sharply)*   Don't you put no such fool notions in Andy's head, Dick—or you 'n' me's goin' to fall out.   *(Then he smiles.)*   You couldn't tempt him, no ways. Andy's a Mayo bred in the bone, and he's a born farmer, and a damn good one, too. He'll live and die right here on this farm, like I expect to.   *(With proud confidence)*   And he'll make this one of the slickest, best-payin' farms in the state, too, afore he gits through!

SCOTT   Seems to me it's a pretty slick place right now.

MAYO   *(Shaking his head)*   It's too small. We need more land to make it amount to much, and we ain't got the capital to buy it.   (ANDREW *enters from the kitchen. His hat is on, and he carries a lighted lantern in his hand. He goes to the door in the rear leading out.)*

ANDREW   *(Opens the door and pauses)*   Anything else you can think of to be done, Pa?

MAYO   No, nothin' I know of.   (ANDREW *goes out, shutting the door.)*

MRS. MAYO   *(After a pause)*   What's come over Andy tonight, I wonder? He acts so strange.

MAYO   He does seem sort o' glum and out of sorts. It's 'count o' Robert leavin', I s'pose. *(To* SCOTT*)* Dick, you wouldn't believe how them boys o' mine sticks together. They ain't like most brothers. They've been thick as thieves all their lives, with nary a quarrel I kin remember.

SCOTT   No need to tell me that. I can see how they take to each other.

MRS. MAYO   *(Pursuing her train of thought)*   Did you notice, James, how queer everyone was at supper? Robert seemed stirred up about something; and Ruth was so flustered and giggly; and Andy sat there dumb, looking as if he'd lost his best friend; and all of them only nibbled at their food.

MAYO   Guess they was all thinkin' about tomorrow, same as us.

MRS. MAYO   *(Shaking her head)*   No. I'm afraid somethin's happened —somethin' else.

MAYO   You mean—'bout Ruth?

MRS. MAYO   Yes.

MAYO   *(After a pause—frowning)*   I hope her and Andy ain't had a serious fallin'-out. I always sorter hoped they'd hitch up together sooner or later. What d'you say, Dick? Don't you think them two'd pair up well?

SCOTT   *(Nodding his head approvingly)*   A sweet, wholesome couple they'd make.

MAYO   It'd be a good thing for Andy in more ways than one. I ain't what you'd call calculatin' generally, and I b'lieve in lettin' young folks run their affairs to suit themselves; but there's advantages for both o' them in this match you can't overlook in reason. The Atkins farm is right next to ourn. Jined together they'd make a jim-dandy of a place, with plenty o' room to work in. And bein' a widder with only a daughter, and laid up all the time to boot, Mrs. Atkins can't do nothin' with the place as it ought to be done. She needs a man, a first-class farmer, to take hold o' things; and Andy's just the one.

MRS. MAYO   *(Abruptly)*   I don't think Ruth loves Andy.

MAYO   You don't? Well, maybe a woman's eyes is sharper in such things, but—they're always together. And if she don't love him now, she'll likely come around to it in time. *(As* MRS. MAYO *shakes her head)* You seem mighty fixed in your opinion, Katey. How d'you know?

MRS. MAYO   It's just—what I feel.

MAYO   *(A light breaking over him)*   You don't mean to say—(MRS. MAYO *nods.* MAYO *chuckles scornfully)* Shucks! I'm losin' my respect for your eyesight, Katey. Why, Robert ain't got no time for Ruth, 'cept as a friend!

MRS. MAYO   *(Warningly)* Sss-h-h! *(The door from the yard opens, and* ROBERT *enters. He is smiling happily, and humming a song to himself, but as he comes into the room an undercurrent of nervous uneasiness manifests itself in his bearing.)*

MAYO   So here you be at last! (ROBERT *comes forward and sits on* ANDY'S *chair.* MAYO *smiles slyly at his wife.)* What have you been doin' all this time—countin' the stars to see if they all come out right and proper?

ROBERT   There's only one I'll ever look for any more, Pa.

MAYO   *(Reproachfully)* You might've even not wasted time lookin' for that one—your last night.

MRS. MAYO   *(As if she were speaking to a child)* You ought to have worn your coat a sharp night like this, Robbie.

SCOTT   *(Disgustedly)* God A'mighty, Kate, you treat Robert as if he was one year old!

MRS. MAYO   *(Notices* ROBERT'S *nervous uneasiness)* You look all worked up over something, Robbie. What is it?

ROBERT   *(Swallowing hard, looks quickly from one to the other of them —then begins determinedly)* Yes, there *is* something—something I must tell you—all of you. *(As he begins to talk* ANDREW *enters quietly from the rear, closing the door behind him, and setting the lighted lantern on the floor. He remains standing by the door, his arms folded, listening to* ROBERT *with a repressed expression of pain on his face.* ROBERT *is so much taken up with what he is going to say that he does not notice* ANDREW'S *presence.)* Something I discovered only this evening—very beautiful and wonderful—something I did not take into consideration previously because I hadn't dared to hope that such happiness could ever come to me. *(Appealingly)* You must all remember that fact, won't you?

MAYO   *(Frowning)* Let's get to the point, son.

ROBERT   *(With a trace of defiance)* Well, the point is this, Pa: I'm not going—I mean—I can't go tomorrow with Uncle Dick—or at any future time, either.

MRS. MAYO   *(With a sharp sigh of joyful relief)* Oh, Robbie, I'm so glad!

MAYO   *(Astounded)* You ain't serious, be you, Robert? *(Severely)* Seems to me it's a pretty late hour in the day for you to be upsettin' all your plans so sudden!

ROBERT   I asked you to remember that until this evening I didn't know myself. I had never dared to dream—

MAYO   *(Irritably)* What is this foolishness you're talkin' of?

ROBERT   *(Flushing)* Ruth told me this evening that—she loved me. It was after I'd confessed I loved her. I told her I hadn't been conscious of my love until after the trip had been arranged, and I realized it would mean—leaving her. That was the truth. I *didn't* know until then. *(As if justifying himself to the others)* I hadn't intended telling her anything but—suddenly—I felt I must. I didn't think it would matter, because I was going away. And I thought she loved—someone else. *(Slowly—his eyes shining)* And then she cried and said it was I she'd loved all the time, but I hadn't seen it.

MRS. MAYO *(Rushes over and throws her arms about him)* I knew it! I was just telling your father when you came in—and, Oh, Robbie, I'm so happy you're not going!

ROBERT *(Kissing her)* I knew you'd be glad, Ma.

MAYO *(Bewilderedly)* Well, I'll be damned! You do beat all for gettin' folks' minds all tangled up, Robert. And Ruth too! Whatever got into her of a sudden? Why, I was thinkin'—

MRS. MAYO *(Hurriedly—in a tone of warning)* Never mind what you were thinking, James. It wouldn't be any use telling us that now. *(Meaningly)* And what you were hoping for turns out just the same almost, doesn't it?

MAYO *(Thoughtfully—beginning to see this side of the argument)* Yes, I suppose you're right, Katey. *(Scratching his head in puzzlement)* But how it ever come about! It do beat anything ever I heard. *(Finally he gets up with a sheepish grin and walks over to* ROBERT.) We're glad you ain't goin', your Ma and I, for we'd have missed you terrible, that's certain and sure; and we're glad you've found happiness. Ruth's a fine girl and'll make a good wife to you.

ROBERT *(Much moved)* Thank you, Pa. *(He grips his father's hand in his.)*

ANDREW *(His face tense and drawn, comes forward and holds out his hands, forcing a smile)* I guess it's my turn to offer congratulations, isn't it?

ROBERT *(With a startled cry when his brother appears before him so suddenly)* Andy! *(Confused)* Why—I—I didn't see you. Were you here when—

ANDREW I heard everything you said; and here's wishing you every happiness, you and Ruth. You both deserve the best there is.

ROBERT *(Taking his hand)* Thanks, Andy, it's fine of you to— *(His voice dies away as he sees the pain in* ANDREW'S *eyes.)*

ANDREW *(Giving his brother's hand a final grip)* Good luck to you both! *(He turns away and goes back to the rear where he bends over the lantern, fumbling with it to hide his emotion from the others.)*

MRS. MAYO *(To the* CAPTAIN, *who has been too flabbergasted by* ROBERT'S *decision to say a word)* What's the matter, Dick? Aren't you going to congratulate Robbie?

SCOTT *(Embarrassed)* Of course I be! *(He gets to his feet and shakes* ROBERT'S *hand, muttering a vague)* Luck to you, boy. *(He stands beside* ROBERT *as if he wanted to say something more but doesn't know how to go about it.)*

ROBERT   Thanks, Uncle Dick.

SCOTT   So you're not acomin' on the *Sunda* with me?   *(His voice indicates disbelief.)*

ROBERT   I can't, Uncle—not now. I wouldn't miss it for anything else in the world under any other circumstances. *(He sighs unconsciously.)* But you see I've found a bigger dream. *(Then with joyous high spirits)* I want you all to understand one thing—I'm not going to be a loafer on your hands any longer. This means the beginning of a new life for me in every way. I'm going to settle right down and take a real interest in the farm, and do my share. I'll prove to you, Pa, that I'm as good a Mayo as you are—or Andy, when I want to be.

MAYO   *(Kindly but skeptically)*   That's the right spirit, Robert. Ain't none of us doubts your willin'ness, but you ain't never learned—

ROBERT   Then I'm going to start learning right away, and you'll teach me, won't you?

MAYO   *(Mollifyingly)*   Of course I will, boy, and be glad to, only you'd best go easy at first.

SCOTT   *(Who has listened to this conversation in mingled consternation and amazement)*   You don't mean to tell me you're goin' to let him stay, do you, James?

MAYO   Why, things bein' as they be, Robert's free to do as he's a mind to.

MRS. MAYO   *Let him!* The very idea!

SCOTT   *(More and more ruffled)*   Then all I got to say is, you're a soft, weak-willed critter to be permittin' a boy—and women, too—to be layin' your course for you wherever they damn pleases.

MAYO   *(Slyly amused)*   It's just the same with me as 'twas with you, Dick. You can't order the tides on the seas to suit you, and I ain't pretendin' I can reg'late love for young folks.

SCOTT   *(Scornfully)*   Love! They ain't old enough to know love when they sight it! Love! I'm ashamed of you, Robert, to go lettin' a little huggin' and kissin' in the dark spile your chances to make a man out o' yourself. It ain't common sense—no siree, it ain't—not by a hell of a sight! *(He pounds the table with his fists in exasperation.)*

MRS. MAYO   *(Laughing provokingly at her brother)*   A fine one you are to be talking about love, Dick—an old cranky bachelor like you. Goodness sakes!

SCOTT   *(Exasperated by their joking)*   I've never been a damn fool like most, if that's what you're steerin' at.

MRS. MAYO   *(Tauntingly)*   Sour grapes, aren't they, Dick? *(She laughs.*

ROBERT *and his father chuckle.* SCOTT *sputters with annoyance.)*
Good gracious, Dick, you do act silly, flying into a temper over nothing.

SCOTT *(Indignantly)* Nothin'! You talk as if I wasn't concerned no-how in this here business. Seems to me I've got a right to have my say. Ain't I made all arrangements with the owners and stocked up with some special grub all on Robert's account?

ROBERT You've been fine, Uncle Dick; and I appreciate it. Truly.

MAYO 'Course; we all does, Dick.

SCOTT *(Unplacated)* I've been countin' sure on havin' Robert for company on this vige—to sorta talk to and show things to, and teach, kinda, and I got my mind so set on havin' him I'm goin' to be double lonesome this vige. *(He pounds on the table, attempting to cover up this confession of weakness.)* Darn all this silly lovin' business, anyway. *(Irritably)* But all this talk ain't tellin' me what I'm to do with that sta'b'd cabin I fixed up. It's all painted white, an' a bran new mattress on the bunk, 'n' new sheets 'n' blankets 'n' things. And Chips built in a book-case so's Robert could take his books along—with a slidin' bar fixed across't it, mind, so's they couldn't fall out no matter how she rolled. *(With excited consternation)* What d'you suppose my officers is goin' to think when there's no one comes aboard to occupy that sta'b'd cabin? And the men what did the work on it—what'll *they* think? *(He shakes his finger indignantly.)* They're liable as not to suspicion it was a *woman* I'd plan to ship along, and that she gave me the go-by at the last moment! *(He wipes his perspiring brow in anguish at this thought.)* Gawd A'mighty! They're only lookin' to have the laugh on me for something like that. They're liable to b'lieve anything, those fellers is!

MAYO *(With a wink)* Then there's nothing to it but for you to get right out and hunt up a wife somewheres for that spick 'n' span cabin. She'll have to be a pretty one, too, to match it. *(He looks at his watch with exaggerated concern.)* You ain't got much time to find her, Dick.

SCOTT *(As the others smile—sulkily)* You kin go to thunder, Jim Mayo!

ANDREW *(Comes forward from where he has been standing by the door, rear, brooding. His face is set in a look of grim determination.)* You needn't worry about that spare cabin, Uncle Dick, if you've a mind to take me in Robert's place.

ROBERT *(Turning to him quickly)* Andy! *(He sees at once the fixed resolve in his brother's eyes, and realizes immediately the reason for it —in consternation.)* Andy, you mustn't!

ANDREW You've made your decision, Rob, and now I've made mine. You're out of this, remember.

ROBERT *(Hurt by his brother's tone)* But Andy—

244   INTRODUCTION TO TRAGEDY

ANDREW   Don't interfere, Rob—that's all I ask. *(Turning to his uncle)* You haven't answered my question, Uncle Dick.

SCOTT   *(Clearing his throat, with an uneasy side glance at* JAMES MAYO *who is staring at his elder son as if he thought he had suddenly gone mad)* O' course, I'd be glad to have you, Andy.

ANDREW   It's settled then. I can pack the little I want to take in a few minutes.

MRS. MAYO   Don't be a fool, Dick. Andy's only joking you.

SCOTT   *(Disgruntledly)* It's hard to tell who's jokin' and who's not in this house.

ANDREW   *(Firmly)* I'm not joking, Uncle Dick. *(As* SCOTT *looks at him uncertainly)* You needn't be afraid I'll go back on my word.

ROBERT   *(Hurt by the insinuation he feels in* ANDREW'S *tone)* Andy! That isn't fair!

MAYO   *(Frowning)* Seems to me this ain't no subject to joke over—not for Andy.

ANDREW   *(Facing his father)* I agree with you, Pa, and I tell you again, once and for all, that I've made up my mind to go.

MAYO   *(Dumbfounded—unable to doubt the determination in* AN-DREW'S *voice—helplessly)* But why, son? Why?

ANDREW   *(Evasively)* I've always wanted to go.

ROBERT   Andy!

ANDREW   *(Half angrily)* You shut up, Rob! *(Turning to his father again)* I didn't ever mention it because as long as Rob was going I knew it was no use; but now Rob's staying on here, there isn't any reason for me not to go.

MAYO   *(Breathing hard)* No reason? Can you stand there and say that to me, Andrew?

MRS. MAYO   *(Hastily—seeing the gathering storm)* He doesn't mean a word of it, James.

MAYO   *(Making a gesture to her to keep silence)* Let me talk, Katey. *(In a more kindly tone)* What's come over you so sudden, Andy? You know's well as I do that it wouldn't be fair o' you to run off at a moment's notice right now when we're up to our necks in hard work.

ANDREW   *(Avoiding his eyes)* Rob'll hold his end up as soon as he learns.

MAYO   Robert was never cut out for a farmer, and you was.

ANDREW   You can easily get a man to do my work.

MAYO   *(Restraining his anger with an effort)* It sounds strange to hear you, Andy, that I always thought had good sense, talkin' crazy like that. *(Scornfully)* Get a man to take your place! You ain't been workin' here for no hire, Andy, that you kin give me your notice to quit like you've done. The farm is your'n as well as mine. You've always worked on it with that understanding; and what you're sayin' you intend doin' is just skulkin' out o' your rightful responsibility.

ANDREW   *(Looking at the floor—simply)* I'm sorry, Pa. *(After a slight pause)* It's no use talking any more about it.

MRS. MAYO   *(In relief)* There! I knew Andy'd come to his senses!

ANDREW   Don't get the wrong idea, Ma. I'm not backing out.

MAYO   You mean you're goin' in spite of—everythin'?

ANDREW   Yes. I'm going. I've got to. *(He looks at his father defiantly.)* I feel I oughtn't to miss this chance to go out into the world and see things, and—I want to go.

MAYO   *(With bitter scorn)* So—you want to go out into the world and see thin's! *(His voice raised and quivering with anger)* I never thought I'd live to see the day when a son o' mine'd look me in the face and tell a bare-faced lie! *(Bursting out)* You're a liar, Andy Mayo, and a mean one to boot!

MRS. MAYO   James!

ROBERT   Pa!

SCOTT   Steady there, Jim!

MAYO   *(Waving their protests aside)* He is and he knows it.

ANDREW   *(His face flushed)* I won't argue with you, Pa. You can think as badly of me as you like.

MAYO   *(Shaking his finger at ANDY, in a cold rage)* You know I'm speakin' truth—that's why you're afraid to argy! You lie when you say you want to go 'way—and see thin's! You ain't got no likin' in the world to go. I've watched you grow up, and I know your ways, and they're my ways. You're runnin' against your own nature, and you're goin' to be a'mighty sorry for it if you do. 'S if I didn't know your real reason for runnin' away! And runnin' away's the only words to fit it. You're runnin' away 'cause you're put out and riled 'cause your own brother's got Ruth 'stead o' you, and—

ANDREW   *(His face crimson—tensely)* Stop, Pa! I won't stand hearing that—not even from you!

MRS. MAYO   *(Rushing to ANDY and putting her arms about him protectingly)* Don't mind him, Andy dear. He don't mean a word he's saying! *(ROBERT stands rigidly, his hands clenched, his face contracted by pain. SCOTT sits dumbfounded and open-mouthed. ANDREW soothes his mother who is on the verge of tears).*

MAYO   *(In angry triumph)* It's the truth, Andy Mayo! And you ought to be bowed in shame to think of it!

ROBERT   *(Protestingly)* Pa!

MRS. MAYO   *(Coming from ANDREW to his father; puts her hands on his shoulders as though to try and push him back in the chair from *which he has risen)*   Won't you be still, James? Please won't you?

MAYO   *(Looking at* ANDREW *over his wife's shoulder—stubbornly)*—The truth—God's truth!

MRS. MAYO   Sh-h-h!   *(She tries to put a finger across his lips, but he twists his head away.)*

ANDREW   *(Who has regained control over himself)*   You're wrong, Pa, it isn't truth.   *(With defiant assertiveness)*   I don't love Ruth. I never loved her, and the thought of such a thing never entered my head.

MAYO   *(With an angry snort of disbelief)*   Hump! You're pilin' lie on lie!

ANDREW   *(Losing his temper—bitterly)*   I suppose it'd be hard for you to explain anyone's wanting to leave this blessed farm except for some outside reason like that. But I'm sick and tired of it—whether you want to believe me or not—and that's why I'm glad to get a chance to move on.

ROBERT   Andy! Don't! You're only making it worse.

ANDREW   *(Sulkily)*   I don't care. I've done my share of work here. I've earned my right to quit when I want to.   *(Suddenly overcome with anger and grief; with rising intensity)*   I'm sick and tired of the whole damn business. I hate the farm and every inch of ground in it. I'm sick of digging in the dirt and sweating in the sun like a slave without getting a word of thanks for it.   *(Tears of rage starting to his eyes —hoarsely)*   I'm through, through for good and all; and if Uncle Dick won't take me on his ship, I'll find another. I'll get away somewhere, somehow.

MRS. MAYO   *(In a frightened voice)*   Don't you answer him, James. He doesn't know what he's saying. Don't say a word to him 'til he's in his right senses again. Please James, don't—

MAYO   *(Pushes her away from him; his face is drawn and pale with the violence of his passion. He glares at* ANDREW *as if he hated him.)* You dare to—you dare to speak like that to me? You talk like that 'bout this farm—the Mayo farm—where you was born—you—you— *(He clenches his fist above his head and advances threatingly on* ANDREW.)   You damned whelp!

MRS. MAYO   *(With a shriek)*   James!   *(She covers her face with her hands and sinks weakly into* MAYO's *chair.* ANDREW *remains standing motionless, his face pale and set.)*

SCOTT   *(Starting to his feet and stretching his arms across the table toward* MAYO)   Easy there, Jim!

ROBERT   *(Throwing himself between father and brother)*   Stop! Are you mad?

MAYO   *(Grabs* ROBERT's *arm and pushes him aside—then stands for a moment gasping for breath before* ANDREW. *He points to the door with a shaking finger.)*   Yes—go!—go!—You're no son o' mine—

no son o' mine! You can go to hell if you want to! Don't let me find you here—in the mornin'—or—or—I'll *throw* you out!

ROBERT   Pa! For God's sake! (MRS. MAYO *bursts into noisy sobbing*).

MAYO   *(He gulps convulsively and glares at* ANDREW.) You go—tomorrow mornin'—and by God—don't come back—don't dare come back—by God, not while I'm livin'—or I'll—I'll— *(He shakes over his muttered threat and strides toward the door rear, right.)*

MRS. MAYO   *(Rising and throwing her arms around him—hysterically)* James! James! Where are you going?

MAYO   *(Incoherently)* I'm goin'—to bed, Katey. It's late, Katey—it's late. *(He goes out).*

MRS. MAYO   *(Following him, pleading hysterically)* James! Take back what you've said to Andy. James! *(She follows him out.* ROBERT *and the* CAPTAIN *stare after them with horrified eyes.* ANDREW *stands rigidly looking straight in front of him, his fists clenched at his sides.)*

SCOTT   *(The first to find his voice—with an explosive sigh)* Well, if he ain't the devil himself when he's roused! You oughn't to have talked to him that way, Andy 'bout the damn farm, knowin' how touchy he is about it. *(With another sigh)* Well, you won't mind what he's said in anger. He'll be sorry for it when he's calmed down a bit.

ANDREW   *(In a dead voice)* You don't know him. *(Defiantly)* What's said is said and can't be unsaid; and I've chosen.

ROBERT   *(With violent protest)* Andy! You can't go! This is all so stupid—and terrible!

ANDREW   *(Coldly)* I'll talk to you in a minute, Rob. *(Crushed by his brother's attitude* ROBERT *sinks down into a chair, holding his head in his hands.)*

SCOTT   *(Comes and slaps* ANDREW *on the back)* I'm damned glad you're shippin' on, Andy. I like your spirit, and the way you spoke up to him. *(Lowering his voice to a cautious whisper)* The sea's the place for a young feller like you that isn't half dead 'n' alive. *(He gives* ANDY *a final approving slap)* You 'n' me 'll get along like twins, see if we don't. I'm goin' aloft to turn in. Don't forget to pack your dunnage. And git some sleep, if you kin. We'll want to sneak out extra early b'fore they're up. It'll do away with more argyments. Robert can drive us down to the town, and bring back the team. *(He goes to the door in the rear, left.)* Well, good night.

ANDREW   Good night. (SCOTT *goes out. The two brothers remain silent for a moment. Then* ANDREW *comes over to his brother and puts a hand on his back. He speaks in a low voice, full of feeling.)* Buck up, Rob. It ain't any use crying over spilt milk; and it'll all turn out for the best—let's hope. It couldn't be helped—what's happened.

ROBERT   *(Wildly)*   But it's a lie, Andy, a lie!

ANDREW   Of course it's a lie. You know it and I know it, —but that's all ought to know it.

ROBERT   Pa'll never forgive you. Oh, the whole affair is so senseless—and tragic. Why did you think you must go away?

ANDREW   You know better than to ask that. You know why. *(Fiercely)* I can wish you and Ruth all the good luck in the world, and I do, and I mean it; but you can't expect me to stay around here and watch you two together, day after day—and me alone. I couldn't stand it—not after all the plans I'd made to happen on this place thinking— *(his voice breaks)*   thinking she cared for me.

ROBERT   *(Putting a hand on his brother's arm)*   God! It's horrible! I feel so guilty—to think that I should be the cause of your suffering, after we've been such pals all our lives. If I could have foreseen what'd happen, I swear to you I'd have never said a word to Ruth. I swear I wouldn't have, Andy!

ANDREW   I know you wouldn't; and that would've been worse, for Ruth would've suffered then. *(He pats his brother's shoulder.)*   It's best as it is. It had to be, and I've got to stand the gaff, that's all. Pa'll see how I felt—after a time. *(As* ROBERT *shakes his head)* And if he don't—well, it can't be helped.

ROBERT   But think of Ma! God, Andy, you can't go! You can't!

ANDREW   *(Fiercely)*   I've got to go—to get away! I've got to, I tell you. I'd go crazy here, bein' reminded every second of the day what a fool I'd made of myself. I've got to get away and try and forget, if I can. And I'd hate the farm if I stayed, hate it for bringin' things back. I couldn't take interest in the work any more, work with no purpose in sight. Can't you see what a hell it'd be? You love her too, Rob. Put yourself in my place, and remember I haven't stopped loving her, and couldn't if I was to stay. Would that be fair to you or to her? Put yourself in my place. *(He shakes his brother fiercely by the shoulder.)*   What'd you do then? Tell me the truth! You love her. What'd you do?

ROBERT   *(Chokingly)*   I'd—I'd go, Andy! *(He buries his face in his hands with a shuddering sob.)*   God!

ANDREW   *(Seeming to relax suddenly all over his body—in a low, steady voice)*   Then you know why I got to go; and there's nothing more to be said.

ROBERT   *(In a frenzy of rebellion)*   Why did this have to happen to us? It's damnable! *(He looks about him wildly, as if his vengeance were seeking the responsible fate.)*

ANDREW   *(Soothingly—again putting his hands on his brother's shoulder)*   It's no use fussing any more, Rob. It's done. *(Forcing a smile)* I guess Ruth's got a right to have who she likes. She made a good choice—and God bless her for it!

ROBERT   Andy! Oh, I wish I could tell you half I feel of how fine you are!

ANDREW   *(Interrupting him quickly)* Shut up! Let's go to bed. I've got to be up long before sun-up. You, too, if you're going to drive us down.

ROBERT   Yes. Yes.

ANDREW   *(Turning down the lamp)* And I've got to pack yet. *(He yawns with utter weariness.)* I'm as tired as if I'd been plowing twenty-four hours at a stretch. *(Dully)* I feel—dead. (ROBERT *covers his face again with his hands.* ANDREW *shakes his head as if to get rid of his thoughts, and continues with a poor attempt at cheery briskness.)* I'm going to douse the light. Come on. *(He slaps his brother on the back.* ROBERT *does not move.* ANDREW *bends over and blows out the lamp. His voice comes from the darkness.)* Don't sit there mourning, Rob. It'll all come out in the wash. Come on and get some sleep. Everything'll turn out all right in the end.   (ROBERT *can be heard stumbling to his feet, and the dark figures of the two brothers can be seen groping their way toward the doorway in the rear as The Curtain Falls.)*

ACT II

SCENE I

Same as Act I, Scene II. Sitting room of the farm house about half past twelve in the afternoon of a hot, sun-baked day in mid-summer, three years later. All the windows are open, but no breeze stirs the soiled white curtains. A patched screen door is in the rear. Through it the yard can be seen, its small stretch of lawn divided by the dirt path leading to the door from the gate in the white picket fence which borders the road.

The room has changed, not so much in its outward appearance as in its general atmosphere. Little significant details give evidence of carelessness, of inefficiency, of an industry gone to seed. The chairs appear shabby from lack of paint; the table cover is spotted and askew; holes show in the curtains; a child's doll, with one arm gone, lies under the table; a hoe stands in a corner; a man's coat is flung on the couch in the rear; the desk is cluttered up with odds and ends; a number of

*books are piled carelessly on the sideboard. The noon enervation of
the sultry, scorching day seems to have penetrated indoors, causing
even inanimate objects to wear an aspect of despondent exhaustion.*

*A place is set at the end of the table, left, for someone's dinner.
Through the open door to the kitchen comes the clatter of dishes being
washed, interrupted at intervals by a woman's irritated voice and the
peevish whining of a child.*

At the rise of the curtain Mrs. Mayo *and* Mrs. Atkins *are discovered sitting facing each other,* Mrs. Mayo *to the rear,* Mrs. Atkins *to
the right of the table.* Mrs. Mayo's *face has lost all character, disinte-
grated, become a weak mask wearing a helpless, doleful expression of
being constantly on the verge of comfortless tears. She speaks in an
uncertain voice, without assertiveness, as if all power of willing had
deserted her.* Mrs. Atkins *is in her wheel chair. She is a thin, pale-
faced, unintelligent looking woman of about forty-eight, with hard,
bright eyes. A victim of partial paralysis for many years, condemned
to be pushed from day to day of her life in a wheel chair, she has developed the selfish, irritable nature of the chronic invalid. Both women
are dressed in black.* Mrs. Atkins *knits nervously as she talks. A ball
of unused yarn, with needles stuck through it, lies on the table before*
Mrs. Mayo.

Mrs. Atkins   *(With a disapproving glance at the place set on the
table)*   Robert's late for his dinner again, as usual. I don't see why
Ruth puts up with it, and I've told her so. Many's the time I've said to
her, "It's about time you put a stop to his nonsense. Does he suppose
you're runnin' a hotel—with no one to help with things?" But she
don't pay no attention. She's as bad as he is, a'most—thinks she
knows better than an old, sick body like me.

Mrs. Mayo   *(Dully)*   Robbie's always late for things. He can't help it,
Sarah.

Mrs. Atkins   *(With a snort)*   Can't help it! How you do go on, Kate,
findin' excuses for him! Anybody can help anything they've a mind to
—as long as they've got health, and ain't rendered helpless like me—
(She adds as a pious afterthought) —through the will of God.

Mrs. Mayo   Robbie can't.

Mrs. Atkins   Can't! It do make me mad, Kate Mayo, to see folks that
God gave all the use of their limbs to potterin' round and wastin' time
doin' everything the wrong way—and me powerless to help and at
their mercy, you might say. And it ain't that I haven't pointed the
right way to 'em. I've talked to Robert thousands of times and told
him how things ought to be done. You know that, Kate Mayo. But
d'you s'pose he takes any notice of what I say? Or Ruth, either—my

own daughter? No, they think I'm a crazy, cranky old woman, half dead a'ready, and the sooner I'm in the grave and out o' their way the better it'd suit them.

MRS. MAYO   You mustn't talk that way, Sarah. They're not as wicked as that. And you've got years and years before you.

MRS. ATKINS   You're like the rest, Kate. You don't know how near the end I am. Well, at least I can go to my eternal rest with a clear conscience. I've done all a body could do to avert ruin from this house. On their heads be it!

MRS. MAYO   *(With hopeless indifference)* Things might be worse. Robert never had any experience in farming. You can't expect him to learn in a day.

MRS. ATKINS   *(Snappily)* He's had three years to learn, and he's gettin' worse 'stead of better. Not on'y your place but mine too is driftin' to rack and ruin, and I can't do nothin' to prevent.

MRS. MAYO   *(With a spark of assertiveness)* You can't say but Robbie works hard, Sarah.

MRS. ATKINS   What good's workin' hard if it don't accomplish anythin', I'd like to know?

MRS. MAYO   Robbie's had bad luck against him.

MRS. ATKINS   Say what you've a mind to, Kate, the proof of the puddin's in the eatin'; and you can't deny that things have been goin' from bad to worse ever since your husband died two years back.

MRS. MAYO   *(Wiping tears from her eyes with her handkerchief)* It was God's will that he should be taken.

MRS. ATKINS   *(Triumphantly)* It was God's punishment on James Mayo for the blasphemin' and denyin' of God he done all his sinful life! (MRS. MAYO *begins to weep softly.*) There, Kate, I shouldn't be remindin' you, I know. He's at peace, poor man, and forgiven, let's pray.

MRS. MAYO   *(Wiping her eyes—simply)* James was a good man.

MRS. ATKINS   *(Ignoring this remark)* What I was sayin' was that since Robert's been in charge things've been goin' down hill steady. You don't know *how* bad they are. Robert don't let on to you what's happenin'; and you'd never see it yourself if 'twas under your nose. But, thank the Lord, Ruth still comes to me once in a while for advice when she's worried near out of her senses by his goin's-on. Do you know what she told me last night? But I forgot, she said not to tell you —still I think you've got a right to know, and it's my duty not to let such things go on behind your back.

MRS. MAYO   *(Wearily)* You can tell me if you want to.

MRS. ATKINS   *(Bending over toward her—in a low voice)* Ruth was almost crazy about it. Robert told her he'd have to mortgage the farm

—said he didn't know how he'd pull through 'til harvest without it, and he can't get money any other way. *(She straightens up— indignantly.)*   Now what do you think of your Robert?

MRS. MAYO   *(Resignedly)*   If it has to be—

MRS. ATKINS   You don't mean to say you're goin' to sign away your farm, Kate Mayo—after me warnin' you?

MRS. MAYO   I'll do what Robbie says is needful.

MRS. ATKINS   *(Holding up her hands)*   Well, of all the foolishness!— well, it's your farm, not mine, and I've nothin' more to say.

MRS. MAYO   Maybe Robbie'll manage till Andy gets back and sees to things. It can't be long now.

MRS. ATKINS   *(With keen interest)*   Ruth says Andy ought to turn up any day. When does Robert figger he'll get here?

MRS. MAYO   He says he can't calculate exactly on account o' the *Sunda* being a sail boat. Last letter he got was from England, the day they were sailing for home. That was over a month ago, and Robbie thinks they're overdue now.

MRS. ATKINS   We can give praise to God then that he'll be back in the nick o' time. He ought to be tired of travelin' and anxious to get home and settle down to work again.

MRS. MAYO   Andy *has* been working. He's head officer on Dick's boat, he wrote Robbie. You know that.

MRS. ATKINS   That foolin' on ships is all right for a spell, but he must be right sick of it by this.

MRS. MAYO   *(Musingly)*   I wonder if he's changed much. He used to be so fine-looking and strong. *(With a sigh)* Three years! It seems more like three hundred. *(Her eyes filling—piteously)* Oh, if James could only have lived 'til he came back—and forgiven him!

MRS. ATKINS   He never would have—not James Mayo! Didn't he keep his heart hardened against him till the last in spite of all you and Robert did to soften him?

MRS. MAYO   *(With a feeble flash of anger)*   Don't you dare say that! *(Brokenly)* Oh, I know deep down in his heart he forgave Andy, though he was too stubborn ever to own up to it. It was that brought on his death—breaking his heart just on account of his stubborn pride. *(She wipes her eyes with her handkerchief and sobs.)*

MRS. ATKINS   *(Piously)*   It was the will of God. *(The whining crying of the child sounds from the kitchen. MRS. ATKINS frowns irritably.)*   Drat that young one! Seems as if she cries all the time on purpose to set a body's nerves on edge.

MRS. MAYO   *(Wiping her eyes)*   It's the heat upsets her. Mary doesn't feel any too well these days, poor little child!

MRS. ATKINS   She gets it right from her Pa—bein' sickly all the time. You can't deny Robert was always ailin' as a child. *(She sighs heavily.)* It was a crazy mistake for them two to get married. I argyed against it at the time, but Ruth was so spelled with Robert's wild poetry notions she wouldn't listen to sense. Andy was the one would have been the match for her.

MRS. MAYO.   I've often thought since it might have been better the other way. But Ruth and Robbie seem happy enough together.

MRS. ATKINS   At any rate it was God's work—and His will be done. *(The two women sit in silence for a moment. RUTH enters from the kitchen, carrying in her arms her two-year-old daughter, MARY, a pretty but sickly and aenemic looking child with a tear-stained face. RUTH has aged appreciably. Her face has lost its youth and freshness. There is a trace in her expression of something hard and spiteful. She sits in the rocker in front of the table and sighs wearily. She wears a gingham dress with a soiled apron tied around her waist.)*

RUTH   Land sakes, if this isn't a scorcher! That kitchen's like a furnace. Phew!   *(She pushes the damp hair back from her forehead.)*

MRS. MAYO   Why didn't you call me to help with the dishes?

RUTH   *(Shortly)*   No. The heat in there'd kill you.

MARY   *(Sees the doll under the table and struggles on her mother's lap.)*   Dolly, Mama! Dolly!

RUTH   *(Pulling her back)*   It's time for your nap. You can't play with Dolly now.

MARY   *(Commencing to cry whiningly)*   Dolly!

MRS. ATKINS   *(Irritably)*   Can't you keep that child still? Her racket's enough to split a body's ears. Put her down and let her play with the doll if it'll quiet her.

RUTH   *(Lifting MARY to the floor)*   There! I hope you'll be satisfied and keep still.   (MARY MAYO *sits down on the floor before the table and plays with the doll in silence.* RUTH *glances at the place set on the table.)*   It's a wonder Rob wouldn't try to get to meals on time once in a while.

MRS. MAYO   *(Dully)*   Something must have gone wrong again.

RUTH   *(Wearily)*   I s'pose so. Something's always going wrong these days, it looks like.

MRS. ATKINS   *(Snappily)*   It wouldn't if you possessed a bit of spunk. The idea of you permittin' him to come in to meals at all hours—and you doin' the work! I never heard of such a thin'. You're too easy goin', that's the trouble.

RUTH   Do stop your nagging at me, Ma! I'm sick of hearing you. I'll do as I please about it; and thank you for not interfering.   *(She wipes her moist forehead—wearily.)*   Phew! It's too hot to argue. Let's talk of something pleasant.   *(Curiously)*   Didn't I hear you speaking about Andy a while ago?

MRS. MAYO   We were wondering when he'd get home.

RUTH   *(Brightening)*   Rob says any day now he's liable to drop in and surprise us—him and the Captain. It'll certainly look natural to see him around the farm again.

MRS. ATKINS   Let's hope the farm'll look more natural, too, when he's had a hand at it. The way thin's are now!

RUTH   *(Irritably)*   Will you stop harping on that, Ma? We all know things aren't as they might be. What's the good of your complaining all the time?

MRS. ATKINS   There, Kate Mayo! Ain't that just what I told you? I can't say a word of advice to my own daughter even, she's that stubborn and self-willed.

RUTH   *(Putting her hands over her ears—in exasperation)*   For goodness sakes, Ma!

MRS. MAYO   *(Dully)*   Never mind. Andy'll fix everything when he comes.

RUTH   *(Hopefully)*   Oh, yes, I know he will. He always did know just the right thing ought to be done. *(With weary vexation)*   It's a shame for him to come home and have to start in with things in such a topsy-turvy.

MRS. MAYO   Andy'll manage.

RUTH   *(Sighing)*   I s'pose it isn't Rob's fault things go wrong with him.

MRS. ATKINS   *(Scornfully)*   Hump! *(She fans herself nervously.)* Land o' Goshen, but it's bakin' in here! Let's go out in under the trees in back where there's a breath of fresh air. Come, Kate. (MRS. MAYO *gets up obediently and starts to wheel the invalid's chair toward the screen door.)* You better come too, Ruth. It'll do you good. Learn him a lesson and let him get his own dinner. Don't be such a fool.

RUTH   *(Going and holding the screen door open for them—listlessly)*   He wouldn't mind. He doesn't eat much. But I can't go anyway. I've got to put baby to bed.

MRS. MAYO   Let's go, Kate. I'm boilin' in here. *(MRS. MAYO wheels her out and off left. RUTH comes back and sits down in her chair.)*

RUTH   *(Mechanically)*   Come and let me take off your shoes and stockings, Mary, that's a good girl. You've got to take your nap now. *(The child continues to play as if she hadn't heard, absorbed in her doll. An eager expression comes over RUTH's tired face. She glances toward the door furtively—then gets up and goes to the desk. Her movements indicate a guilty fear of discovery. She takes a letter from a pigeonhole and retreats swiftly to her chair with it. She opens the envelope and reads the letter with great interest, a flush of excitement coming to her cheeks. ROBERT walks up the path and opens the screen door quietly and comes into the room. He, too, has aged. His shoulders are stooped as if under too great a burden. His eyes are dull and lifeless, his face burned by the sun and unshaven for days. Streaks of sweat have smudged the layer of dust on his cheeks. His lips drawn down at the corners, give him a hopeless, resigned expression. The three years have accentuated the weakness of his mouth and chin. He is dressed in overalls, laced boots, and a flannel shirt open at the neck).*

ROBERT   *(Throwing his hat over on the sofa—with a great sigh of exhaustion)* Phew! The sun's hot today! *(RUTH is startled. At first she makes an instinctive motion as if to hide the letter in her bosom. She immediately thinks better of this and sits with the letter in her hands looking at him with defiant eyes. He bends down and kisses her.)*

RUTH   *(Feeling of her cheek—irritably)* Why don't you shave? You look awful.

ROBERT   *(Indifferently)* I forgot—and it's too much trouble this weather.

MARY   *(Throwing aside her doll, runs to him with a happy cry)* Dada! Dada!

ROBERT   *(Swinging her up above his head—lovingly)* And how's this little girl of mine this hot day, eh?

MARY   *(Screeching happily)* Dada! Dada!

RUTH   *(In annoyance)* Don't do that to her! You know it's time for her nap and you'll get her all waked up; then I'll be the one that'll have to sit beside her till she falls asleep.

ROBERT   *(Sitting down in the chair on the left of table and cuddling MARY on his lap)* You needn't bother. I'll put her to bed.

RUTH   *(Shortly)* You've got to get back to your work, I s'pose.

ROBERT   *(With a sigh)* Yes, I was forgetting. *(He glances at the open letter on RUTH's lap.)* Reading Andy's letter again? I should think you'd know it by heart by this time.

RUTH   *(Coloring as if she'd been accused of something—defiantly)* I've got a right to read it, haven't I? He says it's meant for all of us.

ROBERT   *(With a trace of irritation)* Right? Don't be so silly. There's no question of right. I was only saying that you must know all that's in it after so many readings.

RUTH   Well, I don't. *(She puts the letter on the table and gets wearily to her feet.)* I s'pose you'll be wanting your dinner now.

ROBERT   *(Listlessly)* I don't care. I'm not hungry.

RUTH   And here I been keeping it hot for you!

ROBERT   *(Irritably)* Oh, all right then. Bring it in and I'll try to eat.

RUTH   I've got to get her to bed first. *(She goes to lift MARY off his lap.)* Come, dear. It's after time and you can hardly keep your eyes open now.

MARY   *(Crying)* No, no! *(Appealing to her father)* Dada! No!

RUTH   *(Accusingly to* ROBERT) There! Now see what you've done! I told you not to—

ROBERT   *(Shortly)* Let her alone, then. She's all right where she is. She'll fall asleep on my lap in a minute if you'll stop bothering her.

RUTH   *(Hotly)* She'll not do any such thing! She's got to learn to mind me! *(Shaking her finger at* MARY) You naughty child! Will you come with Mama when she tells you for your own good?

MARY   *(Clinging to her father)* No, Dada!

RUTH   *(Losing her temper)* A good spanking's what you need, my young lady—and you'll get one from me if you don't mind better, d'you hear? (MARY *starts to whimper frightenedly.)*

ROBERT   *(With sudden anger)* Leave her alone! How often have I told you not to threaten her with whipping? I won't have it. *(Soothing the wailing* MARY) There! There, little girl! Baby mustn't cry. Dada won't like you if you do. Dada'll hold you and you must promise to go to sleep like a good little girl. Will you when Dada asks you?

MARY   *(Cuddling up to him)* Yes, Dada.

RUTH   *(Looking at them, her pale face set and drawn)* A fine one you are to be telling folks how to do things! *(She bites her lips. Husband and wife look into each other's eyes with something akin to hatred in their expressions; then* RUTH *turns away with a shrug of affected indifference.)* All right, take care of her then, if you think it's so easy. *(She walks away into the kitchen.)*

ROBERT   *(Smoothing* MARY'S *hair—tenderly)* We'll show Mama you're a good little girl, won't we?

MARY   *(Crooning drowsily)* Dada, Dada.

ROBERT   Let's see: Does your mother take off your shoes and stockings before your nap?

MARY   *(Nodding with half-shut eyes)* Yes, Dada.

ROBERT   *(Taking off her shoes and stockings)* We'll show Mama we know how to do those things, won't we? There's one old shoe off— and there's the other old shoe—and here's one old stocking—and there's the other old stocking. There we are, all nice and cool and comfy. *(He bends down and kisses her.)* And now will you promise to go right to sleep if Dada takes you to bed? (MARY *nods sleepily.)* That's the good little girl. *(He gathers her up in his arms carefully and carries her into the bedroom. His voice can be heard faintly as he lulls the child to sleep.* RUTH *comes out of the kitchen and gets the plate from the table. She hears the voice from the room and tiptoes to the door to look in. Then she starts for the kitchen but stands for a moment thinking, a look of ill-concealed jealousy on her face. At a noise from inside she hurriedly disappears into the kitchen.)*

A moment later ROBERT *re-enters. He comes forward and picks up the shoes and stockings which he shoves carelessly under the table. Then, seeing no one about, he goes to the sideboard and selects a book. Coming back to his chair, he sits down and immediately becomes absorbed in reading.* RUTH *returns from the kitchen bringing his plate heaped with food, and a cup of tea. She sets those before him and sits down in her former place.* ROBERT *continues to read, oblivious to the food on the table.)*

RUTH   *(After watching him irritably for a moment)* For heaven's sakes, put down that old book! Don't you see your dinner's getting cold?

ROBERT   *(Closing his book)* Excuse me, Ruth. I didn't notice. *(He picks up his knife and fork and begins to eat gingerly, without appetite.)*

RUTH   I should think you might have some feeling for me, Rob, and not always be late for meals. If you think it's fun sweltering in that oven of a kitchen to keep things warm for you, you're mistaken.

ROBERT   I'm sorry, Ruth, really I am. Something crops up every day to delay me. I mean to be here on time.

RUTH   *(With a sigh)* Mean-to's don't count.

ROBERT   *(With a conciliating smile)* Then punish me, Ruth. Let the food get cold and don't bother about me.

RUTH   I'd have to wait just the same to wash up after you.

ROBERT   But I can wash up.

RUTH   A nice mess there'd be then!

ROBERT   *(With an attempt at lightness)* The food is lucky to be able to get cold this weather. *(As* RUTH *doesn't answer or smile he opens his book and resumes his reading, forcing himself to take a mouthful of food every now and then.* RUTH *stares at him in annoyance.)*

RUTH   And besides, you've got your own work that's got to be done.

ROBERT   *(Absent-mindedly, without taking his eyes from the book)* Yes, of course.

RUTH   *(Spitefully)* Work you'll never get done by reading books all the time.

ROBERT   *(Shutting the book with a snap)* Why do you persist in nagging at me for getting pleasure out of reading? Is it because— *(He checks himself abruptly.)*

RUTH   *(Coloring)* Because I'm too stupid to understand them, I s'pose you were going to say.

ROBERT   *(Shame-facedly)* No—no. *(In exasperation)* Why do you goad me into saying things I don't mean? Haven't I got my share of troubles trying to work this cursed farm without your adding to them? You know how hard I've tried to keep things going in spite of bad luck—

RUTH   *(Scornfully)* Bad luck!

ROBERT   And my own very apparent unfitness for the job, I was going to add; but you can't deny there's been bad luck to it, too. Why don't you take things into consideration? Why can't we pull together? We used to. I know it's hard on you also. Then why can't we help each other instead of hindering?

RUTH   *(Sullenly)* I do the best I know how.

ROBERT   *(Gets up and puts his hand on her shoulder)* I know you do. But let's both of us try to do better. We can both improve. Say a word of encouragement once in a while when things go wrong, even if it is my fault. You know the odds I've been up against since Pa died. I'm not a farmer. I've never claimed to be one. But there's nothing else I can do under the circumstances, and I've got to pull things through somehow. With your help, I can do it. With you against me— *(He shrugs his shoulders. There is a pause. Then he bends down and kisses her hair—with an attempt at cheerfulness.)* So you promise that; and I'll promise to be here when the clock strikes—and anything else you tell me to. Is it a bargain?

RUTH   *(Dully)* I s'pose so. *(They are interrupted by the sound of a loud knock at the kitchen door.)* There's someone at the kitchen door. *(She hurries out. A moment later she reappears.)* It's Ben.

ROBERT   *(Frowning)* What's the trouble now, I wonder? *(In a loud voice)* Come on in here, Ben. *(BEN slouches in from the kitchen. He is a hulking, awkward young fellow with a heavy, stupid face and shifty, cunning eyes. He is dressed in overalls, boots, etc., and wears a broad-brimmed hat of coarse straw pushed back on his head.)* Well, Ben, what's the matter?

BEN   *(Drawlingly)* The mowin' machine's bust.

ROBERT   Why, that can't be. The man fixed it only last week.

BEN   It's bust just the same.

ROBERT   And can't you fix it?

BEN   No. Don't know what's the matter with the golldarned thing. 'Twon't work, anyhow.

ROBERT   *(Getting up and going for his hat)* Wait a minute and I'll go look it over. There can't be much the matter with it.

BEN   *(Impudently)* Don't make no diff'rence t' me whether there be or not. I'm quittin'.

ROBERT   *(Anxiously)* You don't mean you're throwing up your job here?

BEN   That's what! My month's up today and I want what's owin' t' me.

ROBERT   But why are you quitting now, Ben, when you know I've so much work on hand? I'll have a hard time getting another man at such short notice.

BEN   That's for you to figger. I'm quittin'.

ROBERT   But what's your reason? You haven't any complaint to make about the way you've been treated, have you?

BEN   No. 'Tain't that. *(Shaking his finger)* Look-a-here. I'm sick o' being made fun at, that's what; an' I got a job up to Timms' place; an' I'm quittin' here.

ROBERT   Being made fun of? I don't understand you. Who's making fun of you?

BEN   They all do. When I drive down with the milk in the mornin' they all laughs and jokes at me—that boy up to Harris' and the new feller up to Slocum's, and Bill Evans down to Meade's, and all the rest of 'em.

ROBERT   That's a queer reason for leaving me flat. Won't they laugh at you just the same when you're working for Timms?

BEN   They wouldn't dare to. Timms is the best farm hereabouts. They was laughin' at me for workin' for *you,* that's what! "How're things up to the Mayo place?" they hollers every mornin'. "What's Robert doin' now—pasturin' the cattle in the cornlot? Is he seasonin' his hay with rain this year, same as last?" they shouts. "Or is he inventin' some 'lectrical milkin' engine to fool them dry cows o' his into givin' hard cider?" *(Very much ruffled)* That's like they talks; and I ain't goin' to put up with it no longer. Everyone's always knowed me as a first-class hand hereabouts, and I ain't wantin' 'em to get no different notion. So I'm quittin' you. And I wants what's comin' to me.

ROBERT   *(Coldly)* Oh, if that's the case, you can go to the devil. You'll get your money tomorrow when I get back from town—not before!

BEN   *(Turning to doorway to kitchen)* That suits me. *(As he goes out he speaks back over his shoulder.)* And see that I do get it, or there'll be trouble. *(He disappears and the slamming of the kitchen door is heard.)*

ROBERT   *(As* RUTH *comes from where she has been standing by the doorway and sits down dejectedly in her old place)* The stupid damn fool! And now what about the haying? That's an example of what I'm up against. No one can say I'm responsible for that.

RUTH   He wouldn't dare act that way with anyone else! *(Spitefully, with a glance at* ANDREW's *letter on the table)* It's lucky Andy's coming back.

ROBERT   *(Without resentment)* Yes, Andy'll see the right thing to do in a jiffy. *(With an affectionate smile)* I wonder if the old chump's changed much? He doesn't seem to from his letters, does he? *(Shaking his head)* But just the same I doubt if he'll want to settle down to a hum-drum farm life, after all he's been through.

RUTH   *(Resentfully)* Andy's not like you. He likes the farm.

ROBERT   *(Immersed in his own thoughts—enthusiastically)* Gad, the things he's seen and experienced! Think of the places he's been! All the wonderful far places I used to dream about! God, how I envy him! What a trip! *(He springs to his feet and instinctively goes to the window and stares out at the horizon.)*

RUTH   *(Bitterly)* I s'pose you're sorry now you didn't go?

ROBERT   *(Too occupied with his own thoughts to hear her—vindictively)* Oh, those cursed hills out there that I used to think promised me so much! How I've grown to hate the sight of them! They're like the walls of a narrow prison yard shutting me in from all the freedom and wonder of life! *(He turns back to the room with a gesture of loathing.)* Sometimes I think if it wasn't for you, Ruth, and— *(his voice softening)* —little Mary, I'd chuck everything up and walk down the road with just one desire in my heart—to put the whole rim of the world between me and those hills, and to be able to breathe freely once more! *(He sinks down into his chair and smiles with bitter self-scorn.)* There I go dreaming again—my old fool dreams.

RUTH   *(In a low, repressed voice—her eyes smoldering)* You're not the only one!

ROBERT   *(Buried in his own thoughts—bitterly)* And Andy, who's had the chance—what has he got out of it? His letters read like the diary of a—of a farmer! "We're in Singapore now. It's a dirty hole of a place and hotter than hell. Two of the crew down with fever and we're short-handed on the work. I'll be damn glad when we sail again, although tacking back and forth in these blistering seas is a rotten job too!" *(Scornfully)* That's about the way he summed up his impressions of the East.

RUTH   *(Her repressed voice trembling)* You needn't make fun of Andy.

ROBERT   When I think—but what's the use? You know I wasn't making fun of Andy personally, but his attitude toward things is—

RUTH   *(Her eyes flashing—bursting into uncontrollable rage)* You was too making fun of him! And I ain't going to stand for it! You ought to be ashamed of yourself! *(ROBERT stares at her in amazement. She continues furiously.)* A fine one to talk about anyone else—after the way you've ruined everything with your lazy loafing! —and the stupid way you do things!

ROBERT   *(Angrily)* Stop that kind of talk, do you hear?

RUTH   You findin' fault—with your own brother who's ten times the man you ever was or ever will be! You're jealous, that's what! Jealous because he's made a man of himself, while you're nothing but a—but a— *(She stutters incoherently, overcome by rage.)*

ROBERT   Ruth! Ruth! You'll be sorry for talking like that.

RUTH   I won't! I won't never be sorry! I'm only saying what I've been thinking for years.

ROBERT   *(Aghast)* Ruth! You can't mean that!

RUTH   What do you think—living with a man like you—having to suffer all the time because you've never been man enough to work and do things like other people. But no! You never own up to that. You think you're so much better than other folks, with your college education, where you never learned a thing, and always reading your stupid books instead of working. I s'pose you think I ought to be *proud* to be your wife—a poor, ignorant thing like me! *(Fiercely)* But I'm not. I hate it! I hate the sight of you. Oh, if I'd only known! If I hadn't been such a fool to listen to your cheap, silly, poetry talk that you learned out of books! If I could have seen how you were in your true self—like you are now—I'd have killed myself before I'd have married you! I was sorry for it before we'd been together a month. I knew what you were really like—when it was too late.

ROBERT   *(His voice raised loudly)* And now—I'm finding out what you're really like—what a—a creature I've been living with. *(With a harsh laugh)* God! It wasn't that I haven't guessed how mean and small you are—but I've kept on telling myself that I must be wrong— like a fool!—like a damned fool!

RUTH   You were saying you'd go out on the road if it wasn't for me. Well, you can go, and the sooner the better! I don't care! I'll be glad to get rid of you! The farm'll be better off too. There's been a curse on it ever since you took hold. So go! Go and be a tramp like you've always wanted. It's all you're good for. I can get along without you, don't you worry. *(Exulting fiercely)* Andy's coming back, don't forget that! He'll attend to things like they should be. He'll show what a man can do! I don't need you. Andy's coming!

ROBERT   *(They are both standing.* ROBERT *grabs her by the shoulders and glares into her eyes.)* What do you mean? *(He shakes her violently.)* What are you thinking of? What's in your evil mind, you —you— *(His voice is a harsh shout.)*

RUTH   *(In a defiant scream)* Yes I do mean it! I'd say it if you was to kill me! I do love Andy. I do! I do! I always loved him *(Exultantly)* And he loves me! He loves me! I know he does. He always did! And you know he did, too! So go! Go if you want to!

ROBERT   *(Throwing her away from him. She staggers back against the table—thickly)* You—you slut! *(He stands glaring at her as she leans back, supporting herself by the table, gasping for breath. A loud frightened whimper sounds from the awakened child in the bedroom. It continues. The man and woman stand looking at one another in horror, the extent of their terrible quarrel suddenly brought home to them. A pause. The noise of a horse and carriage comes from the road before the house. The two, suddenly struck by the same premonition, listen to it breathlessly, as to a sound heard in a dream. It stops. They hear* ANDY'S *voice from the road shouting a long hail—"Ahoy there!")*

RUTH   *(With a strangled cry of joy)* Andy! Andy! *(She rushes and grabs the knob of the screen door, about to fling it open.)*

ROBERT   *(In a voice of command that forces obedience)* Stop! *(He goes to the door and gently pushes the trembling* RUTH *away from it. The child's crying rises to a louder pitch.)* I'll meet Andy. You better go in to Mary, Ruth. *(She looks at him defiantly for a moment, but there is something in his eyes that makes her turn and walk slowly into the bedroom.)*

ANDY'S VOICE   *(In a louder shout)* Ahoy there, Rob!

ROBERT   *(In an answering shout of forced cheeriness)* Hello, Andy! *(He opens the door and walks out as the curtain falls.)*

SCENE II

The top of a hill on the farm. It is about eleven o'clock the next morning. The day is hot and cloudless. In the distance the sea can be seen.

The top of the hill slopes downward slightly toward the left. A big boulder stands in the center toward the rear. Further right, a large oak tree. The faint trace of a path leading upward to it from the left foreground can be detected through the bleached, sun-scorched grass.

ROBERT *is discovered sitting on the boulder, his chin resting on his hands, staring out toward the horizon seaward. His face is pale and haggard, his expression one of utter despondency.* MARY *is sitting on the grass near him in the shade, playing with her doll, singing happily to herself. Presently she casts a curious glance at her father, and, propping her doll up against the tree, comes over and clambers to his side.*

MARY   *(Pulling at his hand—solicitously)* Dada sick?

ROBERT   *(Looking at her with a forced smile)* No, dear. Why?

MARY   Play wif Mary.

ROBERT   *(Gently)* No, dear, not today. Dada doesn't feel like playing today.

MARY   *(Protestingly)* Yes, Dada!

ROBERT   No, dear. Dada does feel sick—a little. He's got a bad head-ache.

MARY   Mary see. *(He bends his head. She pats his hair.)* Bad head.

ROBERT   *(Kissing her—with a smile)*   There! It's better now, dear, thank you. *(She cuddles up close against him. There is a pause during which each of them looks out seaward. Finally* ROBERT *turns to her tenderly)*   Would you like Dada to go away? —far, far away?

MARY   *(Tearfully)*   No! No! No, Dada, no!

ROBERT   Don't you like Uncle Andy—the man that came yesterday— not the old man with the white mustache—the other?

MARY   Mary loves Dada.

ROBERT   *(With fierce determination)*   He won't go away, baby. He was only joking. He couldn't leave his little Mary. *(He presses the child in his arms.)*

MARY   *(With an exclamation of pain)*   Oh! Hurt!

ROBERT   I'm sorry, little girl. *(He lifts her down to the grass.)*   Go play with Dolly, that's a good girl; and be careful to keep in the shade. *(She reluctantly leaves him and takes up her doll again. A moment later she points down the hill to the left.)*

MARY   Mans, Dada.

ROBERT   *(Looking that way)*   It's your Uncle Andy. *(A moment later* ANDREW *comes up from the left, whistling cheerfully. He has changed but little in appearance, except for the fact that his face has been deeply bronzed by his years in the tropics; but there is a decided change in his manner. The old easy-going good-nature seems to have been partly lost in a breezy, business-like briskness of voice and gesture. There is an authoritative note in his speech as though he were accustomed to give orders and have them obeyed as a matter of course. He is dressed in the simple blue uniform and cap of a merchant ship's officer.)*

ANDREW   Here you are, eh?

ROBERT   Hello, Andy.

ANDREW   *(Going over to* MARY*)*   And who's this young lady I find you all alone with, eh? Who's this pretty young lady? *(He tickles the laughing, squirming* MARY, *then lifts her up at arm's length over his head.)*   Upsy—daisy! *(He sets her down on the ground again.)* And there you are! *(He walks over and sits down on the boulder beside* ROBERT *who moves to one side to make room for him.)*   Ruth told me I'd probably find you up top-side here; but I'd have guessed it, anyway. *(He digs his brother in the ribs affectionately.)*   Still up to your old tricks, you old beggar! I can remember how you used to come up here to mope and dream in the old days.

ROBERT   *(With a smile)*   I come up here now because it's the coolest place on the farm. I've given up dreaming.

ANDREW   *(Grinning)*   I don't believe it. You can't have changed that much. *(After a pause—with boyish enthusiasm)*   Say, it sure brings back old times to be up here with you having a chin all by our lonesomes again. I feel great being back home.

ROBERT   It's great for us to have you back.

ANDREW   *(After a pause—meaningly)*   I've been looking over the old place with Ruth. Things don't seem to be—

ROBERT   *(His face flushing—interrupts his brother shortly)*   Never mind the damn farm! Let's talk about something interesting. This is the first chance I've had to have a word with you alone. Tell me about your trip.

ANDREW   Why, I thought I told you everything in my letters.

ROBERT   *(Smiling)*   Your letters were—sketchy, to say the least.

ANDREW   Oh, I know I'm no author. You needn't be afraid of hurting my feelings. I'd rather go through a typhoon again than write a letter.

ROBERT   *(With eager interest)*   Then you were through a typhoon?

ANDREW   Yes—in the China sea. Had to run before it under bare poles for two days. I thought we were bound down for Davy Jones, sure. Never dreamed waves could get so big or the wind blow so hard. If it hadn't been for Uncle Dick being such a good skipper we'd have gone to the sharks, all of us, As it was we came out minus a main top-mast and had to beat back to Hong Kong for repairs. But I must have written you all this.

ROBERT   You never mentioned it.

ANDREW   Well, there was so much dirty work getting things ship-shape again I must have forgotten about it.

ROBERT   *(Looking at* ANDREW—*marveling)*   Forget a typhoon? *(With a trace of scorn)*   You're a strange combination, Andy. And is what you've told me all you remember about it?

ANDREW   Oh, I could give you your bellyful of details if I wanted to turn loose on you. It was all-wool-and-a-yard-wide-Hell, I'll tell you. You ought to have been there. I remember thinking about you at the worst of it, and saying to myself: "This'd cure Rob of them ideas of his about the beautiful sea, if he could see it." And it would have too, you bet! *(He nods emphatically.)*

ROBERT   *(Dryly)*   The sea doesn't seem to have impressed you very favorably.

ANDREW   I should say it didn't! I'll never set foot on a ship again if I can help it—except to carry me some place I can't get to by train.

ROBERT   But you studied to become an officer!

ANDREW   Had to do something or I'd gone mad. The days were like years. *(He laughs.)*   And as for the East you used to rave about— well, you ought to see it, and *smell* it! One walk down one of their filthy narrow streets with the tropic sun beating on it would sicken you for life with the "wonder and mystery" you used to dream of.

ROBERT   *(Shrinking from his brother with a glance of aversion)*   So all you found in the East was a stench?

ANDREW   *A* stench! Ten thousand of them!

ROBERT   But you did like some of the places, judging from your letters —Sydney, Buenos Aires—

ANDREW   Yes, Sydney's a good town. *(Enthusiastically)*   But Buenos Aires—there's the place for you. Argentine's a country where a fellow has a chance to make good. You're right I like it. And I'll tell you, Rob, that's right where I'm going just as soon as I've seen you folks a while and can get a ship. I can get a berth as second officer, and I'll jump the ship when I get there. I'll need every cent of the wages Uncle's paid me to get a start at something in B.A.

ROBERT   *(Staring at his brother—slowly)*   So you're not going to stay on the farm?

ANDREW   Why sure not! Did you think I was? There wouldn't be any sense. One of us is enough to run this little place.

ROBERT   I suppose it does seem small to you now.

ANDREW   *(Not noticing the sarcasm in* ROBERT'S *tone)*   You've no idea, Rob, what a splendid place Argentine is. I had a letter from a marine insurance chap that I'd made friends with in Hong-Kong to his brother, who's in the grain business in Buenos Aires. He took quite a fancy to me, and what's more important, he offered me a job if I'd come back there. I'd have taken it on the spot, only I couldn't leave Uncle Dick in the lurch, and I'd promised you folks to come home. But I'm going back there, you bet, and then you watch me get on! *(He slaps* ROBERT *on the back.)*   But don't you think it's a big chance, Rob?

ROBERT   It's fine—for you, Andy.

ANDREW   We call this a farm—but you ought to hear about the farms down there—ten square miles where we've got an acre. It's a new country where big things are opening up—and I want to get in on something big before I die. I'm no fool when it comes to farming, and I know something about grain. I've been reading up a lot on it, too, lately. *(He notices* ROBERT'S *absent-minded expression and laughs.)*   Wake up, you old poetry book worm, you! I know my talking about business makes you want to choke me, doesn't it?

ROBERT   *(With an embarrassed smile)*   No, Andy, I—I just happened to think of something else. *(Frowning)*   There've been lots of times lately that I've wished I had some of your faculty for business.

ANDREW   *(Soberly)*   There's something I want to talk about, Rob—the farm. You don't mind, do you?

ROBERT   No.

ANDREW   I walked over it this morning with Ruth—and she told me about things— *(Evasively)*   I could see the place had run down, but you mustn't blame yourself. When luck's against anyone—

ROBERT   Don't, Andy! It *is* my fault. You know it as well as I do. The best I've ever done was to make ends meet.

ANDREW   *(After a pause)* I've got over a thousand saved, and you can have that.

ROBERT   *(Firmly)* No. You need that for your start in Buenos Aires.

ANDREW   I don't. I can—

ROBERT   *(Determinedly)* No, Andy! Once and for all, no! I won't hear of it!

ANDREW   *(Protestingly)* You obstinate old son of a gun!

ROBERT   Oh, everything'll be on a sound footing after harvest. Don't worry about it.

ANDREW   *(Doubtfully)* Maybe. *(After a pause)* It's too bad Pa couldn't have lived to see things through. *(With feeling)* It cut me up a lot—hearing he was dead. He never—softened up, did he—about me, I mean?

ROBERT   He never understood, that's a kinder way of putting it. He does now.

ANDREW   *(After pause)* You've forgotten all about what—caused me to go, haven't you, Rob? (ROBERT *nods but keeps his face averted.*) I was a slushier damn fool in those days than you were. But it was an act of Providence I did go. It opened my eyes to how I'd been fooling myself. Why, I'd forgotten all about—that—before I'd been at sea six months.

ROBERT   *(Turns and looks into* ANDREW'S *eyes searchingly)* You're speaking of—Ruth?

ANDREW   *(Confused)* Yes. I didn't want you to get false notions in your head, or I wouldn't say anything. *(Looking* ROBERT *squarely in the eyes)* I'm telling you the truth when I say I'd forgotten long ago. It don't sound well for me, getting over things so easy, but I guess it never really amounted to more than a kid idea I was letting rule me. I'm certain now I never was in love—I was getting fun out of thinking I was—and being a hero to myself. *(He heaves a great sigh of relief.)* There! Gosh, I'm glad that's off my chest. I've been feeling sort of awkward ever since I've been home, thinking of what you two might think. *(A trace of appeal in his voice)* You've got it all straight now, haven't you, Rob?

ROBERT   *(In a low voice)* Yes, Andy.

ANDREW   And I'll tell Ruth, too, if I can get up the nerve. She must feel kind of funny having me round—after what used to be—and not knowing how I feel about it.

ROBERT   *(Slowly)* Perhaps—for her sake—you'd better not tell her.

ANDREW   For her sake? Oh, you mean she wouldn't want to be reminded of my foolishness? Still, I think it'd be worse if—

ROBERT   *(Breaking out—in an agonized voice)* Do as you please,

Andy; but for God's sake, let's not talk about it! *(There is a pause. ANDREW stares at ROBERT in hurt stupefaction. ROBERT continues after a moment in a voice which he vainly attempts to keep calm.)* Excuse me, Andy. This rotten headache has my nerves shot to pieces.

ANDREW *(Mumbling)* It's all right, Rob—long as you're not sore at me.

ROBERT Where did Uncle Dick disappear to this morning?

ANREW He went down to the port to see to things on the *Sunda*. He said he didn't know exactly when he'd be back. I'll have to go down and tend to the ship when he comes. That's why I dressed up in these togs.

MARY *(Pointing down the hill to the left)* See! Mama! Mama! *(She struggles to her feet. RUTH appears at left. She is dressed in white, shows she has been fixing up. She looks pretty, flushed and full of life.)*

MARY *(Running to her mother)* Mama!

RUTH *(Kissing her)* Hello, dear! *(She walks toward the rock and addresses ROBERT coldly.)* Jake wants to see you about something. He finished working where he was. He's waiting for you at the road.

ROBERT *(Getting up—wearily)* I'll go down right away. *(As he looks at RUTH, noting her changed appearance, his face darkens with pain.)*

RUTH And take Mary with you please. *(To MARY)* Go with Dada, that's a good girl. Grandma has your dinner most ready for you.

ROBERT *(Shortly)* Come, Mary!

MARY *(Taking his hand and dancing happily beside him)* Dada! Dada! *(They go down the hill to the left. RUTH looks after them for a moment, frowning—then turns to ANDY with a smile.)* I'm going to sit down. Come on, Andy. It'll be like old times. *(She jumps lightly to the top of the rock and sits down.)* It's so fine and cool up here after the house.

ANDREW *(Half-sitting on the side of the boulder)* Yes. It's great.

RUTH I've taken a holiday in honor of your arrival. *(Laughing excitedly)* I feel so free I'd like to have wings and fly over the sea. You're a man. You can't know how awful and stupid it is—cooking and washing dishes all the time.

ANDREW *(Making a wry face)* I can guess.

RUTH Besides, your mother just insisted on getting your first dinner to home, she's that happy at having you back. You'd think I was planning to poison you the flurried way she shooed me out of the kitchen.

ANDREW That's just like Ma, bless her!

RUTH She's missed you terrible. We all have. And you can't deny the farm has, after what I showed you and told you when we was looking over the place this morning.

ANDREW   *(With a frown)* Things are rundown, that's a fact. It's too darn hard on poor old Rob.

RUTH   *(Scornfully)* It's his own fault. He never takes any interest in things.

ANDREW   *(Reprovingly)* You can't blame him. He wasn't born for it; but I know he's done his best for your sake and the old folks and the little girl.

RUTH   *(Indifferently)* Yes, I suppose he has. *(Gayly)* But thank the Lord, all those days are over now. The "hard luck" Rob's always blaming won't last long when you take hold, Andy. All the farm's ever needed was someone with the knack of looking ahead and preparing for what's going to happen.

ANDREW   Yes, Rob hasn't got that. He's frank to own up to that himself. I'm going to try and hire a good man for him—an experienced farmer—to work the place on a salary and percentage. That'll take it off of Rob's hands, and he needn't be worrying himself to death any more. He looks all worn out, Ruth. He ought to be careful.

RUTH   *(Absent-mindedly)* Yes, I s'pose. *(Her mind is filled with premonitions by the first part of his statement.)* Why do you want to hire a man to oversee things? Seems as if now that you're back it wouldn't be needful.

ANDREW   Oh, of course I'll attend to everything while I'm here. I mean after I'm gone.

RUTH   *(As if she couldn't believe her ears)* Gone!

ANDREW   Yes. When I leave for the Argentine again.

RUTH   *(Aghast)* You're going away to sea!

ANDREW   Not to sea, no; I'm through with the sea for good as a job. I'm going down to Buenos Aires to get in the grain business.

RUTH   But—that's far off—isn't it?

ANDREW   *(Easily)* Six thousand miles more or less. It's quite a trip. *(With enthusiasm)* I've got a peach of a chance down there, Ruth. Ask Rob if I haven't. I've just been telling him all about it.

RUTH   *(A flush of anger coming over her face)* And didn't he try to stop you from going?

ANDREW   *(In surprise)* No, of course not. Why?

RUTH   *(Slowly and vindictively)* That's just like him—not to.

ANDREW   *(Resentfully)* Rob's too good a chum to try and stop me when he knows I'm set on a thing. And he could see just as soon's I told him what a good chance it was.

RUTH   *(Dazedly)* And you're bound on going?

ANDREW   Sure thing. Oh, I don't mean right off. I'll have to wait for a ship sailing there for quite a while, likely. Anyway, I want to stay to home and visit with you folks a spell before I go.

RUTH   *(Dumbly)* I s'pose. *(With sudden anguish)* Oh, Andy, you can't go! You can't. Why we've all thought—we've all been hoping and praying you was coming home to stay, to settle down on the farm and see to things. You mustn't go! Think of how your Ma'll take on if you go—and how the farm'll be ruined if you leave it to Rob to look after. You can see that.

ANDREW   *(Frowning)* Rob hasn't done so bad. When I get a man to direct things the farm'll be safe enough.

RUTH   *(Insistently)* But your Ma—think of her.

ANDREW   She's used to me being away. She won't object when she knows it's best for her and all of us for me to go. You ask Rob. In a couple of years down there I'll make my pile, see if I don't; and then I'll come back and settle down and turn this farm into the crackiest place in the whole state. In the meantime, I can help you both from down there. *(Earnestly)* I tell you, Ruth, I'm going to make good right from the minute I land, if working hard and a determination to get on can do it; and I *know* they can! *(Excitedly—in a rather boastful tone)* I tell you, I feel ripe for bigger things than settling down here. The trip did that for me, anyway. It showed me the world is a larger proposition than ever I thought it was in the old days. I couldn't be content any more stuck here like a fly in molasses. It all seems trifling, somehow. You ought to be able to understand what I feel.

RUTH   *(Dully)* Yes—I s'pose I ought. *(After a pause—a sudden suspicion forming in her mind)* What did Rob tell you—about me?

ANDREW   Tell? About you? Why, nothing.

RUTH   *(Staring at him intensely)* Are you telling me the truth, Andy Mayo? Didn't he say—I— *(She stops confusedly.)*

ANDREW   *(Surprised)* No, he didn't mention you, I can remember. Why? What made you think he did?

RUTH   *(Wringing her hands)* Oh, I wish I could tell if you're lying or not!

ANDREW   *(Indignantly)* What're you talking about? I didn't used to lie to you, did I? And what in the name of God is there to lie for?

RUTH   *(Still unconvinced)* Are you sure—will you swear—it isn't the reason— *(She lowers her eyes and half turns away from him.)* The same reason that made you go last time that's driving you away again? 'Cause if it is—I was going to say—you mustn't go—on that account. *(Her voice sinks to a tremulous, tender whisper as she finishes.)*

ANDREW   *(Confused—forces a laugh)* Oh, is *that* what you're driving at? Well, you needn't worry about that no more— *(Soberly)* I don't blame you, Ruth, feeling embarrassed having me around again, after the way I played the dumb fool about going away last time.

RUTH   *(Her hope crushed—with a gasp of pain)* Oh, Andy!

ANDREW   *(Misunderstanding)*   I know I oughtn't to talk about such foolishness to you. Still I figure it's better to get it out of my system so's we three can be together same's years ago, and not be worried thinking one of us might have the wrong notion.

RUTH   Andy! Please! Don't!

ANDREW   Let me finish now that I've started. It'll help clear things up. I don't want you to think once a fool always a fool, and be upset all the time I'm here on my fool account. I want you to believe I put all that silly nonsense back of me a long time ago—and now—it seems—well —as if you'd always been my sister, that's what, Ruth.

RUTH   *(At the end of her endurance—laughing hysterically)*   For God's sake, Andy—won't you please stop talking!   *(She again hides her face in her hands, her bowed shoulders trembling.)*

ANDREW   *(Ruefully)*   Seem's if I put my foot in it whenever I open my mouth today. Rob shut me up with almost the same words when I tried speaking to him about it.

RUTH   *(Fiercely)*   You told him—what you've told me?

ANDREW   *(Astounded)*   Why sure! Why not?

RUTH   *(Shuddering)*   Oh, my God!

ANDREW   *(Alarmed)*   Why? Shouldn't I have?

RUTH   *(Hysterically)*   Oh, I don't care what you do! I don't care! Leave me alone!   *(ANDREW gets up and walks down the hill to the left, embarrassed, hurt, and greatly puzzled by her behavior.)*

ANDREW   *(After a pause—pointing down the hill)*   Hello! Here they come back—and the Captain's with them. How'd he come to get back so soon, I wonder? That means I've got to hustle down to the port and get on board. Rob's got the baby with him.   *(He comes back to the boulder.* RUTH *keeps her face averted from him.)*   Gosh, I never saw a father so tied up in a kid as Rob is! He just watches every move she makes. And I don't blame him. You both got a right to feel proud of her. She's surely a little winner.   *(He glances at* RUTH *to see if this very obvious attempt to get back in her good graces is having any effect.)*   I can see the likeness to Rob standing out all over her, can't you? But there's no denying she's your young one, either. There's something about her eyes—

RUTH   *(Piteously)*   Oh, Andy, I've a headache! I don't want to talk! Leave me alone, won't you please?

ANDREW   *(Stands staring at her for a moment—then walks away saying in a hurt tone:)*   Everybody hereabouts seems to be on edge today. I begin to feel as if I'm not wanted around.   *(He stands near the path, left, kicking at the grass with the toe of his shoe. A moment later* CAPTAIN DICK SCOTT *enters, followed by* ROBERT *carrying* MARY. *The* CAPTAIN *seems scarcely to have changed at all from the jovial, boom-*

ing person he was three years before. He wears a uniform similar to ANDREW'S. *He is puffing and breathless from his climb and mops wildly at his perspiring countenance.* ROBERT *casts a quick glance at* ANDREW, *noticing the latter's discomfited look, and then turns his eyes on* RUTH *who, at their approach, has moved so her back is toward them, her chin resting on her hands as she stares out seaward).*

MARY   Mama! Mama! *(*ROBERT *puts her down and she runs to her mother.* RUTH *turns and grabs her up in her arms with a sudden fierce tenderness, quickly turning away again from the others. During the following scene she keeps* MARY *in her arms).*

SCOTT   *(Wheezily)* Phew! I got great news for you, Andy. Let me get my wind first. Phew! God A'mighty, mountin' this damned hill is worser'n goin' aloft to the skys'l yard in a blow. I got to lay to a while. *(He sits down on the grass, mopping his face.)*

ANDREW   I didn't look for you this soon, Uncle.

SCOTT   I didn't figger it, neither; but I run across a bit o' news down to the Seamen's Home made me 'bout ship and set all sail back here to find you.

ANDREW   *(Eagerly)* What is it, Uncle?

SCOTT   Passin' by the Home I thought I'd drop in an' let 'em know I'd be lackin' a mate next trip count o' your leavin'. Their man in charge o' the shippin' asked after you 'special curious. "Do you think he'd consider a berth as Second on a steamer, Captain?" he asks. I was goin' to say no when I thinks o' you wantin' to get back down south to the Plate agen; so I asks him: "What is she and where's she bound?" "She's the *El Paso,* a brand new tramp," he says, "and she's bound for Buenos Aires."

ANDREW   *(His eyes lighting up—excitedly)* Gosh, that is luck! When does she sail?

SCOTT   Tomorrow mornin'. I didn't know if you'd want to ship away agen so quick an' I told him so. "Tell him I'll hold the berth open for him until late this afternoon," he says. So there you be, an' you can make your own choice.

ANDREW   I'd like to take it. There may not be another ship for Buenos Aires with a vacancy in months. *(His eyes roving from* ROBERT *to* RUTH *and back again—uncertainly.)* Still—damn it all—tomorrow morning is soon. I wish she wasn't leaving for a week or so. That'd give me a chance—it seems hard to go right away again when I've just got home. And yet it's a chance in a thousand— *(Appealing to* ROBERT) What do you think, Rob? What would you do?

ROBERT   *(Forcing a smile)* He who hesitates, you know. *(Frowning)* It's a piece of good luck thrown in your way—and—I think you owe it to yourself to jump at it. But don't ask me to decide for you.

RUTH   (*Turning to look at* ANDREW—*in a tone of fierce resentment*) Yes, go, Andy! (*She turns quickly away again. There is a moment of embarrassed silence.*)

ANDREW   (*Thoughtfully*) Yes, I guess I will. It'll be the best thing for all of us in the end, don't you think so, Rob? (ROBERT *nods but remains silent.*)

SCOTT   (*Getting to his feet*) Then, that's settled.

ANDREW   (*Now that he has definitely made a decision his voice rings with hopeful strength and energy.*) Yes, I'll take the berth. The sooner I go the sooner I'll be back, that's a certainty; and I won't come back with empty hands next time. You bet I won't!

SCOTT   You ain't got so much time, Andy. To make sure you'd best leave here soon's you kin. I got to get right back aboard. You'd best come with me.

ANDREW   I'll go to the house and repack my bag right away.

ROBERT   (*Quietly*) You'll both be here for dinner, won't you?

ANDREW   (*Worriedly*) I don't know. Will there be time? What time is it now, I wonder?

ROBERT   (*Reproachfully*) Ma's been getting dinner especially for you, Andy.

ANDREW   (*Flushing—shamefacedly*) Hell! And I was forgetting! Of course I'll stay for dinner if I missed every damned ship in the world. (*He turns to the* CAPTAIN—*briskly.*) Come on, Uncle. Walk down with me to the house and you can tell me more about this berth on the way. I've got to pack before dinner. (*He and the* CAPTAIN *start down to the left.* ANDREW *calls back over his shoulder.*) You're coming soon, aren't you, Rob?

ROBERT   Yes. I'll be right down. (ANDREW AND THE CAPTAIN *leave.* RUTH *puts* MARY *on the ground and hides her face in her hands. Her shoulders shake as if she were sobbing.* ROBERT *stares at her with a grim, somber expression.* MARY *walks backward toward* ROBERT, *her wondering eyes fixed on her mother.*)

MARY   (*Her voice vaguely frightened, taking her father's hand*) Dada, Mama's cryin', Dada.

ROBERT   (*Bending down and stroking her hair—in a voice he endeavors to keep from being harsh*) No, she isn't, little girl. The sun hurts her eyes, that's all. Aren't you beginning to feel hungry, Mary?

MARY   (*Decidedly*) Yes, Dada.

ROBERT   (*Meaningly*) It must be your dinner time now.

RUTH   (*In a muffled voice*) I'm coming, Mary. (*She wipes her eyes quickly and, without looking at* ROBERT, *comes and takes* MARY'S *hand—in a dead voice.*) Come on and I'll get your dinner for you. (*She walks out left, her eyes fixed on the ground, the skipping*

MARY *tugging at her hand.* ROBERT *waits a moment for them to get ahead and then slowly follows as The Curtain Falls.)*

ACT III

SCENE I

Same as Act II, Scene I—The sitting room of the farm house about six o'clock in the morning of a day toward the end of October five years later. It is not yet dawn, but as the action progresses the darkness outside the windows gradually fades to gray.

The room, seen by the light of the shadeless oil lamp with a smoky chimney which stands on the table, presents an appearance of decay, of dissolution. The curtains at the windows are torn and dirty and one of them is missing. The closed desk is gray with accumulated dust as if it had not been used in years. Blotches of dampness disfigure the wall paper. Threadbare trails, leading to the kitchen and outer doors, show in the faded carpet. The top of the coverless table is stained with the imprints of hot dishes and spilt food. The rung of one rocker has been clumsily mended with a piece of plain board. A brown coating of rust covers the unblacked stove. A pile of wood is stacked up carelessly against the wall by the stove.

The whole atmosphere of the room, contrasted with that of former years, is one of an habitual poverty too hopelessly resigned to be any longer ashamed or even conscious of itself.

At the rise of the curtain RUTH *is discovered sitting by the stove, with hands outstretched to the warmth as if the air in the room were damp and cold. A heavy shawl is wrapped about her shoulders, half-concealing her dress of deep mourning. She has aged horribly. Her pale, deeply lined face has the stony lack of expression of one to whom nothing more can ever happen, whose capacity for emotion has been exhausted. When she speaks her voice is without timbre, low and monotonous. The negligent disorder of her dress, the slovenly arrangement of her hair, now streaked with gray, her muddied shoes run down at the heel, give full evidence of the apathy in which she lives.*

Her mother is asleep in her wheel chair beside the stove toward the rear, wrapped up in a blanket.

There is a sound from the open bedroom door in the rear as if someone were getting out of bed. RUTH *turns in that direction with a look of dull annoyance. A moment later* ROBERT *appears in the door-*

*way, leaning weakly against it for support. His hair is long and un-
kempt, his face and body emaciated. There are bright patches of crimson over his cheek bones and his eyes are burning with fever. He is
dressed in corduroy pants, a flannel shirt, and wears worn carpet slippers on his bare feet.*

RUTH   *(Dully)* S-s-s-h-! Ma's asleep.

ROBERT   *(Speaking with an effort)* I won't wake her. *(He walks
weakly to a rocker by the side of the table and sinks down in it
exhausted.)*

RUTH   *(Staring at the stove)* You better come near the fire where it's
warm.

ROBERT   No. I'm burning up now.

RUTH   That's the fever. You know the doctor told you not to get up and
move round.

ROBERT   *(Irritably)* That old fossil! He doesn't know anything. Go to
bed and stay there—that's his only prescription.

RUTH   *(Indifferently)* How are you feeling now?

ROBERT   *(Buoyantly)* Better! Much better than I've felt in ages.
Really I'm fine now—only very weak. It's the turning point, I guess.
From now on I'll pick up so quick I'll surprise you—and no thanks to
that old fool of a country quack, either.

RUTH   He's always tended to us.

ROBERT   Always helped us to die, you mean! He "tended" to Pa and
Ma and— *(his voice breaks)* —and to—Mary.

RUTH   *(Dully)* He did the best he knew, I s'pose. *(After a
pause)* Well, Andy's bringing a specialist with him when he comes.
That ought to suit you.

ROBERT   *(Bitterly)* Is that why you're waiting up all night?

RUTH   Yes.

ROBERT   For Andy?

RUTH   *(Without a trace of feeling)* Somebody had got to. It's only
right for someone to meet him after he's been gone five years.

ROBERT   *(With bitter mockery)* Five years! It's a long time.

RUTH   Yes.

ROBERT   *(Meaningly)* To wait!

RUTH   *(Indifferently)* It's past now.

ROBERT   Yes, it's past. *(After a pause)* Have you got his two tele-
grams with you? (RUTH *nods.*) Let me see them, will you? My
head was so full of fever when they came I couldn't make head or
tail to them. *(Hastily)* But I'm feeling fine now. Let me read them
again. (RUTH *takes them from the bosom of her dress and hands them
to him.*)

RUTH   Here. The first one's on top.

ROBERT   *(Opening it)* New York. "Just landed from steamer. Have important business to wind up here. Will be home as soon as deal is completed." *(He smiles bitterly.)* Business first was always Andy's motto. *(He reads)* "Hope you are all well. Andy." *(He repeats ironically:)* "Hope you are all well?"

RUTH   *(Dully)* He couldn't know you'd been took sick till I answered that and told him.

ROBERT   *(Contritely)* Of course he couldn't. I'm a fool. I'm touchy about nothing lately. Just what did you say in your reply?

RUTH   *(Inconsequentially)* I had to send it collect.

ROBERT   *(Irritably)* What did you say was the matter with me?

RUTH   I wrote you had lung trouble.

ROBERT   *(Flying into a petty temper)* You *are* a fool! How often have I explained to you that it's *pleurisy* is the matter with me. You can't seem to get it in your head that the pleura is outside the lungs, not in them!

RUTH   *(Callously)* I only wrote what Doctor Smith told me.

ROBERT   *(Angrily)* He's a damned ignoramus!

RUTH   *(Dully)* Makes no difference. I had to tell Andy something, didn't I?

ROBERT   *(After a pause, opening the other telegram)* He sent this last evening. Let's see. *(He reads:)* "Leave for home on midnight train. Just received your wire. Am bringing specialist to see Rob. Will motor to farm from Port." *(He calculates.)* What time is it now?

RUTH   Round six, must be.

ROBERT   He ought to be here soon. I'm glad he's bringing a doctor who knows something. A specialist will tell you in a second that there's nothing the matter with my lungs.

RUTH   *(Stolidly)* You've been coughing an awful lot lately.

ROBERT   *(Irritably)* What nonsense! For God's sake, haven't you ever had a bad cold yourself? *(Ruth stares at the stove in silence. ROBERT fidgets in his chair. There is a pause. Finally ROBERT'S eyes are fixed on the sleeping MRS. ATKINS.)* Your mother is lucky to be able to sleep so soundly.

RUTH   Ma's tired. She's been sitting up with me most of the night.

ROBERT   *(Mockingly)* Is she waiting for Andy, too? *(There is a pause. ROBERT sighs.)* I couldn't get to sleep to save my soul. I counted ten million sheep if I counted one. No use! I gave up trying finally and just laid there in the dark thinking. *(He pauses, then continues in a tone of tender sympathy.)* I was thinking about you, Ruth—of how hard these last years must have been for you. *(Appealingly)* I'm sorry, Ruth.

RUTH   *(In a dead voice)* I don't know. They're past now. They were hard on all of us.

ROBERT   Yes; on all of us but Andy. *(With a flash of sick jealousy)* Andy's made a big success of himself—the kind he wanted. *(Mockingly)* And now he's coming home to let us admire his greatness. *(Frowning—irritably)* What am I talking about? My brain must be sick, too. *(After a pause)* Yes, these years have been terrible for both of us. *(His voice is lowered to a trembling whisper.)* Especially the last eight months since Mary—died. *(He forces back a sob with a convulsive shudder—then breaks out in a passionate agony.)* Our last hope of happiness! I could curse God from the bottom of my soul—if there was a God! *(He is racked by a violent fit of coughing and hurriedly put his handkerchief to his lips.)*

RUTH   *(Without looking at him)* Mary's better off—being dead.

ROBERT   *(Gloomily)* We'd all be better off for that matter. *(With a sudden exasperation)* You tell that mother of yours she's got to stop saying that Mary's death was due to a weak constitution inherited from me. *(On the verge of tears of weakness)* It's got to stop, I tell you!

RUTH   *(Sharply)* S-h-h! You'll wake her; and then she'll nag at me —not you.

ROBERT   *(Coughs and lies back in his chair weakly—a pause)* It's all because your mother's down on me for not begging Andy for help.

RUTH   *(Resentfully)* You might have. He's got plenty.

ROBERT   How can *you* of all people think of taking money from *him?*

RUTH   *(Dully)* I don't see the harm. He's your own brother.

ROBERT   *(Shrugging his shoulders)* What's the use of talking to you? Well, *I* couldn't. *(Proudly)* And I've managed to keep things going, thank God. You can't deny that without help I've succeeded in — *(He breaks off with a bitter laugh.)* My God, what am I boasting of? Debts to this one and that, taxes, interest unpaid! I'm a fool! *(He lies back in his chair closing his eyes for a moment, then speaks in a low voice.)* I'll be frank, Ruth. I've been an utter failure, and I've dragged you with me. I couldn't blame you in all justice—for hating me.

RUTH   *(Without feeling)* I don't hate you. It's been my fault too, I s'pose.

ROBERT   No. You couldn't help loving—Andy.

RUTH   *(Dully)* I don't love anyone.

ROBERT   *(Waving her remark aside)* You needn't deny it. It doesn't matter. *(After a pause—with a tender smile)* Do you know Ruth, what I've been dreaming back there in the dark? *(With a short laugh)* I was planning our future when I get well. *(He looks at her with appealing eyes as if afraid she will sneer at him. Her expression *does not change. She stares at the stove. His voice takes on a note of eagerness.)* After all, why shouldn't we have a future? We're young yet. If we can only shake off the curse of this farm; It's the farm that's ruined our lives, damn it! And now that Andy's coming back —I'm going to sink my foolish pride, Ruth! I'll borrow the money from him to give us a good start in the city. We'll go where people live instead of stagnating, and start all over again. *(Confidently)* I won't be the failure there that I've been here, Ruth. You won't need to be ashamed of me there. I'll prove to you the reading I've done can be put to some use. *(Vaguely)* I'll write, or something of that sort. I've always wanted to write. *(Pleadingly)* You'll want to do that, won't you, Ruth?

RUTH   *(Dully)* There's Ma.

ROBERT   She can come with us.

RUTH   She wouldn't.

ROBERT   *(Angrily)* So that's your answer! *(He trembles with violent passion. His voice is so strange that* RUTH *turns to look at him in alarm.)* You're lying, Ruth! Your mother's just an excuse. You want to stay here. You think that because Andy's coming back that— *(He chokes and has an attack of coughing.)*

RUTH   *(Getting up—in a frightened voice)* What's the matter? *(She goes to him.)* I'll go with you, Rob. Stop that coughing for goodness' sake! It's awful bad for you. *(She soothes him in dull tones.)* I'll go with you to the city—soon's you're well again. Honest I will, Rob, I promise! *(ROB lies back and closes his eyes. She stands looking down at him anxiously.)* Do you feel better now?

ROBERT   Yes. *(RUTH goes back to her chair. After a pause he opens his eyes and sits up in his chair. His face is flushed and happy.)* Then you *will* go, Ruth?

RUTH   Yes.

ROBERT   *(Excitedly)* We'll make a new start, Ruth—just you and I. Life owes us some happiness after what we've been through. *(Vehemently)* It must! Otherwise our suffering would be meaningless—and that is unthinkable.

RUTH   *(Worried by his excitement)* Yes, yes, of course, Rob, but you mustn't—

ROBERT   Oh, don't be afraid. I feel completely well, really I do—now that I can hope again. Oh if you knew how glorious it feels to have something to look forward to! Can't you feel the thrill of it, too—the vision of a new life opening up after all the horrible years?

RUTH   Yes, yes, but do be—

ROBERT   Nonsense! I won't be careful. I'm getting back all my strength. *(He gets lightly to his feet.)* See! I feel light as a feather. *(He walks to her chair and bends down to kiss her smilingly.)* One kiss—the first in years, isn't it?—to greet the dawn of a new life together.

RUTH   *(Submitting to his kiss—worriedly)* Sit down, Rob, for goodness' sake!

ROBERT   *(With tender obstinacy—stroking her hair)* I won't sit down. You're silly to worry. *(He rests one hand on the back of her chair.)* Listen. All our suffering has been a test through which we had to pass to prove ourselves worthy of a finer realization. *(Exultingly)* And we did pass through it! It hasn't broken us! And now the dream is to come true! Don't you see?

RUTH   *(Looking at him with frightened eyes as if she thought he had gone mad)* Yes, Rob, I see; but won't you go back to bed now and rest?

ROBERT   No. I'm going to see the sun rise. It's an augury of good fortune. *(He goes quickly to the window in the rear left, and pushing the curtains aside, stands looking out.* RUTH *springs to her feet and comes quickly to the table, left, where she remains watching* ROBERT *in a tense, expectant attitude. As he peers out, his body seems gradually to sag, to grow limp and tired. His voice is mournful as he speaks.)* No sun yet. It isn't time. All I can see is the black rim of the damned hills outlined against a creeping grayness. *(He turns around; letting the curtains fall back, stretching a hand out to the wall to support himself. His false strength of a moment has evaporated, leaving his face drawn and hollow-eyed. He makes a pitiful attempt to smile.)* That's not a very happy augury, is it? But the sun'll come— soon. *(He sways weakly.)*

RUTH   *(Hurrying to his side and supporting him)* Please go to bed, won't you, Rob? You don't want to be all wore out when the specialist comes, do you?

ROBERT   *(Quickly)* No. That's right. He mustn't think I'm sicker than I am. And I feel as if I could sleep now— *(cheerfully)* —a good sound, restful sleep.

RUTH   *(Helping him to the bedroom door)* That's what you need most. *(They go inside. A moment later she reappears calling back.)* I'll shut this door so's you'll be quiet. *(She closes the door and goes quickly to her mother and shakes her by the shoulder.)* Ma! Ma! Wake up!

MRS. ATKINS   *(Coming out of her sleep with a start)* Glory be! What's the matter with you?

RUTH   It was Rob. He's just been talking to me out here. I put him back to bed. *(Now that she is sure her mother is awake her fear passes and she relapses into dull indifference. She sits down in her chair and stares at the stove—dully.)* He acted—funny; and his eyes looked so —so wild like.

MRS. Atkins *(With asperity)* And is that all you woke me out of a sound sleep for, and scared me near out of my wits?

RUTH I was afraid. He talked so crazy. I couldn't quiet him. I didn't want to be alone with him that way. Lord knows what he might do.

MRS. ATKINS *(Scornfully)* Humph! A help I'd be to you and me not able to move a step! Why didn't you run and get Jake?

RUTH *(Dully)* Jake isn't here. He quit last night. He hasn't been paid in three months.

MRS. ATKINS *(Indignantly)* I can't blame him. What decent person'd want to work on a place like this? *(With sudden exasperation)* Oh, I wish you'd never married that man!

RUTH *(Wearily)* You oughtn't to talk about him now when he's sick in his bed.

MRS. ATKINS *(Working herself into a fit of rage)* You know very well, Ruth Mayo, if it wasn't for me helpin' you on the sly out of my savin's, you'd both been in the poor house—and all 'count of his pigheaded pride in not lettin' Andy know the state thin's were in. A nice thin' for me to have to support him out of what I'd saved for my last days —and me an invalid with no one to look to!

RUTH Andy'll pay you back, Ma. I can tell him so's Rob'll never know.

MRS. ATKINS *(With a snort)* What'd Rob think you and him was livin' on, I'd like to know?

RUTH *(Dully)* He didn't think about it, I s'pose. *(After a slight pause)* He said he'd made up his mind to ask Andy for help when he comes. *(As a clock in the kitchen strikes six)* Six o'clock. Andy ought to get here directly.

MRS. ATKINS D'you think this special doctor'll do Rob any good?

RUTH *(Hopelessly)* I don't know. *(The two women remain silent for a time staring dejectedly at the stove.)*

MRS. ATKINS *(Shivering irritably)* For goodness' sake put some wood on that fire. I'm most freezin'!

RUTH *(Pointing to the door in the rear)* Don't talk so loud. Let him sleep if he can. *(She gets wearily from the chair and puts a few pieces of wood in the stove.)* This is the last of the wood. I don't know who'll cut more now that Jake's left. *(She sighs and walks to the window in the rear, left, pulls the curtains aside, and looks out.)* It's getting gray out. *(She comes back to the stove.)* Looks like it'd be a nice day. *(She stretches out her hands to warm them.)* Must've been a heavy frost last night. We're paying for the spell of warm weather we've been having. *(The throbbing whine of a motor sounds from the distance outside.)*

MRS. ATKINS   *(Sharply)*   S-h-h! Listen! Ain't that an auto I hear?

RUTH   *(Without interest)*   Yes. It's Andy, I s'pose.

MRS. ATKINS   *(With nervous irritation)*   Don't sit there like a silly goose. Look at the state of this room! What'll this strange doctor think of us! Look at that lamp chimney all smoke! Gracious sakes, Ruth—

RUTH   *(Indifferently)*   I've got a lamp all cleaned up in the kitchen.

MRS. ATKINS   *(Peremptorily)*   Wheel me in there this minute. I don't want him to see me looking a sight. I'll lay down in the room on the other side. You don't need me now and I'm dead for sleep.   *(RUTH wheels her mother off right. The noise of the motor grows louder and finally ceases as the car stops on the road before the farmhouse. RUTH returns from the kitchen with a lighted lamp in her hand which she sets on the table besides the other. The sound of footsteps on the path is heard—then a sharp rap on the door. RUTH goes and opens it. ANDREW enters, followed by DOCTOR FAWCETT carrying a small black bag. ANDREW has changed greatly. His face seems to have grown highstrung, hardened by the look of decisiveness which comes from being constantly under a strain where judgments on the spur of the moment are compelled to be accurate. His eyes are keener and more alert. There is even a suggestion of ruthless cunning about them. At present, however, his expression is one of tense anxiety. DOCTOR FAWCETT is a short, dark, middle-aged man with a Vandyke beard. He wears glasses.)*

RUTH   Hello, Andy! I've been waiting—

ANDREW   *(Kissing her hastily)*   I got here as soon as I could.   *(He throws off his cap and heavy overcoat on the table, introducing RUTH and the DOCTOR as he does so. He is dressed in an expensive business suit and appears stouter.)*   My sister-in-law, Mrs. Mayo—Doctor Fawcett.   *(They bow to each other silently. ANDREW casts a quick glance about the room.)*   Where's Rob?

RUTH   *(Pointing)*   In there.

ANDREW   I'll take your coat and hat, Doctor.   *(As he helps the DOCTOR with his things)*   Is he very bad, Ruth?

RUTH   *(Dully)*   He's been getting weaker.

ANDREW   Damn! This way, Doctor. Bring the lamp, Ruth.   *(He goes into the bedroom, followed by the DOCTOR and RUTH carrying the clean lamp. RUTH reappears almost immediately closing the door behind her, and goes slowly to the outside door, which she opens, and stands in the doorway looking out. The sound of ANDREW's and ROBERT's voices comes from the bedroom. A moment later ANDREW reenters, closing the door softly. He comes forward and sinks down in the rocker on the right of table, leaning his head on his hand. His face is drawn in a shocked expression of great grief. He sighs heavily, star-*

ing mournfully in front of him. RUTH *turns and stands watching him. Then she shuts the door and returns to her chair by the stove, turning it so she can face him.)*

ANDREW *(Glancing up quickly—in a harsh voice)* How long has this been going on?

RUTH You mean—how long has he been sick?

ANDREW *(Shortly)* Of course! What else?

RUTH It was last summer he had a bad spell first, but he's been ailin' ever since Mary died—eight months ago.

ANDREW *(Harshly)* Why didn't you let me know—cable me? Do you want him to die, all of you? I'm damned if it doesn't look that way! *(His voice breaking)* Poor old chap! To be sick in this out-of-the-way hole without anyone to attend to him but a country quack! It's a damned shame!

RUTH *(Dully)* I wanted to send you word once, but he only got mad when I told him. He was too proud to ask anything, he said.

ANDREW Proud? To ask *me? (He jumps to his feet and paces nervously back and forth.)* I can't understand the way you've acted. Didn't you see how sick he was getting? Couldn't you realize—why, I nearly dropped in my tracks when I saw him! He looks— *(He shudders)* —terrible! *(With fierce scorn)* I suppose you're so used to the idea of his being delicate that you took his sickness as a matter of course. God, if I'd only known!

RUTH *(Without emotion)* A letter takes so long to get where you were —and we couldn't afford to telegraph. We owed everyone already, and I couldn't ask Ma. She's been giving me money out of her savings till she hadn't much left. Don't say anything to Rob about it. I never told him. He'd only be mad at me if he knew. But I had to, because —God knows how we'd have got on if I hadn't.

ANDREW You mean to say— *(His eyes seem to take in the poverty-stricken appearance of the room for the first time.)* You sent that telegram to me collect. Was it because— (RUTH *nods silently.* ANDREW *pounds on the table with his fist.)* Good God! And all this time I've been—why I've had everything! *(He sits down in his chair and pulls it close to* RUTH'S—*impulsively.)* But—I can't get it through my head. Why? Why? What has happened? How did it ever come about? Tell me!

RUTH *(Dully)* There's nothing much to tell. Things kept getting worse, that's all—and Rob didn't seem to care. He never took any interest since way back when your Ma died. After that he got men to take charge, and they nearly all cheated him—he couldn't tell—and left one after another. Then after Mary died he didn't pay no heed to anything any more—just stayed indoors and took to reading books again. So I had to ask Ma if she wouldn't help us some.

ANDREW   *(Surprised and horrified)* Why, damn it, this is frightful! Rob must be mad not to have let me know. Too proud to ask help of *me!* What's the matter with him in God's name? *(A sudden, horrible suspicion entering his mind)* Ruth! Tell me the truth. His mind hasn't gone back on him, has it?

RUTH   *(Dully)* I don't know. Mary's dying broke him up terrible—but he's used to her being gone by this, I s'pose.

ANDREW   *(Looking at her queerly)* Do you mean to say *you're* used to it?

RUTH   *(In a dead tone)* There's a time comes—when you don't mind any more—anything.

ANDREW   *(Looks at her fixedly for a moment—with great pity)* I'm sorry, Ruth—if I seemed to blame you. I didn't realize— The sight of Rob lying in bed there, so gone to pieces—it made me furious at everyone. Forgive me, Ruth.

RUTH   There's nothing to forgive. It doesn't matter.

ANDREW   *(Springing to his feet again and pacing up and down)* Thank God I came back before it was too late. The doctor will know exactly what to do. That's the first thing to think of. When Rob's on his feet again we can get the farm working on a sound basis once more. I'll see to that—before I leave.

RUTH   You're going away again?

ANDREW   I've got to.

RUTH   You wrote Rob you was coming back to stay this time.

ANDREW   I expected to—until I got to New York. Then I learned certain facts that make it necessary. *(With a short laugh)* To be candid, Ruth, I'm not the rich man you've probably been led to believe by my letters—not now. I was when I wrote them. I made money hand over fist as long as I stuck to legitimate trading; but I wasn't content with that. I wanted it to come easier, so like all the rest of the idiots, I tried speculation. Oh, I won all right! Several times I've been almost a millionaire—on paper—and then come down to earth again with a bump. Finally the strain was too much. I got disgusted with myself and made up my mind to get out and come home and forget it and really live again. *(He gives a harsh laugh.)* And now comes the funny part. The day before the steamer sailed I saw what I thought was a chance to become a millionaire again. *(He snaps his fingers.)* That easy! I plunged. Then, before things broke, I left—I was so confident I couldn't be wrong. But when I landed in New York—I wired you I had business to wind up, didn't I? Well, it was the business that wound me up! *(He smiles grimly, pacing up and down, his hands in his pockets.)*

RUTH   *(Dully)* You found—you'd lost everything?

ANDREW   *(Sitting down again)* Practically. *(He takes a cigar from his pocket, bites the end off, and lights it.)* Oh, I don't mean I'm dead broke. I've saved ten thousand from the wreckage, maybe twenty. But that's a poor showing for five years' hard work. That's why I'll have to go back. *(Confidently)* I can make it up in a year or so down there—and I don't need but a shoestring to start with. *(A weary expression comes over his face and he sighs heavily.)* I wish I didn't have to. I'm sick of it all.

RUTH   It's too bad—things seem to go wrong so.

ANDREW   *(Shaking off his depression—briskly)* They might be much worse. There's enough left to fix the farm O. K. before I go. I won't leave 'til Rob's on his feet again. In the meantime I'll make things fly around here. *(With satisfaction)* I need a rest, and the kind of rest I need is hard work in the open—just like I used to do in the old days. *(Stopping abruptly and lowering his voice cautiously)* Not a word to Rob about my losing money! Remember that, Ruth! You can see why. If he's grown so touchy he'd never accept a cent if he thought I was hard up; see?

RUTH   Yes, Andy. *(After a pause, during which* ANDREW *puffs at his cigar abstractedly, his mind evidently busy with plans for the future, the bedroom door is opened and* DOCTOR FAWCETT *enters, carrying a bag. He closes the door quietly behind him and comes forward, a grave expression on his face.* ANDREW *springs out of his chair.)*

ANDREW   Ah, Doctor! *(He pushes a chair between his own and* RUTH'S*)* Won't you have a chair?

FAWCETT   *(Glancing at his watch)* I must catch the nine o'clock back to the city. It's imperative. I have only a moment. *(Sitting down and clearing his throat—in a perfunctory, impersonal voice)* The case of your brother, Mr. Mayo, is— *(He stops and glances at* RUTH *and says meaningly to* ANDREW*)* Perhaps it would be better if you and I—

RUTH   *(With dogged resentment)* I know what you mean, Doctor. *(Dully)* Don't be afraid I can't stand it. I'm used to bearing trouble by this; and I can guess what you've found out. *(She hesitates for a moment—then continues in a monotonous voice)* Rob's going to die.

ANDREW   *(Angrily)* Ruth!

FAWCETT   *(Raising his hand as if to command silence)* I am afraid my diagnosis of your brother's condition forces me to the same conclusion as Mrs. Mayo's.

ANDREW   *(Groaning)* But, Doctor, surely—

FAWCETT   *(Calmly)* Your brother hasn't long to live—perhaps a few days, perhaps only a few hours. It's a marvel that he's alive at this moment. My examination revealed that both of his lungs are terribly affected.

ANDREW   *(Brokenly)*   Good God!   (RUTH *keeps her eyes fixed on her lap in a trance-like stare.)*

FAWCETT   I am sorry I have to tell you this. If there was anything that could be done—

ANDREW   There isn't anything?

FAWCETT   *(Shaking his head)*   It's too late. Six months ago there might have—

ANDREW   *(In anguish)*   But if we were to take him to the mountains —or to Arizona—or—

FAWCETT   That might have prolonged his life six months ago. (ANDREW *groans.)*   But now— *(He shrugs his shoulders significantly.)*

ANDREW   *(Appalled by a sudden thought)*   Good heavens, you haven't told him this, have you, Doctor?

FAWCETT   No. I lied to him. I said a change of climate— *(He looks at his watch again nervously.)*   I must leave you. *(He gets up.)*

ANDREW   *(Getting to his feet—insistently)*   But there must still be some chance—

FAWCETT   *(As if he were reassuring a child)*   There is always that last chance—the miracle. *(He puts on his hat and coat—bowing to* RUTH.*)*   Good-bye, Mrs. Mayo.

RUTH   *(Without raising her eyes—dully)*   Good-bye.

ANDREW   *(Mechanically)*   I'll walk to the car with you, Doctor. *(They go out of the door.* RUTH *sits motionlessly. The motor is heard starting and the noise gradually recedes into the distance.* ANDREW *re-enters and sits down in his chair, holding his head in his hand.)*   Ruth! *(She lifts her eyes to his.)*   Hadn't we better go in and see him? God! I'm afraid to! I know he'll read it in my face. *(The bedroom door is noiselessly opened and* ROBERT *appears in the doorway. His cheeks are flushed with fever, and his eyes appear unusually large and brilliant.* ANDREW *continues with a groan:)*   It can't be, Ruth. It can't be as hopeless as he said. There's always a fighting chance. We'll take Rob to Arizona. He's *got* to get well. There *must* be a chance!

ROBERT   *(In a gentle tone)*   Why must there, Andy?   (RUTH *turns and stares at him with terrified eyes.)*

ANDREW   *(Whirling around)*   Rob!   *(Scoldingly)*   What are you doing out of bed?   *(He gets up and goes to him.)*   Get right back now and obey the Doc, or you're going to get a licking from me!

ROBERT   *(Ignoring these remarks)*   Help me over to the chair, please, Andy.

ANDREW   Like hell I will! You're going right back to bed, that's where you're going, and stay there!   *(He takes hold of* ROBERT'S *arm.)*

ROBERT   *(Mockingly)*   Stay there 'til I die, eh, Andy?   *(Coldly)*

Don't behave like a child. I'm sick of lying down. I'll be more rested sitting up. *(As* ANDREW *hesitates—violently)* I swear I'll get out of bed every time you put me there. You'll have to sit on my chest, and that wouldn't help my health any. Come on, Andy. Don't play the fool. I want to talk to you, and I'm going to. *(With a grim smile)* A dying man has some rights, hasn't he?

ANDREW   *(With a shudder)* Don't talk that way, for God's sake! I'll only let you sit down if you'll promise that. Remember. *(He helps* ROBERT *to the chair between his own and* RUTH's.) Easy now! There you are! Wait, and I'll get a pillow for you. *(He goes into the bedroom.* ROBERT *looks at* RUTH *who sinks away from him in terror.* ROBERT *smiles bitterly.* ANDREW *comes back with the pillow which he places behind* ROBERT's *back.)* How's that?

ROBERT   *(With an affectionate smile)* Fine! Thank you! *(As* AN-DREW *sits down)* Listen, Andy. You've asked me not to talk—and I won't after I've made my position clear. *(Slowly)* In the first place I know I'm dying. *(*RUTH *bows her head and covers her face with her hands. She remains like this all during the scene between the two brothers.)*

ANDREW   Rob! That isn't so!

ROBERT   *(Wearily)* It *is* so! Don't lie to me. After Ruth put me to bed before you came, I saw it clearly for the first time. *(Bitterly)* I'd been making plans for our future—Ruth's and mine—so it came hard at first—the realization. Then when the doctor examined me, I knew—although he tried to lie about it. And then to make sure I listened at the door to what he told you. So don't mock me with fairy tales about Arizona, or any such rot as that. Because I'm dying is no reason you should treat me as an imbecile or a coward. Now that I'm sure what's happening I can say Kismet to it with all my heart. It was only the silly uncertainty that hurt. *(There is a pause.* ANDREW *looks around in impotent anguish, not knowing what to say.* ROB-ERT *regards him with an affectionate smile.)*

ANDREW   *(Finally blurts out)* It isn't foolish. You *have* got a chance. If you heard all the Doctor said that ought to prove it to you.

ROBERT   Oh, you mean when he spoke of the miracle? *(Dryly)* I don't believe in miracles—in my case. Besides I know more than any doctor on earth *could* know—because I *feel* what's coming. *(Dismissing the subject)* But we've agreed not to talk of it. Tell me about yourself, Andy. That's what I'm interested in. Your letters were too brief and far apart to be illuminating.

ANDREW   I meant to write oftener.

ROBERT   *(With a faint trace of irony)* I judge from them you've accomplished all you set out to do five years ago?

ANDREW   That isn't much to boast of.

ROBERT   (*Surprised*) Have you really, honestly reached that conclusion?

ANDREW   Well, it doesn't seem to amount to much now.

ROBERT   But you're rich, aren't you?

ANDREW   (*With a quick glance at* RUTH) Yes, I s'pose so.

ROBERT   I'm glad. You can do to the farm all I've undone. But what did you do down there? Tell me. You went in the grain business with that friend of yours?

ANDREW   Yes. After two years I had a share in it. I sold out last year. (*He is answering* ROBERT'S *questions with great reluctance.*)

ROBERT   And then?

Andrew   I went in on my own.

ROBERT   Still in grain?

ANDREW   Yes.

ROBERT   What's the matter? You look as if I were accusing you of something.

ANDREW   I'm proud enough of the first four years. It's after that I'm not boasting of. I took to speculating.

ROBERT   In wheat?

ANDREW   Yes.

ROBERT   And you made money—gambling?

ANDREW   Yes.

ROBERT   (*Thoughtfully*) I've been wondering what the great change was in you. (*After a pause*) You—a farmer—to gamble in a wheat pit with scraps of paper. There's a spiritual significance in that picture, Andy. (*He smiles bitterly.*) I'm a failure, and Ruth's another —but we can both justly lay some of the blame for our stumbling on God. But you're the deepest-dyed failure of the three, Andy. You've spent eight years running away from yourself. Do you see what I mean? You used to be a creator when you loved the farm. You and life were in harmonious partnership. And now— (*He stops as if seeking vainly for words.*) My brain is muddled. But part of what I mean is that your gambling with the thing you used to love to create proves how far astray— So you'll be punished. You'll have to suffer to win back— (*His voice grows weaker and he sighs wearily.*) It's no use. I can't say it. (*He lies back and closes his eyes, breathing pantingly.*)

ANDREW   (*Slowly*) I think I know what you're driving at, Rob—and it's true, I guess. (*ROBERT smiles gratefully and stretches out his hand, which* ANDREW *takes in his.*)

ROBERT   I want you to promise me to do one thing, Andy, after—

ANDREW   I'll promise anything, as God is my Judge!

ROBERT   Remember, Andy, Ruth has suffered double her share. (*His voice faltering with weakness.*) Only through contact with suffering, Andy, will you—awaken. Listen. You must marry Ruth—afterwards.

RUTH   *(With a cry)* Rob! *(ROBERT lies back, his eyes closed, gasping heavily for breath.)*

ANDREW   *(Making signs to her to humor him—gently)* You're tired out, Rob. You better lie down and rest a while, don't you think? We can talk later on.

ROBERT   *(With a mocking smile)* Later on! You always were an optimist, Andy! *(He sighs with exhaustion.)* Yes, I'll go and rest a while. *(As ANDREW comes to help him)* It must be near sunrise, isn't it?

ANDREW   It's after six.

ROBERT   *(As ANDREW helps him into the bedroom)* Shut the door, Andy. I want to be alone. *(ANDREW reappears and shuts the door softly. He comes and sits down on his chair again, supporting his head on his hands. His face is drawn with the intensity of his dry-eyed anguish.)*

RUTH   *(Glancing at him—fearfully)* He's out of his mind now, isn't he?

ANDREW   He may be a little delirious. The fever would do that. *(With impotent rage)* God, what a shame! And there's nothing we can do but sit and—wait! *(He springs from his chair and walks to the stove.)*

RUTH   *(Dully)* He was talking—wild—like he used to—only this time it sounded—unnatural, don't you think?

ANDREW   I don't know. The things he said to me had truth in them— even if he did talk them way up in the air, like he always sees things. Still— *(He glances down at RUTH keenly.)* Why do you suppose he wanted us to promise we'd— *(Confusedly)* You know what he said.

RUTH   *(Dully)* His mind was wandering, I s'pose.

ANDREW   *(With conviction)* No—there was something back of it.

RUTH   He wanted to make sure I'd be all right—after he'd gone, I expect.

ANDREW   No, it wasn't that. He knows very well I'd naturally look after you without—anything like that.

RUTH   He might be thinking of—something happened five years back, the time you came home from the trip.

ANDREW   What happened? What do you mean?

RUTH   *(Dully)* We had a fight.

ANDREW   A fight? What has that to do with me?

RUTH   It was about you—in a way.

ANDREW   *(Amazed)* About *me*?

RUTH   Yes, mostly. You see I'd found out I'd made a mistake about Rob soon after we were married—when it was too late.

ANDREW   Mistake? *(Slowly)* You mean—you found out you didn't love Rob?

RUTH   Yes.

ANDREW   Good God!

RUTH   And then I thought that when Mary came it'd be different, and I'd love him; but it didn't happen that way. And I couldn't bear with his blundering and book-reading—and I grew to hate him, almost.

ANDREW   Ruth!

RUTH   I couldn't help it. No woman could. It had to be because I loved someone else, I'd found out. *(She sighs wearily.)* It can't do no harm to tell you now—when it's all past and gone—and dead. *You* were the one I really loved—only I didn't come to the knowledge of it 'til too late.

ANDREW   *(Stunned)* Ruth! Do you know what you're saying?

RUTH   It was true—then. *(With sudden fierceness)* How could I help it? No woman could.

ANDREW   Then—you loved me—that time I came home?

RUTH   *(Doggedly)* I'd known your real reason for leaving home the first time—everybody knew it— and for three years I'd been thinking—

ANDREW   That I loved you?

RUTH   Yes. Then that day on the hill you laughed about what a fool you'd been for loving me once—and I knew it was all over.

ANDREW   Good God, but I never thought— *(He stops, shuddering at his remembrance.)* And did Rob—

RUTH   That was what I'd started to tell. We'd had a fight just before you came and I got crazy mad—and I told him all I've told you.

ANDREW   *(Gaping at her speechlessly for a moment)* You told Rob —you loved me?

RUTH   Yes.

ANDREW   *(Shrinking away from her in horror)* You—you—you mad fool, you! How could you do such a thing?

RUTH   I couldn't help it. I'd got to the end of bearing things—without talking.

ANDREW   Then Rob must have known every moment I stayed here! And yet he never said or showed—God, how he must have suffered! Didn't you know how much he loved you?

RUTH   *(Dully)* Yes. I knew he liked me.

ANDREW   Liked you! What kind of woman are you? Couldn't you have kept silent? Did you have to torture him? No wonder he's dying! And you've lived together for five years with this between you?

RUTH   We've lived in the same house.

ANDREW   Does he still think—

RUTH   I don't know. We've never spoke a word about it since that day. Maybe, from the way he went on, he s'poses I care for you yet.

ANDREW   But you don't. It's outrageous. It's stupid! You don't love me!

RUTH   *(Slowly)* I wouldn't know how to feel love, even if I tried, any more.

ANDREW   *(Brutally)* And I don't love you, that's sure! *(He sinks into his chair, his head between his hands.)* It's damnable such a thing should be between Rob and me. Why, I love Rob better'n anybody in the world and always did. There isn't a thing on God's green earth I wouldn't have done to keep trouble away from him. And I have to be the very one—it's damnable! How am I going to face him again? What can I say to him now? *(He groans with anguished rage. After a pause:)* He asked me to promise—what am I going to do?

RUTH   You can promise—so's it'll ease his mind—and not mean anything.

ANDREW   What? Lie to him now—when he's dying? *(Determinedly)* No! It's *you* who'll have to do the lying, since it must be done. You've got a chance now to undo some of all the suffering you've brought on Rob. Go in to him! Tell him you never loved me—it was all a mistake. Tell him you only said so because you were mad and didn't know what you were saying! Tell him something, anything, that'll bring him peace!

RUTH   *(Dully)* He wouldn't believe me.

ANDREW   *(Furiously)* You've got to make him believe you, do you hear? You've got to—now—hurry—you never know when it may be too late. *(As she hesitates—imploringly)* For God's sake, Ruth! Don't you see you owe it to him? You'll never forgive yourself if you don't.

RUTH   *(Dully)* I'll go. *(She gets wearily to her feet and walks slowly toward the bedroom.)* But it won't do any good. *(ANDREW's eyes are fixed on her anxiously. She opens the door and steps inside the room. She remains standing there for a minute. Then she calls in a frightened voice.)* Rob! Where are you? *(Then she hurries back, trembling with fright.)* Andy! Andy! He's gone!

ANDREW   *(Misunderstanding her—his face pale with dread)* He's not—

RUTH   *(Interrupting him—hysterically)* He's gone! The bed's empty. The window's wide open. He must have crawled out into the yard!

ANDREW   *(Springing to his feet. He rushes into the bedroom and returns immediately with an expression of alarmed amazement on his face.)* Come! He can't have gone far! *(Grabbing his hat, he takes RUTH's arm and shoves her toward the door.)* Come on! *(Opening the door)* Let's hope to God— *(The door closes behind them, cutting off his words as The Curtain Falls.)*

SCENE II

Same as Act I, Scene I—A section of country highway. The sky to the east is already alight with bright color and a thin, quivering line of flame is spreading slowly along the horizon rim of the dark hills. The roadside, however, is still steeped in the grayness of the dawn, shadowy and vague. The field in the foreground has a wild uncultivated appearance as if it had been allowed to remain fallow the preceding summer. Parts of the snake fence in the rear have been broken down. The apple tree is leafless and seems dead.

Robert staggers weakly in from the left. He stumbles into the ditch and lies there for a moment; then crawls with a great effort to the top of the bank where he can see the sun rise, and collapses weakly. Ruth and Andrew come hurriedly along the road from the left.

ANDREW   *(Stopping and looking about him)*   There he is! I knew it! I knew we'd find him here.

ROBERT   *(Trying to raise himself to a sitting position as they hasten to his side—with a wan smile)*   I thought I'd given you the slip.

ANDREW   *(With kindly bullying)*   Well you didn't, you old scoundrel, and we're going to take you right back where you belong—in bed. *(He makes a motion to lift Robert.)*

ROBERT   Don't, Andy. Don't, I tell you!

ANDREW   You're in pain?

ROBERT   *(Simply)*   No. I'm dying. *(He falls back weakly. Ruth sinks down beside him with a sob and pillows his head on her lap. Andrew stands looking down at him helplessly. Robert moves his head restlessly on Ruth's lap.)*   I couldn't stand it back there in the room. It seemed as if all my life—I'd been cooped in a room. So I thought I'd try to end as I might have—if I'd had the courage—alone —in a ditch by the open road—watching the sun rise.

ANDREW   Rob! Don't talk. You're wasting your strength. Rest a while and then we'll carry you—

ROBERT   Still hoping, Andy? Don't. I know. *(There is a pause during which he breathes heavily, straining his eyes toward the horizon.)*   The sun comes so slowly. *(With an ironical smile)*   The doctor told me to go to the far-off places—and I'd be cured. He was right. That was always the cure for me. It's too late for this life—but— *(He has a fit of coughing which racks his body.)*

ANDREW   *(With a hoarse sob)*   Rob! *(He clenches his fists in an impotent rage against Fate.)*   God! God! *(Ruth sobs brokenly and wipes Robert's lips with her handkerchief.)*

ROBERT   *(In a voice which is suddenly ringing with the happiness of hope)*   You mustn't feel sorry for me. Don't you see I'm happy at last—free—free!—freed from the farm—free to wander on and on —eternally! *(He raises himself on his elbow, his face radiant, and points to the horizon.)* Look! Isn't it beautiful beyond the hills? I can hear the old voices calling me to come— *(Exultantly)* And this time I'm going! It isn't the end. It's a free beginning—the start of my voyage! I've won the right to my trip—the right of release—beyond the horizon! Oh, you ought to be glad—glad—for my sake! *(He collapses weakly.)* Andy! (ANDREW *bends down to him.)* Remember Ruth—

ANDREW   I'll take care of her, I swear to you, Rob!

ROBERT   Ruth has suffered—remember, Andy—only through sacrifice —the secret beyond there— *(He suddenly raises himself with his last remaining strength and points to the horizon where the edge of the sun's disc is rising from the rim of the hills.)* The sun! *(He remains with his eyes fixed on it for a moment. A rattling noise throbs from his throat. He mumbles.)* Remember! *(And falls back and is still.* RUTH *gives a cry of horror and springs to her feet, shuddering, her hands over her eyes.* ANDREW *bends on one knee beside the body, placing a hand over* ROBERT'S *heart, then he kisses his brother reverentially on the forehead and stands up.)*

ANDREW   *(Facing* RUTH, *the body between them—in a dead voice.)* He's dead. *(With a sudden burst of fury)* God damn you, you never told him!

RUTH   *(Piteously)* He was so happy without my lying to him.

ANDREW   *(Pointing to the body—trembling with the violence of his rage)* This is your doing, you damn woman, you coward, you murderess!

RUTH   *(Sobbing)* Don't, Andy! I couldn't help it—and he knew how I'd suffered, too. He told you—to remember.

ANDREW   *(Stares at her for a moment, his rage ebbing away, an expression of deep pity gradually coming over his face. Then he glances down at his brother and speaks brokenly in a compassionate voice.)* Forgive me, Ruth—for his sake—and I'll remember— *(*RUTH *lets her hands fall from her face and looks at him uncomprehendingly. He lifts his eyes to hers and forces out falteringly.)* I— you—we've both made a mess of things! We must try to help each other—and—in time—we'll come to know what's right— *(Desperately)* And perhaps we— *(But* RUTH, *if she is aware of his words, gives no sign. She remains silent, gazing at him dully with the sad humility of exhaustion, her mind already sinking back into that spent calm beyond the further troubling of any hope. The Curtain Falls.)*

Questions on *Beyond the Horizon*

A. For Close Reading

ACT I, SCENE 1

1. In the opening dialogue between Andy and Robert, what contrasts are built up between the brothers? What do you learn of their pasts? About their plans for the future? What reasons does Andy give for Robert's going on a trip? What reasons does Robert give? What seems to be on their minds as they part?

2. As Ruth enters, we learn something of her mother; what is her mother like? How does Robert define "the horizon"? When he tells Ruth that he loves her, how does a conflict arise in the play?

SCENE 2

3. What attitude does each character take toward Robert's leaving? What hints do you get that Andy is thinking of something else? What do you learn about the state of business on the farm?

4. What attitude does each character take toward Robert's decision to stay? What reasons does Andy give, at various times in this scene, for his going to sea?

ACT II, SCENE 1

5. What mood is created by the description of the setting? By which key words can you determine the author's purpose for the description?

6. Mrs. Atkins's second speech uses the word, "health." Where, earlier in the play, have there been references to health? Mrs. Atkins was characterized in the first act by Ruth. Is she now acting consistently with that characterization?

7. What is the situation on the farm at this time? What news do we get of Andy? What attitudes do the others take toward his return?

8. What contrasts are built up between Ruth and Robert? What is the dramatic purpose of Ben's speeches?

9. How does Robert now define "the horizon"?

SCENE 2

10. What further contrasts are built up between Andy and Robert?

11. When Andy confesses that he quickly forgot Ruth and wants to tell her of this fact, Robert says, "Perhaps—for her sake—you'd better not tell her." Why does he say that? How does this exchange influence the following scene between Andy and Ruth?

12. In what way is the conversation between Andy and Ruth like that between Robert and Ruth in the opening scene of the play? In what way unlike? What is on Ruth's mind when she says, "What did Rob tell you—about me?" Why is she upset when Andy answers, "Tell? About you? Why, nothing." By what steps, and why, does she finally get hysterical?

13. In what ways is Mary used as a link between Ruth and Robert in this scene? In what ways is she a divisive influence? How would the play be different if Mary were not in it?

ACT III, SCENE 1

14. What mood is created by the description of the setting? What key words create that mood?
15. The opening dialogue between Ruth and Robert is largely expository. What do you learn of their current situation? The dialogue also characterizes them. How has their relationship changed?
16. As Andy and Ruth talk, what more do we learn of their separate situations?
17. When Robert re-enters, he says to Andy, "Listen. You must marry Ruth— afterwards." Then he leaves. How do Ruth and Andy react to his statement? At the end of the scene what is the relationship between Ruth and Andy?

SCENE 2

18. In what way does the setting compare with that of the opening scene of the play?
19. How does Robert now describe "the horizon"?
20. What irony do you find in the contrast between the first scene of the play and the last?
21. At the end of the play what is the relationship between Ruth and Andy?

B. For Writing and Discussion

1. O'Neill begins each scene with a description of the setting to create a mood. How is this mood related to what happens in the scene? How does it reflect the mental states of the characters?
2. In these descriptions O'Neill goes into some detail in telling us about the place, the time, the weather, the season of the year, and the objects on stage. In what ways are the descriptions symbolically prophetic of what is to happen in each scene or indicative of what has happened between scenes?
3. At three different times in the play (I,1; II,1; and III,2) Robert defines what "the horizon" symbolizes for him. Trace his changing attitude toward the surrounding hills each time he talks about them.
4. At what point in the play does Robert make the tragic choice that leads to his ruin? To what extent does the element of fate (events that man cannot control) enter into this choice? To what extent was it determined by Robert's own will?
5. In what ways does fate enter into the affairs of the characters as the play develops?
6. In Act I, Scene 2, Mayo and Scott present different views on man's control over his own destiny. Mayo says, "It's just the same with me as 'twas with you, Dick. You can't order the tides on the sea to suit you, and I ain't pre-

tendin' I can reg'late love for young folks." Then Scott replies, "Love! They ain't old enough to know love when they sight it! Love! I'm ashamed of you, Robert, to go lettin' a little huggin' and kissin' in the dark spile your chances to make a man out o' yourself. It ain't common sense—no siree, it ain't—not by a hell of a sight!" As you look back on the play, which man seems to have had a clearer understanding of what was happening?

7. Another question that must be asked of tragedy is the effect of the suffering it inflicts on the characters of a play. Robert expresses one possible attitude when he says (III,1), "Only through contact with suffering, Andy, will you—awaken." Does his suffering make Robert a better person? Does it improve any of the other characters? What is the evidence?

8. What kind of person are the three major figures, Robert, Ruth, and Andy? Characterize each, proving your general statements by referring to specific incidents. Pay particular attention to the ways in which each changes during the course of the play.

9. What are the dramatic functions of the minor characters of the play? How do they affect the major characters and the unfolding of the plot?

10. Would the lives of all the characters have been different if Robert had gone "beyond the horizon" when he first intended to? Which of them would have been most affected if he had? In what way?

Antigone

(1944)

DURING World War II some French dramatists became interested in adapting Greek myths to new plays because they found in those myths truths that applied to their own lives and world. Jean-Paul Sartre, one of these writers, said in the June, 1946, issue of *Theatre Arts:* ". . . we want to have a theatre of situation; our aim is to explore all the situations that are most common to human experience, those which occur at least once in the majority of lives." What he said applies to the story of Antigone, which for over 2,400 years has symbolized man's revolt against unjust authority. Sophocles wrote his *Antigone* in about 442 B.C.; in 1942 Jean Anouilh adapted the myth to create his own play of the same name.

Greek myths (as you will recall from the introduction to *Oedipus the King)* explained men's relationship to the gods and to one another. Plays based on these myths became a part of Greek religious festivals. Seen collectively, the myths show much about the history and culture of an entire people: how they accounted for suffering or prosperity, what great events they lived through, how they reacted to these events, what they regarded as heroic action. As scholars work with myths, it becomes more and more apparent that some of the narratives contain elements based on historical fact. For example, the ruins of ancient Troy have been uncovered by archaeologists, who dug where Homer said the city was, and the probable course of the voyages of Odysseus have been traced by scholars who combined a knowledge of the winds and ocean currents with descriptions of the lands found in Homer. Fascinating as such discoveries are, however, the enduring appeal of myths lies not in any historical accuracy they may reflect but in their capacity to present timeless truths about human nature.

Along with the twentieth century's academic and archaeological interest in myths, there has also been a keen psychological one, inspired, in part, by the theories of the Swiss psychoanalyst, Carl Gustav Jung, who used the term *archetype* to describe a pattern of plot or character that is part of "racial memory." He meant that certain experiences are common to all people of all times, and that these experiences were related in myths. They dealt, to use Sartre's words again, with "the situations that are most common to human experience, those which occur at least once in the majority of lives." Essentially metaphorical, myths are a link between situations men have faced in the past with those men may encounter in the present or future. Because they concern themselves with the ways in which people all over the world have reacted to basic problems, they make ideal plots for fiction or drama.

Since every society has always been divided into the two classes of the rulers and the ruled, we have always had the question of what rights belong to the governors and what rights to the governed. When a clash comes, the governed are faced with Antigone's problem: Is the conscience of the individual superior to or a stronger force than the established law? Or, to put it another way, when an individual's conscience tells him that the state is doing wrong, what should he do? In choosing the Antigone myth, Anouilh was most interested in what Sartre calls "the situation." Creon, the ruler of Thebes, decrees that Polynices, Antigone's brother, cannot be buried because Creon considers him a traitor to the state. How Antigone reacts to that decree is the subject of the play, which may be seen as a metaphor of how anyone might react to unjust authority.

Jean Anouilh's *Antigone* was first acted in Paris in February, 1944, after the fall of France and during the last six months of the German occupation of that city. Whether Anouilh was commenting on the French situation of that day is not clear, but certainly those citizens connected with the French Resistance movement, who worked in the underground for a free France, would have had little trouble in identifying with Antigone's defiance. Strangely enough, the Nazi censors, who had to approve any play before it could be produced, let this one go on the stage. The explanation may lie in the fact that they could agree with Creon's argument that absolute obedience to the state is fundamental: "You shout an order, and if one man refuses to obey, you shoot straight into the mob. Into the mob, I say!" For those who see the play as a comment on the occupational situation, it expresses the dilemma that anyone would have faced as a French citizen at the time: Should I resist or collaborate? Many of those in the French government did decide to collaborate with the Germans. The spirit of France was kept alive by the underground resistance of those who, like Antigone, decided to say "No."

As has been remarked, the myth that best expressed what was on Anouilh's mind had already been produced some 2,400 years ago in Sophocles' *Antigone,* the story of a daughter of Oedipus. However, Anouilh did not merely retell the story; he recreated it. Though the situation stays much the same as in the earlier version, the religious belief that motivated Sophocles' Antigone is played down in Anouilh's heroine.

When Sophocles wrote his *Antigone,* the religious overtones were unmistakable. His audience would have accepted the idea that to leave the dead unburied was a violation of the law of the gods, and Creon would unquestionably have been considered a villain. His only defense was that he made the decree and that the authority of the state must be obeyed. Antigone buries her brother, in spite of Creon's order, because she chooses to obey the gods—a higher authority than man. This conflict between what a person's conscience tells him is right and what the state says is right will always be with us. It is reflected in the Biblical phrase, "Render therefore unto Caesar the things which are Caesar's; and unto God the things that are God's." The quotation implies that there are areas of life that must yield to the demands of the state and some that belong solely to the individual conscience.

Since the religious motivation that impelled Sophocles' Antigone to action undergoes metamorphosis in Anouilh's version of the story, it is less clear why his heroine acts as she does. Once all the traditional arguments for her actions have been debated by Antigone and Creon and discarded, we find that her opposition is really directed against people who are willing to do what is practical and opportunistic. She represents the young idealist who thinks that life should be better than it is. At one point she reminds Creon of what he himself had been: ". . . a lad named Creon. . . . His mind, too, was filled with thoughts of self-sacrifice." But now Creon is the ruler, the man who assumed the responsibility of governing Thebes after a destructive civil war: "Won't you try to understand me!. . . . There had to be one man who said yes. Somebody had to agree to captain the ship." For him idealism has been replaced by practicality. Antigone feels that practicality is a form of corruption.

With the purity of vision that is characteristic of children, Antigone sees right and wrong in simple terms. Her individualism and humanity conflict with a mechanized world in which human beings do not seem to matter, in which decisions are made for them. The childlike innocence of the heroine is reflected in the language of the play; in the way the Nurse speaks to her and the allusion to her being tucked into bed; in Antigone's plea, "Nanny dear. . . . you must keep me warm and safe. . . ." It is indicative of her nature that she puts earth on the body of Polynices with a toy shovel. You will find examples throughout the play that reflect the way children look at the world, in contrast to the way many adults see it. Even Creon has not completely forgotten what it was like to be young. At the end he says to the Page, "Never grow up if you can help it."

To give the play a sense of being up to date, Anouilh makes deliberate use of anachronisms, things misplaced in time. Though ostensibly the play takes place in ancient Thebes, Creon acts his part in evening clothes; before his death Polynices had smoked cigarettes and driven a car; Eurydice knits and has a room with twin beds; the Guards, the Chorus, and other characters use twentieth century slang and phrasing ("face the music," "beauty sleep," "pals," "ain't got all her marbles").

Antigone is performed on a bare stage except for a semicircular platform in the rear, with three steps leading up to it. As the curtain rises, the cast is sitting on the steps in a tableau. The Chorus, unlike that in a Greek play, is a single person who steps forward and introduces each character by speaking directly to the audience.

Antigone

JEAN ANOUILH

Translator:
Lewis Galantière

CHARACTERS

ANTIGONE, } daughters of Oedipus
ISMENE

CREON, *their uncle and King of Thebes*
EURYDICE, *his wife*
HAEMON, *their son*
NURSE
CHORUS
FIRST GUARD *(Jonas)*
SECOND GUARD
THIRD GUARD
MESSENGER
PAGE

SCENE: THEBES

ANTIGONE, *her hands clasped round her knees, sits on the top step.
The* THREE GUARDS *sit on the steps, in a small group, playing cards.
The* CHORUS *stands on the top step.* EURYDICE *sits on the top step,
just left of center, knitting. The* NURSE *sits on the second step, left of*
EURYDICE. ISMENE *stands in front of arch, left, facing* HAEMON, *who
stands left of her.* CREON *sits in the chair at right end of the table, his
arm over the shoulder of his* PAGE, *who sits on the stool beside his
chair. The* MESSENGER *is leaning against the downstage portal of the
right arch. The curtain rises slowly; then the* CHORUS *turns and moves
downstage.*

CHORUS   Well, here we are.
These people are about to act out for you the story of Antigone.
That thin little creature sitting by herself, staring straight ahead,
seeing nothing, is Antigone. She is thinking. She is thinking that the
instant I finish telling you who's who and what's what in this play, she
will burst forth as the tense, sallow, willful girl whose family would

298

never take her seriously and who is about to rise up alone against Creon, her uncle, the King.

Another thing that she is thinking is this: she is going to die. Antigone is young. She would much rather live than die. But there is no help for it. When your name is Antigone, there is only one part you can play; and she will have to play hers through to the end.

From the moment the curtain went up, she began to feel that inhuman forces were whirling her out of this world, snatching her away from her sister Ismene, whom you see smiling and chatting with that young man; from all of us who sit or stand here, looking at her, not in the least upset ourselves—for we are not doomed to die tonight.

CHORUS *turns and indicates* HAEMON.

The young man talking to Ismene—to the gay and beautiful Ismene —is Haemon. He is the King's son, Creon's son. Antigone and he are engaged to be married. You wouldn't have thought she was his type. He likes dancing, sports, competition; he likes women, too. Now look at Ismene again. She is certainly more beautiful than Antigone. She is the girl you'd think he'd go for. Well . . . There was a ball one night. Ismene wore a new evening frock. She was radiant. Haemon danced every dance with her. And yet, that same night, before the dance was over, suddenly he went in search of Antigone, found her sitting alone —like that, with her arms clasped round her knees—and asked her to marry him. We still don't know how it happened. It didn't seem to surprise Antigone in the least. She looked up at him out of those solemn eyes of hers, smiled sort of sadly and said "yes." That was all. The band struck up another dance. Ismene, surrounded by a group of young men, laughed out loud. And . . . well, here is Haemon expecting to marry Antigone. He won't, of course. He didn't know, when he asked her, that the earth wasn't meant to hold a husband of Antigone, and that this princely distinction was to earn him no more than the right to die sooner than he might otherwise have done.

CHORUS *turns toward* CREON.

That gray-haired, powerfully built man sitting lost in thought, with his little page at his side, is Creon, the King. His face is lined. He is tired. He practices the difficult art of a leader of men. When he was younger, when Oedipus was King and Creon was no more than the King's brother-in-law, he was different. He loved music, bought rare manuscripts, was a kind of art patron. He would while away whole afternoons in the antique shops of this city of Thebes. But Oedipus died. Oedipus' sons died. Creon had to roll up his sleeves and take over the kingdom. Now and then, when he goes to bed weary with the day's work, he wonders whether this business of being a leader of men is worth the trouble. But when he wakes up, the problems are there to be solved; and like a conscientious workman, he does his job.

Creon has a wife, a Queen. Her name is Eurydice. There she sits, the old lady with the knitting, next to the Nurse who brought up the two girls. She will go on knitting all through the play, till the time comes for her to go to her room and die. She is a good woman, a worthy, loving soul. But she is no help to her husband. Creon has to face the music alone. Alone with his Page, who is too young to be of any help.

The others? Well, let's see.

He points toward the MESSENGER.

That pale young man leaning against the wall is the Messenger. Later on he will come running in to announce that Haemon is dead. He has a premonition of catastrophe. That's what he is brooding over. That's why he won't mingle with the others.

As for those three red-faced card players—they are the guards. One smells of garlic, another of beer; but they're not a bad lot. They have wives they are afraid of, kids who are afraid of them; they're bothered by the little day-to-day worries that beset us all. At the same time— they are policemen: eternally innocent, no matter what crimes are committed; eternally indifferent, for nothing that happens can matter to them. They are quite prepared to arrest anybody at all, including Creon himself, should the order be given by a new leader.

That's the lot. Now for the play.

Oedipus, who was the father of the two girls, Antigone and Ismene, had also two sons, Eteocles and Polynices. After Oedipus died, it was agreed that the two sons should share his throne, each to reign over Thebes in alternate years.

Gradually, the lights on the stage have been dimmed.

But when Eteocles, the elder son, had reigned a full year, and time had come for him to step down, he refused to yield up the throne to his younger brother. There was civil war. Polynices brought up allies —six foreign princes; and in the course of the war he and his foreigners were defeated, each in front of one of the seven gates of the city. The two brothers fought, and they killed one another in single combat just outside the city walls. Now Creon is King.

CHORUS *is leaning, at this point, against the left proscenium arch. By now the stage is dark, with only the cyclorama bathed in dark blue. A single spot lights up the face of* CHORUS.

Creon has issued a solemn edict that Eteocles, with whom he had sided, is to be buried with pomp and honors, and that Polynices is to be left to rot. The vultures and the dogs are to bloat themselves on his carcass. Nobody is to go into mourning for him. No gravestone is to be set up in his memory. And above all, any person who attempts to give him religious burial will himself be put to death.

While CHORUS *has been speaking the characters have gone out one by one.* CHORUS *disappears through the left arch.*

It is dawn, gray and ashen, in a house asleep. ANTIGONE *steals in from out-of-doors, through the arch, right. She is carrying her sandals in her hand. She pauses, looking off through the arch, taut, listening, then turns and moves across downstage. As she reaches the table, she sees the* NURSE *approaching through the arch, left. She runs quickly toward the exit. As she reaches the steps, the* NURSE *enters through arch and stands still when she sees* ANTIGONE.

NURSE   Where have you been?

ANTIGONE   Nowhere. It was beautiful. The whole world was gray when I went out. And now—you wouldn't recognize it. It's like a post card: all pink, and green, and yellow. You'll have to get up earlier, Nurse, if you want to see a world without color.

NURSE   It was still pitch black when I got up. I went to your room, for I thought you might have flung off your blanket in the night. You weren't there.

ANTIGONE   *(Comes down the steps)* The garden was lovely. It was still asleep. Have you ever thought how lovely a garden is when it is not yet thinking of men?

NURSE   You hadn't slept in your bed. I couldn't find you. I went to the back door. You'd left it open.

ANTIGONE   The fields were wet. They were waiting for something to happen. The whole world was breathless, waiting. I can't tell you what a roaring noise I seemed to make alone on the road. It bothered me that whatever was waiting wasn't waiting for me. I took off my sandals and slipped into a field. *(She moves down to the stool and sits.)*

NURSE   *(Kneels at* ANTIGONE'S *feet to chafe them and put on the sandals)* You'll do well to wash your feet before you go back to bed, Miss.

ANTIGONE   I'm not going back to bed.

NURSE   Don't be a fool! You get some sleep! And me, getting up to see if she hasn't flung off her blanket; and I find her bed cold and nobody in it!

ANTIGONE   Do you think that if a person got up every morning like this, it would be just as thrilling every morning to be the first girl out-of-doors?

NURSE *puts* ANTIGONE'S *left foot down, lifts her other foot and chafes it.*

NURSE   Morning my grandmother! It was night. It still is. And now, my girl, you'll stop trying to squirm out of this and tell me what you were up to. Where've you been?

ANTIGONE   That's true. It was still night. There wasn't a soul out of doors but me, who thought that it was morning. Don't you think it's marvelous—to be the first person who is aware that it is morning?

NURSE   Oh, my little flibbertigibbet! Just can't imagine what I'm talking about, can she? Go on with you! I know that game. Where have you been, wicked girl?

ANTIGONE   *(Soberly)* No. Not wicked.

NURSE   You went out to meet someone, didn't you? Deny it if you can.

ANTIGONE   Yes. I went out to meet someone.

NURSE   A lover?

ANTIGONE   Yes, Nurse. Yes, the poor dear. I have a lover.

NURSE   *(Stands up; bursting out)* Ah, that's very nice now, isn't it? Such goings-on! You, the daughter of a king, running out to meet lovers. And we work our fingers to the bone for you, we slave to bring you up like young ladies! *(She sits on chair, right of table.)* You're all alike, all of you. Even you—who never used to stop to primp in front of a looking glass, or smear your mouth with rouge, or dindle and dandle to make the boys ogle you, and you ogle back. How many times I'd say to myself, "Now that one, now: I wish she was a little more of a coquette—always wearing the same dress, her hair tumbling round her face. One thing's sure," I'd say to myself, "none of the boys will look at her while Ismene's about, all curled and cute and tidy and trim. I'll have this one on my hands for the rest of my life." And now, you see? Just like your sister, after all. Only worse: a hypocrite. Who is the lad? Some little scamp, eh? Somebody you can't bring home and show to your family, and say, "Well, this is him, and I mean to marry him and no other." That's how it is, is it? Answer me!

ANTIGONE   *(Smiling faintly)* That's how it is. Yes, Nurse.

NURSE   Yes, says she! God save us! I took her when she wasn't that high. I promised her poor mother I'd make a lady of her. And look at her! But don't you go thinking this is the end of this, my young 'un. I'm only your nurse and you can play deaf and dumb with me; I don't count. But your Uncle Creon will hear of this! That, I promise you.

ANTIGONE   *(A little weary)*   Yes. Creon will hear of this.

NURSE   And we'll hear what he has to say when he finds out that you go wandering alone o' nights. Not to mention Haemon. For the girl's engaged! Going to be married! Going to be married, and she hops out of bed at four in the morning to meet somebody else in a field. Do you know what I ought to do to you? Take you over my knee the way I used to do when you were little.

ANTIGONE   Please, Nurse, I want to be alone.

NURSE   And if you so much as speak of it, she says she wants to be alone!

ANTIGONE   Nanny, you shouldn't scold, dear. This isn't a day when you should be losing your temper.

NURSE   Not scold, indeed! Along with the rest of it, I'm to like it. Didn't I promise your mother? What would she say if she was here? "Old Stupid!" That's what she'd call me. "Old Stupid. Not to know how to keep my little girl pure! Spend your life making them behave, watching over them like a mother hen, running after them with mufflers and sweaters to keep them warm, and eggnogs to make them strong; and then at four o'clock in the morning, you who always complained you never could sleep a wink, snoring in your bed and letting them slip out into the bushes." That's what she'd say, your mother. And I'd stand there, dying of shame if I wasn't dead already. And all I could do would be not to dare look her in the face; and "That's true," I'd say. "That's all true what you say, Your Majesty."

ANTIGONE   Nanny, dear. Dear Nanny. Don't cry. You'll be able to look Mamma in the face when it's your time to see her. And she'll say, "Good morning, Nanny. Thank you for my little Antigone. You did look after her so well." She knows why I went out this morning.

NURSE   Not to meet a lover?

ANTIGONE   No. Not to meet a lover.

NURSE   Well, you've a queer way of teasing me. I must say! Not to know when she's teasing me! *(Rises to stand behind ANTIGONE.)* I must be getting awfully old, that's what it is. But if you loved me, you'd tell me the truth. You'd tell me why your bed was empty when I went along to tuck you in. Wouldn't you?

ANTIGONE   Please, Nanny, don't cry any more. (ANTIGONE *turns partly toward* NURSE, *puts an arm up to* NURSE'S *shoulder. With her other hand,* ANTIGONE *caresses* NURSE'S *face.)*   There now, my sweet red apple, do you remember how I used to rub your cheeks to make them shine? My dear, wrinkled red apple! I didn't do anything tonight that was worth sending tears down the little gullies of your dear face. I am pure, and I swear that I have no other lover than Haemon . If you like, I'll swear that I shall never have any other lover than Haemon . Save your tears, Nanny, save them. Nanny dear; you may still need them. When you cry like that, I become a little girl again; and I mustn't be a little girl today.   (ANTIGONE *rises and moves upstage.*)

ISMENE *enters through arch, left. She pauses in front of arch.*

ISMENE   Antigone! What are you doing up at his hour? I've just been to your room.

NURSE   The two of you, now! You're both going mad, to be up before the kitchen fire has been started. Do you like running about without a mouthful of breakfast? Do you think it's decent for the daughters of a king?   *(She turns to* ISMENE.)   And look at you, with nothing on, and the sun not up! I'll have you both on my hands with colds before I know it.

ANTIGONE   Nanny dear, go away now. It's not chilly, really. Summer's here. Go and make us some coffee. Please, Nanny, I'd love some coffee. It would do me so much good.

NURSE   My poor baby! Her head's swimming, what with nothing on her stomach, and me standing here like an idiot when I could be getting her something hot to drink.   *(Exit* NURSE.)

A pause.

ISMENE   Aren't you well?

ANTIGONE   Of course I am. Just a little tired. I got up too early.   (ANTIGONE *sits on a chair, suddenly tired.*)

ISMENE   I couldn't sleep, either.

ANTIGONE   Ismene, you ought not to go without your beauty sleep.

ISMENE   Don't make fun of me.

ANTIGONE   I'm not, Ismene, truly. This particular morning, seeing how beautiful you are makes everything easier for me. Wasn't I a miserable little beast when we were small? I used to fling mud at you, and put worms down your neck. I remember tying you to a tree and cutting off your hair. Your beautiful hair! How easy it must be never to be unreasonable with all that smooth silken hair so beautifully set round your head.

ISMENE   *(Abruptly)*   Why do you insist upon talking about other things?

ANTIGONE   *(Gently)*   I am not talking about other things.

ISMENE   Antigone, I've thought about it a lot.

ANTIGONE	Have you?
ISMENE	I thought about it all night long. Antigone, you're mad.
ANTIGONE	Am I?
ISMENE	We cannot do it.
ANTIGONE	Why not?
ISMENE	Creon will have us put to death.
ANTIGONE	Of course he will. That's what he's here for. He will do what he has to do, and we will do what we have to do. He is bound to put us to death. We are bound to go out and bury our brother. That's the way it is. What do you think we can do to change it?
ISMENE	*(Releases* ANTIGONE'S *hand; draws back a step)* I don't want to die.
ANTIGONE	I'd prefer not to die, myself.
ISMENE	Listen to me, Antigone. I thought about it all night. I'm older than you are. I always think things over, and you don't. You are impulsive. You get a notion in your head and you jump up and do the thing straight off. And if it's silly, well, so much the worse for you. Whereas, I think things out.
ANTIGONE	Sometimes it is better not to think too much.
ISMENE	I don't agree with you! (ANTIGONE *looks at* ISMENE, *then turns and moves to chair behind table.* ISMENE *leans on end of table top, toward* ANTIGONE.) Oh, I know it's horrible. And I pity Polynices just as much as you do. But all the same, I sort of see what Uncle Creon means.
ANTIGONE	I don't want to "sort of see" anything.
ISMENE	Uncle Creon is the king. He has to set an example!
ANTIGONE	But I am not the king; and I don't have to set people examples. Little Antigone gets a notion in her head—the nasty brat, the willful, wicked girl; and they put her in a corner all day, or they lock her up in the cellar. And she deserves it. She shouldn't have disobeyed!
ISMENE	There you go, frowning, glowering, wanting your own stubborn way in everything. Listen to me. I'm right oftener than you are.
ANTIGONE	I don't want to be right!
ISMENE	At least you can try to understand.
ANTIGONE	Understand! The first word I ever heard out of any of you was that word "understand." Why didn't I "understand" that I must not play with water—cold, black, beautiful flowing water—because I'd spill it on the palace tiles. Or with earth, because earth dirties a little girl's frock. Why didn't I "understand" that nice children don't eat out of every dish at once; or give everything in their pockets to beggars; or run in the wind so fast that they fall down; or ask for a drink when they're perspiring; or want to go swimming when it's either too

early or too late, merely because they happen to feel like swimming. Understand! I don't want to understand. There'll be time enough to understand when I'm old. . . . If I ever *am* old. But not now.

ISMENE   He is stronger than we are, Antigone. He is the king. And the whole city is with him. Thousands and thousands of them, swarming through all the streets of Thebes.

ANTIGONE   I am not listening to you.

ISMENE   His mob will come running, howling as it runs. A thousand arms will seize our arms. A thousand breaths will breathe into our faces. Like one single pair of eyes, a thousand eyes will stare at us. We'll be driven in a tumbrel through their hatred, through the smell of them and their cruel, roaring laughter. We'll be dragged to the scaffold for torture, surrounded by guards with their idiot faces all bloated, their animal hands clean-washed for the sacrifice, their beefy eyes squinting as they stare at us. And we'll know that no shrieking and no begging will make them understand that we want to live, for they are like slaves who do exactly as they've been told, without caring about right or wrong. And we shall suffer, we shall feel pain rising in us until it becomes so unbearable that we *know* it must stop. But it won't stop; it will go on rising and rising, like a screaming voice. Oh, I can't, I can't, Antigone!

A pause.

ANTIGONE   How well have you thought it all out.

ISMENE   I thought of it all night long. Didn't you?

ANTIGONE   Oh, yes.

ISMENE   I'm an awful coward, Antigone.

ANTIGONE   So am I. But what has that to do with it?

ISMENE   But, Antigone! Don't you want to go on living?

ANTIGONE   Go on living! Who was it that was always the first out of bed because she loved the touch of the cold morning air on her bare skin? Who was always the last to bed because nothing less than infinite weariness could wean her from the lingering night? Who wept when she was little because there were too many grasses in the meadow, too many creatures in the field, for her to know and touch them all?

ISMENE   *(Clasps* ANTIGONE'S *hands in a sudden rush of tenderness)* Darling little sister!

ANTIGONE   *(Repulsing her)* No! For heaven's sake! Don't paw me! And don't let us start sniveling! You say you've thought it all out. The howling mob—the torture—the fear of death. . . . They've made up your mind for you. Is that it?

ISMENE   Yes.

ANTIGONE   All right. They're as good excuses as any.

ISMENE   Antigone, be sensible. It's all very well for men to believe in ideas and die for them. But you are a girl!

ANTIGONE   Don't I know I'm a girl? Haven't I spent my life cursing the fact that I was a girl?

ISMENE   *(With spirit)* Antigone! You have everything in the world to make you happy. All you have to do is reach out for it. You are going to be married; you are young; you are beautiful—

ANTIGONE   I am not beautiful.

ISMENE   Yes, you are! Not the way other girls are. But it's always you that the little boys turn to look back at when they pass us in the street. And when you go by, the little girls stop talking. They stare and stare at you, until we've turned a corner.

ANTIGONE   *(A faint smile)* "Little boys—little girls."

ISMENE   *(Challengingly)* And what about Haemon?

A pause.

ANTIGONE   I shall see Haemon this morning. I'll take care of Haemon. You always said I was mad; and it didn't matter how little I was or what I wanted to do. Go back to bed now, Ismene. The sun is coming up, and, as you see, there is nothing I can do today. Our brother Polynices is as well guarded as if he had won the war and we were sitting on his throne. Go along. You are pale with weariness.

ISMENE   What are you going to do?

NURSE   *(Calls from off-stage)* Come along, my dove. Come to breakfast.

ANTIGONE   I don't feel like going to bed. However, if you like, I'll promise not to leave the house till you wake up. Nurse is getting me breakfast. Go and get some sleep. The sun is just up. Look at you: you can't keep your eyes open. Go.

ISMENE   And you will listen to reason, won't you? You'll let me talk to you about this again? Promise?

ANTIGONE   I promise. I'll let you talk. I'll let all of you talk. Go to bed, now. (ISMENE *goes to arch; exit.*) Poor Ismene!

NURSE   *(Enters through arch, speaking as she enters)* Come along, my dove. I've made you some coffee and toast and jam. *(She turns towards arch as if to go out.)*

ANTIGONE   I'm not really hungry, Nurse.

NURSE *stops, looks at* ANTIGONE, *then moves behind her.*

NURSE   *(Very tenderly)* Where is your pain?

ANTIGONE   Nowhere, Nanny dear. But you must keep me warm and safe, the way you used to do when I was little. Nanny! Stronger than all fever, stronger than any nightmare, stronger than the shadow of the cupboard that used to snarl at me and turn into a dragon on the bedroom wall. Stronger than the thousand insects gnawing and nibbling in the silence of the night. Stronger than the night itself, with the weird hooting of the night birds that frightened me even when I couldn't hear them. Nanny, stronger than death. Give me your hand, Nanny, as if I were ill in bed, and you sitting beside me.

NURSE   My sparrow, my lamb! What is it that's eating your heart out?

ANTIGONE   Oh, it's just that I'm a little young still for what I have to go through. But nobody but you must know that.

NURSE   *(Places her other arm around* ANTIGONE'S *shoulder)* A little young for what, my kitten?

ANTIGONE   Nothing in particular, Nanny. Just—all this. Oh, it's so good that you are here. I can hold your callused hand, your hand that is so prompt to ward off evil. You are very powerful, Nanny.

NURSE   What is it you want me to do for you, my baby?

ANTIGONE   There isn't anything to do, except put your hand like this against my cheek. *(She places the* NURSE'S *hand against her cheek. A pause, then, as* ANTIGONE *leans back, her eyes shut.)* There! I'm not afraid any more. Not afraid of the wicked ogre, nor of the sandman, nor of the dwarf who steals little children. *(A pause.* ANTIGONE *resumes on another note.)* Nanny . . .

NURSE   Yes?

ANTIGONE   My dog, Puff . . .

NURSE   *(Straightens up, draws her hand away)* Well?

ANTIGONE   Promise me that you will never scold her again.

NURSE   Dogs that dirty up a house with their filthy paws deserve to be scolded.

ANTIGONE   I know. Just the same, promise me.

NURSE   You mean you want me to let her make a mess all over the place and not say a thing?

ANTIGONE   Yes, Nanny.

NURSE   You're asking a lot. The next time she wets my living-room carpet, I'll—

ANTIGONE   Please, Nanny, I beg of you!

NURSE   It isn't fair to take me on my weak side, just because you look a little peaked today. . . . Well, have it your own way. We'll mop up and keep our mouth shut. You're making a fool of me, though.

ANTIGONE   And promise me that you will talk to her. That you will talk to her often.

NURSE   *(Turns and looks at* ANTIGONE*)* Me, talk to a dog!

ANTIGONE   Yes. But mind you: you are not to talk to her the way people usually talk to dogs. You're to talk to her the way I talk to her.

NURSE   I don't see why both of us have to make fools of ourselves. So long as you're here, one ought to be enough.

ANTIGONE   But if there was a reason why I couldn't go on talking to her—

NURSE   *(Interrupting)* Couldn't go on talking to her! And why couldn't you go on talking to her? What kind of poppycock—?

ANTIGONE   And if she got too unhappy, if she moaned and moaned, waiting for me with her nose under the door as she does when I'm out all day, then the best thing, Nanny, might be to have her mercifully put to sleep.

NURSE   Now what has got into you this morning? *(HAEMON enters through arch)* Running around in the darkness, won't sleep, won't eat— *(ANTIGONE sees HAEMON)* —and now it's her dog she wants killed. I never.

ANTIGONE   *(Interrupting)* Nanny! Haemon is here. Go inside, please. And don't forget that you've promised me. *(NURSE goes to arch; exit. ANTIGONE rises.)* Haemon, Haemon! Forgive me for quarreling with you last night. *(She crosses quickly to HAEMON and they embrace.)* Forgive me for everything. It was all my fault. I beg you to forgive me.

HAEMON   You know that I've forgiven you. You had hardly slammed the door, your perfume still hung in the room, when I had already forgiven you. *(He holds her in his arms and smiles at her. Then draws slightly back.)* You stole that perfume. From whom!

ANTIGONE   Ismene.

HAEMON   And the rouge? and the face powder? and the frock? Whom did you steal them from?

ANTIGONE   Ismene.

HAEMON   And in whose honor did you get yourself up so elegantly?

ANTIGONE   I'll tell you everything. *(She draws him closer.)* Oh, darling, what a fool I was! To waste a whole evening! A whole, beautiful evening!

HAEMON   We'll have other evenings, my sweet.

ANTIGONE   Perhaps we won't.

HAEMON   And other quarrels, too. A happy love is full of quarrels, you know.

ANTIGONE   A happy love, yes. Haemon, listen to me.

HAEMON   Yes?

ANTIGONE   Don't laugh at me this morning. Be serious.

HAEMON   I am serious.

ANTIGONE   And hold me tight. Tighter than you have ever held me. I want all your strength to flow into me.

HAEMON   There! With all my strength.

A pause.

ANTIGONE   *(Breathless)* That's good. *(They stand for a moment, silent and motionless.)* Haemon! I wanted to tell you. You know— the little boy we were going to have when we were married?
HAEMON   Yes?
ANTIGONE   I'd have protected him against everything in the world.
HAEMON   Yes, dearest.
ANTIGONE   Oh, you don't know how I should have held him in my arms and given him my strength. He wouldn't have been afraid of anything, I swear he wouldn't. Not of the falling night, nor of the terrible noonday sun, nor of all the shadows, or all the walls in the world. Our little boy, Haemon! His mother wouldn't have been very imposing: her hair wouldn't always have been brushed; but she would have been strong where he was concerned, so much stronger than all those real mothers with their real bosoms and their aprons around their middle. You believe that, don't you, Haemon?
HAEMON   *(Soothingly)* Yes, yes, my darling.
ANTIGONE   And you believe me when I say that you would have had a real wife?
HAEMON   Darling, you are my real wife.
ANTIGONE   *(Pressing against him and crying out)* Haemon, you loved me! You did love me that night, didn't you? You're sure of it!
HAEMON   *(Rocking her gently)* What night, my sweet?
ANTIGONE   And you are very sure, aren't you, that that night, at the dance, when you came to the corner where I was sitting, there was no mistake? It was me you were looking for? It wasn't another girl? And you're sure that never, not in your most secret heart of hearts, have you said to yourself that it was Ismene you ought to have asked to marry you?
HAEMON   *(Reproachfully)* Antigone, you are idiotic. You might give me credit for knowing my own mind. It's you I love, and no one else.
ANTIGONE   But you love me as a woman—as a woman wants to be loved, don't you? Your arms around me aren't lying, are they? Your hands, so warm against my back—they're not lying? This warmth that's in me; this confidence, this sense that I am safe, secure, that flows through me as I stand here with my cheek in the hollow of your shoulder: they are not lies, are they?
HAEMON   Antigone, darling, I love you exactly as you love me. With all of myself.

They kiss.

ANTIGONE   I'm sallow, and I'm scrawny. Ismene is pink and golden. She's like a fruit.

HAEMON   Look here, Antigone—

ANTIGONE   Ah, dearest, I am ashamed of myself. But his morning, this special morning, I must know. Tell me the truth! I beg you to tell me the truth! When you think about me, when it strikes you suddenly that I am going to belong to you—do you have the feeling that—that a great empty space is being hollowed out inside you, that there is something inside you that is just—dying?

HAEMON   Yes, I do, I do.

A pause.

ANTIGONE   That's the way I feel. And another thing. I wanted you to know that I should have been very proud to be your wife—the woman whose shoulder you would put your hand on as you sat down to table, absentmindedly, as upon a thing that belonged to you. *(After a moment, draws away from him. Her tone changes.)* There! Now I have two things more to tell you. And when I have told them to you, you must go away instantly, without asking any questions. However strange they may seem to you. However much they may hurt you. Swear that you will!

HAEMON   *(Beginning to be troubled)* What are these things that you are going to tell me?

ANTIGONE   Swear, first, that you will go away without one word. Without so much as looking at me. *(She looks at him, wretchedness in her face.)* You hear me, Haemon. Swear it, please. This is the last mad wish that you will ever have to grant me.

A pause.

HAEMON   I swear it, since you insist. But I must tell you that I don't like this at all.

ANTIGONE   Please, Haemon. It's very serious. You must listen to me and do as I ask. First, about last night, when I came to your house. You asked me a moment ago why I wore Ismene's dress and rouge. It was because I was stupid. I wasn't very sure that you loved me as a woman; and I did it—because I wanted you to want me. I was trying to be more like other girls.

HAEMON   Was *that* the reason? My poor—

ANTIGONE   Yes. And you laughed at me. And we quarreled; and my awful temper got the better of me and I flung out of the house. . . . The real reason was that I wanted you to take me; I wanted to be your wife before—

HAEMON   Oh, my darling—

ANTIGONE   *(Shuts him off)* You swore you wouldn't ask any questions. You swore, Haemon. *(Turns her face away and goes on in a*

312 INTRODUCTION TO TRAGEDY

hard voice.) As a matter of fact, I'll tell you why. I wanted to be your wife last night because I love you that way very—very strongly. And also because— Oh, my darling, my darling, forgive me; I'm going to cause you quite a lot of pain. *(She draws away from him.)* I wanted it also because I shall never, never be able to marry you, never! (HAEMON *is stupefied and mute; then he moves a step towards her.)* Haemon! You took a solemn oath! You swore! Leave me quickly! Tomorrow the whole thing will be clear to you. Even before tomorrow: this afternoon. If you please, Haemon, go now. It is the only thing left that you can do for me if you still love me. *(A pause as* HAEMON *stares at her. Then he turns and goes out through the arch.* ANTIGONE *stands motionless, then moves to a chair at end of table and lets herself gently down on it. In a mild voice, as of calm after storm.)* Well, it's over for Haemon, Antigone.

ISMENE *enters through arch, pauses for a moment in front of it when she sees* ANTIGONE, *then crosses behind table.*

ISMENE   I can't sleep. I'm terrified. I'm so afraid that, even though it is daylight, you'll still try to bury Polynices. Antigone, little sister, we all want to make you happy—Haemon, and Nurse, and I, and Puff whom you love. We love you, we are alive, we need you. And you remember what Polynices was like. He was our brother, of course. But he's dead; and he never loved you. He was a bad brother. He was like an enemy in the house. He never thought of you. Why should you think of him? What if his soul does have to wander through endless time without rest or peace? Don't try something that is beyond your strength. You are always defying the world, but you're only a girl, after all. Stay at home tonight. Don't try to do it, I beg you. It's Creon's doing, not ours.

ANTIGONE   You are too late, Ismene. When you first saw me this morning, I had just come in from burying him. *(Exit* ANTIGONE *through arch.)*

The lighting, which by this time has reached a point of early morning sun, is quickly dimmed out, leaving the stage bathed in a light blue color. ISMENE *runs out after* ANTIGONE. *On* ISMENE'S *exit the lights are brought up suddenly to suggest a later period of the day.* CREON *and* PAGE *enter through curtain upstage.* CREON *stands on the top step; his* PAGE *stands at his right side.*

CREON   A private of the guards, you say? One of those standing watch over the body? Show him in.

The PAGE *crosses to arch; exit.* CREON *moves down to end of table.* PAGE *re-enters, preceded by the* FIRST GUARD, *livid with fear.* PAGE *remains on upstage side of arch.* GUARD *salutes.*

GUARD   Private Jonas, Second Battalion.

CREON   What are you doing here?

GUARD   It's like this, sir. Soon as it happened, we said: "Got to tell the chief about this before anybody else spills it. He'll want to know right away." So we tossed a coin to see which one would come up and tell you about it. You see, sir, we thought only one man had better come, because, after all, you don't want to leave the body without a guard. Right? I mean, there's three of us on duty, guarding the body.

CREON   What's wrong about the body?

GUARD   Sir, I've been seventeen years in the service. Volunteer. Wounded three times. Two mentions. My record's clean. I know my business and I know my place. I carry out orders. Sir, ask any officer in the battalion; they'll tell you. "Leave it to Jonas. Give him an order: he'll carry it out." That's what they'll tell you, sir. Jonas, that's me—that's my name.

CREON   What's the matter with you, man? What are you shaking for?

GUARD   By rights it's the corporal's job, sir. I've been recommended for a corporal, but they haven't put it through yet. June, it was supposed to go through.

CREON   *(Interrupts)*   Stop chattering and tell me why you are here. If anything has gone wrong, I'll break all three of you.

GUARD   Nobody can say we didn't keep our eye on that body. We had the two-o'clock watch—the tough one. You know how it is, sir. It's nearly the end of the night. Your eyes are like lead. You've got a crick in the back of your neck. There's shadows, and the fog is beginning to roll in. A fine watch they give us! And me, seventeen years in the service. But we was doing our duty all right. On our feet, all of us. Anybody says we were sleeping is a liar. First place, it was too cold. Second place— *(CREON makes a gesture of impatience.)*   Yes, sir. Well, I turned around and looked at the body. We wasn't only ten feet away from it, but that's how I am. I was keeping my eye on it. *(Shouts.)*   Listen, sir, I was the first man to see it! Me! They'll tell you. I was the one let out that yell!

CREON   What for? What was the matter?

GUARD   Sir, the body! Somebody had been there and buried it. *(CREON comes down a step on the stair. The GUARD becomes more frightened.)*   It wasn't much, you understand. With us three there, it couldn't have been. Just covered over with a little dirt, that's all. But enough to hide it from the buzzards.

CREON   By God, I'll—! *(He looks intently at the* GUARD.)   You are
sure that it couldn't have been a dog, scratching up the earth?

GUARD   Not a chance, sir. That's kind of what we hoped it was. But the
earth was scattered over the body just like the priests tell you you
should do it. Whoever did that job knew what he was doing, all right.

CREON   Who could have dared? *(He turns and looks at the* GUARD.)
Was there anything to indicate who might have done it?

GUARD   Not a thing, sir. Maybe we heard a footstep—I can't swear to it.
Of course we started right in to search, and the corporal found a shovel, a kid's shovel no bigger than that, all rusty and everything. Corporal's got the shovel for you. We thought maybe a kid did it.

CREON   *(To himself)* A kid! *(He looks away from the* GUARD.)   I
broke the back of the rebellion; but like a snake, it is coming together
again. Polynices' friends, with their gold, blocked by my orders in the
banks of Thebes. The leaders of the mob, stinking of garlic and allied
to envious princes. And the temple priests, always ready for a bit of
fishing in troubled waters. A kid! I can imagine what he is like, their
kid: a baby-faced killer, creeping in the night with a toy shovel under
his jacket. *(He looks at his* PAGE.)   Though why shouldn't they
have corrupted a real child? Very touching! Very useful to the party,
an innocent child. A martyr. A real white-faced baby of fourteen who
will spit with contempt at the guards who kill him. A free gift to their
cause: the precious, innocent blood of a child on my hands. *(He
turns to the* GUARD.)   They must have accomplices in the Guard itself. Look here, you. Who knows about this?

GUARD   Only us three, sir. We flipped a coin, and I came right over.

CREON   Right. Listen, now. You will continue on duty. When the relief
squad comes up, you will tell them to return to barracks. You will un-
cover the body. If another attempt is made to bury it, I shall expect
you to make an arrest and bring the person straight to me. And you
will keep your mouths shut. Not one word of this to a human soul.
You are all guilty of neglect of duty, and you will be punished; but if
the rumor spreads through Thebes that the body received burial, you
will be shot—all three of you.

GUARD   *(Excitedly)* Sir, we never told nobody, I swear we didn't! Anyhow, I've been up here. Suppose my pals spilled it to the relief; I
couldn't have been with them and here too. That wouldn't be my fault
if they talked. Sir, I've got two kids. You're my witness, sir, it couldn't
have been me. I was here with you. I've got a witness! If anybody
talked, it couldn't have been me! I was—

CREON   *(Interrupting)* Clear out! If the story doesn't get around, you
won't be shot. *(The* GUARD *salutes, turns, and exits at the double.*
CREON *turns and paces upstage, then comes down to end of the
table.)* A child! *(He looks at* PAGE.)   Come along, my lad. Since

we can't hope to keep this to ourselves, we shall have to be the first to give out the news. And after that, we shall have to clean up the mess. (PAGE *crosses to side of* CREON. CREON *puts his hand on* PAGE'S *shoulder.*) Would you be willing to die for me? Would you defy the Guard with your little shovel? (PAGE *looks up at* CREON.) Of course you would. You would do it, too. *(A pause.* CREON *looks away from* PAGE *and murmurs)* A child! (CREON *and* PAGE *go slowly upstage center to top step.* PAGE *draws aside the curtain, through which exit* CREON *with* PAGE *behind him.)*

As soon as CREON *and* PAGE *have disappeared,* CHORUS *enters and leans against the upstage portal or arch, left. The lighting is brought up to its brightest point to suggest mid-afternoon.* CHORUS *allows a pause to indicate that a crucial moment has been reached in the play, then moves slowly downstage, center. He stands for a moment silent, reflecting, and then smiles faintly.*

CHORUS   The spring is wound up tight. It will uncoil of itself. That is what is so convenient in tragedy. The least little turn of the wrist will do the job. Anything will set it going: a glance at a girl who happens to be lifting her arms to her hair as you go by; a feeling when you wake up on a fine morning that you'd like a little respect paid to you today, as if it were as easy to order as a second cup of coffee; one question too many, idly thrown out over a friendly drink—and the tragedy is on.

The rest is automatic. You don't need to lift a finger. The machine is in perfect order; it has been oiled ever since time began, and it runs without friction. Death, treason, and sorrow are on the march; and they move in the wake of storm, of tears, of stillness. Every kind of stillness. The hush when the executioner's ax goes up at the end of the last act. The unbreathable silence when, at the beginning of the play, the two lovers, their hearts bared, their bodies naked, stand for the first time face to face in the darkened room, afraid to stir. The silence inside you when the roaring crowd acclaims the winner—so that you think of a film without a sound track, mouths agape and no sound coming out of them, a clamor that is no more than a picture; and you, the victor, already vanquished, alone in the desert of your silence. That is tragedy.

Tragedy is clean, it is restful, it is flawless. It has nothing to do with melodrama—with wicked villains, persecuted maidens, avengers, sudden revelations, and eleventh-hour repentances. Death, in a melodrama, is really horrible because it is never inevitable. The dear old father might so easily have been saved; the honest young man might so easily have brought in the police five minutes earlier.

In a tragedy, nothing is in doubt and everyone's destiny is known. That makes for tranquillity. There is a sort of fellow-feeling among characters in a tragedy: he who kills is as innocent as he who gets killed: it's all a matter of what part you are playing. Tragedy is restful; and the reason is that hope, that foul, deceitful thing, has no part in it. There isn't any hope. You're trapped. The whole sky has fallen on you, and all you can do about it is to shout.

Don't mistake me: I said "shout": I did not say groan, whimper, complain. That, you cannot do. But you can shout aloud; you can get all those things said that you never thought you'd be able to say—or never even knew you had it in you to say. And you don't say these things because it will do any good to say them: you know better than that. You say them for their own sake; you say them because you learn a lot from them.

In melodrama you argue and struggle in the hope of escape. That is vulgar; it's practical. But in tragedy, where there is no temptation to try to escape, argument is gratuitous: it's kingly.

Voices of the GUARDS *and scuffling sound heard through the archway.* CHORUS *looks in that direction; then, in a changed tone:*

The play is on. Antigone has been caught. For the first time in her life, little Antigone is going to be able to be herself.

Exit CHORUS *through arch. A pause, while the offstage voices rise in volume, then the* FIRST GUARD *enters, followed by* SECOND *and* THIRD GUARDS, *holding the arms of* ANTIGONE *and dragging her along. The* FIRST GUARD, *speaking as he enters, crosses swiftly to end of the table. The* TWO GUARDS *and* ANTIGONE *stop downstage.*

FIRST GUARD   *(Recovered from his fright)* Come on, now, Miss give it a rest. The chief will be here in a minute and you can tell him about it. All I know is my orders. I don't want to know what you were doing there. People always have excuses; but I can't afford to listen to them, see. Why, if we had to listen to all the people who want to tell us what's the matter with this country, we'd never get our work done. *(To the* GUARDS) You keep hold of her and I'll see that she keeps her face shut.

ANTIGONE   They are hurting me. Tell them to take their dirty hands off me.

FIRST Guard   Dirty hands, eh? The least you can do is try to be polite, Miss. Look at me: I'm polite.

ANTIGONE   Tell them to let me go. I shan't run away. My father was King Oedipus. I am Antigone.

FIRST GUARD   King Oedipus' little girl! Well, well, well! Listen, Miss, the night watch never picks up a lady but they say, you better be careful: I'm sleeping with the police commissioner.

The GUARDS *laugh.*

ANTIGONE   I don't mind being killed, but I don't want them to touch me.
FIRST GUARD   And what about stiffs, and dirt, and such like? You wasn't afraid to touch them, was you? "Their dirty hands!" Take a look at your own hands. (ANTIGONE, *handcuffed, smiles despite herself as she looks down at her hands. They are grubby.*) You must have lost your shovel, didn't you? Had to go at it with your fingernails the second time, I'll bet. By God, I never saw such nerve! I turn my back for about five seconds; I ask a pal for a chew; I say "thanks"; I get the tobacco stowed away in my cheek—the whole thing don't take ten seconds; and there she is, clawing away like a hyena. Right out in broad daylight! And did she scratch and kick when I grabbed her! Straight for my eyes with them nails she went. And yelling something fierce about, "I haven't finished yet; let me finish!" She ain't got all her marbles!
SECOND GUARD   I pinched a nut like that the other day. Right on the main square she was, hoisting up her skirts and showing her behind to anybody that wanted to take a look.
FIRST GUARD   Listen, we're going to get a bonus out of this. What do you say we throw a party, the three of us?
SECOND GUARD   At the old woman's? Behind Market Street?
THIRD GUARD   Suits me. Sunday would be a good day. We're off duty Sunday. What do you say we bring our wives?
FIRST GUARD   No. Let's have some fun this time. Bring your wife, there's always something goes wrong. First place, what do you do with the kids? Bring them, they always want to go to the can just when you're right in the middle of a game of cards or something. Listen, who would have thought an hour ago that us three would be talking about throwing a party now? The way I felt when the old man was interrogating me, we'd be lucky if we got off with being docked a month's pay. I want to tell you, I was scared.
SECOND GUARD   You sure we're going to get a bonus?
FIRST GUARD   Yes. Something tells me this is big stuff.
THIRD GUARD   *(To* SECOND GUARD*)*   What's-his-name, you know—in the Third Battalion? He got an extra month's pay for catching a firebug.
SECOND GUARD   If we get an extra month's pay, I vote we throw the party at the Arabian's.
FIRST GUARD   You're crazy! He charges twice as much for liquor as

anybody else in town. Unless you want to go upstairs, of course. Can't
do that at the old woman's.

THIRD GUARD   Well, we can't keep this from our wives, no matter how
you work it out. You get an extra month's pay, and what happens?
Everybody in the battalion knows it, and your wife knows it too. They
might even line up the battalion and give it to you in front of everybody, so how could you keep your wife from finding out?

FIRST GUARD   Well, we'll see about that. If they do the job out in the
barrack yard—of course that means women, kids, everything.

ANTIGONE   I should like to sit down, if you please.

A pause, as the FIRST GUARD *thinks it over.*

FIRST GUARD   Let her sit down. But keep hold of her. *(The two*
GUARDS *start to lead her toward the chair at end of table. The curtain
upstage opens, and* CREON *enters, followed by his* PAGE. FIRST
GUARD *turns and moves upstage a few steps, sees* CREON.) 'Ten-
shun! *(The three* GUARDS *salute.* CREON, *seeing* ANTIGONE *handcuffed to* THIRD GUARD, *stops on the top step, astonished.)*

CREON   Antigone! *(To the* FIRST GUARD) Take off those handcuffs!
*(*FIRST GUARD *crosses above table to left of* ANTIGONE.) What is
this? *(*CREON *and his* PAGE *come down off the steps.)*

FIRST GUARD *takes key from his pocket and unlocks the cuff on* AN-
TIGONE'S *hand.* ANTIGONE *rubs her wrist as she crosses below table toward chair at end of table.* SECOND *and* THIRD GUARDS *step back to
front of arch.* FIRST GUARD *turns upstage toward* CREON.

FIRST GUARD   The watch, sir. We all came this time.

CREON   Who is guarding the body?

FIRST GUARD   We sent for the relief.

CREON *comes down.*

CREON   But I gave orders that the relief was to go back to barracks and
stay there! *(*ANTIGONE *sits on chair at left of table.)* I told you not
to open your mouth about this!

FIRST GUARD   Nobody's said anything, sir. We made this arrest, and
brought the party in, the way you said we should.

CREON   *(To* ANTIGONE) Where did these men find you?

FIRST GUARD   Right by the body.

CREON   What were you doing near your brother's body? You knew what
my orders were.

FIRST GUARD   What was she doing? Sir, that's why we brought her in.

She was digging up the dirt with her nails. She was trying to cover up the body all over again.

CREON   Do you realize what you are saying?

FIRST GUARD   Sir, ask these men here. After I reported to you, I went back, and first thing we did, we uncovered the body. The sun was coming up and it was beginning to smell, so we moved it up on a little rise to get him in the wind. Of course, you wouldn't expect any trouble in broad daylight. But just the same, we decided one of us had better keep his eye peeled all the time. About noon, what with the sun and the smell, and as the wind dropped and I wasn't feeling none too good, I went over to my pal to get a chew. I just had time to say "thanks" and stick it in my mouth, when I turned round and there she was, clawing away at the dirt with both hands. Right out in broad daylight! Wouldn't you think when she saw me come running she'd stop and leg it out of there? Not her! She went right on digging as fast as she could, as if I wasn't there at all. And when I grabbed her, she scratched and bit and yelled to leave her alone, she hadn't finished yet, the body wasn't all covered yet, and the like of that.

CREON   *(To* ANTIGONE*)*   Is this true?

ANTIGONE   Yes, it is true.

FIRST GUARD   We scraped the dirt off as fast as we could, then we sent for the relief and we posted them. But we didn't tell them a thing, sir. And we brought in the party so's you could see her. And that's the truth, so help me God.

CREON   *(To* ANTIGONE*)*   And was it you who covered the body the first time? In the night?

ANTIGONE   Yes, it was. With a toy shovel we used to take to the seashore when we were children. It was Polynices' own shovel; he had cut his name in the handle. That was why I left it with him. But these men took it away; so the next time, I had to do it with my hands.

FIRST GUARD   Sir, she was clawing away like a wild animal. Matter of fact, first minute we saw her, what with the great heat haze and everything, my pal says, "That must be a dog," he says. "Dog!" I says, "that's a girl, that is!" And it was.

CREON   Very well. *(Turns to the* PAGE*)*   Show these men to the anteroom. *(The* PAGE *crosses to the arch, stands there, waiting.* CREON *moves behind the table. To the* FIRST GUARD*.)*   You three men will wait outside. I may want a report from you later.

FIRST GUARD   Do I put the cuffs back on her, sir?

CREON.   No. *(The three* GUARDS *salute, do an about-turn, and exeunt through arch, right.* PAGE *follows them out. A pause.)*   Had you told anybody what you meant to do?

ANTIGONE   No.

CREON   Did you meet anyone on your way—coming or going?

ANTIGONE   No, nobody.

CREON   Sure of that, are you?

ANTIGONE   Perfectly sure.

CREON   Very well. Now listen to me. You will go straight to your room. When you get there, you will go to bed. You will say that you are not well and that you have not been out since yesterday. Your nurse will tell the same story. *(He looks toward arch, through which the* GUARDS *have gone out.)*   And I'll get rid of those three men.

ANTIGONE   Uncle Creon, you are going to a lot of trouble for no good reason. You must know that I'll do it all over again tonight.

A pause. They look one another in the eye.

CREON   Why did you try to bury your brother?

ANTIGONE   I owed it to him.

CREON   I had forbidden it.

ANTIGONE   I owed it to him. Those who are not buried wander eternally and find no rest. If my brother were alive, and he came home weary after a long day's hunting, I should kneel down and unlace his boots, I should fetch him food and drink, I should see that his bed was ready for him. Polynices is home from the hunt. I owe it to him to unlock the house of the dead in which my father and my mother are waiting to welcome him. Polynices has earned his rest.

CREON   Polynices was a rebel and a traitor, and you know it.

ANTIGONE   He was my brother.

CREON   You heard my edict. It was proclaimed throughout Thebes. You read my edict. It was posted up on the city walls.

ANTIGONE   Of course I did.

CREON   You knew the punishment I decreed for any person who attempted to give him burial.

ANTIGONE   Yes, I knew the punishment.

CREON   Did you by any chance act on the assumption that a daughter of Oedipus, a daughter of Oedipus' stubborn pride, was above the law?

ANTIGONE   No, I did not act on that assumption.

CREON   Because if you had acted on that assumption, Antigone, you would have been deeply wrong. Nobody has a more sacred obligation to obey the law than those who make the law. You are a daughter of lawmakers, a daughter of kings, Antigone. You must observe the law.

ANTIGONE   Had I been a scullery maid washing my dishes when that law was read aloud to me, I should have scrubbed the greasy water from my arms and gone out in my apron to bury my brother.

CREON   What nonsense! If you had been a scullery maid, there would have been no doubt in your mind about the seriousness of that edict. You would have known that it meant death; and you would have been satisfied to weep for your brother in your kitchen. But you! You thought that because you come of the royal line, because you were my niece and were going to marry my son, I shouldn't dare have you killed.

ANTIGONE   You are mistaken. Quite the contrary. I never doubted for an instant that you would have me put to death.

A pause, as CREON *stares fixedly at her.*

CREON   The pride of Oedipus! Oedipus and his head-strong pride all over again. I can see your father in you—and I believe you. Of course you thought that I should have you killed! Proud as you are, it seemed to you a natural climax in your existence. Your father was like that. For him as for you human happiness was meaningless; and mere human misery was not enough to satisfy his passion for torment. *(He sits on stool behind the table.)*   You come of people for whom the human vestment is a kind of straitjacket: it cracks at the seams. You spend your lives wriggling to get out of it. Nothing less than a cosy tea party with death and destiny will quench your thirst. The happiest hour of your father's life came when he listened greedily to the story of how, unknown to himself, he had killed his own father and dishonored the bed of his own mother. Drop by drop, word by word, he drank in the dark story that the gods had destined him first to live and then to hear. How avidly men and women drink the brew of such a tale when their names are Oedipus—and Antigone! And it is so simple, afterwards, to do what your father did, to put out one's eyes and take one's daughter begging on the highways.

Let me tell you, Antigone; those days are over for Thebes. Thebes has a right to a king without a past. My name, thank God, is only Creon. I stand here with both feet firm on the ground; with both hands in my pockets; and I have decided that so long as I am king—being less ambitious than your father was—I shall merely devote myself to introducing a little order into this absurd kingdom; if that is possible.

Don't think that being a king seems to me romantic. It is my trade; a trade a man has to work at every day; and like every other trade, it isn't all beer and skittles. But since it is my trade, I take it seriously. And if, tomorrow, some wild and bearded messenger walks in from some wild and distant valley—which is what happened to your dad— and tells me that he's not quite sure who my parents were, but thinks that my wife Eurydice is actually my mother, I shall ask him to do me the kindness to go back where he came from; and I shan't let a little matter like that persuade me to order my wife to take a blood test and the police to let me know whether or not my birth certificate was forged. Kings, my girl, have other things to do than surrender themselves to their private feelings. *(He looks at her and, smiles.)*   Hand *you* over to be killed!   *(He rises, moves to end of table and sits on the top of table.)*   I have other plans for you. You're going to marry Haemon; and I want you to fatten up a bit so that you can give him a sturdy boy. Let me assure you that Thebes needs that boy a good deal more than it needs your death. You will go to your room, now, and do as you have been told; and you won't say a word about this to anybody. Don't fret about the guards: I'll see that their mouths are shut. And don't annihilate me with those eyes. I know that you think I am a brute, and I'm sure you must consider me very prosaic. But the fact is, I have always been fond of you, stubborn though you always were. Don't forget that the first doll you ever had came from me.   *(A pause. ANTIGONE says nothing, rises, and crosses slowly below the table toward the arch. CREON turns and watches her; then:)*   Where are you going?

ANTIGONE   *(Stops downstage. Without any show of rebellion)*   You know very well where I am going.

CREON   *(After a pause)*   What sort of game are you playing?

ANTIGONE   I am not playing games.

CREON   Antigone, do you realize that if, apart from those three guards, a single soul finds out what you have tried to do, it will be impossible for me to avoid putting you to death? There is still a chance that I can save you; but only if you keep this to yourself and give up your crazy purpose. Five minutes more, and it will be too late. You understand that?

ANTIGONE   I must go and bury my brother. Those men uncovered him.

CREON   What good will it do? You know that there are other men standing guard over Polynices. And even if you did cover him over with earth again, the earth would again be removed.

ANTIGONE   I know all that. I know it. But that much, at least, I can do. And what a person can do, a person ought to do.

Pause.

CREON   Tell me, Antigone, do you believe all that flummery about religious burial? Do you really believe that a so-called shade of your brother is condemned to wander for ever homeless if a little earth is not flung on his corpse to the accompaniment of some priestly abracadabra? Have you ever listened to the priests of Thebes when they were mumbling their formula? Have you ever watched those dreary bureaucrats while they were preparing the dead for burial—skipping half the gestures required by the ritual, swallowing half their words, hustling the dead into their graves out of fear that they might be late for lunch?

ANTIGONE   Yes, I have seen all that.

CREON   And did you never say to yourself as you watched them, that if someone you really loved lay dead under the shuffling, mumbling ministrations of the priests, you would scream aloud and beg the priests to leave the dead in peace?

Antigone   Yes, I've thought all that.

CREON   And you still insist upon being put to death—merely because I refuse to let your brother go out with that grotesque passport; because I refuse his body the wretched consolation of that mass-production jibber-jabber, which you would have been the first to be embarrassed by if I had allowed it. The whole thing is absurd!

ANTIGONE   Yes, it's absurd.

CREON   Then why, Antigone, why? For whose sake? For the sake of them that believe in it? To raise them against me?

ANTIGONE   No.

CREON   For whom then if not for them and not for Polynices either?

ANTIGONE   For nobody. For myself.

A pause as they stand looking at one another.

CREON   You must want very much to die. You look like a trapped animal.

ANTIGONE   Stop feeling sorry for me. Do as I do. Do your job. But if you are a human being, do it quickly. That is all I ask of you. I'm not going to be able to hold out for ever.

CREON   *(Takes a step toward her)*   I want to save you, Antigone.

ANTIGONE   You are the king, and you are all-powerful. But that you cannot do.

CREON   You think not?

ANTIGONE   Neither save me nor stop me.

CREON   Prideful Antigone! Little Oedipus!

ANTIGONE   Only this can you do: have me put to death.

CREON   Have you tortured, perhaps?

ANTIGONE   Why would you do that? To see me cry? To hear me beg for mercy? Or swear whatever you wish, and then begin over again?

A pause.

CREON   You listen to me. You have cast me for the villain in this little play of yours, and yourself for the heroine. And you know it, you damned little mischiefmaker! But don't you drive me too far! If I were one of your preposterous little tyrants that Greece is full of, you would be lying in a ditch this minute with your tongue pulled out and your body drawn and quartered. But you can see something in my face that makes me hesitate to send for the guards and turn you over to them. Instead, I let you go on arguing; and you taunt me, you take the offensive. *(He grasps her left wrist.)* What are you driving at, you she devil?

ANTIGONE   Let me go. You are hurting my arm.

CREON   *(Gripping her tighter)*   I will not let you go.

ANTIGONE   *(Moans)*   Oh!

CREON   I was a fool to waste words. I should have done this from the beginning. *(He looks at her.)* I may be your uncle—but we are not a particularly affectionate family. Are we, eh? *(Through his teeth, as he twists.)* Are we? *(CREON propels ANTIGONE round below him to his side.)* What fun for you, eh? To be able to spit in the face of a king who has all the power in the world; a man who has done his own killing in his day; who has killed people just as pitiable as you are—and who is still soft enough to go to all this trouble in order to keep you from being killed.

A pause.

ANTIGONE   Now you are squeezing my arm too tightly. It doesn't hurt any more.

CREON *stares at her, then drops her arm.*

CREON   I shall save you yet. *(He goes below the table to the chair at end of table, takes off his coat, and places it on the chair.)* God knows, I have things enough to do today without wasting my time on an insect like you. There's plenty to do, I assure you, when you've just put down a revolution. But urgent things can wait. I am not going to let politics be the cause of your death. For it is a fact that this whole business is nothing but politics: the mournful shade of Polynices, the decomposing corpse, the sentimental weeping, and the hysteria that you mistake for heroism—nothing but politics.

Look here. I may not be soft, but I'm fastidious. I like things clean, shipshape, well scrubbed. Don't think that I am not just as offended as you are by the thought of that meat rotting in the sun. In the evening, when the breeze comes in off the sea, you can smell it in the palace, and it nauseates me. I refuse even to shut my window. It's vile; and I can tell you what I wouldn't tell anybody else: it's stupid, monstrously stupid. But the people of Thebes have got to have their noses rubbed into it a little longer. My God! If it was up to me, I should have had them bury your brother long ago as a mere matter of public hygiene. I admit that what I am doing is childish. But if the featherheaded rabble I govern are to understand what's what, that stench has got to fill the town for a month!

ANTIGONE   *(Turns to him)*   You are a loathsome man!

CREON   I agree. My trade forces me to be. We could argue whether I ought or ought not to follow my trade; but once I take on the job, I must do it properly.

ANTIGONE   Why do you do it at all?

CREON   My dear, I woke up one morning and found myself King of Thebes. God knows, there were other things I loved in life more than power.

ANTIGONE   Then you should have said no.

CREON   Yes, I could have done that. Only, I felt that it would have been cowardly. I should have been like a workman who turns down a job that has to be done. So I said yes.

ANTIGONE   So much the worse for you, then. I didn't say yes. I can say no to anything I think vile, and I don't have to count the cost. But because you said yes, all that you can do, for all your crown and your trappings, and your guards—all that you can do is to have me killed.

CREON   Listen to me.

ANTIGONE   If I want to. I don't have to listen to you if I don't want to. You've said your *yes*. There is nothing more you can tell me that I don't know. You stand there, drinking in my words.   *(She moves behind chair.)*   Why is it that you don't call your guards? I'll tell you why? You want to hear me out to the end; that's why.

CREON   You amuse me.

ANTIGONE   Oh, no, I don't. I frighten you. That is why you talk about saving me. Everything would be so much easier if you had a docile, tongue-tied little Antigone living in the palace. I'll tell you something, Uncle Creon: I'll give you back one of your own words. You are too fastidious to make a good tyrant. But you are going to have to put me to death today, and you know it. And that's what frightens you. God! Is there anything uglier than a frightened man!

CREON   Very well. I am afraid, then. Does that satisfy you? I am afraid that if you insist upon it, I shall have to have you killed. And I don't want to.

ANTIGONE   I don't have to do things that I think are wrong. If it comes to that, you didn't really want to leave my brother's body unburied, did you? Say it! Admit that you didn't.

CREON   I have said it already.

ANTIGONE   But you did it just the same. And now, though you don't want to do it, you are going to have me killed. And you call that being a king!

CREON   Yes, I call that being a king.

ANTIGONE   Poor Creon! My nails are broken, my fingers are bleeding, my arms are covered with the welts left by the paws of your guards— but I am a queen!

CREON   Then why not have pity on me, and live? Isn't your brother's corpse, rotting there under my windows, payment enough for peace and order in Thebes? My son loves you. Don't make me add your life to the payment. I've paid enough.

ANTIGONE   No, Creon! You said yes, and made yourself king. Now you will never stop paying.

CREON   But God in heaven! Won't you try to understand me! I'm trying hard enough to understand you! There had to be one man who said yes. Somebody had to agree to captain the ship. She had sprung a hundred leaks; she was loaded to the water line with crime, ignorance, poverty. The wheel was swinging with the wind. The crew refused to work and were looting the cargo. The officers were building a raft, ready to slip overboard and desert the ship. The mast was splitting, the wind was howling, the sails were beginning to rip. Every man jack on board was about to drown—and only because the only thing they thought of was their own skins and their cheap little day-to-day traffic. Was that a time, do you think, for playing with words like yes and no? Was that a time for a man to be weighing the pros and cons, wondering if he wasn't going to pay too dearly later on; if he wasn't going to lose his life, or his family, or his touch with other men? You grab the wheel, you right the ship in the face of a mountain of water. You shout an order, and if one man refuses to obey, you shoot straight into the mob. Into the mob, I say! The beast as nameless as the wave that crashes down upon your deck; as nameless as the whipping wind. The thing that drops when you shoot may be someone who poured you a drink the night before; but it has no name. And you, braced at the wheel, you have no name, either. Nothing has a name—except the ship, and the storm. *(A pause as he looks at her.)* Now do you understand?

ANTIGONE   I am not here to understand. That's all very well for you. I am here to say no to you, and die.

CREON   It is easy to say no.

ANTIGONE   Not always.

CREON   It is easy to say no. To say yes, you have to sweat and roll up your sleeves and plunge both hands into life up to the elbows. It is easy to say no, even if saying no means death. All you have to do is to sit still and wait. Wait to go on living; wait to be killed. That is the coward's part. *No* is one of your man-made words. Can you imagine a world in which trees say *no* to the sap? In which beasts say *no* to hunger or to propagation? Animals are good, simple, tough. They move in droves, nudging one another onwards, all traveling the same road.

Some of them keel over, but the rest go on; and no matter how many may fall by the wayside, there are always those few left that go on bringing their young into the world, traveling the same road with the same obstinate will, unchanged from those who went before.

ANTIGONE   Animals, eh, Creon! What a king you could be if only men were animals!

A pause. CREON *turns and looks at her.*

CREON   You despise me, don't you? *(*ANTIGONE *is silent.* CREON *goes on, as if to himself.)*   Strange. Again and again, I have imagined myself holding this conversation with a pale young man I have never seen in the flesh. He would have come to assassinate me, and would have failed. I would be trying to find out from him why he wanted to kill me. But with all my logic and all my powers of debate, the only thing I could get out of him would be that he despised me. Who would have thought that the white-faced boy would turn out to be you? And that the debate would arise out of something so meaningless as the burial of your brother?

ANTIGONE   *(Repeats contemptuously)*   Meaningless!

CREON   *(Earnestly, almost desperately)*   And yet, you must hear me out. My part is not an heroic one, but I shall play my part. I shall have you put to death. Only, before I do, I want to make one last appeal. I want to be sure that you know what you are doing as well as I know what I am doing. Antigone, do you know what you are dying for? Do you know the sordid story to which you are going to sign your name in blood, for all time to come?

ANTIGONE   What story?

CREON   The story of Eteocles and Polynices, the story of your brothers. You think you know it, but you don't. Nobody in Thebes knows that story but me. And it seems to me, this afternoon, that you have a right to know it too. *(A pause as* ANTIGONE *moves to chair and sits.)*   It's not a pretty story. *(He turns, gets stool from behind the table and places it between the table and the chair.)*   You'll see. *(He looks at her for a moment.)*   Tell me, first. What do you remember about your brothers? They were older than you, so they must have looked down on you. And I imagine that they tormented you—pulled your pigtails, broke your dolls, whispered secrets to each other to put you in a rage.

ANTIGONE   They were big and I was little.

CREON   And later on, when they came home wearing evening clothes, smoking cigarettes, they would have nothing to do with you; and you thought they were wonderful.

ANTIGONE   They were boys and I was a girl.

CREON   You didn't know why, exactly, but you knew that they were making your mother unhappy. You saw her in tears over them; and your father would fly into a rage because of them. You heard them come in, slamming doors, laughing noisily in the corridors—insolent, spineless, unruly, smelling of drink.

ANTIGONE   *(Staring outward)* Once, it was very early and we had just got up. I saw them coming home, and hid behind a door. Polynices was very pale and his eyes were shining. He was so handsome in his evening clothes. He saw me, and said: "Here, this is for you"; and he gave me a big paper flower that he had brought home from his night out.

CREON   And of course you still have that flower. Last night, before you crept out, you opened a drawer and looked at it for a time, to give yourself courage.

ANTIGONE   Who told you so?

CREON   Poor Antigone! With her night club flower. Do you know what your brother was?

ANTIGONE   Whatever he was, I know that you will say vile things about him.

CREON   A cheap, idiotic bounder, that is what he was. A cruel, vicious little voluptuary. A little beast with just wit enough to drive a car faster and throw more money away than any of his pals. I was with your father one day when Polynices, having lost a lot of money gambling, asked him to settle the debt; and when your father refused, the boy raised his hand against him and called him a vile name.

ANTIGONE   That's a lie!

CREON   He struck your father in the face with his fist. It was pitiful. Your father sat at his desk with his head in his hands. His nose was bleeding. He was weeping with anguish. And in a corner of your father's study, Polynices stood sneering and lighting a cigarette.

ANTIGONE   That's a lie.

A pause.

CREON   When did you last see Polynices alive? When you were twelve years old. *That's* true, isn't it?

ANTIGONE   Yes, that's true.

CREON   Now you know why. Oedipus was too chicken-hearted to have the boy locked up. Polynices was allowed to go off and join the Argive army. And as soon as he reached Argos, the attempts upon your father's life began—upon the life of an old man who couldn't make up his mind to die, couldn't bear to be parted from his kingship. One after another, men slipped into Thebes from Argos for the purpose of assassinating him, and every killer we caught always ended by confessing who had put him up to it, who had paid him to try it. And it wasn't only Polynices. That is really what I am trying to tell you. I want you to know what went on in the back room, in the kitchen of politics; I want you to know what took place in the wings of this drama in which you are burning to play a part.

Yesterday, I gave Eteocles a State funeral, with pomp and honors. Today, Eteocles is a saint and a hero in the eyes of all Thebes. The whole city turned out to bury him. The schoolchildren emptied their saving boxes to buy wreaths for him. Old men, orating in quavering, hypocritical voices, glorified the virtues of the great-hearted brother, the devoted son, the loyal prince. I made a speech myself; and every temple priest was present with an appropriate show of sorrow and solemnity in his stupid face. And military honors were accorded the dead hero.

Well, what else could I have done? People had taken sides in the civil war. Both sides couldn't be wrong; that would be too much. I couldn't have made them swallow the truth. Two gangsters was more of a luxury than I could afford. *(He pauses for a moment.)* And this is the whole point of my story. Eteocles, that virtuous brother, was just as rotten as Polynices. That great-hearted son had done his best, too, to procure the assassination of his father. That loyal prince had also offered to sell out Thebes to the highest bidder.

Funny, isn't it? Polynices lies rotting in the sun while Eteocles is given a hero's funeral and will be housed in a marble vault. Yet I have absolute proof that everything that Polynices did, Eteocles had plotted to do. They were a pair of blackguards—both engaged in selling out Thebes, and both engaged in selling out each other; and they died like the cheap gangsters they were, over a division of the spoils.

But, as I told you a moment ago, I had to make a martyr of one of them. I sent out to the holocaust for their bodies; they were found clasped in one another's arms—for the first time in their lives, I imagine. Each had been spitted on the other's sword, and the Argive cavalry had trampled them down. They were mashed to a pulp, Antigone. I had the prettier of the two carcasses brought in and gave it a State funeral; and I left the other to rot. I don't know which was which. And I assure you, I don't care.

Long silence, neither looking at the other.

ANTIGONE   *(In a mild voice)*   Why do you tell me all this?
CREON   Would it have been better to let you die a victim to that obscene story?
ANTIGONE   It might have been. I had my faith.
CREON   What are you going to do now?

ANTIGONE   *(Rises to her feet in a daze)* I shall go up to my room.

CREON   Don't stay alone. Go and find Haemon. And get married quickly.

ANTIGONE   *(In a whisper)* Yes.

CREON   All this is really beside the point. You have your whole life ahead of you—and life is a treasure.

ANTIGONE   Yes.

CREON   And you were about to throw it away. Don't think me fatuous if I say that I understand you; and that at your age I should have done the same thing. A moment ago, when we were quarreling, you said I was drinking in your words. I was. But it wasn't you I was listening to; it was a lad named Creon who lived here in Thebes many years ago. He was thin and pale, as you are. His mind, too, was filled with thoughts of self-sacrifice. Go and find Haemon. And get married quickly, Antigone. Be happy. Life flows like water, and you young people let it run away through your fingers. Shut your hands; hold on to it, Antigone. Life is not what you think it is. Life is a child playing around your feet, a tool you hold firmly in your grip, a bench you sit down upon in the evening, in your garden. People will tell you that that's not life, that life is something else. They will tell you that because they need your strength and your fire, and they will want to make use of you. Don't listen to them. Believe me, the only poor consolation that we have in our old age is to discover that what I have just said to you is true. Life is nothing more than the happiness that you get out of it.

ANTIGONE   *(Murmurs, lost in thought)* Happiness . . .

CREON   *(Suddenly a little self-conscious)* Not much of a word, is it?

ANTIGONE   *(Quietly)* What kind of happiness do you foresee for me? Paint me the picture of your happy Antigone. What are the unimportant little sins that I shall have to commit before I am allowed to sink my teeth into life and tear happiness from it? Tell me: to whom shall I have to lie? Upon whom shall I have to fawn? To whom must I sell myself? Whom do you want me to leave dying, while I turn away my eyes?

CREON   Antigone, be quiet.

ANTIGONE   Why do you tell me to be quiet when all I want to know is what I have to do to be happy? This minute; since it is this very minute that I must make my choice. You tell me that life is so wonderful. I want to know what I have to do in order to be able to say that myself.

CREON   Do you love Haemon?

ANTIGONE   Yes, I love Haemon. The Haemon I love is hard and young, faithful and difficult to satisfy, just as I am. But if what I love in Haemon is to be worn away like a stone step by the tread of the thing you call life, the thing you call happiness, if Haemon reaches the point where he stops growing pale with fear when I grow pale, stops thinking that I must have been killed in an accident when I am five minutes late, stops feeling that he is alone on earth when I laugh and he doesn't know why—if he too has to learn to say yes to everything— why, no, then, no! I do not love Haemon!

CREON   You don't know what you are talking about!

ANTIGONE   I do know what I am talking about! Now it is you who have stopped understanding. I am too far away from you now, talking to you from a kingdom you can't get into, with your quick tongue and your hollow heart. *(Laughs)* I laugh, Creon, because I see you suddenly as you must have been at fifteen: the same look of impotence in your face and the same inner conviction that there was nothing you couldn't do. What has life added to you, except those lines in your face, and that fat on your stomach?

CREON   Be quiet, I tell you!

ANTIGONE   Why do you want me to be quiet? Because you know that I am right? Do you think I can't see in your face that what I am saying is true? You can't admit it, of course; you have to go on growling and defending the bone you call happiness.

CREON   It is your happiness, too, you little fool!

ANTIGONE   I spit on your happiness! I spit on your idea of life—that life that must go on, come what may. You are all like dogs that lick everything they smell. You with your promise of a humdrum happiness—provided a person doesn't ask too much of life. I want everything of life, I do; and I want it now! I want it total, complete: otherwise I reject it! I will *not* be moderate. I will *not* be satisfied with the bit of cake you offer me if I promise to be a good little girl. I want to be sure of everything this very day; sure that everything will be as beautiful as when I was a little girl. If not, I want to die!

CREON   Scream on, daughter of Oedipus! Scream on, in your father's own voice!

ANTIGONE   In my father's own voice, yes! We are of the tribe that asks questions, and we ask them to the bitter end. Until no tiniest chance of hope remains to be strangled by our hands. We are of the tribe that hates your filthy hope, your docile, female hope; hope, your whore—

CREON   *(Grasps her by her arms)* Shut up! If you could see how ugly you are, shrieking those words!

ANTIGONE   Yes, I am ugly! Father was ugly, too. (CREON *releases her arms, turns and moves away. Stands with his back to* ANTIGONE.) But Father became beautiful. And do you know when? *(She follows him to behind the table.)* At the very end. When all his questions had been answered. When he could no longer doubt that he *had* killed his own father; that he *had* gone to bed with his own mother. When all hope was gone, stamped out like a beetle. When it was absolutely certain that nothing, nothing could save him. Then he was at peace; then he could smile, almost; then he became beautiful. . . . Whereas you! Ah, those faces of yours, you candidates for election to happiness! It's you who are the ugly ones, even the handsomest of you—with that ugly glint in the corner of your eyes, that ugly crease at the corner of your mouths. Creon, you spoke the word a moment ago: the kitchen of politics. You look it and you smell of it.

CREON   *(Struggles to put his hand over her mouth)*   I order you to shut up! Do you hear me?

ANTIGONE   *You* order me? Cook! Do you really believe that you can give me orders?

CREON   Antigone! The anteroom is full of people! Do you want them to hear you?

ANTIGONE   Open the doors! Let us make sure that they can hear me!

CREON   By God! You shut up, I tell you!

ISMENE *enters through arch.*

ISMENE   *(Distraught)* Antigone!

ANTIGONE   *(Turns to* ISMENE *)* You, too? What do you want?

ISMENE   Oh, forgive me, Antigone. I've come back. I'll be brave. I'll go with you now.

ANTIGONE   Where will you go with me?

ISMENE   *(To* CREON*)* Creon! If you kill her, you'll have to kill me too.

ANTIGONE   Oh, no, Ismene. Not a bit of it. I die alone. You don't think I'm going to let you die with me after what I've been through? You don't deserve it.

ISMENE   If you die, I don't want to live. I don't want to be left behind, alone.

ANTIGONE   You chose life and I chose death. Now stop blubbering. You had your chance to come with me in the black night, creeping on your hands and knees. You had your chance to claw up the earth with your nails, as I did; to get yourself caught like a thief, as I did. And you refused it.

ISMENE   Not any more. I'll do it alone tonight.

ANTIGONE   *(Turns round toward* CREON*)* You hear that, Creon? The thing is catching! Who knows but that lots of people will catch the disease from me! What are you waiting for? Call in your guards! Come on, Creon! Show a little courage! It only hurts for a minute! Come on, cook!

CREON   *(Turns toward arch and calls)* Guard!

GUARDS *enter through arch.*

ANTIGONE   *(In a great cry of relief)*   At last, Creon!

CHORUS *enters through left arch.*

CREON   *(To the* GUARDS)   Take her away!   (CREON *goes up on top step.)*

> GUARDS *grasp* ANTIGONE *by her arms, turn and hustle her toward the arch, right, and exeunt.* ISMENE *mimes horror, backs away toward the arch, left, then turns and runs out through the arch. A long pause, as* CREON *moves slowly downstage.*

CHORUS   *(Behind* CREON. *Speaks in a deliberate voice)*   You are out of your mind, Creon. What have you done?

CREON   *(His back to* CHORUS)   She had to die.

CHORUS   You must not let Antigone die. We shall carry the scar of her death for centuries.

CREON   She insisted. No man on earth was strong enough to dissuade her. Death was her purpose, whether she knew it or not. Polynices was a mere pretext. When she had to give up that pretext, she found another one—that life and happiness were tawdry things and not worth possessing. She was bent upon only one thing: to reject life and to die.

CHORUS   She is a mere child, Creon.

CREON   What do you want me to do for her? Condemn her to live?

HAEMON   *(Calls from offstage)*   Father!   (HAEMON *enters through arch, right.* CREON *turns toward him.)*

CREON   Haemon, forget Antigone. Forget her, my dearest boy.

HAEMON   How can you talk like that?

CREON   *(Grasps* HAEMON *by the hands)*   I did everything I could to save her, Haemon. I used every argument. I swear I did. The girl doesn't love you. She could have gone on living for you; but she refused. She wanted it this way; she wanted to die.

HAEMON   Father! The guards are dragging Antigone away! You've got to stop them!   *(He breaks away from* CREON.)

CREON   *(Looks away from* HAEMON)   I can't stop them. It's too late. Antigone has spoken. The story is all over Thebes. I cannot save her now.

CHORUS   Creon, you must find a way. Lock her up. Say that she has gone out of her mind.

CREON   Everybody will know it isn't so. The nation will say that I am making an exception of her because my son loves her. I cannot.

CHORUS   You can still gain time, and get her out of Thebes.

CREON   The mob already knows the truth. It is howling for her blood. I can do nothing.

HAEMON   But, Father, you are master in Thebes!

CREON   I am master under the law. Not above the law.

HAEMON   You cannot let Antigone be taken from me. I am your son!

CREON   I cannot do anything else, my poor boy. She must die and you must live.

HAEMON   Live, you say! Live a life without Antigone? A life in which I am to go on admiring you as you busy yourself about your kingdom, make your persuasive speeches, strike your attitudes? Not without Antigone. I love Antigone. I will not live without Antigone!

CREON   Haemon—you will have to resign yourself to life without Antigone. *(He moves to left of* HAEMON.*)*   Sooner or later there comes a day of sorrow in each man's life when he must cease to be a child and take up the burden of manhood. That day has come for you.

HAEMON   *(Backs away a step)*   That giant strength, that courage. That massive god who used to pick me up in his arms and shelter me from shadows and monsters—was that you, Father? Was it of you I stood in awe? Was that man you?

CREON   For God's sake, Haemon, do not judge me! Not you, too!

HAEMON   *(Pleading now)*   This is all a bad dream, Father. You are not yourself. It isn't true that we have been backed up against a wall, forced to surrender. We don't have to say *yes* to this terrible thing. You are still king. You are still the father I revered. You have no right to desert me, to shrink into nothingness. The world will be too bare, I shall be too alone in the world, if you force me to disown you.

CREON   The world *is* bare, Haemon, and you *are* alone. You must cease to think your father all-powerful. Look straight at me. See your father as he is. That is what it means to grow up and be a man.

HAEMON   *(Stares at* CREON *for a moment)*   I tell you that I will not live without Antigone. *(Turns and goes quickly out through arch.)*

CHORUS   Creon, the boy will go mad.

CREON   Poor boy! He loves her.

CHORUS   Creon, the boy is wounded to death.

CREON   We are all wounded to death.

FIRST GUARD *enters through arch, right, followed by* SECOND *and* THIRD GUARDS *pulling* ANTIGONE *along with them.*

FIRST GUARD   Sir, the people are crowding into the palace!

ANTIGONE   Creon, I don't want to see their faces. I don't want to hear them howl. You are going to kill me; let that be enough. I want to be alone until it is over.

CREON   Empty the palace! Guards at the gates!

> CREON *quickly crosses toward the arch; exit. Two* GUARDS *release* ANTIGONE; *exeunt behind* CREON. CHORUS *goes out through arch, left. The lighting dims so that only the area about the table is lighted. The cyclorama is covered with a dark blue color. The scene is intended to suggest a prison cell, filled with shadows and dimly lit.* ANTIGONE *moves to stool and sits. The* FIRST GUARD *stands upstage. He watches* ANTIGONE, *and as she sits, he begins pacing slowly downstage, then upstage. A pause.*

ANTIGONE   *(Turns and looks at the* GUARD)   It's you, is it?

GUARD   What do you mean, me?

ANTIGONE   The last human face that I shall see.   *(A pause as they look at each other, then* GUARD *paces upstage, turns, and crosses behind table.)*   Was it you that arrested me this morning?

GUARD   Yes, that was me.

ANTIGONE   You hurt me. There was no need for you to hurt me. Did I act as if I was trying to escape?

GUARD   Come on now, Miss. It was my business to bring you in. I did it.   *(A pause. He paces to and fro upstage. Only the sound of his boots is heard.)*

ANTIGONE   How old are you?

GUARD   Thirty-nine.

ANTIGONE   Have you any children?

GUARD   Yes. Two.

ANTIGONE   Do you love your children?

GUARD   What's that got to do with you?   *(A pause. He paces upstage and downstage.)*

ANTIGONE   How long have you been in the Guard?

GUARD   Since the war. I was in the army. Sergeant. Then I joined the Guard.

ANTIGONE   Does one have to have been an army sergeant to get into the Guard?

GUARD   Supposed to be. Either that or on special detail. But when they make you a guard, you lose your stripes.

ANTIGONE   *(Murmurs)*   I see.

GUARD   Yes. Of course, if you're a guard, everybody knows you're something special; they know you're an old N.C.O. Take pay, for instance. When you're a guard you get your pay, and on top of that you get six months' extra pay, to make sure you don't lose anything by not being a sergeant any more. And of course you do better than that. You get a house, coal, rations, extras for the wife and kids. If you've got two kids, like me, you draw better than a sergeant.

ANTIGONE   *(Barely audible)*   I see.

GUARD   That's why sergeants, now, they don't like guards. Maybe you noticed they try to make out they're better than us? Promotion, that's what it is. In the army, anybody can get promoted. All you need is good conduct. Now in the Guard, it's slow, and you have to know your business—like how to make out a report and the like of that. But when you're an N.C.O. in the Guard, you've got something that even a sergeant-major ain't got. For instance—

ANTIGONE   *(Breaking him off)*   Listen.

GUARD   Yes, Miss.

ANTIGONE   I'm going to die soon.

The GUARD *looks at her for a moment, then turns and moves away.*

GUARD   For instance, people have a lot of respect for guards, they have. A guard may be a soldier, but he's kind of in the civil service, too.

ANTIGONE   Do you think it hurts to die?

GUARD   How would I know? Of course, if somebody sticks a saber in your guts and turns it round, it hurts.

ANTIGONE   How are they going to put me to death?

GUARD   Well, I'll tell you. I heard the proclamation all right. Wait a minute. How did it go now? *(He stares into space and recites from memory.)*   "In order that our fair city shall not be pol-luted with her sinful blood, she shall be im-mured—immured." That means, they shove you in a cave and wall up the cave.

ANTIGONE   Alive?

GUARD   Yes. . . .   *(He moves away a few steps.)*

ANTIGONE   *(Murmurs)*   O tomb! O bridal bed! Alone! (ANTIGONE *sits there, a tiny figure in the middle of the stage. You would say she felt a little chilly. She wraps her arms round herself.)*

GUARD   Yes! Outside the southeast gate of the town. In the Cave of Hades. In broad daylight. Some detail, eh, for them that's on the job! First they thought maybe it was a job for the army. Now it looks like it's going to be the Guard. There's an outfit for you! Nothing the Guard can't do. No wonder the army's jealous.

ANTIGONE   A pair of animals.

GUARD   What do you mean, a pair of animals?

ANTIGONE   When the winds blow cold, all they need do is to press close against one another. I am all alone.

GUARD   Is there anything you want? I can send out for it, you know.

ANTIGONE   You are very kind. *(A pause.* ANTIGONE *looks up at the* GUARD.)   Yes, there is something I want. I want you to give someone a letter from me, when I am dead.

GUARD   How's that again? A letter?

ANTIGONE   Yes, I want to write a letter; and I want you to give it to someone for me.

GUARD   *(Straightens up)* Now, wait a minute. Take it easy. It's as much as my job is worth to go handing out letters from prisoners.

ANTIGONE   *(Removes a ring from her finger and holds it out toward him)* I'll give you this ring if you will do it.

GUARD   Is it gold? *(He takes the ring from her.)*

ANTIGONE   Yes, it is gold.

GUARD   *(Shakes his head)* Uh-uh. No can do. Suppose they go through my pockets. I might get six months for a thing like that. *(He stares at the ring, then glances off right to make sure that he is not being watched.)* Listen, tell you what I'll do. You tell me what you want to say, and I'll write it down in my book. Then, afterwards, I'll tear out the pages and give them to the party, see? If it's in my handwriting, it's all right.

ANTIGONE   *(Winces)* In your handwriting? *(She shudders slightly.)* No. That would be awful. The poor darling! In your handwriting.

GUARD   *(Offers back the ring)* O.K. It's no skin off my nose.

ANTIGONE   *(Quickly)* Of course, of course. No, keep the ring. But hurry. Time is getting short. Where is your notebook? *(The GUARD pockets the ring, takes his notebook and pencil from his pocket, puts his foot up on chair, and rests the notebook on his knee, licks his pencil.)* Ready? *(He nods.)* Write, now. "My darling . . ."

GUARD   *(Writes as he mutters)* The boy friend, eh?

ANTIGONE   "My darling. I wanted to die, and perhaps you will not love me any more . . ."

GUARD   *(Mutters as he writes)* ". . . will not love me any more."

ANTIGONE   "Creon was right. It is terrible to die."

GUARD   *(Repeats as he writes)* ". . . terrible to die."

ANTIGONE   "And I don't even know what I am dying for. I am afraid . . ."

GUARD   *(Looks at her)* Wait a minute! How fast do you think I can write?

ANTIGONE   *(Takes hold of herself)* Where are you?

GUARD   *(Reads from his notebook)* "And I don't even know what I am dying for."

ANTIGONE   No. Scratch that out. Nobody must know that. They have no right to know. It's as if they saw me naked and touched me, after I was dead. Scratch it all out. Just write: "Forgive me."

GUARD   *(Looks at ANTIGONE)* I cut out everything you said there at the end, and I put down, "Forgive me"?

ANTIGONE   Yes. "Forgive me, my darling. You would all have been so happy except for Antigone. I love you."

GUARD   *(Finishes the letter)*   ". . . I love you." *(He looks at her.)* Is that all?

ANTIGONE   That's all.

GUARD   *(Straightens up, looks at notebook)*   Damn funny letter.

ANTIGONE   I know.

GUARD   *(Looks at her)*   Who is it to? *(A sudden roll of drums begins and continues until after* ANTIGONE'S *exit. The* FIRST GUARD *pockets the notebook and shouts at* ANTIGONE.)   O. K. that's enough out of you! Come on!

At the sound of the drum roll, SECOND *and* THIRD GUARDS *enter through the arch.* ANTIGONE *rises.* GUARDS *seize her and exeunt with her. The lighting moves up to suggest late afternoon.* CHORUS *enters.*

CHORUS   And now it is Creon's turn.

MESSENGER *runs through the arch, right.*

MESSENGER   The Queen . . . the Queen!   Where is the Queen?

CHORUS   What do you want with the Queen? What have you to tell the Queen?

MESSENGER   News to break her heart. Antigone had just been thrust into the cave. They hadn't finished heaving the last block of stone into place when Creon and the rest heard a sudden moaning from the tomb. A hush fell over us all, for it was not the voice of Antigone. It was Haemon's voice that came forth from the tomb. Everybody looked at Creon; and he howled like a man demented: "Take away the stones! Take away the stones!" The slaves leaped at the wall of stones, and Creon worked with them, sweating and tearing at the blocks with his bleeding hands. Finally a narrow opening was forced, and into it slipped the smallest guard.

Antigone had hanged herself by the cord of her robe, by the red and golden twisted cord of her robe. The cord was round her neck like a child's collar. Haemon was on his knees, holding her in his arms and moaning, his face buried in her robe. More stones were removed, and Creon went into the tomb. He tried to raise Haemon to his feet. I could hear him begging Haemon to rise to his feet. Haemon was deaf to his father's voice, till suddenly he stood up of his own accord, his eyes dark and burning. Anguish was in his face, but it was the face of a little boy. He stared at his father. Then suddenly he struck him— hard; and he drew his sword. Creon leaped out of range. Haemon went on staring at him, his eyes full of contempt—a glance that was like a knife, and that Creon couldn't escape. The King stood trembling in the far corner of the tomb, and Haemon went on staring. Then, without a word, he stabbed himself and lay down beside Antigone, embracing her in a great pool of blood.

A pause as CREON *and* PAGE *enter through arch on the* MESSENGER'S *last words.* CHORUS *and the* MESSENGER *both turn to look at* CREON; *then exit the* MESSENGER *through curtain.*

CREON   I have had them laid out side by side. They are together at last, and at peace. Two lovers on the morrow of their bridal. Their work is done.

CHORUS   But not yours, Creon. You have still one thing to learn. Eurydice, the Queen, your wife—

CREON   A good woman. Always busy with her garden, her preserves, her sweaters—those sweaters she never stopped knitting for the poor. Strange, how the poor never stop needing sweaters. One would almost think that was all they needed.

CHORUS   The poor in Thebes are going to be cold this winter, Creon. When the Queen was told of her son's death, she waited carefully until she had finished her row, then put down her knitting calmly—as she did everything. She went up to her room, her lavender-scented room, with its embroidered doilies and its pictures framed in plush; and there, Creon, she cut her throat. She is laid out now in one of those two old-fashioned twin beds, exactly where you went to her one night when she was still a maiden. Her smile is still the same, scarcely a shade more melancholy. And if it were not for that great red blot on the bed linen by her neck, one might think she was asleep.

CREON   *(In a dull voice)* She, too. They are all asleep. *(Pause.)* It must be good to sleep.

CHORUS   And now you are alone, Creon.

CREON   Yes, all alone. *(To* PAGE.) My lad.

PAGE   Sir?

CREON   Listen to me. They don't know it, but the truth is the work is there to be done, and a man can't fold his arms and refuse to do it. They say it's dirty work. But if we didn't do it, who would?

PAGE   I don't know, sir.

CREON   Of course you don't. You'll be lucky if you never find out. In a hurry to grow up, aren't you?

PAGE   Oh, yes, sir.

CREON   I shouldn't be if I were you. Never grow up if you can help it. *(He is lost in thought as the hour chimes.)* What time is it?

PAGE   Five o'clock, sir.

CREON   What have we on at five o'clock?

PAGE   Cabinet meeting, sir.

CREON   Cabinet meeting. Then we had better go along to it.

Exeunt CREON *and* PAGE *slowly through arch, left, and* CHORUS *moves downstage.*

CHORUS   And there we are. It is quite true that if it had not been for Antigone they would all have been at peace. But that is over now. And they are all at peace. All those who were meant to die have died: those who believed one thing, those who believed the contrary thing, and even those who believed nothing at all, yet were caught up in the web without knowing why. All dead: stiff, useless, rotting. And those who have survived will now begin quietly to forget the dead: they won't remember who was who or which was which. It is all over. Antigone is calm tonight, and we shall never know the name of the fever that consumed her. She has played her part.

Three GUARDS *enter, resume their places on steps as at the rise of the curtain, and begin to play cards.*

A great melancholy wave of peace now settles down upon Thebes, upon the empty palace, upon Creon, who can now begin to wait for his own death.

Only the guards are left, and none of this matters to them. It's no skin off their noses. They go on playing cards.

CHORUS *walks toward the arch, left, as the curtain falls.*

Questions on *Antigone*

A. For Close Reading

1. In his opening speech what does the Chorus tell us of the past? Of the future? What judgments does he make about what the various characters are like: Antigone? Ismene? Haemon? Creon? Eurydice? the Guards?
2. When the Nurse demands that Antigone explain why she has been out in the night, what contrasts are set up between what the Nurse thinks the situation is and what it really is? Which of Antigone's remarks to the Nurse have a double meaning?
3. In her early scenes with Antigone, what reasons does Ismene give for refusing to help bury their brother? What arguments does Antigone give for defying Creon's order?

4. In Antigone's talks with the Nurse, with Ismene, and with Haemon, cite specific lines and passages that give premonitions of the coming disaster.
5. Judging by the Guard's nervous chatter, what reaction does he expect from Creon to the word he brings of the burial of Polynices' body? How does the Guard defend himself in advance? What is Creon's response to the news?
6. Summarize the definition of tragedy given by the Chorus after Creon learns of the burial of Polynices. What does the Chorus say is the cause of tragedy? Does the definition fit the opening of this play? Is the outcome of the play now "inevitable"? Is "he who kills . . . as innocent as he who gets killed"? How does the Chorus distinguish between tragedy and melodrama?
7. What attitudes do the Guards take toward Antigone and toward what she has done? What irony do you find in their talk? Why is Creon so insistent that the burial attempt be kept quiet?
8. What reasons does Creon give for Antigone's actions and for his own actions? What explanations does Antigone offer for Creon's actions? Trace the arguments carefully.
9. Finding Antigone unpersuaded by his attempts to save her life, Creon asks, "Antigone, do you know what you are dying for?" What answer does he supply to his own question? How does Antigone react to Creon's story of her brothers as "cheap gangsters"?
10. In the speech in which Creon describes the splendid funeral he gave Eteocles (who he says was "just as rotten as Polynices"), he discusses the art of politics. What is that art as he sees it? What does he mean by the phrase, "the kitchen of politics"?
11. Why does Ismene's entrance mark the end of the dialogue between Antigone and Creon? What dose Ismene symbolize at this point?
12. Judging by his discourse with the Chorus and Haemon, what is now on Creon's mind?
13. What arguments are put forward by Haemon for saving Antigone? What is Creon's response?
14. When Antigone is in prison, how does Anouilh make use of the Guard to emphasize her aloneness? How much are they able to communicate with one another? Why does Antigone ask him questions about his age, his children, his length of service in the Guard? Does the letter she dictates throw any light on her character?
15. At one point Creon remarks to Haemon, "Sooner or later there comes a day of sorrow in each man's life when he must cease to be a child and take up the burden of manhood." At the end he says to the Page, "Never grow up if you can help it." How do these comments relate to the total meaning of the play?

B. For Writing and Discussion

1. Reread the Chorus's opening remarks about the characters. Were his judgments accurate? What is the evidence?

2. How would the play be different if the part of the Chorus were left out? Would the omission affect the audience's response to certain scenes?

3. The Nurse is a character who does not appear in Sophocles' *Antigone*. Why do you suppose Anouilh introduced her into his version of the play?

4. The Guard seems to represent the ordinary man, a man with little or no inkling of the tragedy that is being acted out before his eyes but on a level beyond his understanding. What does he know of what actually happens in the play?

5. Is the Guard being used partly for comic relief?

6. In what ways are the Guard and Antigone contrasted? Consider their attitudes toward dying and their reasons for going on living.

7. Comment on the following statement: "The conflict between Creon and Antigone came about because they wanted different things from life."

8. Which of the two, Antigone or Creon, has more freedom of choice in terms of the action each takes?

9. One of Antigone's arguments is against the corrupting quality of life. Has Creon been corrupted by life?

10. As Creon tries to win over Antigone, what does he reveal of his own beliefs about religion, law, government, and family?

11. One of the concepts examined in *Antigone* is that of the nature of kingship. Creon remarks that being a king is an unromantic trade that does not permit a man "to surrender [himself] to [his] private feelings." When Antigone calls Creon "a loathsome man," he replies: "I agree. My trade forces me to be." Are Creon's ideas of what it means to be a leader of people sound, or are they simply excuses to justify his conduct? What evidence does the play supply to support either point of view?

12. Compare and contrast Anouilh's characterization of Creon with that of Sophocles in *Oedipus the King*. In Sophocles' description of Creon is there any indication that Creon was already the kind of man who could act as he does in *Antigone* or has he changed drastically?

13. Could Creon be considered a sympathetic character? Could he have acted in any other way? Is he trapped by circumstances? Was he right in saying, "Somebody had to agree to captain the ship"?

14. Compare the characters of Antigone and Hedda Gabler.

15. What is the effect of the tragedy on Creon? Does he learn anything from it?

16. Is Antigone in any way like Oedipus in her character and predicament?

17. Creon says that Antigone's attempt to bury her brother is "absurd." Is it? Why?

18. Reread the Chorus's definition of tragedy. Has Antigone acted out the import of the last two paragraphs beginning, "Don't mistake me: I said 'shout' . . ."?

19. We know what Antigone is against. What is she for?

20. Shortly before her death, Antigone, in speaking of Oedipus and herself, says to Creon: "Yes, I am ugly! Father was ugly, too. But Father became beautiful. And do you know when? At the very end. When all his questions had been answered." What kinds of questions does Antigone ask during the

play? What answers does she receive? At the end does she, too, become "beautiful"?

21. Although we know that one explanation for Antigone's insistence on being put to death lies in her inability to accept the shabby compromise Creon offers, ambiguities remain. In her letter Antigone says, "I don't even know what I am dying for," and, after her death, the Chorus comments: ". . . we shall never know the name of the fever that consumed her." Creon, however, thinks he knows. Before he condemns her to die he says that she shares Oedipus' "passion for torment," and later he adds: "Death was her purpose . . . Polynices was a mere pretext." For what variety of reasons may Antigone have chosen to die? Is Creon right in saying that Antigone *wanted* to suffer, that "Death was her purpose"?

22. In *Oedipus the King* and in *Hamlet* the suffering of the protagonist causes a change in the world in which he suffered. What is the effect of Antigone's suffering on her world?

23. What answers does the play suggest for the following general questions: What authority does the state have over its citizens? In what area of life does it not have authority? When the state and the individual disagree, how can the argument be settled? If the state gives in, does it lose its authority? What is justice?

Death of a Salesman

ARTHUR MILLER

(1949)

DEATH OF A SALESMAN was first produced in New York on February 10, 1949; in the audience men wept. They wept for Willy, but primarily they wept for themselves. They all knew someone like Willy, and they all saw something of themselves in the action of the play. We are a nation of salesmen, intent like Willy on selling ourselves, on being well-liked, on being impressive. The function of art is to hold the mirror up to life, and many people shuddered when they beheld what Arthur Miller held up. The term "salesman" is in itself symbolic; it represents the man whose only product is himself.

The form of the play is the process of Willy's mind, the mixing of scenes of past and present, of cause and effect, as Willy reveals his present predicament and how he got into it. The action of the play begins about 1945; from there we take excursions into the past. We do not have flashbacks but rather a stream of consciousness technique; a situation in the present reminds Willy of a situation in the past. Sometimes the scene from the past makes a sharp break with the present; sometimes the present and the past merge so that we hear a voice in the present mingling with one in the past. The stage represents the inside of Willy's head. (When Arthur Miller wrote the play he considered calling it *The Inside of His Head*.)

When the curtain went up that winter day in 1949, the audience saw a symbolic setting, a small, transparent house, a mere frame, with a kitchen in the center, the boys' room dimly suggested over the kitchen, and Willy and Linda's room on stage right. Between the house and the audience was stage space to represent the bare backyard. Once dense woods grew there. When Willy bought the house, it had been surrounded by tomato fields. Now apartment houses darken it, and the sky is straight up. The house symbolizes Willy's situation; the world is closing in on him. There are no walls on the outline of the house; when the play is in the present, the characters use the doors and act as though there were walls. When Willy's mind moves into the past, the characters walk through where walls would be. When we are in the past, a gauze curtain falls, blotting out the apartments and suggesting trees.

At times Willy talks to a person who is really there, and at the same time he may be talking to a person whom he only imagines but the audience actually sees. Arthur Miller has said that Willy is one of those ordinary men who we may see any day on a city street, talking to himself. In this play we see the person to whom he is speaking.

The mood is set by a dark stage, a wailing flute, and Willy's slow pace and bent posture as he comes on stage with his heavy sample case and symbolic load of sorrows. He is on stage for only a very few minutes before we know that he is beaten and intent on destroying himself—the rubber hose in the cellar. Arthur Miller said, "I was convinced only that if I could make him remember enough he would kill himself, and the structure of the play was determined by what was needed to draw up his memories. . . ."

The first major division of the play introduces the Loman family: Willy, into whose head the past is intruding; his sons, Biff and Happy, who represent the two major aspects of Willy's own character—the one that wants to get away from it all and the other that needs to fight to the end in a hopeless cause; and Linda, his wife, who like a Greek chorus sees and tells the truth when she must but unlike the Greek chorus is terribly involved in bearing the burden of these three to whom the truth is a curse.

The play recounts what is going on in the mind of this man on the last day of his life. We find out enough of his past to understand his dismal failure. The structure is based on present actions that trigger old memories, all revolving around the question "Why?" and all based on a series of oppositions: past and present, nature and artifice, truth and falsehood, reality and illusion, academic success and athletic success, what can be touched and what is intangible, Ben and Charley, Biff and Bernard. Willy's drive to be impressive and well-liked has left him with nothing but his own loneliness.

The basic principle informing the play is irony, the contrast between what seems to be and what is. Miller continues the tradition of Ibsen, that is, straightforward social criticism of the here and now. *Death of a Salesman* excoriates the pied pipers who control those who do not think, who batter their eyes with images of material goods—the cars, refrigerators and silk stockings that presumably bring both popularity and prestige. It questions the implicit contemporary definition of success and those who believe it. It criticizes a world in which "business is business," in which people who do not produce are thrown aside like worn-out shoes.

In the preface to his *Collected Plays,* Miller has written: "The confusion of some critics in viewing *Death of a Salesman* . . . is that they do not see that Willy Loman has broken a law without whose protection life is unsupportable if not incomprehensible to him and many others; it is the law which says that a failure in society and in business has no right to live." We are moved by the play because, as Willy puts it, "The woods are burning." They burn for all of us who are concerned about man's inhumanity to man.

In trying to put *Death of a Salesman* in perspective, to see it as part of the tradition of tragedy, it is clear that great changes have occurred since Shakespeare's time. The democratization of the masses has made the tragedy of the common man seem at last worth writing about. In the twentieth century a playwright can turn to a Willy Loman. His suffering is considered just as important as the suffering of a "man of high estate," an Oedipus, a

Hamlet, or a Lear. Darwin's theory of evolution and Freud's emphasis on the unconscious mind, moreover, have taken away much of man's pomposity, his sureness about who he is. The effects of the Industrial Revolution have tended to make man a cog in a large machine; one man dies and another takes his place. It has become difficult for the individual to believe in his own importance or that he matters in society. Some great new fate seems to be making man believe that he cannot control what happens to him. Is this prevalent feeling supernaturally enforced, or is it a construct of man himself?

Since art is an imitation of life and since the individual artist is necessarily compelled to imitate the life of his own period, *Death of a Salesman* tells us something of the life of twentieth-century man. One of the first questions it may bring to mind is, where is Willy's concept of individual dignity?

In the fall of Oedipus, dignity, calm, and humility are its very essence. When Oedipus dies (in *Oedipus in Colonnus,* a sequel to *Oedipus the King*), Sophocles writes:

> It was a messenger from heaven, or else
> Some gentle painless cleaving of earth's base;
> For without wailing or disease or pain
> He passed away—an end most marvelous.

And Zeus sent a thunderstorm to hail the event, to relate the death of the hero to the gods and to the state.

Oedipus fell in a search for truth; Willy is unconcerned with truth. His desire for death is at least in part related to his life insurance policy. His death, like his life, is tied up with material gain, or more specifically with grubbing for money. His death does not affect the state; the waters scarcely ripple. Linda says at the funeral, "Why didn't anyone come?" The fact is, who cared?

What is the dramatic effect of such a life? Aristotle pointed out that one requisite of great tragedy is that the individual has to have a chance of winning so that out of his battle against circumstance the spectator will be moved by a sense of terror. But Willy never seems to have a chance, and consequently we tend to be left with no more than a sense of pity. The ending of the play echoes the young T. S. Eliot's lines, "This is the way the world ends/ Not with a bang but a whimper." Obviously we are at a far remove here from the Greek concept of individual dignity.

It is said that when Hitler was about to invade Greece, a Greek statesman remarked, "We have taught the world how to live; we can now teach them how to die." What, we may ask, has such an attitude to teach us in the face of Willy's whining self-pity? The question remains of whether the concept of man's fate that Arthur Miller presents is an altogether fair one. We might translate the problem into social terms by considering the theories of Erich Fromm, who tells us that the major psychological problem of the present day is man's attempt to escape from his own freedom, being unwilling to take the responsibility that liberty demands. Man wants answers and looks for them outside of himself; he wants to hand his problems over to someone else even at the expense of becoming prey to those of an authoritarian character.

David Riesman, in *The Lonely Crowd,* talks of the great increase in our population of "other-directed" people, those who take their code of behavior from others, from their own contemporaries. They do not dare try, as do the "inner-directed" people, to stand alone. Willy Loman symbolizes these attitudes and tendencies in his constant projection of his difficulties onto others, in his constant search for scapegoats, in his insistence on being "impressive" and "well-liked." Environment becomes the villain, replacing the fate that harassed the ancients. In this light, what image of man does *Death of a Salesman* present to us?

Questions on *Death of a Salesman*

A. For Close Reading

ACT I

1. In the first scene (before the shift to the boys' bedroom), what do we learn about the situation that Willy is in?
2. In the scene in the bedroom, what do we learn about Biff and Happy? How are they alike and unlike? What does each want out of life?
3. What signals are given to the audience that Willy's mind is regressing into the past?
4. As we see Willy and the boys as they were in 1928, what do we learn about what they most admired? What connection do you see between their values then and their current predicament?
5. What is the mood of the scene that begins with the car washing? What is the mood at the end of that scene? By what steps does the scene build to a crescendo (a gradual increase in the volume of sound)?
6. In the scene between Willy and Charley, what is on each's mind? In what ways is the imagined Ben worked into this conversation? What values does Ben represent?
7. In the scene between Linda, Biff, and Happy, what else do we learn about Willy's predicament? What is Linda's interpretation of what is wrong with Willy? What is Biff's interpretation? Why do you think that Willy is trying to kill himself?

8. The depressing mood of most of the opening scenes begins to alleviate as we get to the end of the first act. What is Willy hoping for? What are Biff's hopes?

ACT 2

9. What is the mood at the beginning of the act? In what way is Willy's reference to buying seeds symbolic of what is going on at this point in the play? How does the mood of the scene change?
10. In the scene between Howard and Willy, which of Howard's comments make ironic contrasts with Willy's way of life?
11. As Willy speaks of Dave Singleman, he describes his ideal "death of a salesman." How does this ideal fit into the rest of this scene?
12. What connection do you see between Willy's remembering Biff as a football hero and Willy's talk with Howard? Why is the memory summoned up at this point in the play?
13. In what ways does Bernard serve as a contrast to the Loman boys (both here and elsewhere in the play)?
14. Why does Willy refuse Charley's offer of a job? Where, during the scene with Charley, do we get hints that Willy is again thinking of suicide?
15. Earlier we saw what Biff and Happy were like in 1928. In the scene in the restaurant we see them in the present. Has either changed? In what way? How do they react in the discussion with Willy?
16. What similarities and differences do you see between Willy's talk with Howard and Biff's visit to Oliver?
17. When Willy learns about Biff's talk with Oliver, his mind turns back to the young Bernard and to The Woman. How are these two past episodes related to his current predicment? What do they explain about the present?
18. After Biff and Happy return home, what else do we learn about them in their scene with Linda?
19. What is on Willy's mind when he talks with Ben? How do you know?
20. In the next scene, between Linda, Willy, Happy, and Biff, what does Willy learn? Why is he so elated at the end of the scene? Why then does he kill himself?
21. What judgments about Willy's life are made in the Requiem? What does this scene predict about the futures of Biff and of Happy?
22. Summarize what you have learned about Biff, Willy, Happy, and Linda by the end of the play.

B. For Writing and Discussion

1. Where and for what purpose do the following themes recur in the play: pretense, reality, the world of nature, the lack of a world of nature, physical beauty, the need to be liked, the jungle, mechanical devices, academic success, athletic success?
2. In what ways are Linda's comments like those of a Greek chorus? How and when does she keep our minds on the truth of what is happening?

3. How are the names of some of the characters symbolic, that is, how do their names express either their personalities or situations? Consider Loman, Singleman, Biff, and Happy.
4. What comments does the play make on how a man should live his life?
5. Arthur Miller said that when Willy remembered enough, he would kill himself. What does Willy recall that makes him take this step?
6. How does Willy resemble Oedipus and how does he differ?
7. Critics have argued whether this play can be considered a tragedy. In thinking about why that question would arise, consider the following questions: How is fate defined in the play? To what extent is fate responsible for Willy's downfall? How much of his downfall is caused by his own character? How vigorously does he fight back against his fate? In what way is Willy's world affected by his death?